Optiques

CRITICAL AUTHORS & ISSUES

Josué Harari, Series Editor

A complete list of books in the series is available from the publisher.

Optiques

The Science of the Eye and the Birth of Modern French Fiction

ANDREA GOULET

PENN

University of Pennsylvania Press

Philadelphia

Printed in the United States of America on acid-free paper

10 9 8 7 6 5 4 3 2 1

Published by
University of Pennsylvania Press
Philadelphia, Pennsylvania 19104-4112

Library of Congress Cataloging-in-Publication Data

Goulet, Andrea.
Optiques : the science of the eye and the birth of modern French fiction / Andrea Goulet.
p. cm — (Critical authors & issues)
ISBN-13: 978-0-8122-3931-7 (cloth : alk. paper)
ISBN-10: 0-8122-3931-8 (cloth : alk. paper)
Includes bibliographical references and index.
1. French fiction—19th century—History and criticism. 2. French fiction—20th century—History and criticism. 3. Vision in literature. I Title. II. Series
PQ653 .G68 2006
840.9/3561—dc22 2005046708

For my parents:
Denis André Goulet and
AnaMaria Reynaldo Goulet

Contents

Introduction. The Epistemology of Optics: Seeing Subjects, Modern Minds 1

Part I: Realism and the Visionary Eye: Balzac's Optics of Narration

1. Second Sight and the Authorial *chambre noire*: *Les Chouans, Louis Lambert* 19

2. "Tomber dans le phénomène": Afterimages in *La Maison Nucingen* and *Le Bal de Sceaux* 33

3. Alternative Optics: *Séraphîta, La Recherche de l'absolu,* and *La Peau de chagrin* 48

4. "Effets de lumière," or A "Second" Second Sight: *La Fille aux yeux d'or* 59

Part II: Tenebrous Affairs: *Romans policiers* and the Detecting Eye

5. Cuvier, Helmholtz, and the Visual Logics of Deduction: Poe, Doyle, Gaboriau 85

6. Learning to See: *Monsieur Lecoq* and Empiricist Theories of Vision 110

7. Sealed Chambers and Open Eyes: Leroux's *Mystère de la chambre jaune* 137

Part III: Villiers, Verne, and Claretie: Toward a Fin-de-Siècle "Optogrammatology"

8. Death and the Retina: *Claire Lenoir, L'Accusateur,* and *Les Frères Kip* 155

9. Optogram Fiction: Communication, Doubt, and the Fantastic 176

10. Tropical Piercings: Nationalism, Atavism, and the Eye of the Corpse 193

11. The Fin-de-Siècle Logic of the Afterimage: Hysteria, Hallucination, and Villiers's *L'Eve future* 206

Epilogue. The Afterimage of Reference: Optics and the *nouveau roman* 222

Notes 227

Index 261

Acknowledgments 271

Introduction
The Epistemology of Optics: Seeing Subjects, Modern Minds

In *Bouvard et Pécuchet* (1881), Gustave Flaubert pokes fun at the fads and follies of his age by allowing his characters to cycle through a series of dilettantish obsessions. Among the many scientific, pseudoscientific, and philosophical discourses debunked through the heroes' ineptitude, we find a discussion of the nature of light. Bouvard and Pécuchet, who have been roaming about in a hazily metaphysical mood, turn their attention to a candle's flame: "As they watched the candle burn, they speculated as to whether light is found in the object or in our eye. Since stars may already have died out by the time their light reaches us, we may be admiring nonexistent things."[1] This philosophical reverie has two parts. The first asks about light's objective nature: does candlelight find its source in the external world or in the eyes of its perceivers? Such a question raises a centuries-old inquiry into visual perception and its role in the apprehension of reality. In ancient Greece, the question was understood literally: thinkers debated whether the substance of light is emitted by external objects or by the eye itself. Ancient theories of emission were abandoned, for the most part, as knowledge of optical anatomy increased. In eighteenth- and nineteenth-century Europe, however, the question of light's objective nature was rekindled and reformulated by Newtonian physics, which analyzed light as a measurable substance, and by Lockean empiricism, which emphasized the viewer's perception of luminous phenomena. In scientific discussions contemporary with Flaubert, the tension between the objective nature of light and the subjective phenomena of vision frequently resolved itself around the conceit of a candle's flame. For example, Robert-Houdin, in the *Comptes rendus de l'Académie des sciences* of 1869, describes the apparent objectivity of rays emanating from a candle's flame—"these rays . . . appear . . . to be emitted so concretely that one nearly tries to pick them up with one's fingers"—but concludes nonetheless that "this radiant image is purely *subjective*."[2] The notion of a purely subjective image had gained increasing validity within the field of nineteenth-century physiological optics as experimental scientists turned attention to entoptic phenomena—that is, phenomena occurring within the eye, such as floaters, blur circles, sunspots, and afterimages. But as Bouvard and Pécuchet's confusion suggests, the question of objective versus subjective origin for such images had not been definitively resolved by the scientific community in one direction or the other, even at this late date in the century.

In fact, if we look at the second part of Flaubert's passage cited above, we find that the indeterminacy of a luminous image's epistemological status leads to an even more radical ontological crisis: does what we see—a star, for example—even exist? This step in Bouvard and Pécuchet's reasoning is informed by contemporary advances in optics on the physical properties of light. In 1849 and 1869, respectively, the French scientists Fizeau and Foucault had published well-circulated research on measuring the speed of light. Their discoveries act as a topical premise for Bouvard and Pécuchet's doubt and lead to the broader question: given that the distance of astronomical bodies surpasses the speed of light so as to allow us to see stars that no longer exist, how can we be sure that anything we perceive is real? The slippage, so typical of Flaubert's text, from scientific progress to systematic doubt may seem merely comic or clichéd in the context of *Bouvard et Pécuchet*'s deflationary irony.[3] But the very triteness of Flaubert's *idées reçues* affords modern scholars important insights into the vocabularies and premises of scientific discourses circulating in the Europe of his time. *Bouvard and Pécuchet*'s reflection on light crystallizes the substantive epistemological question that gripped contemporary thinkers from Descartes, Condillac, Malebranche, and Buffon to Helmholtz and Giraud-Teulon: how can subjective perception guarantee knowledge of external reality? Or, what is the relation between what the eye sees and what the mind knows?

This book argues that these questions of visual epistemology, while scientific and philosophical in nature, fundamentally structure the semantic and symbolic logic of the modern French novel—not only through the satirical invocations of a *Bouvard et Pécuchet,* but more directly through the shifting elaborations of the narrative subject as defined according to visual paradigms. From Hugo's scenes of hallucinatory blindness, Balzac's elaborations of visionary science, and Villiers' obsessive interest in visual pathology through to the *nouveau roman*'s appeals to pure opticality, nineteenth- and twentieth-century French fiction has harnessed the metaphorics of sight in the service of narrative form. Consider the following topoi of literary studies: the metaphysics of the "visionary novel," the omniscient eye of realist narration, the positivist gaze of scientific naturalism, the hysterical warp of decadent vision, the kaleidoscope of Proustian subjectivity, and the fragmented antiperspectivalism of postmodern fiction. Though locally contested, each of these has become a critical touchpoint in broad histories of the modern French novel—

indeed of modern fiction more generally. But critical and literary histories have not adequately connected the internal tensions of these topoi—each implicitly associating visual perspective with narrative form—to the scientific and philosophical contexts of the shifting history of vision itself. This book pays critical attention to the rich contestations and overlapping debates about the nature of vision and thought—debates increasingly elucidated through the field of "visual studies"—in order to refine and revise a history of narrative perspective.

In one of the most important interdisciplinary initiatives of recent years, scholars of art history, philosophy, and history of science have problematized a static conception of the human seeing subject by calling attention to the changing ways in which vision is imagined, defined, and articulated across various ages and cultures.[4] Contemporary scholars have replaced notions of sight as a biologically constituted, universal faculty with the culturally shaped concept of "visuality," ever-shifting according to different historical circumstances and philosophical frameworks. One of the goals of this book is to emphasize the importance for literary studies of such theorizations of vision—even in the face of a critical counter-eddy against the visual "turn."[5] Among the people now at pains to relativize the paradigmatic dominance of vision, we find Jonathan Crary, who in his most recent book cautions against reducing the rich notion of "embodiment" to mere opticality.[6] Moreover, as Alain Corbin, among others, has reminded us, the nonvisual senses—touch, smell, taste—were never absent from the experiential or discursive ambits of Western thought and therefore deserve critical attention as well.[7] But such reminders paradoxically reinforce the undeniable and continuing centrality of the visual mode for studies of human representation, whether pictorial, literary, or scientific. The field of "visual studies" continues to flourish in the Western academy, as evidenced by new courses, anthologies, and journals[8]—and rightly so, as there is still much work to be done in what might be called the interstices of visual culture, the moments where opticality is neither "dominant" nor "counterhegemonic," but subject to complex and fruitful internal tensions.

By recovering the scientific and philosophical debates about vision that informed nineteenth-century European thought, this book hopes to nuance and revise current critical views on the modern novel, adding historical precision to the oft-cited typing of realism as a "visual" mode. In contrast, for example, to the conceptual vision associated with Proustian modernism, *Optiques* reasserts the materialist bases of realist fiction by establishing a genealogy of popular literary genres as fundamentally optical—that is, as articulated according to bodily notions of sight.

One of the most suggestive moments for the study of visuality is 1830, a date that not only holds literary and historical importance for France (first installments of Balzac's *La Comédie humaine,* publication of Stendhal's *Le Rouge et le noir,* premiere of Hugo's *Hernani,* inauguration of the July Monarchy), but that has also become a marker for the advent of modern visual culture. Jonathan Crary cites events in the 1820s and 1830s as having "produced a new kind of observer" whose subjective bodilyness clashes with previous classical, perspectival models of vision, while for Peter Galison and Lorraine Daston, the date 1830 signals the emergence of modern "objectivity" as a pictorial and philosophical concept.[9] The notable difference, of course, between these characterizations of a key historical moment is that one takes it to mark the epistemological ascendancy of subjectivity and the other, of objectivity. In their introduction to *Picturing Science, Producing Art,* Peter Galison and Caroline Jones reflect on the subjectivity/objectivity stakes of recent art historical discussions over nineteenth-century concepts of the observer, reaching a conclusion that may seem merely to sidestep the argument, but in fact highlights the essentially unavoidable polarity of these terms: "however one considers the particularities of these instances, the broader lesson is clear: the objectivity/subjectivity axis that has so characterized debates over the domains of art and science was itself a historical entity coeval with those debates. It took its defining form in the nineteenth century, and its history forms the backdrop to our own."[10]

Clearly, this history of nineteenth-century conceptions of objectivity and subjectivity is neither simple nor static. But by studying the varied intersections between visual concepts and evolving narrative techniques in nineteenth-century France, we can begin to track some of the terms of debate as they shifted from 1830 to 1910. Starting from the premise that changing notions of how the eye sees have formed and informed articulations of how the mind knows—that optics is directly related to epistemology—this book further connects visual epistemology to the development of the modern novel in its most important transformative stage. It recovers an untold literary history by bringing to bear the scientific and philosophical context of visuality not just on the literary metaphorics of vision but on the very logic of realism and its generic offspring. More specifically, the book finds that post-Lockean debates between objective vision and subjective vision crucially structured narrative tensions: between visionary idealism and realist temporality in Balzac's *Comédie humaine* (1830–50); between a priori deduction and investigative induction in the early French *roman policier* (1860–1910); and between fantastic transcendence and positivist scientism in the "optogram" fictions of Villiers, Verne, and Claretie (1868–1907).

I have chosen the French word *optiques* for the title of this study because its multiple connotations orient the reader toward the overlapping narratological and epistemological questions that underlie my central argument. Unlike its English counterpart *optics*, the word *optiques* is commonly used to refer to perspective—taken either in the concrete sense of "point of view" (that is, in terms of a spatial relation between the subject's eye and the world that is the object of its gaze) or in the abstract sense of an "angle," a way of conceiving or explaining the world; one says, for example, that a speaker has a feminist *optique* or a conservative *optique* on a question. Already, then, *optique* as perspective suggests two ways of defining relations of objectivity and subjectivity: an optical "point of view" implies an observer whose eye neutrally perceives a world spread out in relation to its own position in space, while a mental "worldview" implies a self whose preconceptions code and color his or her interpretation of the world (s)he perceives. Both of these formulations of the relation between subject and world have traditionally informed critical readings of narrative texts. From Fontanier's definition of description as "exposing an object to the eyes," to Hamon's and Genette's discussions of *focalisation*, French theorists of narrative structure have taken up the visual language and logic of point-of-view. Other critics, such as Starobinski and Poulet, have invoked *optiques* in the sense of worldview to describe a stylistic gestalt; their work reveals a textual logic internal and particular to an author's production. This book extends such narratological and phenomenological studies of perspective by putting them into play with another, more technical meaning of the term *optique*: the science of vision.

There have been many attempts to theorize the relation between science and literature, with most current thinkers refusing both inert distinctions between fact and fiction and causal descriptions of unidirectional influence.[11] In this introduction, I want to make clear that this book does not take fictional narrative as merely a playful space for ironizing or vaguely invoking optics, but as a continually evolving mode that reformulates, with new figural and philosophical suggestivity, the rich and complex tensions that have structured changing conceptions of the seeing self. This book aims neither to explain literature by science nor to explain science by literature, but to note a series of conjunctions between the two discourses, conjunctions that nuance and propel our understanding of narrative form and evolving conceptions of the epistemological subject. In the twentieth century, the radical destabilization of a philosophy of the self has informed thinkers like Michel Foucault, with his historicization of the visual logic of the tableau, and Jacques Derrida, with his continually decentered, un-"framed" subject.[12] Although the poststructuralist critique of a subject-centered Cartesian perspectivalism has entered the general academic discourse, its origins in the concrete studies of optics are often forgotten in studies of narrative. Recent works in art history, on the other hand, make interesting use of links between theory and optics, including Foucault's work on the rules of perspective, Lacan's use of the optical concept of anamorphosis, and Derrida's many borrowings from the field of optics.[13] For that reason, my project uses both recent interventions in the field of "visual studies" and nineteenth-century treatises on physiological optics as discursive contexts for studying the links between vision and narrative form. It proposes a new chapter in the study of what Henri Mitterand has called *l'optique romanesque* by exploring how an *optique* on the world—a general conception of the epistemological relation between the subject and perceived reality—shapes the *optique* of a novelistic genre, its representation of the narrative subject through vision, visuality, and perspective.[14] Before turning directly to the literary authors in question, let me outline some of the terms and debates in the history of visual perception that centrally inform the later sections of this book.

Western philosophy has a long tradition of referring to optics as the paradigm for understanding the human subject's relation to the objective world. A recurrent slippage between anatomical physiology and theories of the mind shapes the history of optics, a history whose intellectual legacies remain open to reinterpretation. In order to understand the concept of "visual epistemology," one needs at least a brief overview of the scientific/philosophic background to modern debates about the nature of sight.[15]

1. *The Ancients.* Scholars in antiquity believed optics to be the most fundamental of the sciences, the key to all of nature's secrets. Conflicting theories of visual perception were argued vigorously by competing schools of philosophical thought. In Greece, the debate centered on the nature of visual rays, with Euclid proposing the hypothesis of "extramission" (the emanation of physical rays from the human eye out onto the surfaces of objects in the world) and the atomists maintaining that visual perception occurred through an "intromission" or penetration into the eye by rays originating in the external world. Plato's theory was based on a mutual interaction of "extramissive" and "intromissive" rays, while Aristotle proposed a pneumatic medium that intervened atmospherically between eye and object to enable perception.[16]

But what all of these theorists have in common is a conception of the universe that differs radically from the modern, Cartesian one that separates subject from object, matter from the immaterial. For the ancients, optical rays—whether originating in or out of the body—encompassed both seer and world within a single larger, universal continuum. Thus perception occurred within an undifferentiated spectrum of materiality and immateriality.[17] No substantive distinctions were made in ancient Greek thought between body and spirit, self and world, visible and invisible reality—and in fact, the dualism of subject and object that founds modern metaphysics was inconceivable until centuries later, when Johannes Kepler made a crucial discovery in the field of optics.

2. *Kepler, Descartes, Newton: Classical Optics.* In 1604, Kepler published his theory of retinal images in *De modo visionis.* The discovery that light rays converge through the eye's lens to form reversed images on the surface of the retina constituted, according to Gérard Simon, "an outright epistemological break in the history of optics."[18] What made Kepler's discovery so radical? First of all, Kepler defined optical rays as consisting of light, analyzable according to the abstract and provable laws of mathematics and physics. In ancient Greece, extramissive and intramissive rays had been defined as vague matter allowing direct contact between the body and the world; many ancients even believed that the ("evil") eye could physically harm another body by projecting its rays at it. But the Keplerian theory of retinal images distinguished between subject and object, between the eye as instrument of perception and the external world of geometrical and physical laws, and thus paved the way not only for studies of distance, spatial relations, and perspective, but for a Cartesian rationality that would (theoretically) separate mind and body, matter and spirit, self and world.

Another way to understand the novelty of Kepler's optics is to consider the theoretical model he used to study vision: the camera obscura. Kepler hypothesized that the eye functions analogously to a camera obscura, a closed box with a hole through which light rays enter to form an image on a screen at the other end. This hypothesis allowed him to study the geometrical relations of ray, lens, and retina without actually referring to a physical eye. As I will discuss in later chapters, the camera obscura model was to become a dominant figure for scientists—and, eventually, literary writers like Balzac—as they conceptualized vision. What was revolutionary in Kepler's use of the camera obscura as model for the eye was its abstraction, its separation of optics from the realm of actual visual experience. By isolating the geometrical functioning of the eye from actual sensation and perception, Kepler "reduce[d] physiological optics to inanimate physics," thus breaking radically from his predecessors' emphasis on the living eye.[19]

Kepler's a priori abstraction of sight was taken even further in Descartes's optics, which relied on logical deduction and the study of perspectival laws. In *De la Dioptrique* (1637), Descartes distinguishes between the physiological function of the eye (a faulty organ, prone to error) and the conceptual function of the mind (a faculty better able to access physical laws of vision). There is no necessary homology, proposes Descartes, between the physiological process of visual perception and the structure of mental images. It is therefore possible—and necessary, for the sake of objectivity—to separate the body's experience of visual phenomena from abstract, conceptual analyses of optical truth. As with his broader philosophy, Descartes's optics are based on the separation of an objective "self" from its localized position in the world, in time, and in the body; the resulting abstract detachment is figured as a privileged gaze, one based on a transcendental perspective. For Descartes, reality and truth are assured by reason and not by the evidence of the senses, for "the soul is what feels, not the body."[20] Descartes's separation of mind from body shaped an abstract rationality that was to dominate classical theories of vision in Europe.

Of course, this account of Cartesian optical philosophy as founded on a strict subject/object split and reliant on a decorporealized eye/I has itself been nuanced, particularly by recent art historical debates over the term that Martin Jay's *Downcast Eyes* rendered theoretically current: "Cartesian perspectivalism."[21] Although Cartesianism—that is, the theoretical legacy of the philosopher's work—has emphasized abstraction, objectivity, and the sovereign gaze,[22] attention to Descartes's original writings on optics raises local ambivalences that reposition the knowing subject within the material and spatial conditions of embodied subjectivity. As Lyle Massey points out, the perspectival grid in Descartes's writing consisted not of a purely mental construction, but of a contingent and bodily spatiotemporal form of image making.[23] Similarly, David Summers takes the infinite manipulability of anamorphosis, rather than the ordered grid of perspectivalism, as paradigmatic of Descartes's optics, adding that Descartes was as interested in the physiology of the eye as in the "economy of light."[24] Indeed, accounts of Descartes's optics as purely physical (versus physiological) and idealist (versus empiricist) fail to note the ways in which the *Dioptrique* of 1637 occasionally anticipated concerns that were to take center stage in eighteenth- and nineteenth-century studies of vision. These include Descartes's reliance on the eye's structure to define sensation; here already, vision is inseparable from physiological, anatomical form.

And yet, even as we acknowledge that in practice Descartes's own writings connect the poles of physics/physiology, abstract deduction/empirical method, universality/contingency, and metaphysics/phenomenology, it is important to understand that Cartesian*ism* has traditionally stood in opposition to later empiricist theories of vision and the self. One aspect of Cartesian optics that has most suggestively informed the nineteenth-century French literary and intellectual tradition, for example, is the creation of a tight conceptual nexus between vision and a priori logic. Such a model of vision fits in with the broader deductive method of Cartesianism: we are able to see not because our eyes interact with the world but because our minds are equipped with preexisting, innate ideas. In fact, the experiential and physiological components of sight only interfere, according to this model, with our perception of truth. Thus the classical optics of Kepler and Descartes are understood to be structured not by the lived experience of perception, but by the reasoned deduction of a priori rules and universal categories of vision.

Sir Isaac Newton's optics likewise emphasize the external, objective laws of vision over the experience of perception. In his *Optiks* (1730), Newton published the results of an experiment in which he had analyzed and recomposed the physical properties of light. His materialist conception of light was in keeping with a mathematical optics that held sway in the classical age.[25] In a way, though, Newton acts as a transitional figure between Descartes and the empiricism of the succeeding era. The inductive elements of Newton's methodology in the *Optiks* have led him to be understood as an early participant in a historical move toward the more empirical sciences of observation.

3. *Empiricist Theories of Vision.* Although Cartesian rationality was to hold sway for at least three centuries of scientific positivism, the eighteenth and nineteenth centuries saw a gradual shift in the conception and methodology of optics. The a priori, rational deduction of classical optics was challenged by empiricist theories of vision in well-known philosophical texts by Berkeley (*An Essay Towards a New Theory of Vision,* 1709), Locke (*Essay Concerning Human Understanding,* 1690), and Condillac (*Traité des sensations,* 1754). Berkeley's fundamental thesis on vision explained that the perception of distance is not immediate, but learned through judgment and experience.[26] Locke and Condillac extended this critique of Descartes's belief that bodily perceptions of space and form are "innate" (fully present at birth); their empiricist model of vision described perception as gradually acquired, learned through the application of mental judgment to sensory experience. This regrounding of vision in experience entailed a shift in methodology as well: while Descartes and Newton had studied optics through abstract models of reasoning and the external physics of light, empiricists began to focus on the eye's physiology and on subjective phenomena of vision—that is, on the observation of visual effects rather than on the deduction of abstract causes.

By the end of the eighteenth century, the science of optics in Europe featured a growing interest in the effects that light and color produce on the human observer's eye. Indeed, this was considered the founding age of "L'optique physiologique."[27] The strong legacy of physiological, rather than physical or mathematical, experimentation was to continue into the nineteenth century, with thinkers across Europe turning their attention to the ways in which the anatomy of the eye affects visual perception. In Germany, Goethe's *Theory of Colors* (*Zur Farbenlehre,* 1810) opposed Newton by studying colors not as the physical components of light but as phenomena in which shadows, darkness, illusion, and the bodily pulses of the perceiver play a part. In France, Chevreul examined color contrasts in the tapestries woven at Les Gobelins; his *De la loi du contraste simultané des couleurs* (1839) explains how our eyes' perception of colors, shadings, and tones is due to optical effects rather than to actual physical differences of color. By the time Hermann von Helmholtz wrote his extensive *Treatise on Physiological Optics* in 1867, a large body of optical experimentation had been devoted to experiential topics like human binocularity, depth and color perception, retinal accommodation, and nerve stimulation. Not only did nineteenth-century opticians like Purkinje, Young, Hering, Brewster, and Helmholtz turn their new instruments onto the various pathologies of the eye, they also studied everyday "subjective" visual phenomena that had been previously dismissed as inessential aberrations of the body: blur circles, sunspots, floaters ("mouches volantes"), and positive and negative afterimages.

It may be useful at this point to summarize, in schematic form, the oppositions that developed in nineteenth-century thought between idealist and empiricist theories of vision, as they form the underlying (though contested) binary structures that inform this book's critical readings of the French novel after 1830:

Idealist theories of vision	*Empiricist theories of vision*
Cartesian rationality	Lockean empiricism
a priori deduction	observation of experiential facts
vision as abstract, mental	vision as corporeal
laws of physics	physiological phenomena
objective thought	subjective experience
atemporality	temporal logic
innate, immediate perception	sight as gradual acquisition of facts

It should be made clear that the distinctions between these categories will be continually questioned throughout the chapters of this book, for they intersected and blurred in various ways and at various moments. In fact, their very systematization relies on the a posteriori prism of Helmholtzian polemics.[28] And yet these binaries remain essential to understanding certain nineteenth-century intellectual habits, such as the epistemological tension between *voyance* (second sight) and observation of the material world that manifests itself throughout Balzac's *Comédie humaine.* What this table should not be taken to indicate is a well-defined and unidirectional historical shift from idealism to empiricism, though I believe that Jonathan Crary's *Techniques of the Observer* was right in pointing to ways in which nineteenth-century physiological optics increasingly called attention to subjective, experiential vision. The scientific elaborations of embodied optical phenomena remain key to a study of nineteenth-century

French literature not only because they provided new fodder for the novelistic imagination (double vision and the stereoscope, optical illusions and fantasmagoria, blur circles and afterimages all made their way into popular fiction of the time), but because their premises allow us to reexamine persistent and fundamental questions of narrative objectivity and subjectivity. Rather than claim a dismissal of objective laws in favor of subjective phenomena, a nuanced history of optics allows us to chart the rising importance of subjectivity as the ground for both a skeptical erosion and a perennial reassertion of the founding subject/object distinction in modern Western thought and artistic representation. In the end, this study finds that historically fixable tensions between the a priori deduction of physical optics and the inductive empiricism of physiological optics crucially underwrite formal and thematic narrative choices particular to the developing genres of the modern novel, from realism to the fantastic. Moreover, it proposes that the philosophies of the self that underlie these competing models of vision serve as an important backdrop to understanding twentieth-century formulations of the narrative subject that developed in opposition to the high realism of the novel's *âge d'or*.

From today's perspective, nineteenth-century optics appears as a sort of protophenomenology: its attention to subjective visual *phenomena* suggests a corporeal, rather than conceptual, epistemology. But on the other hand, nineteenth-century philosophers of vision retained confidence in the mastering, objective gaze of science: a gaze that allowed humans to study the world as a stable object, governed by universal laws and organized according to bounded and coherent schemata. Nineteenth-century optics, then, might be understood as a transitional phase between (a) the abstract rationality and apriority of the classical age; and (b) the corporeal subjectivity of twentieth-century phenomenology. The thinkers of the nineteenth century, of course, had no such hindsight; to them, body and mind, matter and spirit, perception and conception were tightly woven in a continuously reexamined relation. Not until the next century would the very foundations of visual epistemology be put into question.

The radical critique of a positivist visuality did not come from the realm of strict scientific optics, which continued (and continues) to refine knowledge about physics and physiology. Nor did it surface in the field of psychology of vision, which focused its studies on optical illusions, gestalt theory, and so on. Instead, the double strand of philosophy and optics was taken up in the twentieth century by philosophers and psychoanalysts like Maurice Merleau-Ponty and Jacques Lacan. Less interested in the mechanics of vision than in the way visual models define how we understand our subject-relation to the world, these thinkers nonetheless entered into direct dialogue with previous philosophers and scientists of optics.

Twentieth-century phenomenology, for example, combined optics with Husserlian philosophy in order to interrogate the Cartesian distinction between abstract thought and sensory perception. Where once the eye and the mind were considered incompatible organs of knowledge (the former susceptible to sensory error and the latter capable of transcending bodily location), phenomenology proposed that our knowledge of the world cannot help but be imprinted by the particularity of our bodies. We are corporeal entities, bodies in the world, situated in time and in space. All that we can know, therefore, must come directly from lived experience. As formulated by Merleau-Ponty, the phenomenological method disdained conceptual constructions of knowledge in favor of direct experience of the world through the senses, especially sight. Such a method flies in the face of the Cartesian "gaze from above" (*le survol*) implied by perspectival optics; it also critiques nineteenth-century scientific positivism, with its faith in the neutral, objective eye. But Merleau-Ponty's thought has its antecedents: he takes up and radically extends a strand of physiological optics that can be traced back to Goethe's *Theory of Colors*.[29]

It is possible to understand several other strains of twentieth-century thought as variations on the basic challenge to the objectively centered visual subject. Freudian psychology explored the pathologies of vision and revealed ways in which subconscious irruptions into the psyche follow a visual logic. Sartre's philosophical discussion of the gaze, *le regard*, exposed the eye's role in intersubjective relationships of power.[30] And Lacanian psychoanalysis theorized a "field of vision" that denies the possibility of optical mastery by trapping the human subject in a radically nonhuman gaze.[31] Although Freud, Sartre, Merleau-Ponty, and Lacan emphasize different aspects of visuality, they share a fundamental questioning of the possibility of the visual subject's grasp over his own identity and over an objective reality—a questioning that was to structure novelistic forms of the mid-twentieth century from the *nouveau roman* on.[32]

If we examine Lacan's formulations against the concept of visual mastery, we find that much twentieth-century thought on vision and visuality has grown out of and against the history of optics. For Lacan, the Cartesian *cogito* can be understood in visual terms as "consciousness's illusion of *seeing itself see itself* [*se voir se voir*]"; to see oneself in the process of seeing oneself is to conceive, abstractly—and, as it were, inauthentically—of a self that can comprehend, grasp, and master the object of its own gaze.[33] Moreover, for Lacan, this mastering gaze finds its figurative structure in Descartes's geometrical optics, which analyzes vision according to mathematical laws of perspective. Lacan cites Descartes's *Dioptrique* as well as Diderot's *Lettre sur les aveugles*, in which Diderot claims that a blind man can comprehend an entire perspectival system, to show that geometrical optics constructs an abstracted spatiality that has nothing to do with vision as experienced perception. As with Merleau-Ponty, a particular form of optics (perspectivalist, classical, deductive) comes to signify the myth of conceptual mastery that a positivist philosophy of the self propounds. And similarly, Lacan's reaction against the geometrical abstraction of classical (Cartesian, Newtonian) optics comes out of a countertradition that can be traced back to Goethe. In a persuasive analysis, Stephen Melville traces this anti-Newtonian current in twentieth-century thought through the mediation of a Heideggerian metaphorics of light. His formulation provides us with a way to understand the affinities between psychoanalytical and phenomenological conceptions of vision: "Heidegger's *Lichtung* is not Newtonian, not an empty space traversed by lines of light, but a welling up of light in an interplay with darkness that is generative of a multicolored world of things, and Lacan, no doubt with a push from Bataille, is also fundamentally oriented to this space or place of light (light is something we enter or that enters us, not something that shines upon us). This is the point of Lacan's strictures on Descartes, Diderot, and 'geometral perspective'—all of which are, in his view as in Goethe's—'simply the mapping of space, not sight.'"[34] Light, then, becomes one of the defining figures of a lineage—from Goethe through Merleau-Ponty, Heidegger, and Lacan—that is opposed to the Cartesian perspectival tradition. This brings us back to the objective light/subjective light distinction raised by Flaubert's Bouvard and Pécuchet in their questions about the candle. Do we see with our minds or with our eyes? The distinction centrally shapes our changing views on human perception. As Melville's description of Heideggerian light suggests, the metaphorics of such a distinction are multiple: gridded space versus fluid experience, purity versus shadow, white light versus multicolored world, illumination from above versus being-within. Moreover, these particular figural logics course through the literary language of the nineteenth- and twentieth-century French novel. By bringing into rigorous focus the physiological underpinnings of modern visual thought, this book proposes to move beyond vague appreciations of the science/literature nexus. It examines a suggestive set of intersections between metaphors of human knowledge and representations of light, color, and visuality in the modern French novel.

This historical overview, centered primarily on Western Europe and particularly France, gives us a sense of the broad epistemological debates that have underlain optical discourse across many centuries. In the modern age, we can discern a generalized move from seventeenth-century Cartesian abstraction to nineteenth-century physiological optics to twentieth-century phenomenology—or, to take up Merleau-Ponty's terms, from the dominance of "l'Esprit" to the grounding of vision in "l'Œil." It is important, though, to think about the historical blind spots that such a diachronic study of visuality implies, in addition to the broad heuristic advantages it provides. The emphasis in histories of optics on ruptures between "scopic regimes"—perspectivalism in the classical age of Descartes, empiricism in the nineteenth century, anti-ocularcentrism in the twentieth—creates a hermeneutic fiction, a useful tool for thinking of the theoretical implications of particular patterns and practices. The historical perspective from which we perceive broad shifts in dominant visual modes makes manifest the tensions and terms at stake in particular moments of discourse; Goethe's 1810 anti-Newtonian *Theory of Colors*, for example, seems anomalous in a positivist age, but it takes on importance and retrospective coherence in light of twentieth-century phenomenological theory. Generalizations are useful, but as Jonathan Crary reminds us, any overly broad characterization of an age's visuality leaves out "the marginal and local forms by which dominant practices of vision were resisted, deflected, or imperfectly constituted."[35] At no given moment does one particular figure or text actually embody the dominant "scopic regime." In contrast to the physiological studies that were to follow, Newton's optics can be read as perspectival and Cartesian for their residual abstraction; on the other hand, Newton's inductive methodology can be taken as precedent for the empiricism that was eventually to promote physiological studies of vision. Even within the writings of a particular thinker, certain strains may be occluded or reinterpreted by a generalized discussion of the writer's place in a larger history. Descartes may have considered his anatomical experiments on a cow's eye to be methodologically empirical, but his broader deductive philosophy and the nineteenth century's later experiments on living, human eyes allow the bovine model to be seen retroactively as abstract and "incorporeal." Aspects of particular texts can be found to prefigure later developments, as when Descartes's *Dioptrique* turns to the entoptical subjective phenomena (afterimages, or the lights and colors we continue to see after closing our eyes) that were to become central to physiological, empiricist—and "anti-Cartesian"—studies of vision. Whereas a diachronic, historical view can take two epistemological moments as successive and mutually exclusive, a synchronic study of particular texts and their contexts such as this book undertakes reveals a structure of overlap rather than of rupture.

The chapters that follow use close textual exegeses combined with attention to scientific context in order to focus on literature's interaction with a mixed inheritance of visual theory. With the understanding that both conjunctions and disjunctions exist between the history of the French novel and the history of optics in Europe, the book examines the ways in which particular literary texts and their implied generic affiliations are structured around terminological and conceptual fault lines produced by the epistemological debates of optics in their time.

Part I, "Realism and the Visionary Eye," focuses primarily on Balzac's *La Comédie humaine* (1830–50) as paradigmatic of a broader ambivalence between visionary insight and empirical observation. Poised between Hugo's transcendent visuality and Zola's physical optics, Balzac's texts straddle fantastic and realist modes in their depictions of the seeing subject; textual tensions between these two modes reflect the fundamental objectivity/subjectivity split that structures modern visual thought. Moreover, this section situates Balzac as the source point for a proliferation of fictional subgenres whose formulas are structured by a specific visual and narrative logic.

Part II, "Tenebrous Affairs," proposes a new reading of the early *roman policier* as it developed in France. Partly because the detective genre inherits (from texts like Balzac's 1841 *Une Ténébreuse affaire* and Féval's 1863 *Les Habits noirs*) a traditional figuration of light as truth, its epistemological thrust has been typed in terms of pure Cartesian rationality and the abstract sublimation of the bodily senses. But by resituating it in the context of nineteenth-century physiological optics, we can identify an alternative, antirevelational, and empiricist visuality as the genre's crucial structuring model.

Part III, "Toward a Fin-de-Siècle 'Optogrammatology,'" studies literary topoi in the fiction of Villiers de l'Isle-Adam, Jules Claretie, and Jules Verne that have been borrowed from the field of physiological optics: the optogram (photo in/of an eye), the retinal afterimage, the stereoscope, the ophthalmascope, and the visual hallucination. The chapters in this section unite to identify a late nineteenth-century "optogram moment" that combines the optical tropes of hysteria and of physiological science with a philosophical exploration of the tug between (objective) idealism and (subjective) solipsism.

The book's Epilogue grows out of this section, arguing that the gap between real and unreal in the "optogrammatic" fiction of the fin de siècle prepares the terrain for an eventual twentieth-century move toward textual self-referentiality and phenomenologies of vision—features of the *nouveau roman* that would once again redefine narrative and its long entanglement with the science of sight.

Part I
Realism and the Visionary Eye: Balzac's Optics of Narration

Chapter 1

Second Sight and the Authorial *chambre noire*: *Les Chouans, Louis Lambert*

Commonplace distinctions between romantic and realist fiction in the nineteenth century have figured literary practice as a visual matter, invoking an apparent relation between narrative form and authorial vision: the poetic thrust of the romantic novel implies a visionary eye, attuned to the realm of mystical revelation, while the descriptive logic of the realist or naturalist novel implies a scientific eye, trained for the positivist observation of details in the world. One need only read the titles of two well-known critical works on Hugo and Zola to recognize the competing poles of visuality at stake: *Victor Hugo and the Visionary Novel* (1984) and *The Visual Novel: Emile Zola and the Art of His Times* (1992). Victor Brombert's study of Hugo emphasizes a transcendent and transgressive visuality, one that exceeds mere ocular perception; themes of temporal boundlessness, spiritual turbulence, and hallucinatory revelation invest the Hugolian narrative "eye" with a visionary consciousness.[1] By contrast, the eye in Zola's novels belongs to a precisely located materiality. As William Berg convincingly demonstrates, contemporary scientific theories of optical perception—Taine's writings on retinal sensations; Chevreul's, Maxwell's, and Rood's principles of complementary colors; Young's and Helmholtz's experiments in physiological optics—shaped Zola's avowed authorial goal of "direct observation."[2]

Honoré de Balzac's *La Comédie humaine* might well be said to straddle the two poles of Hugo's mysticism and Zola's scientism. As Balzac's stories shift quickly from ultrarealist depictions of daily life to fantastic scenes of hallucinatory confusion, they register a continual dialogue between the competing modes of *sight* and *vision*, of observation and revelation. Certainly, the long-standing "querelle Balzac-réaliste/Balzac-visionnaire" has cast the author's narrative range in visual terms, assigning the fantastic and philosophical elements of his writing to the logic of *voyance* and its historico-sociological themes to the classificatory eye of the *observateur*.[3] This opposition is solidified by the critical tendency to classify the different works in *La Comédie humaine* according to their position on a realist-to-visionary spectrum. The historical and sociological themes in

Les Chouans, Illusions perdues, Splendeurs et misères des courtisanes, and *Le Père Goriot* place them on the Balzac-*observateur* side, while works with fantastical or philosophical themes—*Séraphîta, La Peau de chagrin, Louis Lambert*—fall on the side of Balzac-visionnaire.

Such divisions can only be artificial, of course, for each of Balzac's novels slides continuously between a totalizing realist observation and the mystical élan of revelation. As indicated in its *Avant-propos* of 1842, *La Comédie humaine* aims to combine precise descriptions of the contemporary world with an intense interest in the mystical essences underlying visible appearance.[4] Consequently, most critics today would agree that the "querelle Balzac-observateur/Balzac-visionnaire" is no longer pertinent in its attempt to categorize Balzac and his work according to an either/or of realist observation and transcendent vision. But is it enough to say that *vue* and *vision* coexist in Balzac's textual universe? Or can attention to the scientific context of Balzac's thinking—particularly in the field of experimental optics—allow us to elucidate more precisely the contours of tension in his texts between physical sight and mystical vision?

I contend that we need to get beyond the temperate acknowledgment that "Balzac was both an observer who looked at the world with the exact eye of a scientist and a seer who gazed with inspired clarity into the depths of the human spirit and beyond."[5] By associating one kind of vision with science and another with mysticism, this seemingly indisputable formulation promotes a distinction that was not observed in much intellectual discourse of Balzac's time, nor in his *Avant-propos de la Comédie humaine.*[6] Moreover, it fails to take into account the particular, ambivalent status of vision *within* nineteenth-century science itself. For Balzac is writing at a moment when a tension between empiricism and idealism pulls the scientist's eye in what may seem to us to be two directions at once: toward the ephemeral details of the visible world as well as toward the eternal truths that subtend them.[7] Even more pertinent to a study of visuality in Balzac than the methodological double thrust of the sciences in general is the ambivalence that inhabited the field of optics at the beginning of the nineteenth century. From the philosophers of vision Locke, Diderot, and Condillac to the authors of optical treatises Monge, Hassenfratz, and l'Abbé Nollet, the thinkers who influenced Balzac's visual theories were poised between an idealist concept of vision (as the innate apperception of abstract laws) and an empiricist definition of sight (as subjective and physiological experience).[8]

The Scottish philosopher Thomas Reid, who indirectly influenced Balzac's notion of second sight,[9] exemplifies the dual nature of this transitional moment of optics. In fact, Reid's theories of visual perception, elaborated in *An Inquiry into the Human Mind on the Principles of Common Sense* (1764), allow us to locate Balzac's concept of *la seconde vue* in the overlapping conceptual space between Cartesian and empiricist optics.[10]

In "Of Seeing," Reid resists the subjectivist conclusions of Locke's and Addison's studies on sensation by reaffirming certain Cartesian standards, such as the idea that a blind man can conceive the phenomena and laws of optics, thereby supporting the dissociation of vision's essence from its physiological basis.[11] But Reid also disagrees with Descartes on certain important points—ones that end up aligning him with Balzac's defense of materialism in the *Avant-propos.* Whereas Descartes wrote famously that "our senses deceive us," Reid defends sensory observation as a reliable witness to the realm of truth. When errors are made, it is because of defective reasoning rather than an inherent faultiness of the senses and their technological extensions.[12] Reid takes the realm of appearance as a necessary and useful tool (or language, as he calls it) for understanding its underlying truths. Indeed, in this way, his conception of the visible world may well be understood to inform that of the *Comédie humaine,* where deceptive appearances abound (think of the many-masked Vautrin), but where each material object acts a sign available to interpretation.

But who does the interpreting? Who really sees? For Thomas Reid, whose philosophy resists both poles, idealism and empiricism, the model of vision is not limited to common, quotidian acts of perception. Reid's synthesis of the topic begins by evoking those whose inspiration surpasses the need for physical eyesight—intuitive "seers"; it also discusses the field of optics in relation to *les aveugles*—blind seers; and it includes, as noted, a reference to the *philosophe initié*—the trained "seer." A spectrum of visual possibilities is laid out, then, blurring the distinctions between physical, physiological, mystical, and conceptual vision.[13] Balzac similarly blurs those lines and provides various models for seeing through the characters of *La Comédie humaine.* His spectrum of seers recalls Reid's: the inspired *voyants* (Louis Lambert, Victor Morillon), those initiated through art or science (Balthazar DeClaës, Frenhofer), the blind seer (Facino Cane), and all of the regular heroes whose ungifted eyes are gradually trained to perceive the workings of society (Lucien de Rubempré, Eugène de Rastignac, Raphaël de Valentin).[14] The double-stranded context of Reid's theory allows us to elucidate the range of optical models—from an idealized, visionary mode to a more material, temporal conception of sight—at work in *La Comédie humaine,* without losing track of how these models crystallize a Balzacian interest in the connection between phenomenal appearance and underlying truth. Optical discourses of the time, in other words, provide us with a new way to understand *La Comédie humaine*'s visual double thrust: its *ténébreuses affaires* and its *recherche de l'absolu.*

And indeed, the narrative choices that Balzac makes in his *Comédie humaine* ratify the scientific synthesis between physical sight and mystical vision, as he not only thematically multiplies and overlaps visual types throughout his novels, but also (in the Preface to *La Peau de chagrin*) defines the authorial project as combining "observation" with "a sort of second sight."[15] The synthesis is not an easy one, however. One may note, for example, the awkwardness of Balzac's language as he pairs observation with the communication of "the vividness of primordial sensations" before further linking this quality to second sight as "an unheard-of, unaccountable, moral phenomenon poorly grasped by science." The vagueness with which he ascribes this "sort of second sight" to "some unknown power" of spatial displacement indicates the ambivalence underlying Balzac's conception of literary vision as both physical and mystical. In order really to understand this ambivalence, let us examine Balzac's representation of two fictional geniuses, the "visionary" authors Victor Morillon and Louis Lambert.

Victor Morillon

Balzac's first signed novel, *Les Chouans* (1828), foregrounds visuality from the start, with its pictorial descriptions of the Fougères and Alençon regions of Brittany. The story begins by following a regiment of republican soldiers and their recruits as they wind their way through a landscape that changes according to their visual perspective: "Though they had come from Fougères, where the tableau now before their eyes could also be seen, albeit altered by the differences forced upon it by the change in perspective, they could not help but admire it one last time."[16] Though shifting by virtue of the observers' placement, the landscape remains a "tableau" whose color contrasts and spatial dispositions follow the rules of visual representation. Nature, here, affects the soul as it affects the eye: "Here and there, dark-slated roofs giving off wisps of white smoke and the sharp-edged, silvery ditches left behind by the Couesnon's meandering streams caught the eye in an optical trap [*une de ces pièges d'optique*] of the kind that, without our knowing why, render us irresolute and prone to reverie" (58). In this idyllic setting, the magnetizing powers of a *piège d'optique* echo the tortuousness of the stream to foreshadow a slightly menacing atmosphere. And in fact, visual effects carry *Les Chouans* beyond the picturesque, for the story turns out to be about power and deception, spying and surveillance, suspicious gazes and hidden glances. Corentin, the government spy who, with Peyrade, mismanages *Une Ténébreuse affaire*, makes his appearance here as one of the many characters whose identity is cloaked in mystery. The melodramatic love story between the "shadowy and sly" (*ténébreusement rusé*) (67) Montauran and the lively-eyed Marie de Verneuil plays itself out under the suspicious gazes of Madame du Gua, Corentin, the Chouans, and the government forces. In his introduction to *Les Chouans*, the critic Maurice Ménard notes the complex play of gazes in this tale, adding that "Balzac multiplies the play of fascinated gazes in his novel before sharing with us the spectacle being played out before his own fascinated gaze."[17] This fascination occurs already at the level of landscape, where optical traps attract the eye and the soul, "without our knowing why."

Ménard's remark points us to something found throughout Balzac's work: the desire to communicate images, that is, to make a scene accessible to the reader's eye through the intermediary of a character's visual perception. *Les Chouans* problematizes that exchange, however, through its constant reminders that the reader can only imagine what the characters can actually see. In other words, there is an inescapable gap between the immediate sensation of the eye and the mimetic imaging of the mind. The following passage uses references to painting, drawing, and memory to make this point:

> Even if a contemplative mind were to fully perceive the dappled interplay of shadow and light, the mountains' misty horizons, the uncanny views to be seen in treeless stretches where the waters ramble beguilingly; if memory were able to color in, so to speak, this fleeting picture, which is no sooner seen than it disappears; persons touched by these tableaux would still have no more than an imperfect notion of the magic spectacle that burst upon the still-impressionable souls of the young soldiers. (58)

What Balzac seems to be saying in this rather convoluted sentence is that even a concentrated effort of imagination, whereby a reader embellishes (or "colors in") a fleeting memory, would be incapable of capturing the full spectacle that assaulted the senses of the young soldiers at that particular moment. The "magic" of that spectacle may in fact reside in its resistance to representation—although more directly, it resides in the immediate complexity and richness of the scene. In either case, the reader is excluded from the sublime vision in all of its fullness.

Balzac's idealized author, on the other hand, is gifted with a perfect capacity to envision a scene—not through reconstruction of a memory image, nor by perceptual contact with the world, but through the intuitive gift of second sight. In the "Avertissement du Gars," the preface to what would become *Les Chouans*, Balzac pretends to introduce the author of "Le Gars," a young orphan genius whom he calls Victor Morillon. The false biography of this author figure focuses on his *imagination fantasmagorique* (419). This prodigious imagination allows Victor to envision "magic spectacles" as vividly as the soldiers of *Les Chouans*; but while they perceived landscapes with their eyes, Victor sees a world of images that transcends the visible. In fact, Victor's "sight" constitutes a rejection of all sensory perception, of all bodily matter: "he grew, plant-like, given up to endless contemplation, possessed by a strange hatred for brute realities and bodies, unaware of his own physical existence; he lived, so to speak, exclusively through the forces of the inner senses that, in his view, made up a second being within man" (417).

The interior perception that allows Victor "a deep intuition into things" is equivalent to second sight, a visionary gift that Balzac will explore more explicitly in *Louis Lambert*. Although the term *seconde vue* is not used in the "Avertissement du Gars," Victor Morillon certainly marks the first instance of Balzac's discussion of the concept. In fact, the young author is described in terms that link him to the definition of *La Spécialité*, Balzac's alternative name for second sight: "this generous life, clear and deep like a calm, secluded lake bearing the reflections of thousands of images, . . . His soul was, as Leibniz put it so beautifully, *a concentric mirror of the universe*" (420). Suzanne Bérard has traced this image from Leibniz's *Monadology* through Balzac's texts; in *Séraphîta*, the mirror is used to describe "Le Voyant" and in the Preface to *La Peau de chagrin*, the ideal author "must have within himself some kind of concentric mirror in which . . . the universe is reflected."[18] The figuration of creative imagination as a mirror—that is, as a surface in which images are reflected—acquires even more visual force in the etymological comment Balzac makes in *Louis Lambert*: "Specialité, *species*, sight, speculate, to see everything, and all at once [*d'un seul coup*]; *speculum*, mirror or means of judging an object *by seeing it in full*" (my emphasis). To see an object in its entirety, to capture its wholeness, is to accede to the Saint-Hilairien realm of *unité* evoked in the *Avant-propos*. But there is, in addition, an immediacy to that vision—"to see everything, *and all at once*." The mirror of the universe abolishes both fragmentation and time; its image is eternal and complete.

This ideal of instantaneous and whole knowledge severed from the physical perception of optical reality links Balzac's image to a more general Cartesian concept of vision. The Leibnizian mirror partakes of a Cartesian logic of immediacy; in fact, Leibniz was one of the best-known defenders and developers of Descartes' theory of innate ideas.[19] In his optics, Descartes emphasized the preexisting mental faculties that allow us to make judgments concerning the percepts available to the eye. Without innate ideas about form, distance, and coherence, the mind would be incapable of processing those often conflicting and jumbled images. Innate ideas allow an immediate interpretation of perceptual facts; because of them, we see the world "d'un seul coup." Balzac's notion of *Spécialité*, then, taps into a theory of optics that elides the temporality of phenomenal perception to focus instead on an inner—and instant—revelatory faculty.

In science and philosophy, the Cartesian theory of direct vision was already losing its position of uncontested dominance by the time Balzac was writing. Locke, for example, had rejected the concept of innate ideas, claiming instead that all perception is based on the gradual acquisition of interpretive skills. For empiricists following Locke, visual judgments occur not *d'un seul coup*, but through the incremental experience of reality.[20] The empiricist notion of visual perception differs from Balzac's *Spécialité* in both coherence and immediacy: for Lockeans, the resolution of jumbled precepts into a coherent image occurs only a posteriori, once the mind—trained by experience—applies its judgments to the eye's sensation. This typically modern conception of vision attends to the experiential reality of the eye, to its relation with the phenomenal world. Balzac, on the other hand, with his theory of second sight, displays a sort of nostalgia for an idealized, classical vision, one that bypasses the material world of perception to access directly a realm of coherent revelation.

Although it may seem inappropriate to assimilate a mystical theory of second sight to an optical discussion of visual perception, in fact—and we see this in Leibniz's intervention through innate ideas into discussions of sensory perception—the distinction between mystical vision and physical eyesight was not strictly upheld in the century preceding Balzac. For many philosophers influencing Balzac, including Thomas Reid, the intuitive powers of genius were analogous to the physical faculties of vision. Reid, as we have seen, links mystical vision to physical perception to mental conception, discussing all three under the rubric "De la vue." For him, sight and second sight exist on a conceptual continuum. Just as the chosen few endowed with *l'inspiration* can directly perceive truths that most cannot see, the sighted can perceive forms, lights, and colors that the blind cannot see. The inspired communicate their revelations to the sighted; and the sighted communicate what they have learned through perception to the blind, who are themselves perfectly capable of conceiving of optical truths. Reid demystifies the gift of second sight, pointing out that people with ordinary vision must seem to the blind like "a pack of prophets, holy men and visionaries": "We know that inspiration grants man no new ability: it merely communicates to him, in odd and extraordinary ways, what common human abilities are able to understand, and what he is able to communicate to others through ordinary means."[21] The difference, then, between "seers" and the sighted is merely a question of mode of access.

If, for Thomas Reid, sight and second sight are not of a radically different order, it is because both of these forms of vision are concerned with accessing ideal forms of truth. Although he incorporates empiricist facts of vision into his discussions, Reid remains committed to a Cartesian validation of the mind's role in the perceptual process. In fact, writes Reid, visual perception often consists of *ignoring* what the eye sees, of getting beyond the visible, phenomenal appearance of the world. If one were to look at a book, for example, under changing conditions of light and perspective, its appearance would change but its essential color and form would in fact remain unaltered. In other words, a gap exists between how things are and how they look. And for Reid it is the former that counts: essence is more important than appearance. Even in daily visual perception, we ignore the visible appearance of things in order to access the truth to which they refer. To perceive is always already to conceive, for while Reid distinguishes lexically between perception and conception, he asserts that the former cannot exist without the latter.[22] Although perception occurs through the medium of the sensory organs, it is primarily defined by Reid as a mental faculty (understood as apprehension of objective fact, not subjective "sensation"): "The perception of external objects by our senses is an operation of the mind" (3: 24).[23]

Beyond merely stating, then, that Reid's visual studies informed Balzac's theory of second sight, we can identify their common subordination of the visible, phenomenal world in favor of conceptual truth. Indeed, Balzac's imagined young author-seer Victor Morillon takes Reid's dismissal of materiality to its logical extreme. While Reid's seer looks past the visible world to the essences underlying it, Victor does not engage with that world at all. His images are fully conceptual, having no basis in perceptual reality. The "Avertissement du Gars" evokes the power of Victor's pure imagination. Although he has lived in poverty and isolation, the young genius is capable of describing a life of unbounded luxury in opulent sensory detail:

> He described the delights of an immense fortune with an astonishing intensity of color; told . . . of the ecstasies to be experienced at balls . . . painted the luxurious quarters he lived in, their furnishings, their extravagant china and beautiful paintings, the patterns on silk dresses and carpets, detailed the features of sumptuous carriages, Arabian steeds, . . . fashions . . . , the selection of fabrics, canes, and jewels . . . *without ever having seen any of it with his outer, visible eye.* (417–18; my emphasis)

The rich descriptive detail of Victor's imagination relies on a complete elimination of the perceptual mode. Victor's *inner* eye bypasses the visible world of lived experience (which, for Victor, is colorless and empty) and goes directly to an abstract realm existing only in the mind. As with Reid's description of vision as conceptual, Balzac's description of Victor's *voyance* emphasizes his separation from the corporeal realities of the physical world. In this earliest fictional incarnation of Balzac's theory of *voyance*, the sumptuous visuality of description is purified of external perception.

Thus a "Cartesian" suspicion of visible phenomena appears essential to Balzac's youthful idea of artistic genius. Victor Morillon embodies an ideal of authorial imagination whose very effectiveness lies in its direct route from envisioning to communication—without the intermediate step of sensory perception. In the descriptive passage from *Les Chouans* discussed above, we saw a gap between (a) nature's *magique spectacle* as it appeared to the soldiers' eyes and (b) the imagined recreation of the scene as constructed by the reader's memory. That gap occasioned an *image imparfaite.* The fictionalized author-figure of Victor Morillon, on the other hand, represents the possibility of perfect images—of scenes whose richness and colors avoid the gap between sensory experience and remembered vision. Paradoxically, to capture scenes in their pictorial fullness—to see *tout et d'un seul coup*—entails a rejection of colors and forms as they assault the eye. Victor does not need to see the world to envision it; his purified model of imagination is Cartesian in its double repudiation of the temporal delay of memory's recreation and of the limited perspective of an observing eye.

Victor Morillon embodies an ascetic ideal, one that is, after all, related to the desire to control one's own imaginary space. In reducing the life of his fictional alter ego to reclusion and second sight, Balzac seems to fulfill a fantasy of the god-like creation of a world out of nothingness. Victor's rejection of lived experience allows him to invent an entire, alternate, literary reality that recalls Balzac's project of the *Comédie humaine.* In an imagined letter, Victor writes: "The solitude and silence of the countryside, the habit I adopted of creating, for my own enjoyment, characters and events placed within a fanciful invention, and my enjoyment of lengthy historical research have led me to embark upon the monumental work whose first installment is before you. . . . I have fought mightily against my inclination to finish up a tableau only after looking at it from all angles at great length" (426). To turn around a "tableau," to encompass it in its entirety before presenting it to the world, is to be seer as master. Balzac's *voyance,* then, has more to do with the reasoned, sovereign control of a created universe than with a Hugolian submission to the oceanic divine. Victor Morillon *sees* neither through experiential empiricism nor mystical self-subjugation; his vision—unlike Louis Lambert's, as we shall see—is pure and abstract, controlled and "Cartesian."[24]

Louis Lambert

In Balzac's philosophical reverie *Louis Lambert* (1832), the titular figure is a childhood friend of the author's, recalled as a doomed genius. Louis Lambert, whom Mme. de Staël described as "a true seer," shares with

Victor Morillon the ability to imagine vivid scenes without having actually perceived them:

By the age of twelve his imagination, stimulated by his ever-active mind, had developed sufficiently to enable him to have such accurate intuitive knowledge of objects he perceived only through reading, that the image of them imprinted upon his soul was just as real as if he had actually seen them. This happened either by analogical reasoning or by endowment with a kind of second sight through which he took in the natural world.[25]

Lambert's second sight seems to fit the model of *voyance* suggested by "L'Avertissement du Gars," in which the perceptible world is bypassed in favor of abstract imagination. The young genius, for example, is astounded one day to find himself visiting a landscape that had previously appeared to him in a dream. He concludes from the uncanny familiarity of the scene that his spirit had actually moved through space while he was asleep, taking a voyage unfettered by the limitations of body and time. Musing on the possibility of movement without space and vision without light, Louis concludes that "we may have internal senses that are independent of external physical laws" (622). The notion of internal senses that parallel those of the body belongs to a long mystical tradition.[26] Lambert follows that tradition in taking vision above the other senses as the privileged medium for mystical revelation: "If apparitions are not impossible," Lambert said, "they must occur through an ability to perceive ideas that represent mankind in its pure essence, and whose existence . . . eludes our outer senses but may be perceived by the inner self during moments of great ecstasy or clarity of sight" (629–30). Ideas are presented here as pure essence, free of the distracting errors of the visible world.[27] As with Victor Morillon and his ideal vision, Lambert's second sight seems disconnected from the mechanics of perception: "'The corsets of sight and hearing,' he said, amused at his turn of phrase, 'are probably what constrict our wondrous minds!'" (623).

The images that interest Louis Lambert are those of the mind, not of the eye. In fact, to access his inner vision, Lambert figuratively shuts off his external senses: "'When I wish to,' he told me in his odd way . . . , 'I draw a veil over my eyes. I quickly withdraw into myself, *where I find a camera obscura*; there, the phenomena of nature are reproduced in a form purer than that in which they first appeared to my external senses.'" (593, my emphasis) This formulation of second sight as a *purer*, non-corporeal type of vision employs a charged metaphor to identify the locus of inner vision: the *chambre noire,* or camera obscura.

As discussed in the Introduction to this book, the camera obscura model of vision promoted a primarily Cartesian conception of vision as reasoned abstraction rather than as physiological phenomenon.[28] The *chambre obscure* isolates the observer from the external world and presents vision not as temporal, bodily sensation but as ideal, purified illumination. This Cartesian subtext does initially appear to correspond to Louis Lambert's retreat from the phenomenal world into a purified space of interiority. As with Victor Morillon, this gifted seer taps into images of a "purer form" than those available to the eye—so that abstraction underlies Balzac's ideal of artistic inspiration. But as Crary reminds us, the implications of the camera obscura model were in flux by the early to mid-1800s, when Balzac was beginning to write the novels of *La Comédie humaine.* Although traditionally associated with a noncorporeal purity of vision, the camera obscura image would eventually be recuperated into empiricist notions of visual perception that take account of temporality and bodily experience.[29] And in fact, if we look again at the *Louis Lambert* passage, we see that his *chambre obscure* already deviates somewhat from the Cartesian ideal as well as from the visionary ideal represented by Victor Morillon. While Morillon was able to access his inner vision directly, Louis Lambert sees with his mind only after seeing with his eyes. His mental images, says Lambert, have a purer form than "that in which they *first appeared* to my external senses" (593; my emphasis). In other words, this visionary does not completely bypass the physical world of phenomenal experience. His "second sight" is structured according to the "first" sight of the bodily eye.

If we take, then, the historical spectrum of theories of visual perception as moving from a seventeenth-century Cartesian idealism (mind over eye) to a nineteenth-century empiricism (eye over mind), Balzac's Victor Morillon represents the former while Louis Lambert begins to incorporate elements of the latter. For, as I have begun to suggest, Lambert's description of his own second sight allows elements of materiality and experience to seep into the idealized model of mystical vision figured by the *chambre obscure*; as the second event in a sequence, his inner vision partakes of an empiricist temporality rather than a Cartesian immediacy. One might even take Balzac's preference for the term "seconde vue" over the contemporary synonym "clairvoyance" as an implicit nod toward vision as empirical acquisition rather than innate revelation. After all, the Cartesian ideal of transparent vision (unimpeded by the potential errors of physical senses) appears in the term "*clair*-voyance," while "seconde vue" retains an echo of "la première vue"—physical sight.[30]

And in fact, throughout *Louis Lambert* the representation of "second sight" remains connected to a physiological, phenomenal visuality. The schoolboy Lambert's keen eyesight, for example, is instrumental in his astounding capacity for learning: "He had developed the curious phenomenon of being able to absorb ideas through reading; his eye took in seven or eight lines at a glance, and his mind took in their meaning at equal speed" (16–17). Eye and mind work in conjunction here; physical perception is not skipped over in Balzac's conception of genius. Lambert's eyesight is emphasized as its own faculty, much as in the description of Etienne, the visionary title character of Balzac's story "L'Enfant maudit": "Like all men whose souls dominate their bodies, he had keen eyesight and could easily discern from great distances the most fleeting nuances of light, the most transient stirrings of water" (391). Such emphases on the physical properties of eyesight—its relation to distance and to light—may seem out of place in the description of men whose souls "dominate" their bodies. But it underlines the fact that Balzac's understanding of *vision* is not a decorporealized one. The eye may act as privileged intermediary between body and *esprit*, but it does not do so as a transparent gate or window to the other world; rather, it retains its physiological characteristics.[31]

Of course, *Louis Lambert* is a rather unsystematic text, influenced by Swedenborgian and Mesmerist mumbo-jumbo and by the temporal distance separating the author's memory from Lambert's theoretical proclamations. It would, therefore, be a mistake to try to extract a coherent doctrine out of Louis Lambert's often contradictory musings on the relation between mind and matter, *voyance* and physical sensation. But that incoherence itself argues against a purified, sublimated mysticism that bypasses physicality altogether. Balzac presents the gift of second sight in *Louis Lambert* as an unexplained phenomenon whose makeup defies rigorous distinctions between matter and spirit. At the end of his narrative about Louis Lambert's short, doomed life, the narrator proposes a distillation of Lambert's revelations, which includes this definition of second sight, or *Specialité*: "*Specialité* consists of seeing objects in the material world as well as those in the spiritual world in their primordial and logical ramifications" (688). Two aspects of this definition go beyond the explicitly mystical, purely eternal character of the faculty of second sight. First, the seer is understood to have access not only to a transcendent, spiritual realm, but to the hidden meanings of the *material* world as well. The revelation of occult, or hidden, causes in the daily, physical world undermines any theoretical separation between the "Balzac-réaliste" and "Balzac-visionnaire." Second, the vision is not an atemporal revelation but an understanding of origins and consequences—that is, of past and future; the role of the seer is not incompatible with the human experience of time. In this way, *vue* (sight, with all its physiological implications) imprints itself onto *vision* (revelatory vision).

This implicit incorporation of sight into vision is in keeping with the *Avant-propos*' more deliberate defense of materialism. In that text, the search for metaphysical truths implies—necessitates, even—the close observation of the material world. If thought is like light, as the *Avant-propos* asserts, it is because both are substances whose materiality acts as impetus—not obstacle—to revelation. One does not, as Descartes implied, have to bypass the body to get to the mind. I am suggesting a link between this philosophical materialism and more specifically optical theories of vision as a context for Balzac's use of the term "second sight." Louis Lambert's great moment of revelation comes with his dramatic formulation of the *Avant-propos* analogy between thought and light: "'To think is to see!' [*Penser, c'est voir!*], he told me one day in a fury" (*AP*, 615). This assertion should be taken as more than just an instance of the familiar trope in which vision is used as metaphorical figure for understanding. Instead of evacuating the optical meaning from the term "to see" (as happens when one says "I see!" to mean "I understand"), this statement materializes the term "to think": thought is no longer to be understood as purely incorporeal, but as a substance analogous to light. Thomas Reid, as noted above, writes that all perception presupposes conception—but Louis Lambert's "Penser, c'est voir!" makes the opposite point: conception is necessarily shaped according to the forms of perception. As in the *Avant-propos*, Balzac refuses to abandon the physical world to a rarefied concept of pure philosophy. Even in the revelations of his spiritualist hero-*voyant*, matter retains a hold.

In the end, then, *Louis Lambert* complicates the opposition of spirit to matter. Louis is presented as "soul-dominant" like the *enfant maudit* and Séraphîta, beings whose angelic nature dooms them to eventual exclusion from the base, physical world. The narrator—Balzac as a child—represents the materialist counterpart to Lambert's spiritualism: "He was a spiritualist; but I was bold enough to contradict him by using against him his own observations that intelligence was an entirely physical product" (*LL*, 615). The extremes of this argument (mind as pure spirit, mind as pure matter) are consistently and explicitly denounced with Balzac's general defense of the imbrication of spirit and matter: "We were both right." What to make, then, of the fact that the materialist narrator survives, while the spiritualist seer goes mad and dies? Certainly, the text presents itself as a nostalgic elegy for the pure spirit that cannot make it in this world; like Séraphîta's ascension, Lambert's tragic death reflects an incompatibility between Ideal and Real. But Balzac's text also puts into question the utility of a pure model of *voyance*, of vision unmarred by the material world. Lambert's obsessive worldly passion with Pauline (initiated, significantly, through the eyes) is presented as the beginning of a downfall into madness and death. No productive legacy is left behind, beyond the incoherent musings collected posthumously by his narrator-friend. It is in fact this narrator who survives—survives to become Balzac, the writer of the *Comédie humaine*. In a certain sense, materialism has won out in the world, even while idealism remains an object of nostalgic mourning.

If the fictional Victor Morillon represents an ideal horizon of pure, noncorporeal vision, *Louis Lambert* tells how the gift of second sight plays out in the world. Victor as author can be seen as a preempiricist ideal, a fantasy creator, given that Balzac's own writing was in fact supported by actual experience and observation. Once applied to a real life, that of Louis Lambert, the concept of second sight takes on the thickness and impurity of the material world. With his paean to Lambert's *voyance*, Balzac strains toward a visionary ideal; but the sheer materiality of his realist oeuvre taps into an alternative mode of visuality that engages the bodily eye, not just the mental one.

Chapter 2

"Tomber dans le phénomène": Afterimages in *La Maison Nucingen* and *Le Bal de Sceaux*

> *It often happens that we look at a dress, a tapestry, or a blank sheet of paper so absentmindedly that we do not immediately perceive a shape or glittering spot thereupon that later strikes our eye all of a sudden, as if it had appeared there at the very moment we noticed it.*
>
> —Le Bal de Sceaux

Many of us, as Balzac suggests in the above passage, have turned our attention away from a particular object and encountered the delayed visual impression of a blurred shape or a spot of bright light. The effect is even more dramatic when one has purposely focused on an especially contrasting and luminous image, such as the pattern of dark window frames against a light window. The resulting effect (with the light/dark pattern reversed) is called a "retinal afterimage," an optical phenomenon with a telling history.

Before the eighteenth century, the "afterimage effect" had been dismissed as illusory and therefore inconsequential for serious studies of vision, concerned as they were with the objective nature of the physical world. After Peiresc described afterimages of windows in 1634, the phenomenon became a sort of parlor trick.[1] And although the "illusion" attracted the scientific attention of thinkers like Mariotte, Newton, and de la Hire, it was not until the eighteenth century that the retinal afterimage became an object of study as one of several subjective phenomena of vision. No longer was the science of optics concerned only with the physics of objective reality and the rational laws governing a normative concept of vision; Locke's empiricism had turned attention to the subjective experience of seeing. Illusory appearances like blur circles (the "haloes" formed around distant lights), floaters (*mouches volantes,* or "flying gnats"), and retinal afterimages became part of a larger inquiry into the ways in which our bodily eyes affect how we see the world. In 1743, Buffon (the naturalist whose work interested a young Balzac) published his "Dissertation sur les couleurs accidentelles," a term he coined to describe the afterimages of colors as distinguished from the objective colors we first perceive. "Les couleurs accidentelles" are effects of the eye, depending on our organ of sight rather than on the properties of light; they are verified through the observation of subjective experience. Buffon's observation of retinal afterimages paved the way for a growing interest among nineteenth-century scholars, such as Goethe, whose definition of the phenomenon locates it in the observer's body: "Let the observer look steadfastly on a small coloured object and let it be taken away after a time while his eyes remain unmoved; the spectrum of another colour will then be visible on the white plane . . . it arises from an image which now *belongs to the eye*."[2] And it was, indeed, to the physiology of the eye itself that nineteenth-century scientists like Purkinje, Aubert, and Helmholtz turned for explanations, as they performed numerous experiments designed to test the neurological effects of retinal stimulation by light and electrical sparks. Despite the many advances in the field, however, even as late as 1867 Helmholtz decried the incompleteness and inexactitude of scientific knowledge on afterimages. The problem, explains Helmholtz, lies in the limitations of the observer's body: "generally these experiments soon prove to be so trying to the eyes that severe and dangerous ocular and nervous trouble may ensue if they are pursued too long."[3] Thus the very thing that made afterimages a new object of study—their corporeality—also limited the means of acquiring knowledge about them. As scientific inquiry about vision moved gradually from Cartesian abstraction to an experience-based empiricism, the body became both object and tool for the study of vision. Cartesian models had swept away anomalies, pulses, and bodily eccentricities in order to create a rationalized, idealized model of vision, but empiricist theories of vision brought them back, attempting to explain the eye's functions through observation of how and what a living subject's eye actually sees under changing conditions.

And in fact, it was their groundedness—in the body, in time—that made afterimages such a suggestive phenomenon for empiricist theorists of vision. Afterimages carried important theoretical implications for the study of perception and cognition: as phenomena produced through an interaction of light and the bodily eye, afterimages are subjective; as delayed responses to an initial luminous impression, afterimages exist within a sequential temporality.[4] Both characteristics imply a new way of understanding how we see—and know—the world: through experience, through time. Thus within scientific discourse, the study of afterimages signals an important epistemological shift away from objectivity and atemporality, away from the kind of abstract purity of the camera obscura model that Balzac nostalgically invoked to depict Louis Lambert's visionary gift.

So what does it mean when Balzac calls our attention to the experience of afterimages? Surely, in the passage cited above, Balzac is not entering into a scientific debate about methodology in the field of optics. He neither identifies the phenomenon as an "afterimage" nor invests his reference with any explicit epistemological weight. And yet the narrative context of these optical images can tell us something new not only about Balzac's conception of vision and its relation to knowledge, but also about what visual epistemology has to do with his literary project itself. The conjunction of visual figure and narrative form begins to emerge, for example, in another text featuring a retinal afterimage: *La Maison Nucingen* (1838).

La Maison Nucingen

La Maison Nucingen is the rather convoluted story of Eugène de Rastignac's rise to fortune through the financial dealings of his lover's husband, the Baron de Nucingen. It is narrated as an overheard tale told by a dinner reveler, Bixiou, to his Parisian buddies in a restaurant. Bixiou and his friend Blondet have promised to satisfy their friends' curiosity with a detailed narration of the banking deals that propelled Rastignac upward through the layers of French society, leading to a tale full of secondary characters and seemingly unrelated events.

One episode concerns a ball at which a mediocre young Parisian named Godefroid de Beaudenord becomes enamored of a lovely—and unmarried—young lady. Godefroid, a superficial fop who ends up being the dupe of Rastignac's financial machinations, is convinced by a friend that he should ask for the lady's hand in marriage. As Bixiou tells it, the lovestruck Godefroid can think only of the object of his affections, Isaure, for several days after the ball: "For three days, *in the camera obscura of his mind,* Godefroid saw *his* Isaure with her white camellias, and her head's noble bearing, *as when, after looking at a brightly-lit object for a long time, we see it again with our eyes closed in a smaller, radiant, and colored form, sparkling among the shadows*" (353, my emphasis).[5] The reader will recognize the two optical phenomena in this comparison: the camera obscura (here, as with *Louis Lambert,* compared to the dark enclosure of one's mind) and the retinal afterimage (a bright object reappears as a persistent, blurred image once one's eyes are closed). Their coexistence reminds us that Balzac is writing during a period of flux in theories of vision, when the implied mastery of Cartesian perspectivalism overlaps with the subjective corporeality of empiricism.[6]

When the passage in *La Maison Nucingen* moves from the *chambre obscure* to the effects of afterimages, it reinserts the temporal, bodily, phenomenal world into an abstracted, Cartesian model of vision (and recapitulates in miniature the drift of nineteenth-century science). This point is made clearer when we compare the passage directly to the one from *Louis Lambert* cited in Chapter 1: "I quickly withdraw into myself, *where I find a camera obscura; there, the phenomena of nature are reproduced in a form purer* than that in which they first appeared to my external senses" (*LL*, 593; my emphasis). Both Louis Lambert and Godefroid perceive mental images in the figural camera obscura of their minds. The image of a darkened chamber signals a distance from the external, physical world. For Louis Lambert, the distance is caused by an ascetic retreat from the physical world, and for Godefroid it is brought about by the physical absence of the woman he admires. But while Lambert's *chambre noire* allows a purified image of the world to develop, Godefroid's is modified, as though by the subjective phenomenon of afterimages: compare the "purer" form of Lambert's mental image to Godefroid's "smaller, radiant, and intensely-colored form, sparkling among the shadows." The latter description recalls the language used to describe retinal afterimages, in which the bright blots of color appear shaky and hazy because of the eye's twitches and the semi-obscurity of the closed eyelid. Balzac's language deviates from the conventional way in which the camera obscura had been used to figure vision—that is, as a chamber whose minute opening allows a ray of light to project an accurate image to the retina while shutting out any disruptive, extraneous phenomena. In the passage from *La Maison Nucingen*, the *chambre obscure* of the mind is compared to a *closed* eye, one whose nerves and pulses blur the shrunken, shimmering image. From pure blackness (Louis Lambert's "chambre noire") to shadowy obscurity (Godefroid's "chambre obscures" and "ténèbres"), the two passages echo a subtle ambivalence in optical discourse between the clearcut purity of abstracted vision and the bodily disturbances of experiential sight.

It is only fitting, of course, that the spiritual visionary Lambert be associated with an atemporal model of revelation while the lovestruck Godefroid is associated with a corporeal and subjective perception. After all, Lambert is gifted with the inner vision of "second sight," while Godefroid—propelled by his libidinal stirrings and blind to the ways in which he is being manipulated—has a real lack of vision; the two characters lie on either side, as it were, of normal visual perception. What I find interesting, however, is that this difference manifests itself even in the casual and seemingly similar use of an optical phenomenon, the camera obscura, to refer to their mental processes. While Lambert "sees" the abstract truths of a burgeoning philosophy in his purified mind, Godefroid sees Isaure, the conventionally pretty and conveniently rich young lady he wants to marry. Bixiou calls Godefroid's attraction to Isaure "l'idéal ascétique"—a possible indication of a link to Lambert's visionary mode—but the phrase can only be taken as irony, since Godefroid's rather bumbling courtship shows no signs of pure artistic, ascetic, or amorous genius. Even if Godefroid's *cerveau* is initially pure, it is soon affected by the afterimages of time and the body in the form of libidinal interest and manipulations of financial timing.

La Maison Nucingen is, after all, a story about cynical intrigue and enterprising venality. Through a series of complex investments, divestments, false rumors, and delays, the Baron de Nucingen uses underhanded financial intrigue to ensure Eugène de Rastignac's rise to fortune. Speculation here takes on a joint financial and visual meaning, with the chance effects of the market combining with conscious distractions of Godefroid's focus of attention in order to blind, *aveugler*, the victims of the capitalist ruses. The move in visuality from absolute essence to phenomenal appearances corresponds, in a sense, to the move in early nineteenth-century finance from a confidence in stable values to a more fluid conception of the relation between monetary units and their changing appearances (in the stock market, for example). With their "fausse faillite" [fraudulent bankruptcy] scheme, Rastignac and de Nucingen are able to manipulate those appearances because they have abandoned an absolutist belief in transcendental value.[7] Similarly, the scientists of empiricist vision turn their attention away from abstract models of vision and toward the shifting, pulsing phenomena of visual experience. Rather than pin down a transcendental physics of vision, they allow temporality to affect its study. The interest in retinal afterimages, or "les couleurs accidentelles," rests on the fact that they function according to temporal delays and to an element of chance—much as Rastignac's manipulation of Godefroid's investment relies on chance and temporal delay for its success.

This may seem like a negative shift—from an idealized, pure image to "une forme moindre" [a lesser form] of a previous ideal, but there may be more at stake here than just a nostalgic glance at purer forms of ascetic vision and value. We should remember that *La Maison Nucingen* is a tale within a tale: the framing scenes take place at a restaurant, where an unidentified narrator has overheard a story told by the young man-about-town Bixiou and his friends. The narrator then recounts the story, with a full staging of its narration, complete with details about Bixiou's voice, his gestures, and interruptions from his listeners. In a way, then, *La Maison Nucingen* is a story about storytelling. As the main internal author-figure, Bixiou is materially incorporated into the very production of the tale—unlike Victor Morillon, who is given a fictional role external to the story of *Les Chouans.*

Bixiou's listeners continuously attack his storytelling technique as *marivaudage* (narrative affectation). For example, when he begins to expound upon the camellias worn by Isaure at a ball, Bixiou is interrupted by his companion Blondet: "Here we go again with Sancho's three hundred goats!" (351), an allusion to Don Quixote's exhortation to Sancho Panza to get to the point. Bixiou defends the value of pleasure over brevity in literature and Blondet apologizes for the interruption. Bixiou is interrupted again, however, right after he compares Godefroid's mental image of Isaure to the effects of afterimages:

> [Bixiou:] Godefroid saw *his* Isaure with her white camellias, and her head's noble bearing, as when, after looking at a brightly lit object for a long time, we see it again with our eyes closed in a smaller, radiant, and colored form, sparkling among the shadows.
>
> "Bixiou," said Couture, "you're lapsing into pointless details [*tu tombes dans le phénomène*], how about putting them together into scenes[*tableaux*] for us?" (353)

"Tu tombes dans le phénomène"—Well, precisely! At the very moment that he invokes the subjective phenomenon of vision we call an afterimage, Bixiou is accused of paying attention to the world of appearances, of inessential phenomena, of details that do not matter. Or to return to the terms used by Thomas Reid, he is accused of pausing at the level of *apparences visibles* before getting on to what they signify. The centuries-long philosophical debate between unifying essence and diversity of forms gets applied here to the realm of narrative—through a visual figure. Bixiou has gone beyond a conventional description of imagined love by appealing to our own visual experience, to the way in which an idealized image—rather than remaining stable in the abstract vacuum of a pure camera obscura—is distorted, blurred, changed by the mechanisms of our bodily eye. Couture's impatient reaction to this appeal signals a desire to pull Bixiou back to a less visual narrative essence and away from "des tableaux" of overpainted, colored narrative. In other words, Couture wants Bixiou to eliminate distracting details drawn from the material (sensory, phenomenal) world and to pass directly to the story's essence—just as an idealist theory of vision tries to eliminate the phenomenal distractions of sensory perception from an idealized and instantaneous form of vision.

But Bixiou, the storyteller, defends his narration. The material world cannot be skipped over, for it comprises the tale itself. In the realist mode of storytelling, the details *do* count, the phenomena of the visible world do "matter." The material particulars—like the number of Isaure's camellias or the way in which Godefroid's imaging of her recalls our own visual experience—are not to be skipped over in the service of brevity any more than the visible world is to be skipped over in the service of a theoretical purity of vision.

In short, Balzac's own narrative project is at stake in Bixiou's defense of "phenomenal" narration. Bixiou embodies the author function not as isolated *voyant* but as effective guide to the labyrinthine realities of society. He is no fictional Victor Morillon, pure spirit and ideal horizon of artistic production as imagined in a Preface draft. Bixiou belongs to the real cast of characters populating Balzac's *Comédie humaine.* And his narrative project has less to do with providing a distillation of a sweeping historical event (as *Les Chouans* was meant to do) than with providing the reader with the sense of a particular atmosphere at a particular moment; as readers we are given enough details to identify with the narrator, sated by an elegant Parisian restaurant meal, listening from behind a curtain to intriguing and intrigue-filled gossip.

As his themes and methods move away from idealized overviews and toward daily dealings and contemporary experience, Balzac closes a gap that had been established in the Preface to *Les Chouans* between visionary author and worldly reader. In that Preface, Balzac described Victor Morillon as a publicity-shy seer, reluctant to tarnish the purity of his vision by allowing mercenary publishers to share his stories with the world: "If he were to describe the images best kept within his soul, the hastily sketched tableaux, no sooner drawn than erased, that passed through his innermost thoughts bearing the charm of daybreak, exposing them for all to see, he would witness the loss of their virginal bloom" (414). This early, melodramatic description of the images wrought by gifted inspiration emphasizes their purity, their protection from the eyes of the public, their isolation in a sort of *chambre noire* of the soul—so much so that contact with the world necessarily defiles them. With Bixiou, on the other hand, there is no such imaginative purity: his tale of Rastignac's rise to fortune is based on what he has directly observed, heard, witnessed. The scene of narration itself is meant to be visualized, so that the reader may phenomenologically enter the experience not only in the tale but *of* the tale.[8] Where *Les Chouans*'s unidentified narrator had lamented the impossibility of a reader seeing the story's introductory landscape, *La Maison Nucingen* presents the reader with sensory connections to every element of the story. Bixiou's narration functions according to the empirical logic of observation and experience. Unlike the abrupt revelation of images in Victor Morillon's mental sanctuary (his "virginal bloom"), Bixiou's story comes to the reader slowly, with interruptions and delays, temporal mediation and sensory screens. If Victor represents the visionary purity of second sight, *La Maison Nucingen* casts aside that purity in favor of a temporal logic of narration, a series of *after*-images rather than one pure "second sight." And its figural move from *camera obscura* to afterimage indicates a shift from atemporal illumination to bodily vision elaborated over time.

What are the implications of this textually encoded move in Balzac from one mode of seeing to another? Might we not read *La Maison Nucingen* as an exploration of the "modern observer"—that is, of the seeing subject as bodily, temporally grounded and implicated in a nexus of political and economic forces that strip the subject of perspectival mastery? I think so, for a variety of reasons. For one thing, the multiple, framed narration (by Bixou, Blondet, Finot, and Couture) implies the abdication of a single, all-knowing perspective. As with changing theories of optics, an objective, mastering gaze is decentered, and Reason is replaced with the experience of individuals. This narrative "democracy" is in keeping with Bixiou's defense of the story's flow as against the voiced desire by his listeners for a narrative purity, one that follows only the "essence" of the tale. Further, the move away from pure, essential value is echoed in the financial themes of the tale, where relativism and speculation determine the rise and fall of fortunes. And finally, the narrative and financial flux are linked to new modes of government. After having heard the ins and outs of the financial rigmarole that allowed Nucingen and Rastignac to make their fortunes, Blondet proclaims that the only way to eliminate financial corruption is to go back to absolute rule: "Back to absolute government, the only one that can repress the strivings of the Spirit against the Law!" (392). He adds that all healthy societies go back to a monarchy in one form or another. With Blondet's outburst, *La Maison Nucingen* ends on a note of nostalgia for the stable purity of a political absolutism. But its narrative form belies that nostalgia, proposing instead a forward flow whose implications include the following substitutions: (a) history for transcendence; (b) empirical methodology for a priori deduction; (c) speculation for absolute monetary value; (d) gradual sight for visionary illumination; (e) multiple narration for unifying perspective; (f) bodily flux for abstract purity; and (g) (semi-) democratic regimes for absolute monarchy.

This may seem a lot to hang on a minor short story like *La Maison Nucingen*, but I want with this list to show how thoroughly a visual tension—between transcendental "second sight" and physiology-based optics—inflects the broader historical, philosophical, and narrative ambivalences that course through *La Comédie humaine*. There is no doubt that Balzac, writing at a time of postrevolutionary flux, was looking both backward and forward. While texts like *Les Chouans*, *Louis Lambert*, and *Séraphîta* exist under the sign of a dominant nostalgia, other texts exhibit a forward propulsion that reflects the modernizing impulses of empiricism. Among these I would count *Le Bal de Sceaux*, an analysis of which will both clarify this point and extend the connections between visual and political ambivalences in Balzac.

Le Bal de Sceaux

Le Bal de Sceaux was written in 1829, soon after *Les Chouans.* But while *Les Chouans* is set in 1800, at the end of an era (note the original title, "The *Last* Chouan"), *Le Bal de Sceaux* takes place in 1815, at the beginning of the Restoration reign of Louis XVIII—a time of transition, of change, and of a sense of inevitable progress. It is the story of Emilie de Fontaine, the elegant and beautiful youngest daughter of a royalist count, Monsieur de Fontaine. A Bourbon loyalist, Fontaine had lost a fortune fighting bravely for the king during Napoleon's first rise to power. Such selflessness had won him the consideration of the other courtiers as "the purest of the Vendeans"—but that consideration included as well a bit of sneering at such absolute *purity.* Slowly, the count begins to realize that those who had joined the king in exile had received far more compensation than those who had bravely fought at home. As a result, Fontaine decides to emigrate with the court during the second royal exile (1814–1815); in other words, he learns from experience. He learns so well, in fact, that he returns to France with the court, after Napoleon's defeat, as one of Louis XVIII's closest advisors. Despite having once balked at any hint of dilution of monarchical power, he eventually accepts representative rule: "This philosopher prince [Louis XVIII] had taken pleasure in converting the Vendean [Fontaine] to the ideas imposed by the nineteenth century's progress and the monarchy's restoration" (117).[9] Fontaine has observed his surroundings and allowed experience to modify an originally pure political model.

Fontaine's daughter, Emilie, is another story. Among the favors that Louis XVIII has granted to Fontaine is the promise that his children will marry wealthy bourgeois mates. But as *Le Bal de Sceaux* begins, we learn that his youngest child, Emilie, refuses all proposed matches because she considers them beneath her station. The count's move to a progressive political stance included the acceptance of a new definition of nobility, based not only on aristocratic birth but on merit and even on wealth. Emilie, on the other hand, clings to the most traditional, essentialist definition of nobility taught to her by her aristocratic mother: to be a nobleman, one must be born a nobleman. Emilie has in mind an image (we could say a "preimage") of her ideal mate: he must be rich, elegant, handsome, svelte, and a Peer of France—that is, of the highest nobility.

Notably, Emilie wants her ideal suitor's nobility to be visually apparent. She seems especially interested in the arms emblazoned on her future spouse's carriage as a visible sign of his standing: "I would find it intolerable," she announces, "not to see my coat of arms painted on the panels of my carriage amid the flowing folds of an azure cloak" (123).

The lucky position of judgment from which this young lady rejects all suitors is set up by Balzac in visual terms: "The young man who did not, at first glance, meet the required conditions was not favored with a second look."

Emilie herself, like so many of Balzac's characters, displays the traits of her personality so that they can be perceived by the eye. Haughtiness and disdain, for example, manifest themselves in her height, her "piercing eyes," and even a rather long neck, which allows her to survey the world (and her suitors) from above. From her position of superiority, Emilie masters the social spectacle of her time, where seeing and being seen determine every intrigue, amorous or political. Her father, though, worries that the world might tire of "someone who remains onstage for so long without putting an end to the play in which she performs," for if Emilie's power lies in her visibility, it also relies on a certain blindness in her audience: "the count sensed that his daughter's pretensions, the absurdity of which was sure to become apparent [*visible*] to certain ladies who were as observant [*clairvoyantes*] as they were unkind, would in time become a fatal subject of mockery" (124). Emilie has turned the serious business of marriage into a game whose investment in the visual realm is threatened by the emptiness of optical illusion. Her father still hopes that the suitors he presents to his daughter will have a chance, "that his gathering of would-be lovers would not turn out, this time, to be a mere fantasmagoria for his daughter" (125). A fantasmagoria—that is, a purely superficial distraction for the eyes, to be dismissed as amusing illusion.[10]

The visual mastery that Emilie exerts over her private domain, however, is doomed to be toppled at the ball of the story's title. As Anne-Marie Meininger proposes in her introduction to *Le Bal de Sceaux*, the choice of this particular ball reveals Balzac's interest in social and political questions that surpass the private romance of a young lady:

> the Sceaux ball is not merely the place where Emilie . . . sees Longueville for the first time. It is, above all, a site for a symbolic encounter between the past and the future; it is the "fascinating mêlée" of the aristocracy and the masses, of those who watch and those who move, of those coming from manors where things are preserved and those from the fields and offices or shops where things are acquired, of the class in decline and the class on the rise. (*BS*, 98)

But if the ball marks a link between past and future, manorial aristocracy and commercial class—as indeed the outcome of the story confirms—Emilie arrives at Sceaux blind to the potential blurring of the boundaries she holds so dear. In fact she has decided to attend this provincial country dance for the simple amusement of displaying her radiant beauty. Emilie is certain that the townsfolk will be devoid of interest for her, other than as objects of ridicule: "Mlle de Fontaine amused herself by imagining how the townsfolk would look; laughing in advance at the affected dancers sure to be present, she saw herself [*elle se voyait*] leaving the memory of her enchanting gaze and smile in many a bourgeois heart" (133)."She saw herself": as both subject and object of her imagined visuality, Emilie puts herself in the Cartesian position of visual control through abstraction of the self. The perspective external to her own body allows Emilie to imagine the effect that her own charming glances will have on the bourgeois population. They, she is sure, will be "magnetized"—that is, subjugated by her visible radiance and rendered incapable of turning away their own eyes. Emilie's haughty eye will, in short, direct a play of gazes. At least, that is what the young coquette expects from her country outing.

But something unexpected happens to Emilie as she makes her rounds at the modest ball—something that is presented initially as an optical phenomenon familiar to the reader:

> It often happens that we look at a dress, a tapestry, or a blank sheet of paper so absentmindedly that we do not immediately perceive a shape or glittering spot thereupon that later strikes our eye all of a sudden, as if it had appeared there at the very moment we noticed it; by means of a somewhat similar moral phenomenon, Mlle de Fontaine recognized in a young man the very image of the external perfection she had dreamed of for so long. (134)

This passage, which I cited as epigraph to this chapter, returns us to retinal afterimages. As with the comparison in *La Maison Nucingen* between Godefroid's mental image and the common phenomenon of afterimages, this description of Emilie's perception of a young man appeals to the readers' visual experience. The "shapes" or "spots" (*taches*) and "glittering spots" in Balzac's analogy recall the physiological effects of retinal stimulation described by scientists of vision like Buffon and Helmholtz. Remember that Cartesian optics dismissed such phenomena as irrelevant to the study of vision. For empiricist theories of vision, on the other hand, these seemingly unimportant specks on the eye are essential indicators of optical physiology. Balzac's use of afterimages in this comparison emphasizes this central significance: Emilie's expectations that nothing in the "blankness" of the ball will attract her attention is belied by the eventual importance of the young man who appears to her as though he were an afterimage. We are being told, in effect, to pay attention to the details, to the phenomena of the visible world, because they are what motivate Balzac's story and the society it describes.

Let me add a further nuance to my reading of this passage. Balzac's announced parallel of optical phenomena (the spots and lights that "strike our eye all of a sudden") and moral phenomena ("a somewhat similar moral phenomenon") does not actually hold up as a rigorous comparison. One would expect the second term of the comparison to refer to Emilie's eventual recognition that a handsome man had crossed into her field of vision without her having initially noticed him. Instead, Balzac tells us that Emilie came across a man who fit the imagined ideal that she had mentally formed in advance. One might paraphrase Balzac's sentence thus: "just as something we hadn't consciously perceived (although it had crossed our field of vision) appears retrospectively to the eye, Emilie perceived a visual image whose existence she had earlier only imagined." If a déjà vu, a "have-seen," exists for Emilie, it is only because of her imagination's force—not because of any real similarity of structure between the optical experience of afterimages and her described visual interaction with the *jeune homme.* The result is a catachresis in which the physiological term (a young man passes through Emilie's scopic field) is left out entirely. The "monstrosity" of the figure as well as the hesitancy of Balzac's "somewhat similar" (*assez semblable*) point to a conceptual tension—between two models of vision. For in fact, the two sides of Balzac's equation are anything but "semblable," in that they invoke two different types of seeing: the "*pre*-image" of a Cartesian apriority, in which visual truths are deduced from pre-existing abstract models; and the *after*-image of empiricist induction, in which optical phenomena are studied for what they can tell us about visual functioning. Emilie's absolute adherence to a preexisting image of her ideal suitor belongs to a Cartesian logic of abstraction. Balzac's rhetorical appeal to the reader in this passage, on the other hand, privileges the empiricist model as useful for his telling of the story—a story that ends up undermining Emilie's absolutist visuality.

How is Emilie toppled from her high perch of visual mastery? It begins with the passage above, which alerts the reader to the importance of Emilie's first visual contact with the young man at the ball. Then, as though the textual structure itself were recreating the double temporality of an afterimage, we get a longer, second version of that moment, stretched out over a more detailed description. First, Emilie is seated in a position of visual mastery over the scene:

> she had stationed herself at the edge of the group formed by her family so that she could stand up or move forward as she wished, interacting with the living tableaux and groups gathered in the room as if she were visiting a museum exhibition; she boldly peered through her lorgnon at someone standing right beside her and pondered him as if critiquing or praising a study of a head or a genre scene. (134)

Through this analogy of country dance to museum exhibit, the narrator transforms human subjects into static "tableaux," framed visual objects of Emilie's art-critic eye.[11]

But this eye does not keep its privileged position: "*Her gaze,* after wandering over this immense animated canvas, *was suddenly seized* by a figure that seemed to have been deliberately placed in a corner of the tableau, to the best possible advantage, like a character *out of all proportion to those around him.* The stranger . . . was standing with his arms crossed while bent forward slightly, as if placed there to have his portrait painted" (134, my emphasis). Emilie's gaze, starting out as grammatical subject and sign of her visual mastery, loses its status quickly; it is "seized" or "seized upon," controlled externally, taken into a perspective other than its own. And taken by what? By something that exceeds the picturesque framing of Emilie's country scene: by an alternate subject existing outside the rules of proportion and perspective set up by Emilie's smug art-viewer position. According to the rules of perspective for painting that were drawn up by Brunelleschi and Alberti in the Renaissance (and that dominated classical theories of art), a single element that is out of proportion in a painting destabilizes the entire work. It provokes a *désaxement,* a discrepancy vis-à-vis the origin point that is meant to organize the represented space. The "stranger" (*inconnu*) at the Bal de Sceaux is presented as just such an element, one whose disproportion will overturn and trouble the "tableau" that is Emilie's world. Moreover, it is disproportionate only in relation to Emilie's position; in and of himself, the "inconnu" embodies the perfect ideal of esthetic form: "His trim, elegant figure recalled the splendid proportions of Apollo" (135).

Emilie is used to being the center of interest and attention. She usually wields control over her suitors by magnetizing them, attracting their desiring gazes. But this stranger, far from succumbing to Emilie's scopic field, is gazing entrancedly at another: "His fixed gaze was following the movements of a particular dancer, disclosing as it did so a deeply felt emotion" (135). And Emilie's own gaze is seized and led in to *his* visual vector: "Mlle de Fontaine then followed the young man's gaze and espied the reason for his indifference to her" (136). Emilie is marginalized by the young man's inattention at the same time that she is becoming enraptured by his perfect appearance, at the moment when her haughty "survol" is troubled by desire for the first time in her life.

Naturally, Emilie will do all she can to regain her elevated position. Her amusing, bumbling attempts to do so occur, once again, in terms of visual mastery. First, our young coquette wanders apparently aimlessly over to the area where the young man is standing. Although she feigns indifference, "by means of an optical contrivance [*artifice d'optique*] women often use, not one of the young man's movements escaped her notice" (136). She later proposes to her brother a promenade around the handsome stranger "under the pretext of wanting to observe the garden's varied perspectives [*points de vue*]" (136–37). Emilie is used to surveying her sea of suitors from the "points de vue" of her whims, as though the people around her were sculptures in an art gallery. But even her attempt to recreate the control through a contrived perspectival walk fails. Through the stranger's indifference, Emilie's visual field has become uncertain, destabilized.

To a certain extent, Emilie's *effets d'optique* do end up capturing the young man's attention; he comes calling a few days later. The story unfolds with a series of encounters that leaves Emilie more and more enamored of the young man, Maximilien, though she is unable to discover his rank. Maximilien seems to fit her preordained ideal to perfection: he is stunningly rich, meltingly handsome, talented at dancing, generous, and good—and he loves Emilie sincerely. It is only a matter of time before the young couple fall in love. But it is a love based on a mutual blind spot: his *punctum caecum* is her snobbery, which he keeps hoping does not really exist; and hers is his nonnoble rank, which she allows herself to deny. They avow their love for each other in a tender engagement scene, but the luster soon fades when Emilie is confronted with visual proof that her fiancé is not a nobleman: she sees him selling cloth in a bourgeois boutique. Emilie's disappointment is enormous, and despite her love for Maximilien, she cruelly rejects him, even after learning that his lowly employment is due to a generous sacrifice by Maximilien for his older brother to attain the Peerage—the title, that is, that Emilie finds so essential to her union. The tragicomic dénouement has Emilie, age twenty-two, marrying her eighty-year-old great-uncle and—to top it off—learning too late that Maximilien has inherited the title Pair de France from his father and older brother.

This somewhat amusing comeuppance of a snobby young lady relates the story's progressive political moral through the figural decentering of a visual subject. If *Le Bal de Sceaux* is a political fable, it is also a fable of visibility, of the relations between seeing and knowing. The great disappointment in Emilie's life is due to a social upheaval that changes the rules of perspective that had governed her idealized world. First, Maximilien's appearance indicates nobility to Emilie; then, when she sees him selling merchandise, she believes that her initial assessment was wrong. The gap between how he seems and what he is confounds Emilie's hopes for a happy marriage. As a result, she ends up wishing for a relation between essence and appearance that would guarantee that a suitor's beauty and elegance be commensurate with his rank. This wish takes the form of nostalgia for an era when social hierarchies were confirmed by visible signs:

> If she were able to influence the Chamber as her father had, she said, she would call for a law requiring tradespeople . . . to be branded on their foreheads, as sheep were in Berry, until they had reached their third generation. . . . In her

view, it may well have been to the monarchy's disadvantage that there was no visible difference between a merchant and a peer of France. (158)

Political absolutism is linked here to stable visuality.[12] Horrified by the social mobility of this postrevolutionary age, Emilie wants to legislate appearances, to ensure a transparent relation between what things are and how they appear to the eye.

But the political flexibility of Louis XVIII's reign indicates a new, troubled status of the privileged seeing subject. No longer able to take in the world at a *coup d'œil* (as Emilie did when she first saw Maximilien at the ball), the modern observer must gain experience with the subtle, changing phenomena of social appearances in order to interpret them. Emilie's *coup d'œil*, based as it is on an absolute, preexisting image of the world as it should be, recalls the Cartesian aprioristic conception of innate, idealized vision.[13] Her father, on the other hand, has a vision of the world that incorporates learning and experience; his acceptance of historical flux recalls the empiricist concept of vision as gradual acquisition. Emilie has resisted the progress that attempts to pull her away from a static hierarchical conception of the world. But her visuality is at odds with a world coming to terms with the gaps between absolute essence and phenomenal variety. In Balzac's optical and philosophical contexts, the uniform perspective of absolute mastery was giving way to a changing conception of bodily subjects-within-the-world; theories of perception, as I have suggested, were leaning toward a subjective visuality that allows optical phenomena (shadows, sunspots, afterimages) to shape definitions of vision. The "phénomène" of Maximilien as he first appeared to Emilie at the ball, like the spots that appear in one's eyes, signifies an irruption of the body into the purified, abstracted, absolutist space of the Ideal.

What the afterimages in *La Maison Nucingen* and *Le Bal de Sceaux* suggest is an alternative visuality to the transcendental *voyance* of second sight. While visionaries like Victor Morillon, Louis Lambert, and—in a more angelic mode—Séraphîta represent a vertical thrust toward transcendent illumination, the physical world represented in *La Comédie humaine* imposes itself as necessary object of observation. Indeed, the material, visible world is not merely a transparent phenomenal indicator of what lies behind it; rather, it functions as an empirical object of observation, modifying the ways that conceptual, underlying truth is perceived.[14] Throughout the Balzacian text, physical vision structures the spiritual search for truth. If Victor Hugo wrote that "Contempler les choses, / c'est finir par ne plus les voir," Balzac, on the other hand, gave us the visionary dictum "Penser, c'est voir":—a reminder that images of the mind are grounded in images of the eye, that "*second* sight" necessarily follows a first.

Chapter 3

Alternative Optics: *Séraphîta, La Recherche de l'absolu,* and *La Peau de chagrin*

When Balzac was taken to task in Alain Robbe-Grillet's 1963 *Pour un nouveau roman,* it was not only because the nineteenth-century author's realist notions of form, character, and plot exemplified a genre ripe for renewal, but also because the mimetic project itself had come to imply a particular ideology of vision, one that privileged understanding over perception. Observation of the physical world may have played a key role in *La Comédie humaine,* but Balzac's descriptions of that world seemed always to lead necessarily to a metaphysical beyond, an *au-delà* that the Ecole de Minuit hoped to purge from its own antirepresentational fiction. In his 1964 *Essais critiques,* Roland Barthes joined Robbe-Grillet in calling for a textual mode that would replace the visionary symbolics of Balzacian realism with a registration of perception unencumbered by the myths of underlying essence, of metaphorical symbolism, and of anthropomorphic projection: "la description optique."[1]

And though both Barthes and Robbe-Grillet would later disavow the simplistic neutrality of "optical description," their initial characterization of realist visuality led to a generation of scholarly projects emphasizing a "readable" [*lisible*] Balzac, one whose novelistic descriptions follow the revelatory logic of *la physiologie.* The fact that visible signs in *La Comédie humaine*—the gloves on a parvenu, the color of a villain's eyes, the cut of a dandy's coat—seem to lead invariably to knowledge of the *in*visible hierarchies of social life allowed latter-day critics to represent nineteenth-century realism, with Balzac as its figurehead and whipping boy, as a mode that used vision in the service of metaphysical knowledge, a genre in which the act of seeing (whether social, scientific, or visionary) slipped automatically into the epistemological register.

Even Lucien Dällenbach, who swung the pendulum away from the structuralist, *lisible* Balzac toward a poststructuralist, less totalizing one, takes *La Comédie humaine*'s link between seeing and knowing as emblematic of the Balzacian project.[2] Citing Balzac's statement, "Seeing has been my sole ambition. For isn't seeing the same as knowing" [*Voir n'est-ce pas savoir?*], Dällenbach likens Balzac's visual epistemology to that of the *nouveau romancier* Claude Simon. Like Balzac's, "Simon's *optique* . . . consists above all in a *will to see* [*un vouloir voir*] that spies and scrutinizes passionately . . . and that ceaselessly seeks to extend the domain of the visible—better yet, to see past sight itself."[3] Though working from opposite ends of the mimetic spectrum, the two authors seem to share across a century the very visuality that Robbe-Grillet denounced as realism's foible:

Gaining access to the hidden heart of things, breaking through appearances, sounding the depths concealed behind or underneath an observable surface, exploring behind the scenes, rending all kinds of veils and curtains, glorifying screens the better to pass through them, . . . : all these are manifestations of a never-satisfied desire to go deeper, to penetrate, that relates the act of seeing in Simon's writings more closely to Balzac than to Robbe-Grillet. (48)

Thus, for Dällenbach, Balzac's literary project lies essentially in the potential thrust of vision beyond sight, of meaning beyond perception.[4] But while it is certainly true that Balzac sets up his fiction's visual stakes in epistemological terms—"Voir n'est-ce pas savoir?"—we should not forget this famous formulation's interrogative form, for it appears significantly in a text that very much calls into question the seeing/knowing nexus: *La Peau de chagrin*.[5]

The question ("Voir n'est-ce pas savoir?") is posed by the antique shop dealer in the novel's key set-up scene, as the *antiquaire* explains to Raphaël de Valentin why he himself has never entered into *Peau de chagrin*'s diabolical bargain of fulfilled desires in exchange for shortened life. The old man has tried at all costs, he says, to avoid the (literally) exhausting excesses of *vouloir* and *pouvoir*, preferring the perpetual calm of *savoir*, which he describes as a purified life of the mind, an "intellectual pleasure" whose enjoyment stems neither from the "heart, which can be broken" nor in the "senses, which can be dulled," but in the "mind, which never wears out and outlasts all else" (40). In this contrast of the mind against both passions and senses, even travel and exotic adventures—mountain climbing in Asia, haggling in China, sleeping in an American wigwam—become decorporealized pleasures. The sensual and the sensory are not eliminated (the *antiquaire* is no ascetic), but rather subsumed by the mind; why tire the body when one can indulge in a "harem of the imagination," why lose oneself in feeling when one can invent stories with one's *vision intérieure*? The *antiquaire*'s reference to interior vision (one of many in Balzac) suggests that there is more than one way to see, and indeed his entire system rests on the distinction between two modes of vision: (a) an enervating vision shot through with desire and the will to possess, and (b) a contemplative vision driven by tranquil and uninvested thought ("Thought is the key to all treasure" 86). When the antique dealer says, then, "Seeing has been my sole ambition. For isn't seeing the same thing as knowing?" he is invoking an abstracted, purified model of vision that replaces passion with temperance and—more importantly—physiology with philosophy.

Indeed, this "seeing" that the dealer claims as his sole ambition has very little to do with actual eyesight, as we see from the old man's inversion of optical logic in a key formulation: "Isn't it true that the brightest light of the ideal world gently caresses one's sight, while the faintest shadows of the physical world never fail to injure it[?]" (87). The full weight of this paradox lies in its reversal of the visual organ's response in the real world, in which light can blind and shadow rests the eye. The antique dealer's idealized vision counters (or confirms by negation) the danger for physical sight that Balzac evokes elsewhere, in a confession written to Doctor Benassis while composing *Le Médecin de campagne*: "A dreadful tale! It's about a man who has, for several months, delighted in all that nature offers, all of the effects of sunlight on display in a luxuriant countryside, and who loses his sight."[6] In the physical world, the light of the sun can blind, as various contemporaries of Balzac warned in optical and philosophical treatises.[7]

Balzac gives these warnings a moral cast throughout *La Comédie humaine*, where ambition, greed, and lust become the too bright lights that threaten spiritual calm, figured as vision-beyond-sight. In *La Recherche de l'absolu*, for example, the modest purity of the young lovers Marguerite Van Claës and Emmanuel is contrasted with Balthazar's overreaching philosophical ambition through the symbol of the flower garden and its effects on the eye. Of Balthazar's prize tulips, the humble Emmanuel says, "These flowers blind me [*m'éblouissent*]. My habit of working in the small, dark room where I live . . . no doubt leads me to prefer that which is less dazzling to the eye."[8] Marguerite gracefully suggests that they distance themselves from the tulips' offending brightness: "From this spot, . . . you won't see the tulips so close up, and they will tire your eyes less. You're right, their colors sparkle and hurt the eye" (743).[9] Emmanuel makes explicit the connection between visual *éblouissement* (blindness caused by a dazzling sight) and moral choices when he adds: "Perhaps that's why I prefer a daisy, overlooked by others, . . . to these fine tulips bursting with gold and crimson color, and with the sapphires and emeralds that bespeak a life of ostentation, just as the daisy bespeaks the peaceful and patriarchal life of the poor teacher I shall be" (744). The ancient injunction against looking into the Light is translated into a botanical allegory about optical danger, as Emmanuel's quiet and "patriarchal" life is contrasted with the life of the Van Claës patriarch, for Balthazar's unfettered desire for knowledge (described as "voyance") renders him metaphorically blind to the material exigencies and affective ties of the world.

The dangers of desiring vision are made even clearer in *Facino Cane,* in which it literally deprives the narrator of physical eyesight. Driven by specular gold-lust, Facino Cane's optical reserves are depleted by the strain of searching for gleam in shadows: "You'll soon see how fully God has punished me. . . . I would attribute my infirmity to my time in the dungeon, to my underground labors, if it weren't for the fact that my ability to see gold implied an abuse of visual power that predestined me to lose my eyesight."[10] *Facino Cane*'s narrator embodies, in other words, the worldliness that *La Peau de chagrin*'s *antiquaire* reviles—and his optical vulnerability follows the logic underlying the *antiquaire*'s warning against nonspiritual vision.

Let us look again at the optical terms of that warning: "Isn't it true that the brightest light of the ideal world gently caresses one's sight [*la vue*], while the faintest shadows of the physical world never fail to injure it[?]" Here "la vue" must refer not to common eyesight, for which the laws of physical optics dictate an opposite reaction to light, but an ideal vision, one suited to the "monde idéal"—and therefore regulated by an *alternative optics* that we might call revelational rather than physiological.

Balzac will develop more systematically this revelational form of vision through the strange optics of his famously Swedenborgian story *Séraphîta.* In this mystico-philosophical tale, the angelic androgyne Séraphîta/Séraphîtus discloses the secrets of the ideal, heavenly realm to the young mortals Minna and Wilfred, reminding them that man's understanding is limited by the boundaries of external vision. The angel's interior, spiritual vision allows it to transcend the vexing problems that stall mankind, problems like the (false) matter/spirit distinction or the (inessential) physical laws of optics. Séraphîta proclaims to the humans:

> Your laws on Acoustics and Optics are disproven by the sounds that you hear within yourselves while you sleep and by the light from an electrical sun whose rays often dazzle you. You are no more aware of how light turns into intelligence inside you than you are of the simple, natural process that changes it into rubies, sapphires, opals, and emeralds on the neck of a bird in the Indies while it remains grey and dusky on that of the same bird under the cloudy skies of Europe, nor do you understand how it remains white here, in the polar landscape. You cannot make up your minds whether color is a faculty with which the body is endowed or whether it is an effect produced by the affusion of light.[11]

In typically enigmatic fashion, *Séraphîta* is referring to actual debates of Balzac's time on the nature of light and color,[12] while suggesting that those debates completely miss the point in a higher sphere of understanding. For Swedenborg, the Swedish mystic whose writings inspired *Séraphîta,* light and color exist differently on the spiritual plane, where they are perceived by "discernment-sight," than on the physical plane, where they are perceived by "eyesight."[13] Although the two corresponding sorts of vision are interrelated, they nevertheless exist within two separate systems of luminosity: "There are in fact two lights, one proper to this world, from the sun, and one proper to heaven. . . . There is no discernment within this world's light, but there is discernment within heaven's light" (123). Like the *antiquaire*'s desire-free vision, Swedenborg's "discernment-sight," an inner vision more spiritually evolved than mere eyesight, is soothed by celestial brilliance and clouded by earthly shadow.

Swedenborg's optical cosmology goes even further, describing the unworldly brilliance of lights and colors that abound in heaven's "parklike gardens"; the flowers in these gardens "could scarcely be grasped by any earthly perception, and particular ones glowed with an incomprehensible radiance because they came from heaven's light," while "there are also colors that people observe in the other life that so surpass in brilliance and splendor the luster of colors in this world that there is scarcely any comparison" (137–38). The Swedenborgian heavens provide us with a metaphysical context for the figural "éblouissement" of Emmanuel's eyes in *La Recherche de l'absolu.* While the young man's proclaimed preference of daisies (associated by nickname with Marguerite) over tulips (associated with her father's heritage and ambitions) is easily explained as a lover's sweet gallantry, his extreme visual sensitivity to the tulips' colored brilliance might seem mere hyperbolic flourish without the extratextual hypothesis of heavenly optics; as earthbound (though pure-hearted) mortals, Emmanuel and Marguerite simply cannot tolerate the tulips' gemlike brilliance of hue, for these flowers are defined by a celestial chromatic perfection—"in this flower, dubbed *tulipa Claësiana,* were united the seven colors" (103)—better suited to the eyes of Balthazar, himself described as resembling "a seer from the Church of Swedenborg" (45).

In a similar but even more explicit manner, *Séraphîta* incorporates Swedenborg's distinction between human visual perception and celestial luminescence. The androgyne's angelic nature is revealed early in the story by its ability to look into the brilliant polar-white light of the mountains and to face their "blinding abyss[es]" (738). Minna and Wilfred, on the other hand, can barely tolerate the sight of Séraphîta's ascension: "They no longer dared ask it anything or look upon it, and remained in its shadow as one remains under the tropical sun's scorching rays without daring to raise one's eyes, for fear of losing one's sight" (852). At their own moment of revelation, from which point on they will be described as "voyants," the brightness Wilfred and Minna perceive surpasses anything that they had previously understood as light, and indeed, the appearance of "La Vraie Lumière" allows the mortals to recognize the puerility of human sciences—including, as we saw earlier, the science of optics (853–55). In a way, then, *Séraphîta* can be understood as an optical bildungsroman, the description of two humans' successful ascension from the worldly/scientific to the celestial/spiritual plane of visual perception.

The "blinding, eternal lights" of Balzac's Swedenborgian fantasy may represent the extreme horizon of purity (858). Most of *La Comédie humaine,* however, takes place in the very real world of illusion, confusion, desire, and shadow. In this world, one can only get glimpses—through the eyes of a visionary like Louis Lambert, for example—of the alternative realm existing for Balzac beyond the derisory limits of physics and physiology. Although not generally understood as a visionary, the *antiquaire* in *La Peau de chagrin* provides such a glimpse into an alternative realm of vision, which he describes not in Swedenborgian terms of celestial enlightenment, but in terms of an ideal optics attained through divestment from desire.[14]

Of course the *antiquaire*'s purified model of vision is doomed to failure in *La Peau de chagrin,* a text organized around life's untenable balance of (specular) desire and fulfillment. At the end of the novel, the dealer's chaste philosophy is toppled, as Raphaël's revenge wish leads the *antiquaire* into a tumultuous affair with the courtesan Euphrasie. Fittingly, this entry—or descent—into the specular realm of worldly desire is revealed to the reader and to Raphaël as a scene to be seen: the decrepit old man with his fresh, lovely lover makes a spectacle of himself at an ultimate space of spectacle, the foyer of the theater Les Italiens. The *antiquaire*'s manifesto of abstraction and abstention had been underwritten by a model of ideal vision as both untainted by libidinous, acquisitive impulses and unaffected by the laws of human perception. But now, as he struts with a bought woman on his arm, the old man's entrance into the realm of illusion is underlined by the shifty optical effects of his artificially colored hair: "His eyebrows and hair . . . were dyed black; but, since it had apparently been applied to hair that was too white, the dye had yielded a purplish, ersatz color whose hues shifted according to the varying brightness of the light reflecting off of it" (176). Black dye on (overly) white hair has created a third color whose tones shift in the play of light, an effect that had stimulated scientific debate in the study of physiological optics. The history of color-contrast theory tells us that Aristotle stated (without being able to prove beyond doubt) that "blue could be obtained by mixing white and black."[15] In the eighteenth and early nineteenth centuries, there were two schools of thought on whether the "shadow color" (Aristotle's blue or the *antiquaire*'s purple) existed objectively or was the result of subjective perception.[16] By Balzac's time, most had adopted the subjective hypothesis that "contrast is due to a change in sensation"; thus, Balzac's description of the "purplish color" as both false and shifting supports the newer subjective theory of perception while emphasizing the pretense that marks the antique dealer's new lifestyle.

In other words, optics underwrites the figural logic of the *antiquaire*'s moral descent into temptation.

Visual perception acts as the flashpoint for Raphaël's ethical choices as well. On the same evening at Les Italiens, Raphaël tries to extend his life by combating the temptations of the eye. Seated in his loge, "he wore a lorgnon whose artfully arranged microscopic lens ruined the harmony of any beautiful traits, rendering them hideous" (180). Despite the device of optical distortion, however, Raphaël becomes aware through the audience's glances that a ravishing beauty must be seated beside him in his own box. He tries not to look, but unable to ignore the seduction of his other senses—touch ("either the stranger's hair or her feather-soft dress brushed against Raphaël's head, causing him to feel a voluptuous sensation"), hearing ("the folds of her dress . . . gave off a feminine rustle, a slight shiver full of languid allure") and smell ("her haunting aloe-scented perfume captivated Raphaël completely")—Raphaël turns his eyes to see his beloved Pauline, in a dramatic moment of visual revelation and recognition. This brief vision sparks enough desire to send Raphaël back to the Peau, as he makes the wish that will end his life: "I want Pauline to love me."

Even before Raphaël first strikes the Peau's diabolical bargain, he can only see the world not with the *antiquaire*'s proposed visual disinterest, but through a relation of absorption, desire, and fascination. *La Peau de chagrin* is a story about a young man's will (or lack of it, as will-sapping desires displace his work on the *Théorie de la volonté*), but also about his eyes. Raphaël's distorting lorgnon tips us off to the importance of the visual sense as entry point for external temptations and influences, but it is even earlier in the book that a link is set up between visual disturbance and the hero's troubled state of mind—namely, in the pivotal antique shop scene.

"Phénomènes d'optique"

The *magasin d'antiquités* acts as a threshhold space in *La Peau de chagrin* between Raphaël's life before and after the magic influence of the skin. In this famous scene of the *roman philosophique*, the human senses are immediately foregrounded, as the despairing "inconnu"—later to be introduced as the protagonist Raphaël de Valentin—enters the shop "wishing to feed his senses" (22). "Inebriated" by his own liminal position between life and death, Raphaël "soon grew dizzy again, and continued to see objects in a different light" [*d'apercevoir les choses sous d'étranges couleurs*], a phrase whose literal meaning we may want to reactivate, as it implies a sensationalistic harmony between mental state and visual perception of the world. It seems, indeed, that Raphaël's perceptions are affected by both his morbid frame of mind and the sluggish flow of blood in his tired body: "He . . . continued to see objects in a different light, or as if they were moving about slightly; this was no doubt caused by irregular circulation of his blood, which at times churned like a waterfall, and at other moments was as calm and tame as lukewarm water" (22). Balzac's casual "no doubt" might distract the reader from the surprising causality that this passage proposes: the static antique objects in the cluttered shop appear to move because Raphaël's blood pulses with its own ebbs and flows. Body alters perception. The interconnectedness between bodily and mental states, on the one hand, and the perception of objects in the world, on the other, recalls Condillac's sensationalistic epistemology, which both assimilates understanding to sensation and attributes knowledge of the world to sensory processes.[17] Through Balzac's description, the antique shop becomes a full sensorium for Raphaël, a place of nourishment for both "the senses" (22) and "the soul" (23), highlighting the juxtaposition of matter and abstraction in the phrase "philosophical compost heap." This is no site of decorporealized philosophy, but a place in which Raphaël's "burning imagination" stimulates him to smell ("a plaited mat . . . still gave off the scent of sandalwood"), to touch ("he stroked a tomahawk from Illinois"), to experience bodily sensation ("he shivered as he watched the snow fall"). Aural, mental, and visual perceptions exist on the same discursive plane: "His ear thought it heard broken-off cries; his mind thought it perceived half-committed crimes; his eye thought it saw indistinct glimmerings of light" (24). Rather than impose a rigorous mind/eye division, reminiscent of a Cartesian epistemology, the passage melds thought with sensation in the manner of empiricist theories of perception.

This is not to propose a simple correspondence between Balzac's poetics and any particular philosopher of perception, whether Locke, Condillac, or Reid, but rather to say that *La Peau de chagrin* capitalizes on post-Cartesian thought—and more precisely on its explorations of sensory experience—to represent a pivotal, life-altering moment for its protagonist, one that destabilizes easy correlations between will and action, subject and world. In fact, if the space of the antique shop is particularly disorienting, that may be because it contracts the subject's experience into two terms of uncertain (ontological) status—the perceiving self and the objects of perception. Which is the anchor of knowledge? How do mind and body interact to perceive the objective world? Rather than answer these questions, Balzac heightens the instability of both subject and object: Raphaël is put into a state of emotional crisis, mental fatigue, and bodily distortion, while the material world is made aggressive in its objectness—multiple, disparate, and monstrously jumbled.

Though all of the senses are put into play in the antique shop scene, the question of subject/object relations is most suggestively filtered (as in contemporary philosophical discourses) through the visual mode. The visual stage is set for Raphaël's hallucinatory reverie as he lets his exhausted gaze wander "across the fantasmagorias of this panorama of the past" (30), a phrase that combines two optical devices that helped define early nineteenth-century perceptual experience. Donata Campagnoni analyzes nicely the way in which this Balzacian phrase joins the complementary meanings associated with *fantasmagoria* and *panorama*: "The first one ushers the reader into the protagonist's mental universe, into a hazy scene where specters from the ruins of the past are coming back to life. The other metaphor, involving the panorama, places Raphaël in the center of history's broad, continuous, and circular canvas."[18] The term *fantasmagoria* evokes the psychological present of the protagonist, filled as it is with confusion and evanescent visions, while the panorama evokes an uninterrupted sequence, writes Campagnoni, of "images external to the protagonist, real, concrete objects with clear and well-defined outlines" (136). Simply put, *fantasmagoria* emphasizes subjective perception, while *panorama* emphasizes the objective world.[19] Their coexistence in Balzac's phrase implies a continual interaction of internal state with external images, so that one might read the scene as a refusal to settle on either subject or object as prime mover of perception.

Indeed, the fantastic effects and unsettling distortions of Raphaël's experience in the antique shop are assigned both subjective and objective causes, often simultaneously:[20]

> The paintings lit up, the modeled heads of the Virgin smiled at him, and the statues took on an illusory hue of life. *Half-hidden in shadow and impelled to move by the frantic torment seething within his shattered mind*, these works of art stirred and whirled before him; every gewgaw sent a grimace his way, and the figures represented in the paintings closed their tired, long-open eyes. . . . But *these optical phenomena* [phénomènes d'optique], *brought on by fatigue, by the tension of ocular forces, or by the vagaries of twilight*, did not alarm the stranger. (30, my emphasis)

The hallucinatory animation of painted faces and sculpted bodies may be due to external effects of shadow ("à la faveur de l'ombre," "les caprices du crepuscule") and light: "These monstrous paintings were also subjected to innumerable effects of light through an odd profusion of colors caused by a jumble of hues, a stark opposition of light and dark tones" (24). Or they may be the result of physiological effects: the "frantic torment . . . within his shattered mind, . . . fatigue, . . . the tension of ocular forces." The "either/or" of the final phrase—either objective light effects or the subject's body—allows no resolution between the two sorts of perceptual stimulus.[21]

Moreover, the very interrelation of ocular tension and crepuscular caprice should signal to the reader a full discursive context for Balzac's phrase "phénomènes d'optique," for it is within the studies of subjective phenomena in eighteenth- and nineteenth-century physiological optics that we find perception defined as the intersection of anatomy and light. Physiologists like Buffon, Monge, Nollet, and Serre D'Uzes called attention to various illusory effects of the eye's interaction with the world by studying the distortions of ocular fatigue, pulsings of the retina, and the subjective "auréoles" of complementary colored light.[22] As for Raphaël in the antique shop, visual perception is anything but clear and distinct. His dreamlike impressions follow "the unhurried waning of the light," as a red-illumined skeleton seems to warn him off with a nod and as night falls, he senses indistinctly "the phantoms surrounding him"; at the deepest moment of fugue, declares the narrator, the young man "had no clear perception of earthly things" (31). The skeleton and ghosts, the darkness of Raphaël's deathly vision, certainly echo the morbid tropes of a typical fantasmagoric spectacle (as put on by the showman Etienne-Gaspard Robertson), but they also evoke what the optical physiologist Giraud-Teulon was to call "ocular specters," the ghostly and illusory after-images that appear on one's retina through a combination of light and nervous pulsings. In fact, when the *antiquaire* finally appears to the dazed Raphaël, he has all the characteristics of subjective phenomena of vision, from the blinding (rather than illuminating) effect of light in a dark optical chamber to the colored halo that shimmers around him: Raphaël "closed his eyes, as rays from a bright light were blinding him. In the shadows, he saw a reddish sphere glowing; in its center was a small, elderly man who was standing upright and shining a lamp onto his face" (31). The old man will soon deliver to Raphaël his moralistic sermon about desire-free vision, but at the first moment of his appearance, he is far from the embodiment of idealized optics that we analyzed earlier in this chapter. Instead, he appears to Raphaël as an "kind of phantom," with a staging—closed eyes, blinding light, and colored spheres—that makes him an optical effect similar to the "luminous impressions" that Helmholtz describes as typical of subjective perception. The antique shop is no Swedenborgian paradise-garden of purified optics; instead, it remains a place of earthly vision in which bodily pulsings combine with material objects to unsettle perception.

Raphaël's "vision," then, inhabits the common early nineteenth-century space of fantasmagoric spectacle and physiological optics. Both of these take the eye as a site of interaction between the self and the world that destabilizes easy distinctions between reality and unreality. By 1830, the disorienting effects of the *chambre noire* are to be found not in a technical device but in the optical chamber as the uncertain point of interaction between bodily pulse and objective images. *L'optique* is no longer merely an "illusory art," but a primal indicator of the epistemological uncertainty inherent to human perception. It is only fitting that at the end of Raphaël's fantasmagoric vision in *La Peau de chagrin,* the narrator invokes a Descartes of doubt (rather than mastery), while posing the question of hallucination as an unresolved scientific conundrum: "during the brief interval separating his somnambulistic life from his waking life, he retained the philosophical doubt recommended by Descartes and in those moments was, despite himself, ruled by inexplicable hallucinations, the mysteries of which are proscribed by our pride, or that our pitiful knowledge attempts fruitlessly to understand" (31). Raphaël's experience exposes the limits of knowledge. His is not the visionary's "disordering of the senses" that M. H. Abrams identifies with Romantic revelation,[23] but rather an anti-epiphanic entry into the most troubled form of perception, an experience that exposes the illusions looming at the edge of every subject's encounters with the objective world.

The antique shop passage in *La Peau de chagrin* emphasizes the enigmatic quality of hallucinations, their inexplicable status between dream and waking, between the real and the unreal (in the midst of all the objective materiality of the shop, the apparition of the *antiquaire* is described as "magique," "fantastique," "surnaturel"). As Tony James explains, Balzac's use of the word "hallucination" reflects the emergence of medical and scientific analyses of hallucinatory phenomena; in *La Peau de chagrin,* the term slides from earlier supernatural connotations to more technical ones, without yet carrying any of the explanatory power that it will have later in the century.[24] Similarly, I am suggesting that Balzac's text inhabits an intermediate philosophical space between idealism and empiricism that reveals itself through the subject/object visual relations of his characters. At a time when the optical study of subjective phenomena was posing key questions about reality and perception, Raphaël's hallucinatory experience in the antique shop remains poised between the real and the fantasmagorical; moreover, the text has traditionally been understood as generically hybrid, straddling the two narrative modes of realism and the fantastic. In this way, *La Peau de chagrin* may well be understood as a "hinge" for the *Comédie humaine*'s double project of realist observation and visionary revelation, one that encapsulates the very ambivalence of Balzac's visual epistemology by posing—and preserving in the interrogative—the question, "Voir n'est-ce pas savoir?"

Chapter 4
"Effets de lumière," or a "Second" Second Sight: *La Fille aux yeux d'or*

If *Louis Lambert* and *Séraphîta* are the stories of Balzac's mystical seers, or *voyants, La Fille aux yeux d'or* is one of the many stories about *les initiés,* characters like Eugène de Rastignac, Lucien de Rubempré, and Raphaël de Valentin, whose comprehension of the social landscape dawns only gradually. Lacking a masterful vision, the *initiés* nonetheless experience moments of insight into the inner workings of the Parisian world they are trying to decipher. Typical in its visual figuration of the young *ambitieux*'s rise in society is *Le Père Goriot,* in which the provincial Rastignac finds the doors of nobility opened to him by his relation to the Vicomtesse de Beauséant. Her noble name acts as a "touch from a magic wand" that transforms Rastignac's "mind [*esprit*]" and his visual relation to the urban promised land: "a flash of light helped him see more clearly into the still-murky [*ténébreuse*] atmosphere of Parisian high society."[1] This sudden light means momentary mastery for Rastignac—over his own *esprit,* over the audience made captive by a name, over the tenebrous atmosphere of Parisian society. The moment recirculates an Enlightenment metaphor of light as mental clarity, but while Rastignac will struggle throughout the novel to regain its pure and lucid power, his experiential contact with the reality of Parisian high society belies the theoretical ideal of illumination. Morally discouraged by the "élégant parricide" in which Delphine de Nucingen involves him, Eugène sees the world as an "ocean of filth" through which man must slog (276). The narrator continues: "'Only petty crimes are committed there!' he told himself. But Vautrin is bigger than that. He had witnessed [*Il avait vu*] society's three great expressions: Obedience, Struggle, and Revolt; the Family, the World, and Vautrin" (276).

Vautrin's cynical vision is contrasted with muddy, petty mediocrity. Larger than life, Vautrin has the power to encompass all of society, to categorize and allegorize it in an overarching vision—the same overarching perspective, with its visual organization of a complex world into legible categories, that will become Rastignac's mode of triumphant access at the end of the novel. *Le Père Goriot*'s final scene, in which our hero looks down on the city from the heights of the Père-Lachaise cemetery, has come to exemplify the representation of visual-epistemological mastery in the nineteenth-century French novel. With its final words, the novel presages its protagonist's social successes to come: "Over this buzzing hive, he leveled a gaze that seemed to relieve it of its honey in advance, and uttered these grandiose words: 'It belongs to both of us now!'" Paris has become a chamber whose honeyed pleasures are destined to be extracted solely by the powers of Rastignac's gaze from above.

Knowledge and control are thus marked in Balzac's narrative by the panoramic overview ([*survol*] or "overarching gaze" [*regard surplombant*]) that has come to be associated with the Cartesian logic of perspective—an all-knowing gaze from above contrasted with the subject's experiential entry into a muddy and confusing world. Rastignac's survey of Paris represents the antithesis of Fabrice del Dongo's confused experience at Waterloo in Stendhal's *La Chartreuse de Parme*, in which, even after the fact, the battle's incoherence resists both visualization and conceptual perspective. Rastignac's position of visual transcendence seems predestined: like Louis Lambert, Rastignac possesses a gift of inner vision tightly linked to his superior eyesight: "His moral sight shared the lucid scope of his lynx-like eyes. Each of his dual senses exhibited the mysterious range and flexibility so remarkable in superior beings" (114). What is this moral—rather than spiritual—second sense that shadows Rastignac's lynx-like eyes? Throughout *La Comédie humaine*, the theme of second sight is assigned varying degrees of philosophical import; certainly, the idea of a "moral" second sight seems to carry less weight than that of a pure and mystic interior vision.[2] Still, it signals here a certain superiority of perception that marks Rastignac as uncommon. Rather than transcend the physical world to a realm of divine essence, Rastignac's "moral sight" casts its "lucid scope" on society itself; his is the second sight of a worldly hero.

Perhaps the most worldly of Balzac's society heroes is Henri de Marsay, who appears as prime minister in *Béatrix*, *Les Secrets de la Princesse de Cadignan*, and *Une Ténébreuse affaire*. Unlike Eugène de Rastignac, Lucien de Rubempré, and Raphaël de Valentin, this young dandy's initiation comes quickly, with no illusions to be lost; by the beginning of his adventures in *La Fille aux yeux d'or*, he already possesses the confident and cynical gaze of the best of Vautrin's disciples. His is the story of an alternative second sight, a vision that functions at the opposite pole from Louis Lambert's or Séraphîta's pure *voyance*, but in a different visual register from both Rastignac's clear glimpses of light and his mastering overview of the city laid out beneath him.

La Fille aux yeux d'or: Seeing Paris

La Fille aux yeux d'or tells the story of Henri de Marsay, the gorgeous but fatuously self-important bastard son of a British lord, and his amorous encounters with a mysterious beauty, the golden-eyed girl of the title. Before introducing the reader to de Marsay, however, Balzac provides us with a vast, classificatory description of Paris and its inhabitants, entitled "Physionomies Parisiennes." As the subtitle's reference to Lavater's system suggests, the description of Paris is based on a logic of direct relation between visible surface and invisible truth—the same transparent relation between appearance and underlying essence that the *Avant-propos à la Comédie humaine* promotes. The legibility of the city relies on this relation; upon seeing the multiple faces of Paris, one should be able to infer, à la Lavater, the city's underlying, unified character.

When it comes to the actual description, though, Balzac seems continually tempted to invert the order, moving deductively from invisible cause to visible symptoms rather than vice versa. In the first two pages of the long passage, for example, he announces that "a few observations on Paris's spirit may explain the reasons behind its cadaverous physiognomy," and promises to "indicate the general cause" that colors its inhabitants "before analyzing the causes underlying the particular physiognomy of this nation's every tribe."[3] Balzac's explanatory pronouncements suggest that he has already analyzed and classified Paris's characteristics so as to be able to present an allegorical overview of the many-tiered urban inferno. With the overarching vision that Rastignac ascribes to Vautrin in *Le Père Goriot,* the narrator lays out Paris's classes in ascending order of wealth—from the working class, through the petite bourgeoisie, to the haute bourgeoisie, and finally to the aristocracy (with a short detour for artists). Whereas in *Illusions perdues* and *Splendeurs et misères des courtisanes,* Lucien de Rubempré's localized encounters with individuals of diverse rank determine the order in which the social classes of France and Paris are described, *La Fille aux yeux d'or*'s preface gives us a journalistic synthesis of the city and its inhabitants from—as Christopher Prendergast puts it—the "high point" of panoramic vision.[4]

Combined with the avowed transparency of the physiognomic relation between Paris and its people, this aerial perspective takes on the traits of a "Cartesian" visuality. The city is mapped out allegorically, ordered by an overarching a priori logic, while the mastery implied by the Cartesian *survol* is taken up by Balzac's confidence in the direct relation between cause and effect, comprehension and communicability: "This *view* [vue] of moral Paris proves that physical Paris could be no different than it is" (1051, my emphasis). Even the invisible causes motivating the city's visible characteristics are presented as coherent and visually graspable, so that the prefatory "vue" would seem to contrast formally with the second part of the tale, which will follow de Marsay's wanderings from the limited perspective of his particular experience.

The Paris description, however, already deviates from its announced panoramic logic in various ways. For one thing, the narrator's frequent use of second-person address blurs the distinction between an aerial, omniscient perspective and a localized, subjective one by placing the reader in the "down below, wandering along the streets" [*en bas, au fil des rues*] position, as we are directed to see the city not from above but from within: "Take up these two words [*gold* and *pleasure*] before you like a torch and wander through this enormous plaster cage, this hive through which somber streams flow, and track therein the serpentine meanderings of this thought that besets, rouses, obsesses it? See [*Voyez*]" (1040–41). As with the description at the end of *Le Père Goriot*, Paris is compared to a beehive, but this one is labyrinthine and incoherent—a black-rivered hive agitated by the snakings of a thought—rather than spread out for the taking. Compare it to the object of Rastignac's ambitious gaze: "Over this buzzing hive, he leveled a gaze that seemed to relieve it of its honey *in advance*, and uttered these grandiose words: 'It belongs to both of us now!'" (my emphasis). In *La Fille aux yeux d'or*, we are denied such a priori mastery, that of a gaze capable of extracting the essence of Paris. In fact, any close study of *La Fille aux yeux d'or*'s urban description will unsettle its apparently cohesive status as introductory tableau, for even within this "view from above," the text articulates—through questions of visualizability—a series of tensions central to Balzac's entire literary project and to its epistemological context: localized experience versus organizing unity, empiricism versus deduction, details versus the whole.

The first sentence of *La Fille aux yeux d'or* describes the Paris population as a "spectacle to be seen," but as Prendergast nicely observes, both the mastering (objective, totalizing, scientific) perspective and the visual coherence implied by the term *spectacle* are undermined by the text's "rapid, hectically garrulous movement through a flux of verbal registers and figures in which the framing and taming claims of science are left far behind" (54). Indeed, Prendergast is right to link the question of scientific mastery to the passage's style, which has as its most notable feature the massive accumulation of words. The sentences pile up, filled to bursting with lists numbering up to twenty-five elements, so that their very clutter evokes the teeming crowds of the city population. Faced with the impossibility of representing sheer quantity by one-to-one nominational correspondence—it is not an easy task "to depict the two or three thousand most noteworthy figures of an era" (*AP*, 27)—the narrator of *La Fille aux yeux d'or* alternates groupings by *type* with a jumble of generalizations, individual cases, collective movements, and "a-day-in-the-life-of" narratives.

Grammatically, there is no clear movement between specific and general, example and group. The working class appears variably as a singular type ("the worker," "the manufacturer"), as a plural subject ("these quadrumanes," "these men") and as a collective ("this dynamic part of Paris," "She"), each granted its own long list of active verbs, while descriptions of the other classes just as inconsistently jumble grammatical plurals and singulars into a thematic hodgepodge of collectives and individuals. Why is this notable? Because it problematizes, within the scope of narrative description, the methodological tension underlying Balzac's proposed "constructional unity." If, indeed, the world is composed of a hidden unified structure and a manifest plurality of forms, how does one go about knowing—and describing—it? Does one observe, inductively, its multiple parts and add them up to form a sense of the whole, or does one deduce the individual forms from a preexisting theory of the whole?

These questions were central to Balzac's engagement with the contemporary naturalists Georges Cuvier (whose inductive approach emphasized diversity) and Geoffroy Saint-Hilaire (whose deductive method emphasized unity). The "querelle Cuvier-Saint-Hilaire," which came to a head at the Académie des Sciences in 1830, had to do with a difference in emphasis: Cuvier focused on visible distinctions among species, while Saint-Hilaire drew out the hidden similarities that testified to their "compositional unity."[5] The latter's deductive methodology appeals to Balzac's interest in unity, as Françoise Gaillard reminds us in her rigorous and nuanced article on science and the *Avant-propos*: "For [Balzac], compositional unity is *the invisible reason for the visible*, that which gives *sens* (in its double meaning of signification and direction) to the world of phenomena and its movements."[6] The visual modality of Gaillard's statement allows us to connect Balzac's representational problem (induction versus deduction) to the question of alternative modes of seeing, as the Cuvier-Saint-Hilaire conflict finds its logic in a question of visual epistemology: does seeing truth consist of attentive observation of the exterior forms of the visible world? Or do those forms only make sense in light of preexisting laws that are themselves inaccessible to the physical eye? The easy answer in terms of *La Comédie humaine* is "both"—after all, Balzac's precise sociological observations combine with allusions to underlying order, and his crowning of Saint-Hilaire in the *Avant-propos* is balanced by effusive paeans to Cuvier throughout the novels.[7] But the awkward and disorderly language of the Paris description in *La Fille aux yeux d'or* indicates the strain that this double answer implies—a strain, I would argue, particular to the early nineteenth-century moment in scientific thought.

After all, not long after Balzac's time, attempts would be made in the sciences to reconcile inductive and deductive methodologies. In the 1870s, for example, Michel-Eugène Chevreul (who is known in the field of optics for his research on simultaneous color contrast) identified the sciences according to whether they moved from the general to the particular (a priori method) or from the particular to the general (a posteriori).[8] Chevreul's positivistic systematization of these two competing methods identifies the grammatical terms that map onto the concepts of *general* and *particular*: "le substantif appellatif" (collective nouns, such as those which refer to class, order, genus, and species) and "le substantif propre" (proper nouns referring to individuals). Scientific methods of experimentation and verification proceed from one to another—from *substantif appellatif* to *substantif propre*, or vice versa. But in Balzac's text, appearing well before Chevreul's systematization, we find a far less orderly use of collective nouns and individual cases, as the *Fille* passage shuttles between unified groups and diverse individuals, between a coherent vision of Paris's "soul" and a detailed description of its inhabitants. This conceptual and grammatical lack of systematization situates Balzac's text, then, still and squarely within the unresolved problematics of the Cuvier-Saint-Hilaire debate.

Françoise Gaillard argues that the *Avant-propos à la Comédie humaine* relies conceptually on Saint-Hilaire's theory, whose emphasis on unity justifies Balzac's conservative faith in historical continuity, while Cuvier's theory, by contrast, is incapable of furnishing Balzac with the sense of Totality he desires—both conceptually (society as consistent) and aesthetically (his literary project as all-encompassing). But as she suggests in her article's open-ended conclusion, it is a different matter when it comes to actual textual practice (83). Indeed, as I have been proposing in these chapters on *La Comédie humaine*, Balzac's descriptive method—doubly determined as it is by realist and revelational goals—is unable to disentangle the parts (the diversity of phenomenal appearances) from the whole (the underlying unity of cause) in favor of either as originary.

In *La Fille aux yeux d'or*'s Paris description, the implicit fusion of Saint-Hilaire's deductive reasoning (coherence as governing principle of variety) with a Cuvierian empiricism (descriptive inventory of parts) has its counterpart in the tense conjunction of two visual models: (a) totalizing pictoriality, with its implied spatial simultaneity; and (b) fragmented perspective, with its temporal sequence. Continually addressing the reader of this passage, the narrator offers to introduce us to Paris's classed population by means of a spatially figured journey through the city's alleyways and streets. Rather than overlook the urban scene, as Rastignac did from atop the hill, the reader is to enter the scene corporeally, through the use of all the senses—but especially the visual, as the narrator exhorts us to see: "Voyez." Despite the narrator's command, however, this Paris is decidedly difficult to visualize. A plaster cage, a black-streamed hive tossed about by the snakings of thought—the image combines thick animality with abstraction, as thought acquires a serpentine physicality to produce an impression of clotted, crowded space that defies pictorial representation. And if the talismanic words *or* and *plaisir* are to light our way, it is only with the tarnished luster of ugliness, greed, passion, and need: the infernal glow that permeates this description of Paris and its hideous folk. So the reader should view this double lantern suspiciously, remembering that Balzac himself sees by a different light ("I write by the light of two eternal truths—Religion and the Monarchy," he claims in the *Avant-propos*). As counterweight to this ideal illumination, our lantern of *or et plaisir* casts Paris as an erroneous space antithetical to eternal truth. Like navigating the monstrous "plaster cage/hive" landscape, then, reading the Paris description in *La Fille aux yeux d'or* is disorienting.

As will be the case for de Marsay in the story's second part, the reader is frustrated in the desire for visual mastery and for the coherent totality afforded by a panoramic view. *La Fille aux yeux d'or* may be dedicated to Delacroix and may strain toward pictoriality, but it tells the story of writing's failure to cross over the gap separating it from the perspectival space of mastery and coherence. Balzac's writing in fact opens up an alternative spatiality, whose limits are not determined according to a Cartesian grid of imposed order. Pertinent in this regard is Le Huenon and Perron's reading of *La Maison du chat-qui-pelote*: "The narrative offers itself as an initial emplacement of a complete, ordered, and measurable spatial device that, due to an ill-timed accident, will be transformed into a troubling, misframed, and fragmented space of alterity, an indecisive and undecidable libidinal space where the subject cannot be constituted."[9] *La Fille aux yeux d'or* seems explicitly to enact this dissolution of space, beginning as it does with a portrait of Paris, turning to the disquieting erotic journey of a blinded hero, and ending with a literal—bodily, bloody—fragmentation of a subject. Understood as separate parts, the description of Paris and the narration of de Marsay's tale can be taken as emblems of the conflicting moments described by Le Huenon and Perron: first, an ordered and coherent (descriptive) space; then, a decentered and fragmentary (narrative) space. But, as we have seen, the Paris that opens *La Fille aux yeux d'or* belies such a static conception of description. Hinting at what is to come, it already represents a fragmented space, in which attempts at unity are fated to fail. If there is an element of consistency between the main story and its tacked-on introduction, in other words, it lies precisely in a visual incoherence, a spatiality that does not conform to the regulated frame of a "tableau."

Even the sentence linking the two parts of the tale—the Paris description and de Marsay's story—reenacts the tension between visual coherence and incoherence.

> Thus [*Or*], on one of these fine spring mornings when the leaves have opened but are not yet green; when the roofs are ablaze with sunshine and the sky is blue; when the people of Paris crawl from their honeycombs, buzzing along the boulevards, gliding along like a multicolored serpent, . . . on one such lovely day, a young man, whose beauty matched that of the day itself, as he was dressed most tastefully and was graceful in manner, a love child (let us keep the secret no longer), the illegitimate son of Lord Dudley and the famous Marquise de Vordac, was strolling in the *grande allée* of the Tuileries. (1054)

The description of a sunny spring day begins with a picturesque tableau, in which each element is nicely assigned its own color, but turns quickly to a much less visualizable description of the population as a buzzing mass that transforms itself into a thousand-colored serpent winding its way through the streets. The rather monstrous image combines the bees and snakes from the hive-cage passage into a fantastical creature that slithers joyfully through the city, a beast whose multicolored skin alludes to the diversity of its symbolic human parts. Only from above could one see the sun flaming on the roofs and the winding path of the "snake"; and yet, the muddled agglomeration of "mille couleurs" resists the coherent scenography of a panoramic view.

This slippage occurs even at the level of the first word in the transitional passage: *Or*. This word literally and figurally links the two parts of the story, recalling the lantern of *or et plaisir* that guides the reader through the Paris description, and reviving the *fille aux yeux d'or* of the title for the tale to follow. Shoshana Felman points out that the *Or* at the beginning of this sentence is ambiguous; its potential meanings as conjunction ("thus," "however")—rather than as the symbolic gold "taken as a light"—subvert the luminous and authoritative logic of the Paris description.[10] I would add that the polyvalence of gold and light throughout the story, their refusal to fit the easy symbolic relation of the tableau and the transparent logic of "la physiognomie," undermine a classical conception of vision in which light is equivalent to knowledge. The transitional sentence above pretends at once to refer to clarity and to embody it: as the sun of a clear blue sky illuminates the city roofs on a beautiful spring day, the narrator presents de Marsay to the reader with a gesture of transparent communication—"a love child (let us keep the secret no longer)." The parenthetical aside suggests an open disclosure, a bringing to light of any skeletons in our hero's closet. But as anyone who has read *La Fille aux yeux d'or* knows, the open secret of de Marsay's birth only screens a more complex secret destined to stay veiled until the end of the tale. Apparent clarity is narrative deception. And the thousand-colored serpent, snaking its way through this lovely tableau of one-to-one correspondence, may in fact prefigure the epistemological—and visual—confusion to follow, when the light of the sun will not always lead to clear blue skies, when clouds and veils and optical effects will trouble the eye, when the sunlike light of *Or* will give way to the gold-gleam of seduction.

Desiring Vision: Henri de Marsay

With his seductive blue eyes, curled black hair, fine girlish skin, svelte build, and beautiful hands, the Parisian rake Henri de Marsay has reason to be self-satisfied. Like the lovely Emilie in *Le Bal de Sceaux*, de Marsay relishes his beauty's power of visual attraction; "For a woman, merely to see him was to be madly in love with him" (1057). The reader of *La Fille aux yeux d'or* first meets de Marsay as he strolls along the Tuileries, a place of ultimate visual display, where the fashionable come to see and be seen; it is a place where communication occurs through the eyes, as in this nonverbal exchange between de Marsay and a promenading acquaintance: "'What brings you here on a Sunday?' the Marquis de Ronquerolles asked Henri as he passed by. 'There's fish in the trap,' the youth replied. This exchange of thoughts took the form of two meaningful glances, which Ronquerolles and Marsay sent without giving the slightest hint that they were acquainted" (1058). The meaning of exchanged glances is clear—to the glancers, to the narrator, to the reader seeing de Marsay in the mind's eye. By interpreting the "meaningful glances," the narrator signals the possibility of transparent visual communication. Still, a *coup d'œil* can lead to interpretive mistakes: "at first glance, one naturally thinks that the two types of young people who live a fashionable life are quite distinct from each other; . . . But observers who look beyond the surface of things are soon convinced that the differences between them are purely moral in nature, and that nothing is more deceptive than this lovely outer layer" (1059–60). Indeed, it will take Henri quite a while to learn the lesson that looks can be deceiving. Recounting the haphazard meeting in the gardens of his eventual lover Paquita to his friend Paul de Manerville, de Marsay displays a cocky conviction that he has been able to read accurately the meaning of *l'inconnue*'s body language; he interprets her stillness as the effect of astonishment and reads her face as expressing the following desire-driven monologue: "Why, there you are, the being who haunts my thoughts, my dreams morning and night. How did you get there? . . . Take me, I'm yours, et cetera!" (1064). Arrogant and assured, de Marsay imputes a precise motivation to the young girl's profound reaction: she has recognized in him the embodiment of her preexisting mental *ideal.* Assuming her state of purity, de Marsay attributes Paquita's apparent recognition of him to the existence of an idealized abstraction rather than to any personal experience. But precisely what his interpretation misses is that her initial shock of recognition comes from experience: her desiring glance comes not because de Marsay matches up to some abstract ideal, but because he resembles so closely the person with whom she has already enjoyed the pleasures of the flesh. De Marsay wrongly attributes, in other words, a deductive rather than inductive logic to the girl's visual subjectivity; his interpretation is based on a narrative repression, an abstraction of physical, bodily experience. In fact, it is a double repression—of the blood-link between de Marsay and his half-sister and of the latter's shared intimacies with Paquita.

Meanwhile, though, the tension between abstraction and experience, idealization and physicality makes its way through the text's visual logics. If anyone is projecting a preexisting ideal onto the other during the lovers' first encounter, it is de Marsay onto *l'inconnue* and not vice versa. In this case, the ideal form takes the shape of a preexisting visual representation, a painting: in the *fille*, de Marsay has discovered "the original of the frenzied painting entitled *Woman Caressing Her Chimera*" (1065). In *S/Z*, Barthes notes Balzac's habitual references to the anterior cultural code of painting in his textual descriptions: rather than take reality as referent, the comparison of a textual character to a painting merely creates a circularity of artistic codes, ungrounded in any extra-representational order.[11] De Marsay's description of Paquita as "l'original" of the Pompeiian fresco entitled *Woman Caressing Her Chimera* attempts to deny this circularity. In fact, de Marsay insists that she is "an ideal woman" whose form is "prostituted by those who have copied it for frescoes and mosaics." But despite his conviction that, as seeing subject of this lovely feminine object, he is accessing an ideal referent, de Marsay's own language reveals another possibility. With flippant optimism, Henri extends his comparison of *la fille*, putting himself in the potential position of the painted *chimère* of the fresco: "So here I am, today, awaiting this girl whose chimera I am [*cette fille dont je suis la chimère*]; all I ask is to stand in for the monster in the fresco" (1065). "Je suis la chimère" may be meant as the boast of a man who is sure he will soon be the object of amorous caresses, but the phrase also allows a misreading of the verb as *suivre*, to follow. The two possibilities, paraphrased, are these: "I am this girl's fantasy-ideal and am happy to oblige," or, "I am waiting for this girl whose monstrous dream I follow." The first grounds itself in the (Cartesian) "Je suis" and the conviction that he can know the framed boundaries of this girl's existence. The second possibility suggests that de Marsay is to follow a dream that is not even his own, that he will be led into a realm that exceeds his own volition. The story's outcome will confirm the latter possibility; as with Emilie in *Le Bal de Sceaux*, de Marsay will end up pulled out of an idealized frame of understanding.

De Marsay's idealism, as we have seen, is based on preexisting knowledge and a perspectivalist control over his environment. Paris, for de Marsay, is a world of transparent signs, of faces, glances, and language that he can read with epistemic confidence, as he wields a control figured as supremely, divinely visual:

> Henri could do as he pleased in indulging his pleasures and egotism. His invisible influence on the social world had empowered him with real, but concealed grandeur, . . . His opinion of himself was not like that of Louis XIV, but rivaled that of the proudest Caliphs, Pharaohs, Xerxes who thought themselves members of a divine race, when they imitated God by veiling themselves before their subjects, claiming that their gaze had the power to give death. (1085)

De Marsay's belief in the power of his own gaze justifies his deceptive actions, his "self-veiling" as secret sovereign. But the many other veils in *La Fille aux yeux d'or* will in fact call into question de Marsay's mastery. For while he believes that he will blind the many-eyed monster, it will turn out that de Marsay himself will be blinded—literally blindfolded—and led on an adventure that exceeds his control.

Veils and Vision: Balzac After Rousseau

In one of *La Fille aux yeux d'or*'s narrative digressions, Balzac praises Jean-Jacques Rousseau's celebrated novel *Julie; ou, La Nouvelle Héloïse*:

> While Rousseau was clearly inspired by Richardson's work [*Clarissa*], he departed from it in countless details that lend his monument a magnificent originality; he commended it to posterity through grand ideas that are difficult to tease out through analysis when, in one's youth, one reads this work in hopes of encountering an impassioned portrayal of our most physical sensations, whereas serious-minded, philosophical writers never use such images except as the consequence and necessity of vast thought; and Milord Edouard's adventures are one of this work's most Europeanly subtle ideas. (1092)

I will return to Milord Edouard (whose adventures comprise the end to *Julie; ou, La Nouvelle Héloïse*), but for now let me point out that Balzac's praise focuses on the fact that Rousseau grounds his representation of sentiment and passion in a preexisting system of thought.[12] The valorization of Rousseau's serious, philosophical side seems a bit out of place in *La Fille aux yeux d'or*, constructed as it is on such a lush and sensual "impassioned portrayal of our most physical sensations." It seems worth exploring, therefore, Balzac's explicit reference.

After all, *Julie; ou, La Nouvelle Héloïse* acts as suggestive intertext for *La Fille aux yeux d'or* in that its own idealism—its justification of physical sentiment by conceptual system, as Balzac puts it—carries a particular visual logic. In *Jean-Jacques Rousseau: la transparence et l'obstacle* (1957) and *L'Œil vivant* (1961), Jean Starobinski analyzes the way in which Enlightenment idealism underlies Rousseau's pervasive valorization of transparent communication in *La Nouvelle Héloïse.* In Rousseau's novel, clarity in Nature reflects directly an honesty of the soul; "A limpid space where the transparency of the soul opens onto the transparency of air."[13] The figure of the veil takes on central importance in Starobinski's reading as obstacle to knowledge, both intersubjective and divine. And as with Balzac's theory of the visionary's "second sight," Rousseau's ideal vision entails a transcendence of the visible, material world: "Everything to which we immediately respond is, in reality, an obstacle (a veil) between God and ourselves" (*Transp*, 144). Rousseau's logic is embedded not only in a vague mysticism but in the Cartesian ideal of panoramic vision, with its negation of the body anchored in space and time.[14] As Starobinski points out, Julie's husband Wolmar dreams of controlling his realm, an ambition that manifests itself in the figure of an omniscient eye, "l'œil vivant" that catapults him to the position of God (*Transp*, 144). As we saw above, Balzac's Henri de Marsay, like Rousseau's Wolmar, attributes to himself the role of the invisible all-seer, like those who imitate God "by veiling themselves before their subjects, claiming that their gaze had the power to give death." The main difference here may lie in the final word, "death" in the place of "life." Where Rousseau's novel ends in Julie's transcendent death, which rends the veils of mediation and obstruction to salvation, the end of *La Fille aux yeux d'or* brings de Marsay face to face with his own contingency, his particular boundedness in brute body and matter.

Henri de Marsay may share Wolmar's ambition of visual transcendence, but *La Fille aux yeux d'or* turns out to be one long drawn-out limit-case to Balzac's own professions of faith in the power of the gaze: a "moment . . . when looking produces not clarity and mastery but trouble, the inability to see, and the disempowerment of the observer."[15] De Marsay's visual disempowerment, as we shall see, is intertwined with a more general visual metaphorics that goes against the "transparence et obstacle" logic of Rousseau's poetics and of Descartes' optics. Veils and screens abound in *La Fille aux yeux d'or,* but their relation to truth and knowledge is not always obstructive, and even the figure of Light appears not only as guarantee of knowledge but as an obstacle in its own right to clear and distinct ideas.

As de Marsay comes closer to seducing the young girl he had met on his stroll, he is drawn away from his known territory, pulled mysteriously into Paquita's realm by the power of her eyes, "whose rays appeared to have the same nature as those thrown out by the sun" (1073). This is not a sun whose light affords transparent knowledge, but one whose rays trouble and confuse the viewer. At his first rendezvous with Paquita,

Henri is guided up a tenebrous, dank stairway to a dark and seedy room; he feels uneasy, unknowing. Paquita, on the other hand, enjoys the freedom of a sun in its own orbit; reclining on a divan in a voluptuous peignoir, she is "free to cast about her golden, fiery glances . . . , free in her luminous movements" (1079). In relation to her light, to the open presence of her gaze, de Marsay loses his usual self-assurance and hesitates to approach the woman he had so ardently desired. The experience of coming face to face with the once distant object of desire is compared by the narrator to the contemplation of a clear sky: "At first glance, nature appears as if covered by a gauzy veil, the firmament's azure appears black, *the heightened brightness like shadows*" (1080, my emphasis). The optical experience of temporary disorientation and semiblindness brought on by the extreme light of a cloudless sky becomes a figure for the emotional confusion of facing a desired object free of obstacles. In Rousseau's logic, the ideal of transparent communication is figured by a bright sky. Here, on the other hand, we have the illusion of darkness produced by the very intensity of light. Light is not dispelling shadows here, but causing them. De Marsay's usual clarity of purpose, his confidence as experienced seducer, is confounded by sunlike, luminous rays.

Despite de Marsay's apparent gifts of perception (he is, claims the narrator, among those who can see the "result in causes that are hidden to the eyes of others, but discernible to their own" 1080), he loses both foresight and insight when confronted with Paquita's eyes, from which "sparks flew." These brilliant sparks create the optical effects of a *fantasmagorie,* a light-filled spectacle of illusions that veils the ominous presence of Paquita's chaperone:

> [Paquita] then seemed so wondrously beautiful to Henri that the whole fantasmagoria of rags, age, worn red garments, . . . all of her frail, pained ostentation immediately disappeared. *The salon brightened* [s'illumina], *he no longer could see except through a cloud* the terrifying harpy, immobile, perched in silence atop her red divan, and whose yellow eyes revealed her servile devotion. (1081, my emphasis)

Again, the presence of light causes an effect of shadow in the observer's eye, as de Marsay struggles to regain the mastering perspective of the sovereign subject, "like an Oriental king calling for an amusement" (1082).

For a moment, however, Henri's evaluative and knowledgeable gaze puts Paquita back in the object-position, turning her into a useful specimen rather than an acting, desiring subject. "He saw all of this within this young woman more distinctly that ever before, for she gave herself up to be seen, happy to be admired. De Marsay's admiration became a secret passion, *and he unveiled her completely,* with a glance that the Spaniard recognized" (1082, my emphasis). With his gaze of possession, de

Marsay thinks he controls the veiling (of himself) and the unveiling (of his desired object), but he makes a mistake that leads to a subjectivity tug-of-war. He announces to Paquita that if anyone else were to possess her, he would kill her. "Hearing this, Paquita veiled her face with her hands and cried out . . .! " She veils herself, taking back the subject-position not only of veiling but of seeing, since she is the one now who knows the truth of de Marsay's rival, while Henri remains blind to all of the hints that follow, bedazzled as he is by the fantasmagoric atmosphere of shadowy lights and sparkling screens.

The central point to note here is that whenever *la fille aux yeux d'or* appears, veils and filmy vapors combine with *effets de lumière* to create a dreamy world of optical illusion. In her richly ornamented boudoir, "The shimmering tapestry, which changed color according to the direction of one's gaze, turning all white or all pink, harmonized with the effects of the light infusing the chiffon's diaphanous flutings, offering a hazy vision" (1088). The room's *effets de lumière* create an optical realm of subjective perception, as the color of the wall hanging changes according to the viewer's position while the gauzy veils diffuse the soft light through the room. Similarly, when Paquita kneels by him in her white peignoir, de Marsay is pulled into a sensationalism removed from the stability of objective reality: "Perhaps due to the contrast between the shadows he had just left and the light flooding his soul, . . . he felt the kind of delightful sensation that only true poetry can provide" (1089). Luminous reflections and sparkling vapors combine to rid de Marsay of his initial cocky arrogance: "When he saw, in the midst of this alcove born of a fairy's wand . . . this girl . . . whose soft skin, glowing slightly from the red reflections and from the effusion of some mysterious vapor of love, sparkled as if it were reflecting rays from lights and colors, all of his anger, desire for vengeance, and wounded pride fell away" (1089). The golden-eyed girl's reflections of rays and colors dissipate de Marsay's sovereign gaze, providing an alternate visual experience to his imagined mastery. Where Rousseau's Wolmar is allowed to cling to his Cartesian, transparent optics, de Marsay is introduced to an alternative, sensationalist optics by the magnetizing pull of bodily desire. Paquita is no transparent object, no simple embodiment of his preexisting mental ideal; her own subjecthood and bodily experience reflect back the shimmering rays of light that might have allowed him to know her.

In *La Fille aux yeux d'or*, then, Balzac corporealizes light, anchoring its symbolics in the bodily logic of perception. Contrast, for example, the motif of the "dream-veil" in his text with Rousseau's. In *Julie; ou, La Nouvelle Héloïse*, Saint-Preux has a nightmare in which an ominous veil separates him from Julie on her deathbed: "ever this same device of death, ever this impenetrable veil leaves my hands and hides from my eyes the dying object it covers."[16] Saint-Preux's dream comes to him in a moment of bitter nostalgia for his lost moments with Julie; as darkening omen of death, the veil represents an insurmountable distance between the desiring subject and his pure object. In *La Fille aux yeux d'or*, de Marsay also dreams of a veil, after his first visit to Paquita's boudoir. But unlike Saint-Preux, he has fallen asleep full of brash confidence in his amorous exploits to come. "He dreamed of the *fille aux yeux d'or* . . . he saw monstrous images, elusive oddities, *full of light*, that revealed invisible worlds but always incompletely, for *an interposed veil changes optical conditions*" (1085, my emphasis) Unlike Rousseau's dark and heavy symbol, this *voile* is luminous and gauzy, casting its optical effects in a disorienting, rather than directly obstructive, way. De Marsay's dream-vision is suffused with light, but the light takes part in the monstrous atmosphere rather than existing behind it as some unattainable realm of pure and total revelation. Where Rousseau's metaphysics anchor the figure of light in God, *La Fille aux yeux d'or* leaves light untethered and changeable according to the conditions of its perception.

This fictional emphasis on light as physiological effect rather than as stable physical entity mobilizes the burgeoning optics of Balzac's time. Johannes Müller, for example, defined vision in terms of subjective sensation rather than through Descartes' innate ideas: in the *Handbuch des Physiologie des Menschen* (1833), he proposed an optics in which "the experience of light becomes severed from any stable point of reference or from any source or origin around which a world could be constituted and apprehended."[17] Similarly, light in *La Fille aux yeux d'or* is disconnected from the sun-God position that de Marsay imagines himself inhabiting before his adventure—just as the empiricist emphasis on bodily sensation as necessary mode of knowledge was posing threats to the Cartesian system of idealism. In *La Fille aux yeux d'or*, Balzac praises Rousseau for anchoring the representation of sensation in a coherent system of ideas; but his own book depicts—perhaps as warning—the effects of entering into a realm of pure sensation.

After all, de Marsay's dream does not act as revelation: he wakes up blithely to a day of gaming in anticipation of a night of pleasure. The optical effects of de Marsay's dream, meanwhile, have hinted at the vaporous, screenlike nature of desire's illusory realm. *La Fille aux yeux d'or* has been described as an infernally lit space, where "what appears to be light is merely fire and flame, that which burns and consumes";[18] I would characterize the lighting in the tale less as the burning fires of hell than as the diaphanous, sparkling lights of optical illusion, the fascinating powers of changing appearances, as experienced through the screens and blurs of the bodily eye. From Rousseau to Balzac, we have moved from "l'œil vivant" and its transcendental Light to the optical illusions of subjective vision.

Let us take a brief second look at Balzac's digressive reference to Rousseau's *Julie; ou, La Nouvelle Héloïse,* which comes at a moment when de Marsay is displaying a postcoital callousness coupled with the passive acceptance of being blindfolded by his lover. Sated with pleasure and lazily assailed by vaguely ignoble feelings, de Marsay experiences a moral ambiguity defined as the disjunction of sentiment from the grounding principles of God's light: "The certainty of this mental state, which is a chaotic but real one in souls that are neither illuminated by this celestial light nor scented with the holy balm that brings us pertinacity of sentiment, no doubt imposed upon Rousseau the adventures of Milord Edouard that close the letters of *La Nouvelle Héloïse*" (1092). It is here that the narrator adds his comment on Rousseau's idealism as justification of his novelistic depiction of passionate sentiment or sensation. But the sensationalistic adventures of Milord Edouard seem an odd segment of *La Nouvelle Héloïse* for Balzac to mention, especially if, as Raymond Trousson writes, "Balzac clearly felt that he was one of these serious-minded and philosophical writers who use sentiment only to serve a broader, deeper purpose."[19]

"Les Amours de Milord Bomston" appears at the end of *La Nouvelle Héloïse,* in the form of a summarized appendix to the long novel. In the novel itself, Edouard Bomston is Saint-Preux's English friend and confidant, serving as link between the introspective hero and society in his role as addressee for many of Saint-Preux's confessional letters. But in the book's appendix, Rousseau tells the story of Bomston's entanglement in a love triangle. A beautiful marquise, whom he loves but will not possess because she is married, offers him the services of a young prostitute, Laure, as a hand-picked outlet for his sexual frustrations. Laure, in turn, falls in love with him and renounces her debased state to join a convent. Bomston ends up publicly embroiled in these two affairs from which he reaps no sexual benefit—the first because of his own virtue and sublimation of desire, the second because of the chastity imposed by Laure's newfound self-respect. The marquise's presentation to Bomston of Laure as an acceptable but exclusive object of his sexual desires creates a dynamic charged with jealousy, transference, and objectification—in some ways reminiscent of *La Fille*'s love triangle. But most suggestive for an intertextual reading is the marquise's use of Laure as a sort of *femme-écran,* a screen-woman. We encounter this term in Balzac's text when de Marsay, swaggering in his postseduction vanity, gives his friend de Manerville a short discourse on discretion; the best way, he says, to avoid the discovery of an adulterous affair is to employ a *femme-écran*—that is, a woman of no attachment to distract from the true object of interest.

The Rousseauian intertext allows us to identify Paquita's role in *La Fille aux yeux d'or* as that of "narrative *femme-écran,*" less in the sense that de

Marsay proposes (as alibi for cynical adultery) than as Rousseau's marquise uses Laure: as an outlet for desire while the real object of interest is unattainable. And who is the reader's "real" object of interest in *La Fille aux yeux d'or*? Oddly enough, another marquise. When de Marsay first tells Paul de Manerville, in the Tuileries, of having seen the mysterious *fille aux yeux d'or*, his friend responds that he himself had recently seen her accompanied by a woman whose attractiveness far surpasses Paquita's. De Manerville describes this second woman as a black-eyed, fiery beauty bearing a striking resemblance to Henri de Marsay. Henri, vain as ever, retorts "you flatter her!" and when his friend continues to describe this unknown woman, exclaims with impatience, "Come on, old boy, what do I care about someone I've never seen!" (1064). Only by entering into his visual field will an object merit de Marsay's attention—and his annoyed dismissal of a woman on whom he's never laid eyes encourages the reader of *La Fille aux yeux d'or* to experience a similar blindness to her potential significance. Upon first reading the story, the resemblance between the unknown woman and de Marsay seems a gratuitous coincidence, as do later details in the text: the fact that Paquita is in contact with a marquise from Spain, where Henri's father had sired an illegitimate daughter, for example, or Paquita's sexual savoir-faire and acknowledgment of having been taught to hate men. Premonitional clues are sidelined as the reader's eyes, like de Marsay's, are directed toward the fascinating *fille aux yeux d'or*, with her sparkling light effects and veiled mystery. At the story's end, the gory, climactic description of Paquita's mutilated body and her room's painterly pattern of blood creates a scene of visual interest as Henri enters her room.[20] Paquita is dead, but her corpse continues to speak as object of an attentive gaze: "Her body, slashed to ribbons . . . told how fiercely she had fought for a life that Henri had made so precious to her." Murdered, the *fille aux yeux d'or* appears to have become legible text for Henri's eyes, as she seemed to be at their first encounter.

But at this point, de Marsay has not seen all there is to see, for the "spectacle presented to his gaze astonished . . . him for more than one reason" (1106). Gradually, he and the reader become aware of the marquise as she stands in silent, torn triumph over her bloodied victim. The marquise, Paquita's former lover, is as irresistibly drawn to the visual image of the *fille aux yeux d'or* as is her rival de Marsay: only after minutes spent contemplating the corpse of their mutually desired victim are de Marsay and the marquise finally able to tear their eyes away from her mesmerizing presence. Only then can the narrative reveal its deferred and hidden truth, as Henri and the marquise look each other in the eye and see their own traits reflected in each other's faces. After this moment of brutal recognition that the two share not only the same lover but the same father, a rushed dénouement informs us that the marquise will enter a convent and that de Marsay has returned to his promenades in the Tuileries. In the end, then, de Marsay retreats to the realm whose visible signs he believes he can interpret at first glance.

After the dramatic discovery that ends *La Fille aux yeux d'or,* the reader realizes that clues to the marquise's identity had been scattered throughout the text, overshadowed by Paquita's brilliant presence as material being, as object of de Marsay's desires and projections, as evident impetus for the sensationalistic plot. As the focal point throughout the story, the *fille aux yeux d'or* functions as a narrative screen-object, blocking out the clues, distracting the reader from the unseen woman—for we, like de Marsay, have asked as we read along, "Come on, . . . what do I care about someone I've never seen!" The marquise is de Marsay's double, his identical rival, the hidden pole in the triangle of relations with Paquita in the center. Rousseau's marquise in "Les Amours de Milord Bomston," meanwhile, had proposed Laure as a safe (she thinks) object on which Bomston can discharge his sexual energy; the young prostitute serves as a physical intermediary between two lovers who cannot consummate their passion. Paquita plays a similar role, as the physical and sexual connection between a man and a woman who are at once linked and separate; it is as *narrative femme-écran* that *la fille aux yeux d'or* fulfills her deceptive and gleaming goldlike destiny.

"Les Amours de Milord Bomston" ends with a compact moral that could as easily serve as epigraph to *La Fille aux yeux d'or.* "In our blindness, we . . . all spend [our lives] chasing our chimeras" (771). In a way, we could take this story as an antisensationalist lesson, a warning to the reader not to focus our eyes on the illusory realm of appearances, of lights and shadows, of sentiment and passion—not to fall for the *fantasmagorie.* To follow the chimerical object of visual desire, the *fille aux yeux d'or,* is to be blind to the true nature of things. As well as connoting illusion, the chimera represents a monstrous dual composite. As we have seen, Paquita herself has a dual nature; in her, we find "The truly bizarre union of the mysterious and the real, of shadow and light, of the appalling and the beautiful, of pleasure and danger, of Heaven and Hell" (1091).[21] The conjunction of light and shadow in one being is "bizarre," monstrous; it disassembles the hierarchical system of dichotomy that holds together Rousseau's idealism, for example, where light is assigned to transcendence and darkness to the limited realm of human sensation. Confusion and hybridization in the visual realm become indicators for all kinds of other blurrings that the story addresses, including homosexuality's potential to blur clear distinctions between sexual purity and experience. Balzac's tale thus straddles an idealized metaphysics of moral ideas and their sensual, sensationalistic *mise en question.*

Indeed, this may be the real key to why Balzac names "Les Amours de Milord Bomston" in his moral justification of Rousseau's idealism. Originally, the adventures of Milord Bomston had been intended as an integral part of *La Nouvelle Héloïse.* In the end, though, Rousseau decided to cut the letters relating to the adventure from the main text because their tone would clash with the more philosophical parts of the novel. What we have, instead, is a synoptic version of Milord's adventures, relegated to an appendix in *La Nouvelle Héloïse* because of their overly "romanesque" nature (759). The adventures of Milord Bomston can only exist *en marge,* as excess; unable to fit into *La Nouvelle Héloïse*'s harmonious simplicity; writes Rousseau, they are "bizarres." In point of fact, the adventures are not actually more shocking in themselves than the affair between Julie and Saint-Preux, except that they lack an explicit philosophizing context. While Rousseau's reaction to the *bizarre* tale is to excise it from the naturalistic chronological order of the letters, Balzac implicitly reintegrates it into Rousseau's philosophical project. The justification would extend to *La Fille aux yeux d'or,* whose sensationalistic content might seem to conflict with the more idealistic parts of Balzac's own project.

The "Second" Sight of Realism

After all, *La Fille aux yeux d'or* is in some ways the anti-*Séraphîta*—a story driven by the most sensual, bodily desires instead of angelic, transcendent purity. Though differently elaborated, *Séraphîta*'s Swedenborgian metaphysics are compatible with the logic of transparency that Starobinski traces in Rousseau: unfettered by the limitations of the bodily senses, the angelic spirit possesses the pure internal eye of second sight and ascends at the end of the novel into "La Vraie Lumière."[22] Let us recall Séraphîta's tirade against the limitations of human understanding, as it focuses on the particular debates going on in the field of optics at the time. Addressing the humans, (s)he cites the controversy over the definition of color as an example of our inability to escape the matter/spirit divide: "You cannot make up your minds whether color is a faculty with which the body is endowed or whether it is an effect produced by the affusion of light."[23] The definition of color, like the definition of light, divided idealists from sensationalists at the end of the eighteenth and beginning of the nineteenth centuries: believers in objective vision like Newton and Descartes identified color as an inherent, stable quality of objects in the real world, analyzable according to laws of physics and the decomposition of the spectrum; post-Lockean empiricists interested in subjective vision, on the other hand, studied the ways in which colors were perceived differently under changing optical circumstances. *Séraphîta* imagines a transcendental realm where this conflict between objective vision and subjective vision makes no sense. As pure spirit, Séraphîta escapes the quandary posed by the philosophers of Balzac's time: if human understanding is located in our minds, why do we access the world through our sensory organs of perception? Are these organs the route to knowledge or a distraction from it? *Séraphîta* elides the epistemological struggle that occupied Locke, Condillac, Berkeley, and Leibniz by imagining direct, transparent communication unmediated by the bodily organs of sensation in the material world.

In *La Fille aux yeux d'or,* on the other hand, the ideal of transparent communication grapples continuously with an alternative mode of physicality. In this story of desiring, bodily human subjects, the conflict between objective vision and subjective vision still pertains.

If de Marsay possesses a second sight, it is not the unmediated perception of the visionary eye. Rousseau's "principle of immediacy" (*Transp,* 132), Descartes' theory of innate ideas, Séraphîta's timeless illumination, all give way in *La Fille aux yeux d'or* to a temporal (which is to say, narrative) logic of visuality. After de Marsay's first visit to Paquita's golden boudoir, he still thinks she is merely an insignificant conquest, whose fearful prophecies are unfounded. The next day, however, he takes a second look at the previous night's events. After a bout of callous bragging, he sits back and begins "to view the events of the night before in an odd light [*sous un singulier jour*]." Note that the word *jour* is being used as a synonym for light; Balzac might instead have written "sous une singulière lumière." By juxtaposing "jour" to de Marsay's "nuit," Balzac underlines the temporal aspect of his hero's revelation. In other words, a visual concept (light) has been replaced by a temporal one (day), so that the understanding that arises is not figured as sudden illumination (a *vision*) but as temporal process, as day following night. De Marsay's "second sight" (a spatial concept of interior vision) requires a "second glance" (temporally, a second moment) to flourish: "As is true for many great minds, his perspicacity was not spontaneous; he did not immediately get to the heart of the matter. Like all personalities endowed with the ability to live largely in the present, to squeeze out and drink down its juices, so to speak, *his second sight* required a type of sleep in order to become identified with causes" (1096, my emphasis). A variant in Balzac's manuscript of *La Fille aux yeux d'or* explains that de Marsay's "second sight was not involved during the event itself; it needed a type of sleep during which it became identified with things, and led him to them a posteriori."[24] The empiricist logic of the a posteriori, the need for a "second time around" for true understanding, grounds de Marsay's "second sight" in a human temporality. This is not the instant insight of a visionary like Louis Lambert, but a gradual comprehension of the ways of the world.

In fact, de Marsay's a posteriori vision is figured even before the story's grand finale, in the two scenes of a blindfolded voyage. As de Marsay is pulled away from his own turf, into the confusing world of *la fille aux yeux d'or*, he is forced to relinquish visual control over his surroundings. If ever our hero needs access to an "inner vision," it is during these voyages, when his external organs of perception are blocked by a band of white silk. And indeed the narrator proposes that there is no reason for him not to be able to situate himself within the grid of Paris's streets while riding passively in the coach, for "all he needed to do was to concentrate and to count, based on the number of street gutters crossed, the streets they would pass in front of on the boulevards" (1086–87) in order to recognize the streets taken by the carriage and thus ascertain his location in the city. The erection of a mental grid to take the place of visual cues supports the Cartesian idea that spatial orientation and visual perception in general are innate and ideational rather than tied to the sensory organ. A lucid mind should be able to compensate for the loss of sensory perception. But in de Marsay's case, wounded pride and passionate desire get in the way: "But the violent emotion . . . , the fury he felt due to his wounded dignity, the ideas of vengeance he gave himself up to, his suspicions about the meticulous care taken by this mysterious girl in making him come to her, all of this kept him from experiencing the blind attentiveness he needed in order to concentrate his mind and to have perfect insight" (1087). "Blind attentiveness" may suggest the notion, popularized in Diderot's *Lettre sur les aveugles*, that the blind are capable of producing visual meaning out of abstract contextual and formal relations. Against this Cartesian ideal of spatial understanding, Locke argued that perceptual experience was indispensable to the comprehension of visual concepts. The blindfolded scene in *La Fille aux yeux d'or* clings to the Cartesian premise of an ideal mental capacity, since on his second voyage, de Marsay succeeds in creating a mental picture of his route. But his comprehension remains limited, leading the narrator to comment on the imperfection of human understanding in general: "Had he been free, or if he had walked, he could have broken off a branch of shrubbery, gazed upon the type of sand clinging to his boots; but now, transported aerially, one might say, to inaccessible lodgings, his good fortune was to be what it had been up to that point: a dream. But it is man's despair that he can do nothing that is not imperfect, for either good or evil. All of his intellectual or physical endeavors bear a stamp of destruction" (1098). This pessimistic conclusion characterizes the moral system of *La Fille aux yeux d'or*, for it is the story of the sensory realm, where human passions and desires have come untethered from the light of divinity ("What do you call light?" asks de Marsay; answers Paquita, "You, my handsome Adolphe!" 1100). De Marsay has no inner "second sight"—

only a "second" second sight, an imperfect understanding that comes a posteriori, after a temporal delay. Into the ideal of a mentally constructed spatial grid enters the temporal logic of the bounded human body.

The coupling of de Marsay's limited viewpoint with the retained ideal of a mental perspectival overview might be linked to Leibniz, whose *New Essays on Human Understanding* (1765) stated an intermediary opinion between Locke and Condillac's empiricism and Descartes' belief in innate ideas.[25] Leibniz accepts Locke's theory of unnoticed perceptual judgments, but insists that ideas of geometrical form, extension, and spatial orientation exist independently of perception by the sensory organs.[26] In other words, the blind (or blindfolded, like de Marsay) should be capable of accessing relational ideas of space, although human understanding can never fully control the perceptual realm. Leibniz's philosophy attempts to reconcile idealism, figured by a universal, absolutely privileged point of view, with the limitations of mankind, figured in our multiple points of view.[27] Balzac's representations of the visionary eye, especially in *Louis Lambert* and *Séraphîta*, suggest the possibility of escape from a finite, human viewpoint, but the eye in *La Fille aux yeux d'or* remains temporally bounded and susceptible to the illusions and veils of the physiological organ of sensation.

If, as William Paulson suggests, the visionary mode of "second sight" can be linked to Balzac's Romantic writing, the temporality of de Marsay's alternative "second" second sight seems, rather, linked to the sequential temporality of Balzac's realist narration. *La Fille aux yeux d'or*'s narrative structure hinges on a temporal logic of sequentiality, a logic of two moments that replaces the instantaneous, revelatory model of its initial "tableau." De Marsay's gift of second sight depends on a temporal delay. Only after going back over, mentally, the previous evening's experience can he understand, partially, his own lack of control: "At that moment, de Marsay realized that he had been played for a fool by the *fille aux yeux d'or*" (1096). Retrospectively, de Marsay is able to see the night "in its entirety." Balzac describes this delayed revelation in terms of reading: "then he was able to read into this shining, showy page, to divine its hidden meaning" (1096). The sentence provides a hint to the reader to go back, give the pages he has read a second look, and to find the hidden enigma. De Marsay was at first blinded by the light of his enigmatic lover, but in retrospect, he is able to find the hidden meaning. When he re-"reads" his visit to Paquita's lair, "a few words, obscure at first but now clear . . . all of it proved to him that he had been standing in for another person" (1096). The words—like the phenomena of colors and light in this tale—have no stable form; their meaning depends on a shift in perspective, on the lighting effects ("obscure at first but now clear") of the moment. The *optique*-changing veils that de Marsay encountered on his visits to his lover have their counterpart in the narrative veiling of this text's enigma.

In the end, transcendent vision is replaced by an optical experience that incorporates the phenomenal world. Immediate revelation is not the currency of the *Comédie humaine.* As de Marsay approaches Paquita's room at the end of the story, he brags to his companion Ferragus, leader of the secret society that calls itself les Treize, "we, and we alone, can foresee all." But the boast is immediately refuted by the bloody dénouement, unforeseen by de Marsay. Neither *prévoyance* nor *voyance* pertain, but the novel does propose a sort of "post-*voyance,*" a temporal second sight that accords with the complexities of worldly optics and that embodies the realism of the Balzacian text, its need to "tomber dans le phénomène" of narration in order to grasp the absolute. Henri de Marsay will go on to become one of the most successful readers of Parisian society, appearing as the minister in *Une Ténébreuse affaire* who has understood the story's mystery and gives its a posteriori explanation at the end of the book. But already in *La Fille aux yeux d'or,* de Marsay is learning the lesson that life is a "tenebrous affair": that knowing and seeing mean having to take shadows into account as unavoidable modes of perception, rather than clinging blindly to an idealistic realm of transparency, clarity, and light as pure absence of darkness.

Part II

Tenebrous Affairs: *Romans policiers* and the Detecting Eye

Chapter 5

Cuvier, Helmholtz, and the Visual Logics of Deduction: Poe, Doyle, Gaboriau

Long before one could hire a private eye to act as paid organ of sight; before the Série Noire in France concretized a semantic link between mystery and darkness; before a magnified eye became an immediately recognizable symbol of detectives and their tales—the *roman policier* had established its own narrative logic of visuality. With its dual parentage of nineteenth-century French popular fiction (from Balzac's 1841 *Une Ténébreuse affaire* and other "judiciary novels" to the serial fluff of Paul Féval's 1863 *Les Habits noirs*) and the Anglo-American gothic novel (from Radcliffe to Poe), the *roman policier* inherited a conventional metaphorics in which truth is equivalent to light, knowledge to visual revelation. As this book has been proposing, however, such a simple formula fails to take into account important variations in nineteenth-century conceptions of vision, variations that shaped both scientific and literary conventions and forms. An exemplary model of the modern epistemological subject, the fictional detective allows us to reexamine the preeminently visual logic of observation and inquiry. For if "eureka" is the cry of triumph for a Balzacian scientist-sage, "I see" marks the moment at which the *roman policier*'s mystery-solver has attained the knowledge necessary to re-create the steps of a crime.

From the first universally acknowledged detective story, Poe's "The Murders in the Rue Morgue" (1841), the work of the fictional detective has consisted in seeing what others are unable to see.[1] The detective Dupin's famed confidence contrasts with the apparent blindness of all around him, while Holmes's avowed mission to trace "the scarlet skein of murder running through the colourless skein of life" reminds us that solving a mystery requires a certain visual aptitude, both rare and specialized. Consider the classic instance of Watson's frustration with his mentor's superior insight: "I had heard what he had heard," writes Sherlock Holmes's assistant, "I had seen what he had seen, and yet from his words it was evident that he saw clearly not only what had happened, but what was about to happen, while to me the whole business was still confused and grotesque!"[2] Like Poe's Dupin, Holmes possesses a certain kind of vision that allows him to perceive the broadest implications in the simplest facts. Most often, these facts are visible ones, as in "A Scandal in Bohemia," where Holmes amazes Watson with spontaneous insight into the latter's private life. Holmes explains his process of deduction: "my eyes tell me that on the inside of your left shoe, . . . the leather is scored by six almost parallel cuts. Obviously they have been caused by someone who has very carelessly scraped round the edges of the sole in order to remove crusted mud from it" (5). When Watson protests that his eyes are as good as his mentor's, Holmes replies: "Quite so, . . . You see, but you do not observe. The distinction is clear" (6). But what is, exactly, this "clear" distinction between sight as visual perception and vision as observational process? Given that Holmes often closes his eyes to think through a case, and that Dupin finds darkness inspirational of clear thought, it seems that mere ocular registration has little to do with the detective's superior *vision.* Certainly, Holmes seems to set the work of the mind above the work of the eye. In "The Adventure of the Blue Carbuncle," he comforts Watson, who has been complaining that when faced with a man—or a clue or a hat—he can see nothing. Says Holmes: "On the contrary, Watson, you can see everything. You fail, however, to reason from what you see. You are too timid in drawing your inferences" (156). Holmes opposes the logical act of reasoning, with its steps and abstractions, to a certain immediate sensory knowledge that Watson seems to want. "Observation" appears to entail mental action alone. Yet, that action is rooted in visual perception: it is "from what you see" that you are to reason. The recurring thematics of vision in Doyle's texts (Watson is often "all in the dark," wondering if Holmes "can see a spark where all is dark to me"), coupled with Holmes's rigorously optical methods (his magnifying glass becomes a trademark), keep the detective's eye from being eclipsed by his mind.

Rather than take the detective genre's double interest in visual and mental functions as mere unsystematic oscillation, this chapter proposes reading the *roman policier* in the context of nineteenth-century sciences of vision, which give as large a role to cognitive inference as to the optical organ. Within this context, both *seeing* and *observing* can be understood as integral to the logics of detection—in other words, Holmes's distinction becomes less than perfectly "clear." By way of the scientific writings of Cuvier (who represents, according to Foucault, a radically modern way of seeing the world) and Helmholtz (for whom to see is to "observe" through rigorous induction), this chapter explores a textual kinship between the analytical processes of deduction in the early *roman policier* and the epistemological concerns of science in its time. More particularly, it reasserts the importance of "experience" as a key term for understanding the genre's scientific roots. Recalling its double meaning in French, *experience* should be taken here to refer not just to lived reality, but to an experimental method—and indeed, to the very method that bases itself precisely in experience: that is, empiricist investigation. By drawing out the conflicting deductive and inductive drives of the empirical method, we restore a sense of vibrant debate often missing from accounts of nineteenth-century literature as reflecting a smooth triumph of positivistic science. We begin, then, with the commonplace analogy between the fictional detective and an empirical scientist, Georges Baron Cuvier.

The Detective's Bones: Clues and Cuvier

In "The Murders in the Rue Morgue," the detective Dupin, seeking to identify his case's guilty party as not a man but a species of "Orang-Outang" from Borneo, consults the zoological writings of the French naturalist Georges Baron Cuvier (1769–1832). Cuvier serves as authoritative back-up and explicatory reference to Dupin's own observations at the scene of the crime (of a too large hand imprint and orange-colored hair). Cuvier's appearance in this founding fictional text must have seemed quite apt, for both of Poe's direct heirs in the writing of detective novels, Emile Gaboriau and Sir Author Conan Doyle, also mentioned the famous French anatomist in their fictions. But they went even further than Poe, invoking Cuvier not merely as positivist depository of arcane biological knowledge, but as the very model of the detective at work: in Gaboriau's *Monsieur Lecoq* and Doyle's "Five Orange Pips," the detective is described as reconstructing a crime from a clue just as a naturalist reconstructs an entire animal from a single bone fragment. This latter feat had been associated with Cuvier ever since his famous boast in the 1812 Preface to *Recherches sur les ossemens fossiles de quadrupèdes* of being able to recreate the entire bodily structure of a disappeared species based on the form of a single, partial fossil. The analogy between the naturalist's reconstruction and that of the detective works clearly, as in both cases the form of a past event is indicated by the fragmentary material evidence left behind.

But there is more to this analogy than the mere theme of reconstruction. Indeed, attention to the methods invoked in *Monsieur Lecoq* and "The Five Orange Pips," when combined with analysis of the Cuvierian context, will expose a *visual* logic of reasoning that anchors the *roman policier* genre in the "empirico-transcendental doublet" of nineteenth-century thought: that is, in the insoluble double bind between induction and deduction that marks the modern epistemology of the age.[3]

As we saw in Part I of this book, Cuvier's thought had directly influenced literary imagination before, as in Balzac's *La Comédie humaine,* where it stands both as foil to Saint-Hilaire's "compositional unity" and as inspirational source of resurrection for lost epochs. In the *Avant-propos* evocation of the famous naturalists' *querelle*, Cuvier is associated with the systematic description of visible differences among species, while Saint-Hilaire is understood to emphasize their underlying, *in*visible affinities. But in *La Peau de chagrin*'s famous ode (the passage that more directly pertains to the *roman policier* analogy), what makes Cuvier "the greatest poet of our century" is actually his ability to conjure all that is hidden under the surface of the earth's crust: that which we cannot see.

It is this latter "Cuvier of the invisible" that inspired Foucault, in *Les Mots et les choses*, to describe Cuvierian biology as having opening up a new epistemological space at the start of the nineteenth century, one that looks for knowledge in the *unseen* workings of the world, the body, and the universe.[4] Where seventeenth-century natural history had focused on visible surfaces (classifying birds, for example, according to similar feather shapes and colors), the nineteenth century brought an interest in anatomy, in the internal workings of plants, animals, and man. Foucault takes Cuvier as a threshold figure for this new age of the nonvisible. As though underlining his interest in hidden systems (alimentary, circulatory), Cuvier is said to have actually broken the transparent test tubes of his predecessors—an iconoclastic act that Foucault equates with the end of history (knowledge of the visible) as opposed to philosophy (knowledge of the invisible).[5] Cuvier's work marks, then, a moment of rupture; it ushers in a new "space of knowledge" that founds classification on organization rather than on the description of what can be seen (239). By examining functions (i.e., what an element of anatomy *does*, not what other element it looks like), this new system of natural classification escapes "le régime du visible."

Up to a certain point, Foucault's characterization of Cuvier as scientist of the invisible helps us to understand the naturalist's own most ambitious claims—as they appear, for example, in the *Discours préliminaire* to *Recherches sur les ossemens fossiles de quadrupèdes*, the text that presents his theory of the reconstruction of animals from their fossils.[6] In the *Discours*, Cuvier dramatically announces his contribution to recent advances in the study of the earth and the universe, proclaiming that the modern scientific mind has finally comprehended that which the eye is unable to see. Whether discussing biology, astronomy, or geology, Cuvier consistently calls us to look beyond appearances: beyond the formal similarities of animals, beyond what is visible in the night sky, beneath the crust of the earth. The mundane and visual scientific work of *observation* is given far less attention in the *Discours* than are the glorious and abstract workings of the mind. In other words, Foucault's point that Cuvier is interested in invisible connections can be extended to include not only

Cuvier's choice of subjects, but also his rhetorical emphasis on mental operations, on mind over eye.

Indeed, the question of visibility is crucially linked to the question of methodology—that is, to the ways in which Cuvier, along with his scientific contemporaries, theorizes the interaction of deductive reasoning and inductive observation. In the *Discours*, Cuvier seems to validate the former over the latter, as he lavishes praise on the ways in which man's rational faculties have compensated for inadequacies in his sensory capabilities. In discussing astronomy, for example, Cuvier marvels at what "reasoning" has been able to reveal about the mechanical workings of the world: "We admire the energy with which the human mind has measured the movements of spheres that nature had seemingly hidden from our sight forever" (3). Contemporary science has been able to make "visible" (comprehensible) that which the eye cannot see, as the mind (*l'esprit*) takes over where the physical senses have left off. And yet, Cuvier's language cannot help but attribute a visual component to the mental process, for he continues: "a few observations developed through reasoning have unveiled the workings of the world" (3). "Observations" and "unveiled" seem here to be meant in a non-optical sense, but the words resound metaphorically with a residual visuality. If the mind is what makes visible that which had been hidden from sight, its processes cannot be taken as radically distinct from those of the senses.

In fact, Cuvier's language in the *Discours* generally reveals the eye and the mind to be continually interactive, rather than exclusionary or unidirectional, tools of scientific discovery. As the self-proclaimed Newton of the natural sciences, for example, Cuvier brags that reasoning has allowed him to generalize about the Earth's development from the "primary illuminations" that observation of fossils provides (36).[7] He also credits "reasoning" for the development of his geological cataclysm theory, but Cuvier ends, nonetheless, his demonstration of that theory with an optical rather than mental metaphor: "These tremendous and terrifying events are inscribed everywhere in plain sight for the eye that is able to read their story in the monuments they left behind" (12). Here is an eye that penetrates beyond what is immediately visible, that stands in for Cuvier's conception of the trained and gifted scientific mind capable of making the leaps of reasoning to unveil earthly secrets.

This particular figuration of mind as eye is based on Cuvier's apparent conception of the visual observation as mere supplement to mental reasoning. In discussing the reconstruction of animal morphology from bone fragments, Cuvier explains that organic theories are insufficient in themselves. This is a concession, made after the more confident and dramatic proclamation that upon finding the tiniest fragment of bone, "the person whose mind was able to fully grasp the laws of organic economy could extrapolate the entire animal from it" (61). The rational laws are not quite enough after all, Cuvier admits. Making a distinction between theory and observation, between the mental reasoning and the visual examination that leads to deductions, Cuvier expands upon the principle he has just put forward: "but when it is to be applied, in many cases our theoretical knowledge of relationships between forms is insufficient when it is not firmly grounded on observation" (61). So the observation of facts supports the theoretical work of the mind (just as, in the *roman policier* that developed later in the century, the observation of clues supports the detective's acts of ratiocination).

Cuvier returns to the relation between observation and theory in his continuing justification of the claim to re-create an entire animal from "the tiniest fragment of bone": "Thus, by adopting in this way the method of observation as a supplementary means when theory deserts us, we learn astonishing details" (65). Where earlier, in his discussion of astronomy, Cuvier had suggested that the mind takes over where the eye leaves off, here we have the eye taking over where the mind leaves off. These two formulations may seem to imply a reversed relation between theory and observation, but both in fact give more importance to the mind's work than to the painstaking observation of facts. Only the mind, for Cuvier, is capable of making the analogical leaps that result in dramatic advances in our knowledge of the Earth and the universe. Observation remains essential as a tool for the scientist, but it is "a supplementary means," a crutch; the eye itself already acts as a kind of prosthetic—even before the addition of microscopes, telescopes, and other scientific instruments that extend the powers of vision.

Later, of course, Freud would suggest a link between the technology of visual aids and the logic of prosthesis. In *Civilization and Its Discontents*, telescopes, microscopes, and cameras are listed among the tools that civilized man has created to perfect and extend the powers of his own organs; as "auxiliary organs," these technologies make him feel closer to the ideal of omnipotence, but the feeling of magnificence is tempered by the fact that prosthetics make up for a basic inadequacy—in this case, the limitations of the eye.[8] Let me suggest that in Cuvier's rhetoric, visual observation, even without the aid of scientific instruments, already partakes of this logic. If, further, we take Cuvier's description of observation as a "supplementary means" in light of Derrida's conception of supplementarity as indicative of lack and excess, we can reinterpret what seems to be Cuvier's unsystematic use of visual language as a particularly charged version of the uneasy relation between eye and mind.[9]

With rhetorical flights that vaunt the mind's analogical prowess, Cuvier is in effect sublimating the physical work of the eye, with all of its limitations. But, when Cuvier presents his case for the reconstruction of animals from a single bone, the eye comes back, inflated to grand proportions, as a figure for the mind: "These tremendous and terrifying events are recorded everywhere in plain sight for the eye that is able to read their story in the monuments they left behind" (12). In other words, while Cuvier's rhetoric seems to attribute his success to abstract reasoning, the sensory side of observation refuses to be dismissed altogether.

To recap, then, Cuvier's appeals to the methodological abstraction of reasoned generalization seem to align him more with the Saint-Hilairian "invisible reason for the visible" than the terms of the "querelle" would indicate. However, as I suggested above, even Cuvier's most theoretical and deductive text does not completely sublimate the eye in favor of the mind. An *œil* still serves as figure for the scientific observer, as the very idea of making the invisible visible relies on the validation of visibility. The scientific observer for Cuvier is not a "disembodied" mind, separated off from the physical supports of the senses. Indeed, even while veering toward the mind in its description of the act of observation, the text continually asserts the (supplementary) necessity of visual attention to keep theory from being unhinged. If Foucault's categorical distinctions between an epistemology of the visible and an epistemology of the invisible are useful, it is as direction of emphasis, rather than as exclusionary demarcation.[10] Ocular observation and inductive processes remain essential to Cuvier's scientific method and epistemology.

Why, then, is Cuvier taken as model for the detective, that pure reasoner whose reputation and success lie in startling mental feats of deduction rather than in the dogged observation of minutiae? The answer should be clear by now: Cuvier's combination of actual inductive method with overt claims to deductive boldness captures the particular logic of fictional detection in the latter half of the nineteenth century.

After all, from its start, the detective novel has allowed material clues to drive the plot while disavowing their importance vis-à-vis the detective's deductive skills. In "The Murders in the Rue Morgue," Poe's Dupin holds forth in praise of the analytical and imaginative powers of the mind; the famous scene in which he "reads" his assistant's mind starts from a minor observation (of the narrator's discomfiture at having been bumped by a fruit cart) and recreates an impressive series of logical steps based on preexisting (i.e., a priori) knowledge. In Sir Arthur Conan Doyle's first Sherlock Holmes novel, *A Study in Scarlet*, the detective is introduced as the author of an article entitled "The Science of Deduction and Analysis," an indication that real detection results not from hound-like diligence, but from the detective's powers as thinker, problem solver. Indeed, the detective's analytical powers are often defined as abstract and disconnected from the physicality of the senses, as when Gaston Leroux's detective Rouletabille claims to rely on reasoning "in its purest state," governed more by the laws of logic than by the material traces of a crime. He invents a whole topography of the mind, drawing an imaginary circle around the two bumps ("bosses") of his forehead in order to "approach reason from the right end." Emile Gaboriau's detective Lecoq, meanwhile, turns not to phrenological geometry, but to the abstraction of algebra: "investigating a crime is nothing less than finding the solution of an algebraic problem." Once one knows of the crime, one has the constants; but we still need to find, continues Lecoq, "the third term, the *X*, the unknown; that is, the guilty party." Rouletabille's and Lecoq's appeals to mathematical logic suggest a desired link to theoretical, rather than empirical, modes of scientific inquiry.

This is the side of the *roman policier* as *genre scientifique* that has traditionally been emphasized in critical studies. For Dorothy Sayers, the detective acts as modern hero-protector, whose tools of science and reason replace the *chevalier*'s ancient sword as his reign of Order cathartically dispels murder's terror. Sayers defines the genre as analytical, pointing out that Poe founded the genre by moving from romantic sensationalism to a classic novel of intellection.[11] Boileau-Narcejac's "Que sais-je" series perpetuates the distinction between sense and reason with its definition of the *roman policier* as a transformation of mystery (belonging to "the tangible order") into solvable problem (belonging to the order of rational thought). The detective novel, write Pierre Boileau and Thomas Narcejac, allows the sensorial, physical incomprehensibility of murder to be subdued by the abstract order of intellection. "This is the *roman policier*'s metaphysical taproot: we are creatures dedicated, at all costs, to extracting the intelligible from the tangible."[12] Whether conceived as the orderly reassertion of social regulations after a cathartic release of mayhem or as the transformation of incomprehensible mystery into algebraically solvable *problème*, the main action of the *roman policier* is taken to be the mental reconstruction of the steps leading up to a crime. Uri Eisenzweig writes that the *roman policier* is centered not on the crime itself, but on "the [apparently] coherent elucidation of a mystery."[13] The detective novel's emphasis on reason has allowed for strict judgments on the "purity" of the genre. Régis Messac, for example, reserves the term "detective novel" for texts consisting only of "the element of deduction"; for him, Gaboriau does not count as a detective novelist because he drowns his plot of analysis in a "welter of details straight out of a serial novel."[14] Neither romantic, spiritualist, sensationalist, nor visionary, the "novel of analysis" belongs to an ordered world of rationality, in which precise intellection conquers the sensory, passionate mysteries of murder. Moreover, it has been characterized as having brought the rigors of deduction to the murky methods of empiricism. Fereydoun Hoveyda, for example, distinguishes the modern detective from the (fictional and real) *espions* and ex-bandits who preceded the genre's arrival in the mid-nineteenth century. The investigations of the "predetective" Vidocq, writes Hoveyda, rely on empirical—as opposed to deductive—methods; rather than solving crimes through analysis, the former criminal would frequent his old haunts, overhear details about a crime, and often end up obtaining the criminal's confession on the spot. Hoveyda contrasts this method with the "scientific methods" of Alphonse Bertillon, who added to the police arsenal techniques such as *l'anthropométrie* (the study of proportions in the human body) to identify criminals and photography to record scenes of the crime; such preexisting grids allowed for a priori identification based on ordered rules rather than on random tavern hopping and overheard leads.

A key element of the genre's rise, then, lies in a new authority and dignity accorded to the detective's work based on its scientifically inflected, deductive methodological rigor. Despite its roots in *feuilleton* sensationalism, the nineteenth-century detective novel invents a thinking hero, whose abstract ratiocinations cut through the criminal confusion of his time. Such a model underlies Régis Messac's early history of the genre, *Le "Detective Novel" et l'influence de la pensée scientifique* (1929). As the title suggests, Messac aligns detective fiction with the dissemination of scientific theories in the nineteenth century, citing the influence both of officially approved theories by Lavater, Gall, and Cuvier and of less-accepted branches of science like mesmerism, Swedenborgianism, and divination. Despite noting the influence of the latter "pseudosciences," however, Messac emphasizes the rational, systematic side of the scientific detective novel. In his view, rigorous reflection is the essential characteristic of the detective novel. Yet even while defining the genre according to its claims of scientism, Messac already tips us off to its self-delusion: the conflict, that is, between its claims to pure reasoning and the actual practice of detection in its fictions. The nineteenth-century "vulgarization" of scientific knowledge that undergirds the genre's rise implies a dilution, for not only did writers like Walter Scott and Conan Doyle get their science wrong, writes Messac, the detectives themselves are often much less rigorous in their thinking than the narration suggests. Poe's Dupin, for example, despite his talk of differential calculus and algebra, ends up finding solutions more literary than mathematical.

Messac's questioning of the genre's supposed logical rigor usefully signals another locus of its self-definition: "deduction." Deductive reasoning, long considered the detective's sine qua non, consists in drawing specific conclusions from a preexisting abstract rule. As Messac points out, however, the typical *roman policier* actually unfolds through induction, moving from precise observations of a particular case to general conclusions about its cause. (Thus, of course, the apparent aptness of the Cuvier analogy.)

Both Conan Doyle and Gaboriau use the term "deduction" to describe mental progress from the known to the unknown, a formulation Messac calls "somewhat inexact." But Messac's quibble might be read as a bit stringent, for the accepted meaning of the word—then as now—refers primarily to the use of rigorous reasoning to draw a conclusion from observed facts. It is only when contrasted with induction that deduction acquires the specialized restriction of moving from the general to the particular. Still, it is worth noting the distinction, because it furnishes the term "deduction" with implications relevant to detective method and its scientific models. In the nineteenth-century classification of the sciences, inductive processes defined the empirical sciences (natural history, zoology, anatomy) while deduction characterized the "pure," theoretical sciences (mathematics, physics).[15] The distinction was based on an association between induction and the particularity of experience, with deduction linked to pure mental reason. The deductive move from general to particular is often conceived as rooted in abstraction, as in this 1869 definition in Buckle's *Civilization*: "By deduction we descend from the abstract to the concrete."[16] Whereas induction begins with the concrete "matter" of experience, deduction originates in abstract thought. A critical definition, then, of the *roman policier* as "novel of deduction" reinforces the genre's self-presentation as rigorously abstract and rational. But in fact, despite their overt appeals to the abstraction of algebraic thought, detective fictions of the time do not really activate the scientific methods and results of the exact or "pure" sciences. As Messac suggests, the move from particular facts (clues) to general conclusions (crime) ties the fictional detective, rather, to the inductive or "experimental" sciences: *les sciences physiques et naturelles.* As such, it has more in common with empiricism than with a Cartesian or Kantian apriorism.

The main points to take from the apparent slipperiness of the terms "induction" and "deduction" as they are applied categorically to the branches of science are twofold: first, that we must avoid a simple model of scientific thought as "pure" and abstract deduction; and second, that it is worth looking at the methodological instabilities *within* the deductive and inductive sciences and not merely *between* them. That is why this chapter takes the example of Cuvier as a scientific model for the detective's logic; like Cuvier's text, the *roman policier* presents an uneasy but inextricable relation between ratiocination and observation, abstract logic and empirical evidence, mind and eye.

Let us look more closely, then, at the fictional passages where Cuvier is invoked, beginning with *Monsieur Lecoq,* in which Emile Gaboriau describes the necessarily interactive "series of interconnected inductions and deductions" in the solution of a crime.

Gaboriau and Cuvier

Gaboriau's *Monsieur Lecoq* (1869) is the story of the titular policeman's first successful murder case. At one point, after frustrating weeks of dead ends and red herrings, Lecoq finds himself turning to his experienced mentor, Père Tabaret, for confirmation of his hunches about the murderer's identity. The two begin discussing the mysterious absence of the judge who had originally been assigned to the case and Tabaret immediately announces that not only had the judge faked his reason for absence but was himself implicated in the events surrounding the murder. At this point, Lecoq expresses his doubts—the judge in question is, after all, a well-respected magistrate. Tabaret laughs at Lecoq's hesitation, exclaiming, " This, from you? . . . from you, the man I thought would succeed me and continue my inductive method; how can it be that you, of all people, are asking me this ridiculous question!"[17]

After this introduction of a "méthode d'induction," the reader might expect a rigorous demonstration of Tabaret's steps of reasoning—one following the model, for example, of Dupin's virtuoso reconstruction of his friend's thoughts in "The Murders in the Rue Morgue." Instead, we get a somewhat rambling set of suppositions, sprinkled with advice to the admiring Lecoq. When Tabaret explains his theory about the judge's implication, Lecoq imagines a comparison between his mentor's "méthode d'induction" and the Cuvierian method: "Lecoq was enthralled by the amazing investigational abilities of this eccentric policeman who, based on circumstances of which he (Lecoq) had taken no notice, reconstructed the drama of truth. In doing so he was not unlike naturalists who, after inspecting no more than two or three bones, are able to sketch out a picture of the entire animal to which they once belonged" (218). What impresses Lecoq in both Tabaret and the naturalists is the mental reconstitution of a larger truth from few facts. In both cases, the truth emanates from the past: the bones are clues to the now vanished animal and the circumstances on which Tabaret bases his conclusions are clues to the suspects' previous actions. The narrator reiterates Lecoq's admiration: "he greatly esteemed this swift and wondrous labor of induction."

As noted above, the use of the term *induction* in general discourse of the time implied a certain precision that *deduction* did not; where *deduction* was often used to describe reasoning in general, *induction* appeared primarily in distinction to the deductive move from general to particular. But Gaboriau is unsystematic, at one point letting Tabaret vaunt "the logic of my deduction" (215). And indeed, despite his more frequent appeal to *induction,* Tabaret's process actually seems to consist of its opposite; all of his conclusions are based on the following—antivisual—a priori rule, the one "principle" that existed "at the beginning": "Take special care not to trust in appearances; believe the exact opposite of what appears to be true or merely likely." Both in form (a priori rule) and in content ("not to trust in appearances"), this "principle" renders visual observation (the basis for induction) unnecessary. In fact, Tabaret says he does not even need to see the characters involved to know what has happened: "I wasn't there on the spot as you were, I wasn't able to make any judgments based on what I saw; but solely on the basis of what you've told me, I can replay the scene as it unfolded. It's almost as if I see it" (217). This general independence from direct visual evidence support's Tabaret's rule: that one must always assume the opposite of what seems to be—of what appears likely (*vraisemblable*).

But does Tabaret actually stick to that rule in his reasoning? At first, yes: it is precisely, explains Tabaret, because of the *vraisemblance* (likelihood) of the judge's excuse of having broken his leg that in fact he must not have broken his leg. But as he continues to reconstruct the judge's likely actions, Tabaret moves back toward *vraisemblance*, not its opposite, as probable truth. What would you have done in his situation? he repeatedly asks Lecoq. Not only Lecoq, but his dim-witted assistant Absinthe both reply that in the judge's shoes, they would reveal nothing. This, to Tabaret, is proof that the judge indeed remained silent. And he continues his demonstration by putting Lecoq in the judge's shoes: you would have done this, you would have done that . . . Tabaret's appeal to the "normal" response depends precisely on a belief in the *vraisemblable*—that is, on the opposite of his a priori rule. To deduce the judge's actions based on what any man might do in his place is to assume a commonality of human response, a norm which must certainly extend to the judge in question. In fact, it works somewhat like Cuvier's induction, in its search for commonality (in function/action) behind appearances of difference (Lecoq, Absinthe, the judge). Though staking claim to a method of deductive reasoning, with its fidelity to an a priori rule of *invraisemblance*, Tabaret reverts to a logic based on experience—and in this way reverts in practice to his earlier claim of a "méthode d'induction."

It is, notably, the category of *experience* that Tabaret identifies as the missing link between Lecoq's limited ingenuity and his own successful *méthode*. "You've got talent" he tells the younger detective, " . . . there's no denying it; you have the nose for it [*le flair*], the eye [*le coup d'œil*], you can deduce the unknown from the known . . . all you need is experience" (214). In Lecoq's "science" then, we find the eye (visual observation) and the mind (rational deduction), but something is still missing: experience. In other words, an element of empiricism. As I will argue in the next chapter, Lecoq's entire narrative of detection mobilizes crucial elements of the empiricist theory of visual perception.

To be sure, Gaboriau uses terms like "deduction" and "induction" without much rigor. I do not want to imply by my reading that the *feuilletoniste* is engaged in some subtle verbal play in order to deconstruct the scientific methods of his century. But the very confusion of his language suggests two things. The first hardly needs repeating: namely, that while masterful demonstrations of abstract deduction were part of the genre's mystique and success from the beginning, the inductive analyses performed by fictional detectives do not actually hold up to strict standards of logical reasoning.

The second point is an alternative reading of these "lapses" in scientific rigor, based on the way in which an indiscriminate use of the terms induction and deduction ends up destabilizing distinctions between abstract theory and direct (visual) observation. The genre partakes of and provides a concrete narratological instance of a larger unresolved question in nineteenth-century human sciences: the methodological ambivalence between abstraction and empiricism. If Messac is right that the detective novel is imbued with "trickle-down" science, then it is not surprising to find in it traces of a scientific debate between a priori and a posteriori reasoning, between Kantian apriority and the empiricism of Wheatstone and Helmholtz, for example.

This particular debate occurred with vigor in the study of physiological optics at the end of the nineteenth century. On the side of empiricism were Charles Wheatstone, whose invention of the stereoscope "gave a powerful incentive to the investigation of the influence of experience on our visual apperceptions," and Helmholtz, who elaborated an entire empirical theory of perception as learned, gradual, experiential.[18] They were opposed by followers of Hering's *innate* or *intuitive* theory, which came out of a Kantian epistemology, as Helmholtz explains in this passage: "KANT had briefly represented space and time as given forms of all apperception, without going farther and investigating how much might be derived from experience in the more minute formation of individual apperceptions of space and time. . . . Thus, for example, he regarded the geometrical axioms as being propositions in space-apperception which were given to start with;—a view which is not at all settled yet" (2: 36). Visual perception in this debate functions as a case study of epistemology in general: the idea of innate and immediate vision maps onto a (Kantian) transcendental conception of knowledge, while the delayed temporality of gradual sight belongs to a (Lockean) corporealized empiricism. Helmholtz's three-volume *Treatise on Physiological Optics* sets out to debunk completely the intuitive theory of visual perception, but while he disproves many of its tenets, he cannot absolutely refute a priori visuality. The vigor of this debate, with concessions grudgingly made on either side, argues for Foucault's formulation of modern (post-1800) epistemology as caught in an "empirico-transcendental doublet."

The Doublet

In *Les Mots et les choses,* Foucault writes of modern truth's fundamental division between (a) historical analyses that show human knowledge to be historically determined, and (b) empirical analyses that operate within the space of the body, that came about by studying perception and sensorial mechanisms, and that led to the discovery that the conditions of knowledge are determined by anatomy and physiology.[19] But there is a further, more fundamental division, continues Foucault, on which both of these conceptions of human knowledge (as historical and as bodily) rely. This division appears in the order of discourse. Modern discourse is ambiguous because "either this true discourse is founded upon and modeled after this empirical truth whose natural and historical origin it retraces, resulting in a positivist analysis . . . ; or the true discourse anticipates this truth whose nature and history it defines, sketching it out in advance and spurring it on from afar, resulting in an eschatological discourse" (331). In other words, either it proceeds by induction or it proceeds by deduction. Either it is empiricist or it is transcendental. Either it reasons a posteriori from physical observation or it reasons from a priori laws. Foucault transforms all of these either/or propositions into a coterminous ambiguity identified as inherent to modern epistemology. "In truth," he writes, "this is less an alternation than the oscillation inherent to any analysis that emphasizes the empirical on the transcendental level" (331). Hence the empirico-transcendental "doublet," the indissociability within modern discourse of empirical positivism and critical transcendentalism: "This is why modern thought cannot help . . . seeking the site of a discourse that involves neither reduction [i.e., positivist, empirical] nor promise [i.e., transcendental, eschatological]: a discourse whose tension would keep separate the empirical and the transcendental while making it possible to allude to both of them at the same time" (331).

The *roman policier* registers and encodes this epistemological double bind. There is, on the one hand, the mystique of the detective as abstract and deductive reasoner, performing virtuoso feats of the mind without leaving his armchair. In "The Purloined Letter," which Poe considered his best "tale of ratiocination," for example, Dupin's reasoning succeeds where the most detailed and exhaustive search—with the aid of "a most powerful microscope"—had failed.[20] On the other hand, the detective relies on tangible clues to reconstitute a posteriori the events leading up to a crime. For example, in the conclusion to *A Study in Scarlet,* Sherlock Holmes explains that he used "reasoning backwards" to identify and catch the murderer Mr. Jefferson Hope. Holmes identifies his own reasoning here as *analytical* as opposed to *synthetic.* In other words, rather than immediate, it proceeds gradually, step by step—that is, empirically. The "Bi-Part Soul" of the detective novel, its narrative tension, may in fact result from this uneasy coexistence of empirical with critical thought.

Certainly Poe's Dupin seems aware of such an ambivalence—a modern ambivalence that, as Foucault puts it, comes out in a discourse that wants it both ways: abstract *and* physical, deduced from general rules *and* true to experience. In "The Murders in the Rue Morgue," for example, Dupin explains his seemingly preternatural mental acumen as "analysis," a faculty that relies on both observations and inferences. Although invigorated by mathematical study, says Dupin, this faculty is not equivalent to mere mathematical calculation; it requires true imagination rather than simple ingenuity. To illustrate the difference, Dupin points to chess as a game of mere calculation and to whist as a game of true analysis in that it requires deductions external to the game. In whist, he continues, one must observe the interplay of glances around the table, the way in which each player holds the cards, and so on. In short, Dupin's conception of the detective's analytical powers combines the mental with the visual, inferences with observations, deductions with glances. Even in "The Purloined Letter," where, as we know, Dupin's intellect outdoes the police's diligent visual search, Poe's detective rejects the idea of a purely abstract reasoning. In a rather huffy rebuttal to the narrator's suggestion that mathematical reason is paramount, Dupin rails at the "egregious" error of thinking that abstract or general truths can be found in the "purest" algebra.[21] It is only in *relation* that these truths hold, says he, not in application to the world. It is fortunate then, in the estimation of Poe's famous detective, that the character under discussion is "both mathematician and poet" (19). In other words, the detective straddles theoretical and experiential registers of knowledge.

What is manifest in Poe's text operates as a kind of latent narrative principle in Gaboriau's novels. Gaboriau's detectives, both the young Lecoq and the experienced Tabaret, seem to lack the sophisticated self-awareness of a Dupin. The text's oscillation between the promise of a rigorous "méthode inductive" and the realities of experience appears unintended and confused. But this very ambivalence is what makes the *roman policier* an important example of the narrative embodiment of nineteenth-century science's most basic theoretical predicaments. The narrative thrust of the genre is, after all, epistemological: to solve a mystery, to reveal a hidden truth, to make known the unknown. At some level, then—whether in Dupin's explicit and authoritative pronouncements or in Lecoq's hesitating feints—the *roman policier* must enquire into and manifest the modes of knowing.

With this in mind, let us take a second look at Tabaret's advice to Lecoq: "You've got talent, there's no denying it; you have the nose for it, the eye, you can deduce the unknown from the known . . . all you need is experience" (406b). Lecoq has the eye and the mind—faculties that correspond to Foucault's dichotomy of empirical and transcendent thought—but still lacks experience. What Gaboriau appears to gesture at here is a third term that would itself break out of the empirico-transcendental double bind. Consider, in this context, Foucault's identification of lived experience as a "third term" in modern thought: "It's clear that the analysis of lived experience is established in modern thought as a radical questioning of positivism and eschatology; that it attempts to restore the forgotten dimension of the transcendental; that it seeks to exorcise the naive discourse of a truth reduced to the empirical" (332). The attempt described here fails, of course; as a discourse, the analysis of experience remains as ambiguous as the systems it seeks to topple. Nor does experience resolve the empirico-transcendental tensions in *Monsieur Lecoq*. Nevertheless, the term holds a tantalizing place on the horizon of the work of detection. Experience is what Gaboriau's titular detective lacks throughout the novel as he strives to make a name for himself—and experience is what Tabaret can provide. The ideal detective, we are led to believe, combines the contradictory powers of deduction and induction with experience, and with the knowledge acquired through that experience. If we turn to Sir Arthur Conan Doyle's invocation of Cuvier, we can further examine the fraught role that experience plays in the methodologies of both detective and naturalist.

Doyle and Cuvier

"The Five Orange Pips" is a tale whose explanation, admits Watson, is "founded rather upon conjecture and surmise than on that absolute logical proof which was so dear to [Holmes]" (102). In fact, to clear up the story's central mystery of "who is KKK?" Holmes has only to recall his preexisting knowledge of an American secret society by that name. So it is no surprise that his own "discourse on method" moves from pure reasoning to a reliance on what one already knows. Here is what Holmes (in his armchair, with eyes closed) tells his assistant:

> The ideal reasoner . . . would, when he had once been shown a single fact in all its bearings, deduce from it not only all the chain of events which led up to it, but also all the results which would follow from it. As Cuvier could correctly describe a whole animal by the contemplation of a single bone, so the observer who has thoroughly understood one link in a series of incidents, should be able to accurately state all the other ones, both before and after. We have not yet grasped the results which *the reason alone* can attain to. Problems may be solved in *the study which have baffled all those who have sought a solution by the aid of their senses.* To carry the art, however, to its highest pitch, it is necessary that the reasoner should be able to utilize all the facts which have come to his knowledge,

and this in itself implies . . . *a possession of all knowledge*, which, even in these days of free education and encyclopedias, is a somewhat rare accomplishment.[22]

Prior knowledge, then, is supplementary to pure reason: it brings deduction to the level of an art, but is not thereby rigorously necessary. In fact, Holmes is saying, reason alone can perform quite impressive feats, especially when compared to reliance on one's senses. The distinction Holmes makes between reason and the senses colors his use of the term "observer." To Holmes, the "observer" is precisely *not* involved in direct observation of the facts; instead, the observer comprises the "ideal reasoner" who can theoretically generalize from the smallest link to the full chain of its being.

This "great chain" is a concept familiar to Conan Doyle's readers, as it appears in *A Study in Scarlet*'s discussions of detection as scientific method. In this first Sherlock Holmes novel, the detective is introduced to the narrator Watson as a doctor and "enthusiast in some branches of science"; their first encounter occurs at a hospital laboratory, over test-tubes.[23] By the second chapter, "The Science of Deduction," Holmes has begun to instruct Watson in his theories of analytical reasoning: he shows him a self-authored article that sets out to impress upon its readers how much a man can learn by the systematic examination of what he observes. In it, Holmes makes a claim that, judging from Watson's reaction ("ineffable twaddle!"), fails to ring of established scientific truth: "from a drop of water, a logician could infer the possibility of an Atlantic . . . all life is a great chain, the nature of which is known whenever we are shown a single link of it."[24] Watson's skepticism, of course, serves only to dramatize Holmes's superiority throughout the series, and by the time the image reappears in "The Five Pips," Watson is all deference. Although Cuvier is not mentioned in Holmes's initial "Science of Deduction and Analysis," the inference of an oceanic truth from a tiny fact comes from the naturalist's famous boast of recognizing an entire animal from a single bone. Cuvier's feat of synecdochal reasoning is based on his first principle that every organism forms a unique and closed system in which all parts correspond. Any one characteristic of an organism "entails all of its properties" and thus serves as a link indicating the form of an entire "chain" to which it belongs.[25] Cuvier's theoretical move from link to chain comprises what Doyle's Sherlock Holmes defines as rigorous logical reasoning.

The attribution by Holmes of Cuvier's skill to the "ideal reasoner" or "logician" might perhaps have pleased the naturalist, whose goals included introducing mathematical rigor into the study of natural history. Cuvier hoped to bring quantification and rigorous thought to anatomy, which had long been considered a science of mere observation. Fittingly, then, Cuvier's new anatomical science went beyond the act of description: "The raw data obtained by dissection and observation had to be generalized by comparison and then interpreted by the application of the principle of correlation of parts."[26] In other words, the initial step of empirical observation was to be followed by both comparison (analogical thinking) and application of a preexisting law of logic (deductive thinking).

However, this ideal of a harmonious balance between observation and ratiocination (a dialectically reconciled version of Foucault's "empirico-transcendental doublet") did not actually characterize Cuvier's own method or discourse. As indicated earlier, Cuvier's manifesto the *Discours préliminaire*, reflects an ambivalent identification of observation as supplementary to theory; the two modes appear in problematic equipoise, not in synthesis. And if Cuvier's method lay somewhere between pure empiricism and pure deduction (as compared, for example, with those of Geoffroy Saint-Hilaire, who proposed laws in direct contradiction to evidence),[27] the combination was not always free of tension.

In his theory of the reconstruction of animals from fossil debris, for example, "Cuvier proposed the principle of the correlation of parts as the theoretical basis of this work, but in practice he relied heavily upon direct (and indirect) comparison of the ancient pieces with those from similar modern animals."[28] In the *Discours préliminaire*, Cuvier acknowledged "his very real dependence upon observed correlations."[29] It is here, as we saw, that Cuvier writes of observation as making up for the failure of theory. Coleman reads Cuvier's statement that observation serves to establish empirical laws (as opposed to rational laws) as a "restriction upon the applicability of purely rational principles" (120). Further, Coleman points out that Cuvier's theoretical writings confuse reconstruction with identification; whereas a naturalist might be able to identify an already known species from a single bone, only a paleontologist having "long experience" with fossils would be able to reconstruct an unknown, ancient animal's form on the basis of a fragment (121). "*All depended on experience*," explains Coleman, "and Cuvier's reconstruction 'principles' were really rationalizations after the fact." So, in spite of Cuvier's theoretical reliance on his two anatomical principles, the fact remains that his work was possible only because of a previous knowledge of existing anatomy (139, my emphasis).

Cuvier's unacknowledged reliance on experience and previous knowledge returns us to Gaboriau (whose Tabaret advises "experience" to Lecoq) and to Doyle (whose Holmes advocates the acquisition of knowledge as supplementary to deduction). It is evident that even in *A Study in Scarlet* Sherlock Holmes is not, as Doyle had claimed, "a mere calculating machine."[30] Watson's famous list of Holmes's fields of expertise (under the categories "Nil," "Some," and "Profound" knowledge) demonstrates that the detective comes to mysteries with more than just a capacity to reason. His impressive description of the as-yet-unknown murderer in *A Study in Scarlet,* for example, relies on specialized knowledge of types of cigar ashes and of German lexographical habits. Even his theorizations are based on evidence; when Watson asks for an initial opinion of the case, Holmes replies, "No data yet" and, "It is a capital mistake to theorize before you have all the evidence. It biases the judgement." But of course, *all* the evidence, just like "a possession of all knowledge," is never available. Theorizing—hypothesizing from partial evidence—occurs nonetheless. Otherwise, of course, there would be no need for astounding feats of abstract deduction. Although the cards are stacked (Doyle, for example, usually provides Holmes with mysteries that require his own particular esoteric knowledge), the detective's method (and the resulting narrative) must bridge the gap between known and unknown, visible and invisible. And it is that gap, I suggest, that marks the point of contact between the *roman policier* as a genre and the scientific enquiries of its time: both reside in the epistemological space between evidence and conjecture. What Cuvier brings to early texts of detection, in addition to his suggestive feat of reconstruction from part to whole, may in fact be his position between *géologie positive* (observational or experimental science depending uniquely upon facts) and *géologie explicative* (the discipline seeking to explain these facts).[31]

As I have suggested, the poles between which resides the deductive logic of the *roman policier* can be formulated in various ways, including the following: empiricism and transcendentalism, a posteriori and a priori reasoning, observation and theory, description and explanation, materiality and abstraction. These oppositions represent the fault lines along which, while the *roman policier* genre was beginning to develop, the science of optics was starting to split—especially as understood through the polemical prism of Hermann von Helmholtz, proponent of the distinction between idealist and empiricist theories of vision. With its new physiological interests, optics as a field could no longer be categorized as purely deductive (like mathematics or physics), but its methods retained the deductive legacy even within an inductive thrust. As such, the physiological optics of the nineteenth century merits a privileged position as context for understanding the "visual logics"—that is, the way in which visuality intersects with the inductive/deductive double bind—of early detective fiction in England and France. So we turn from Cuvier to Helmholtz, from geology to the "slow vision [*vision lente*]" of empiricist optics.

"Une Vision Lente": The *roman policier* and Empiricist Theories of Visual Perception

In Balzac's *Louis Lambert,* the title character provides an unusual definition of poetry by contrasting its rapid vision with the slow vision of the human sciences: "All of man's knowledge is based on deduction, which is a slow vision through which we move downward from cause to effect, through which we move upward from effect to cause; or, to state it more broadly: all poetry, like any work of art, proceeds from a swift seeing of things."[32] This rather enigmatic statement rests on various suggestive presuppositions. Note, for example, the fluid use of the term "deduction." As a means of reasoning, it can go in two directions: "down" from cause to effect or "up" from effect to cause. The concept thus contains the possibility of both a priori and a posteriori thought. In either case, the gradualism of reasoning involved in "deduction" distinguishes it from an immediacy of perception belonging to the arts. No need, in poetry, for climbing or descending the steps between cause and effect—its knowledge comes in a flash. Two modes of perception, then, are being compared: a slow acquisition of knowledge through reasoning, and an immediate comprehension of things.

Where would the *roman policier* fit into this somewhat whimsical distinction between science and poetry? It declares itself a scientific genre, but fiction undermines theory in every case. Meanwhile, as "œuvre d'art," it is most often considered a degraded form, a popularized genre belonging to the category of *paralittérature,* whose appeal has less to do with any authorial genius than with the gimmick of criminal deduction.[33] Let us, then, for the sake of argument, consider the *roman policier* in light of Louis Lambert's dichotomy as being on the side of human science's *déduction*: on the side, that is, of a "slow" rather than a rapid vision. As we recall, Lecoq's *coup d'œil* was considered insufficient in Gaboriau's *Monsieur Lecoq*; it had to be followed through with deduction, and with the slow, gradual acquisition of knowledge through experience. And in fact, the classical structure of the *roman policier* follows the first model of perception in Louis Lambert's opposition, guiding the reader slowly through delays, obstacles, and detours from effect to cause: from the material clues of the corpse to the identification of its killer—and from cause to effect: from the detective's hypotheses to their proof. Knowledge (about the crime) is presented not in an immediate flash, but step by step. Moreover, it is precisely the acquisition of that knowledge that comprises the *roman policier*'s narrative action; the genre's epistemological mode is that of *la déduction,* of Louis Lambert's "slow vision."

But what is this *lente vision* that Balzac contrasts with art's rapid glance? What might *lente vision* mean in a nineteenth-century European context?

Let me suggest a possible answer by turning to the contemporary debates in the science of physiological optics, where two conceptions of visual perception came into conflict: one "rapid," immediate, innate, and the other, "slow," gradual, and *deductive.*

Theorists of visual perception were far from consensus in the second half of the nineteenth century, when Herman von Helmholtz compiled an authoritative summary of all previous theories into his three-volume *Treatise on Physiological Optics.* Proponents of the "intuition" or "innate" theory of vision (including Müller, Steinbuch, Porterfield, Bartels, Volkmann, and Tourtual, most of whom published their findings in the 1820s and 1830s) believed that the visual organs possess, a priori, the innate ability to sense depth, spatial location, form, and three-dimensionality. For these "sensationalists," perception occurs directly and instantaneously. The contrary view (espoused in the mid-1800s by Meissner, Herbart, Czermak, Brücke, and Helmholtz, among others) goes back to Locke's opinion that all knowledge of form in visual perception is dependent on experience.[34] Spatial forms and relations, according to the "empiricists," can only be coherently interpreted according to *learned* laws of "illumination, shading, atmospheric haze, geometrical, perspective, concealment of one body by another, the sizes of men and animals, etc."[35] The existence of optical illusions supports the position that visual percepts, though seemingly communicated to us directly and immediately, are in fact interpreted according to mental processes.[36] So, while the "innate theory" conceives of visual perception as immediate sensation, the "empirical theory" takes visual perception to be an active mental process.

For Helmholtz, then, vision is a mental—rather than primarily sensory—action. Here is his fundamental thesis on the empirical theory of visual perception: "The sensations of the senses are tokens for our consciousness, it being left to our intelligence to learn how to comprehend their meaning" (§33, 553). As mere "tokens," visual sensations cannot in themselves constitute vision; to "see" is not just to receive pulses of light but to interpret them mentally. Although, then, Helmholtz and physiological optics are generally associated with a "bodilyness," a corporeality in distinction to Cartesian theory or abstraction, they actually emphasize the mental act of seeing, the "consciousness" that allows us to interpret as coherent objects the random colors and forms that assault our retinas.

Helmholtz provides many examples of the gap between "raw" visual data and the conclusions we draw from them. These may involve Colors (an apple appears gray in low lighting, but we interpret it as red-in-darkness), Forms (we see an angled parallelogram, but interpreting it as a table, we take it to be square), Perspective (we see a tiny human figure at the base of a tree and assume it has normal adult proportions and is far away, rather than that it is a two-inch elf). Vision, then, in its most ordinary forms, always involves a conceptual act. Helmholtz's empirical theory is consistent with Sully's proposed definition in 1884 of perception as "a complex mental act or process,"[37] but where Sully remains rather vague on the actual procedure of thought (it involves discrimination, identification, and "integration"), Helmholtz provides a very specific model of reasoning to explain what happens when we "see": *induction.*

Explaining the analytical process that goes into the ordinary acts of vision, Helmholtz notes that what we call visual perceptions are actually "ideas"—formed conceptions that enable us to interpret sensations as indicative of the existence, form, and position of external objects (3: 1). We are most often unaware of the complex logical processes governing our vision, but they allow us to form conclusions about what we are seeing. "These unconscious conclusions derived from sensation," continues Helmholtz, "are equivalent in their consequences to the so-called *conclusions from analogy*" (4). By analogy, Helmholtz means comparison—of a present visual situation with similar ones we have encountered in the past. Through these comparisons, we train ourselves to interpret raw visual percepts as something other than what they seem (as coherent objects rather than inconsistent blotches of light and color). In other words, in accordance with the empirical theory of perception, we see by making inferences according to previous experience. Moreover, the acquisition of experience is a "psychic activity," more psychological than physiological. The distinction is important, as it denies the sensationalism of the innate theory. "We are not simply passive to the impressions that are urged on us, but we *observe,* that is, we adjust our organs in those conditions that enable them to distinguish the impressions most accurately" (14). Not only, then, is vision "slow"; it is conscious, active, and reliant on the comparative process of thought that Helmholtz names "induction."

The term arises when Helmholtz announces a methodological step in his own argument: "We must speak now of the manner in which our ideas and perceptions are formed by inductive conclusions" (3: 24). "Ideas," remember, are actually synonymous with visual perceptions. And though the mental steps we take to reach perceptual conclusions are "unconscious" (through experience, they have become automatic and it is only when faced with ambiguous situations—an optical illusion, an unidentifiably shadowy figure—that we become aware of our interpretive judgments), Helmholtz proposes to expose the logical steps of thought involved. To do so, he turns to John Stuart Mill's *Logic,* an analysis of inductive logic that allows Helmholtz to assert that our mental conclusions about the visible world are neither arbitrary nor external to it, but are dictated by reality. The result is an apparent circularity or self-evidence of reasoning: "As long as the premise of the conclusion is not an injunction imposed by outside authority for our conduct and belief, but a statement related to reality, which can therefore be only the result of experience, the conclusion, as a matter of fact, does not tell us anything new or something that we did not know already before we made the statement" (3: 25). But Helmholtz's example (from Mill) is not exactly a tautology:

Major: All men are mortal.
Minor: Caius is a man.
Conclusion: Caius is mortal.

In fact, as formulated here, this is actually *de*duction, going from an a priori rule to a specific example, from cause (the law of mortality) to effect (this particular Caius will die). *But,* as Helmholtz explains, the major premise was not in fact established a priori, but arrived at empirically: "Observers have learned by experience that Lucius, Flavius, and other individuals of their acquaintance, no matter what their names are, have all died" and have thus "felt justified in explaining this general law as being valid also for all those cases which might come up for observation hereafter" (3: 25). The general law acts as a sort of mnemonic distillation of accumulated experience, allowing for a rapid deduction that, for example, Caius will die. In other words, our memory has compiled all of the specific, observed examples in our experience into a general law to be applied to future cases.

Moreover, adds Helmholtz, the development of such general principles is the norm, not only in conscious logical thinking, but in sense-perception as well. As we look at the world around us, we are continually making visual judgments consisting of generalizations from previous experience with similar sensations and conclusions about the present sensations based on those generalizations. Whether the generalization is consciously stated as an abstract rule or not, it splits the logical process into two parts. His empirical theory of perception can allow for no a priori visual rules, so it is important to Helmholtz to prove that all conclusions are made experientially. For this reason, he practically dismisses the generalized rule as an intermediary step of no consequence: when we allow a general rule to stand in for the accumulated experience of many past examples, "there is much gain in the convenience and certainty of the process; but nothing essentially new is added that did not exist already in the conclusions which were reached by analogy without reflection" (3: 26). In other words, the establishment of the rule—along with the deductive process that follows from that rule—is merely supplemental to the empirical process. In order to avoid giving any role to deductive reasoning, Helmholtz calls the resulting conclusions "inductive conclusions unconsciously formed." In effect, he is claiming that whether directly or indirectly, our minds process new information by comparing it with previous experience—that is, inductively.

There is a similarity between Helmholtz's epistemology of perception and that of the natural sciences in general. More precisely, visuality acts as a case study of wider epistemological questions in nineteenth-century science. In our daily visual interactions with the world, according to Helmholtz, we are constantly making the same sorts of judgments about our sensations as scientists make about observable facts in nature. Over and over in our lives, we put our visual experience to the test: "It is only by voluntarily bringing our organs of sense in various relations to the objects that we learn to be sure as to our judgments of the causes of our sensations. This kind of experimentation begins in earliest youth and continues all through life without interruption" (3: 30–31). We adhere, then, to principles of scientific experimentation throughout our lives, observing objects while changing the various conditions (variables) under which they are perceived. Through experience, experimentation, and reasoning, we acquire visual knowledge.

Cuvier's description of his own gradual acquisition of knowledge about the natural world follows a similar pattern. Observation and comparative description of animals, for example, leads inductively to the establishment of a generalized rule (or, in this case, the two laws of anatomy), from which all future conclusions will be deduced. But where Helmholtz obscures the deductive step of this reasoning, Cuvier deemphasizes inductive observation to play up the dramatic force of deductions from his two rules. Observation is declared supplementary to the theories made possible by the two laws. The fact that these had previously been established by empirical means is acknowledged, but it is not given prominence within the declaration of method. Many of Cuvier's conclusions come directly from comparison with previous cases rather than from the established rules.

Cuvier and Helmholtz each refer to a cycle that includes both inductive and deductive processes. For Cuvier, it is a methodological cycle, involving detailed observation of various cases, comparison and generalization, and application to new cases. For Helmholtz, it is a perceptual cycle (it is important to remember that Helmholtz is not here discussing his own empirical methods as a scientist, but the methods employed by sighted people to see the world), involving experiential observation of various cases, comparison and generalization, and application to new cases. The cycle does not end with the deductive conclusion; in formulating a general principle, notes Helmholtz, "we are led to test accurately every new case that occurs, with reference to the correctness of the generalization" (3: 26). The testing of hypotheses involves further acts of comparison, observation, and analysis. The cycle continues—and rather than consist entirely of "pure" deduction or "pure" induction, it combines the two modes of reasoning.

Similarly, the investigative processes of detectives in the early *roman policier* involve a complex cycle of reasoning rather than a unidirectional move from mystery to solution. As (Cuvierian) scientists and (Helmholtzian) seers—that is, active observers—detectives combine a priori with a posteriori thought, empirical with abstract reasoning, material observations with hypothetical conjectures. Sherlock Holmes's methods in *A Study in Scarlet,* for example, have been analyzed by Bonfantini and Proni as interweaving the three forms of logic identified by C. S. Peirce: induction, abduction (or hypothesis), and deduction.[38] In *A Study in Scarlet,* three of Holmes's hypotheses about his suspect are confirmed by the murder of a second victim, named Stangerson:

(a) A hotel page saw the murderer escape and *confirms* that the man is tall and high-complexioned.
(b) A telegram in Stargeson's [*sic*] possession *confirms* that "J.H. is in Europe." (We do not know who this is at this point in the story but Holmes does.)
(c) A box containing two pills *confirms* the use (the attempted use this time) of poison.[39]

Notice, from the parenthetical indication of knowledge possessed by Holmes but not by the reader, that the detective novel performs its own version of mystification of method. Indeed, the typical detective plot presents both clues and gaps in such a way as to require (by both reader and detective) not only the scientific aplomb of a Cuvier, but the active interpretation of a Helmholtzian empirical observer. And like both of these scientific discourses, naturalist and optical, the *roman policier* can function only by alternately highlighting and obscuring the logical processes of induction and deduction.

To summarize, then, a combined contextual attention to Cuvier's logics of invisibility and Helmholtz's empiricist theory of visual perception allow us to understand more clearly the visual logic of the emergent detective genre. As with the naturalist and the optical discourses of that time, the detective novel inhabits an epistemological space that shuttles uneasily between empirical induction and abstract deduction. To this unresolved tension between the terms of evidence and thought, the *roman policier* adds Foucault's third term, experience: the shape and temporality of its narrative follows the individual detective's process of knowledge acquisition. Thus, by following the detective's mental moves in a field of mystery, the detective novel creates and enacts a nineteenth-century conception of how one comes to see and to know the world. It is within the context of that "slow" scientific vision that the following chapter proposes Gaboriau's *Monsieur Lecoq* as a paradigmatic example of the *roman policer* as visual bildungsroman.

Chapter 6

Learning to See: *Monsieur Lecoq* and Empiricist Theories of Vision

When John Locke published "Molyneux's problem" in his *Essay Concerning Human Understanding* (1690), he sparked a philosophical debate that was to enflame Europe for two centuries. Suppose, went the question, one were to restore sight to a man born blind. If he had previously been taught to distinguish by touch between a cube and a sphere, would he now be able to distinguish them merely by sight? Locke answered with a forceful, but hypothetical, no. In agreement with Molyneux, he proposed that a recently resighted man would have had no way to obtain the experience necessary to distinguish forms, distance, and three-dimensionality; he would not have *learned* to separate and organize his visual stimuli into a comprehensible order.[1] Along with Molyneux and Locke, Berkeley supported the empiricist theory of visual perception as learned, rather than innate. His 1709 *Essay Towards a New Theory of Vision* was introduced in France by Voltaire in 1738 and was to dominate scientific and philosophical discussions of sight for over a century, leading Mill to announce in 1842 that the theory had emerged as "one of the least disputed doctrines in the most disputed and most disputable of all sciences,—the science of man."[2]

Proponents of Berkeley's theory included Condillac in the eighteenth century and, in the nineteenth, Reid, Müller, Mill, and Helmholtz. Among Berkeley's evidence for the experiential acquisition of perception was his citation of an intriguing case that was to become a *cause célèbre* in Europe: the story of a blind boy whose sight had been surgically restored in 1728 by the physician William Cheselden. The Cheselden case, as it became known, provided a direct test of Molyneux's hypothesis and details from the case—the fact that the boy described seen things as "touching" his eye, and his inability to distinguish visually between a cat and a dog—were used by Berkeley and many others after him to support the claim that visual perception is learned.[3]

The gradualist version of visual perception refutes a revelational or divine model of vision.[4] Unlike Malebranche, for example, who in the 1670s invoked God's intervention to unravel the mystery of sight, optical theorists of the eighteenth and nineteenth centuries systematically traced the eye's physics and physiology to explain perception. Stories of the re-sighted were not mere anomalies, but the very basis for a theory of normal sight as a learned behavior consisting of perceptual skills developed in infancy and early childhood. The documentation of the Cheselden case, for example, presents the move from blindness to sight as a frustratingly slow process rather than a miraculous moment of illumination.

Helmholtz cites a similar case, the Wardrop case of 1826, in his compendious *Treatise on Physiological Optics*.[5] With its emphasis on the piecemeal acquisition of visual skills, the case supports Helmholtz's empiricist theory, in which vision is understood to be composed of distinct, analyzable parts; only through the learned synthesis of various discrete actions and perceptions (light refraction, color distinction, muscular movements, nerve impulses, depth measurement) can the illusion of an immediate, "whole" perceptual experience be produced. The emphasis on training sets Helmholtz in opposition to proponents of the innate theory of perception. In order to debunk the innate (or "nativistic") theory, Helmholtz cites evidence from cases of the resighted and extends the arguments of Locke and Molyneux. While conceding that experience may not account for all elements of visual perception, Helmholtz maintains that it is only through *inductive* learning that one comes to understand perspective and form (3: 220–31). All of us, like the formerly blind, have *learned* to see.

In the context of the empiricist theory's dominance, I propose a reevaluation of the detective fiction genre as it emerged in the latter half of the nineteenth century. As argued in Chapter 5, the detective novel is saturated with visual images and scientific self-stylizations that entangle it in an unresolved epistemological bind; its narrative tensions between mind and eye, abstraction and physicality, deduction and induction are shaped by the methodological and rhetorical ambivalences of a gradual acquisition of knowledge. My larger hypothesis is that the detective novel, with its serial form and sensationalist roots, partakes of a scientific conception of vision that counters both a Cartesian logic of innate perception and a visionary optics of revelation. Although the *roman policier* has been conceived by critics according to Hugolian antitheses of light and darkness, good and evil, white and black, the genre's form and content actually present the world of crime and investigation in shades of gray.[6] It is no accident that Balzac's *Une Ténébreuse affaire*, with its shadowy title and themes, inspired many books of crime and deduction, nor that it is often regarded as a precursor to the genre of detective fiction. The mysterious textual space of the *roman policier* is indeed shadowy, indistinct, difficult to navigate visually. It is the work of the fictional detective to illuminate the dark corners of crime, exposing webs of murder and deceit to the "light" of rationality, morality, and law. His is the eye of the Police, figured as singular by Balzac ("this famous eye, the police's formidable emblem, invented during the Revolution") and as multiple by Foucault ("a faceless gaze that transforms the entire social body into a perceptual field: eyes by the thousands").[7]

But for all its apparent mastery, the eye of the detective is not omnipotent. The work of the detective (and the narrative structure that engenders him), like that of the eye's mechanisms according to Helmholtz, is gradual, confused, and complex. The dilatory structure of the classical detective novel—in which an initial shocking discovery is followed by delays, red herrings, and analytical steps of reasoning—follows the non-instantaneous model of vision as learned. Just as the eye gradually learns to make sense of a sequential set of percepts, the detective novel plays out its tale of illumination through a series of facts and clues whose relation to each other must be retrospectively interpreted. In other words, rather than associate the detective genre with a Cartesian logic of a priori deduction, this chapter proposes that the structure of the *roman policier*, with its hermeneutic delays, follows an empiricist model of vision. By extension, an empirical conception of the subject shapes the genre's narrative ambiguity. For the fictional detective progressively filters clues, bodies, suspects, and leads in much the same way that a human eye collects and interprets visual percepts. Truth, in this genre, appears not innately or immediately, but at the end of a search, through an a posteriori reconstitution of the facts.

Gaboriau's Visual Bildungsroman: *Monsieur Lecoq*

Edgar Allan Poe famously inaugurated the nineteenth-century detective novel with his invention of the Frenchman Dupin, but it was the less-known author Emile Gaboriau who was subsequently dubbed "the father" of the detective novel in France. Gaboriau had been writing popular *romans-feuilleton* (serial novels) for years when, inspired by Poe's Dupin stories, he penned *L'Affaire Lerouge* (1866), considered by most historians of the genre to be the first full-length detective novel. The novel's immediate success led Gaboriau to write a series of stories in the following decade that repeated its basic structure of an opening crime and a step-by-step inquiry. In France and in England, Gaboriau's formula took off, and imitators ranging from Fortuné du Boisgobey and Eugène Chavette to Sir Arthur Conan Doyle abounded in the final decades of the century.[8]

Gaboriau's fifth *roman-feuilleton*, *Monsieur Lecoq*, was first published in serial form in 1869 in the aptly titled journal *Le Soleil* (The Sun). Apt, because the blinding effects of the sun's light undergird the novel's metaphorics of knowledge and detection. Like so many *affaires ténébreuses,* the plot of *Monsieur Lecoq* begins on a dark, foggy Paris night, when out of the blue, a loud cry attracts a police patrol to La Poivrière, a seedy cabaret in a seedier part of town. As the agents arrive at the scene, we share their rushed curiosity, but the text delays their visual access (and ours) to what lies inside. Although described as "hermetically sealed," the tavern does in fact provide an opening through which light can be seen: "reddish glimmers of light filtered through heart-shaped openings in the shutters, as if from something on fire."[9] The country-kitchen quaintness of heart-shaped shutters is belied by the sinister red light escaping through them. As sounds of a scuffle inside are heard, one of the police agents, as yet unidentified, stands on tiptoe to peer through one of these heart-shaped openings. No description immediately follows, only the agent's outburst, "Horrible! It's horrible!" The cops' hesitation at the threshold, along with the agent's reaction, builds visual suspense as the narrative delay moves the reader's curiosity from the question "what caused the cry?" to "what horror does the agent *see*?"

The peculiarly visual nature of this delay exemplifies the visuality inherent in the entire *roman policier*'s "delayed decoding" of the hermeneutic function.[10] If the mystery is to remain a mystery until the end of the book, screens must be erected to obscure the vision of detective and reader. And in fact, the young agent straining to see inside the murky *cabaret* turns out to be the young and untested Lecoq himself, hero of *Monsieur Lecoq*. Gaboriau's novel is a bildungsroman, an allegory of the development both of the genre itself (as test case for emerging conventions) and of its protagonist (who, by the end of the initiation plot, will have earned the *Monsieur* which graces his name in subsequent texts).[11] Before his formation as detective begins, however, Lecoq is identified merely as an eye. A privileged eye, perhaps—for he is the only agent to peep through the hole in the tavern shutters to observe the scene of the crime, the first to witness its spectacle.

After the story's notable delay, the main officer Gévrol finally breaks through the main door of the tavern: "The low-ceilinged room of the Poivrière displayed a spectacle so appalling that all of the Sûreté employees, along with Gévrol himself, stood motionless for a time, frozen in place by unspeakable horror" (14). Once again, we encounter a reaction to the scene before its description, as the men are immobilized by a "spectacle" that stalls the narrative's progression, while drawing on a conventional Medusa trope that concretizes the dangers of visual perception. The visual shock of a murder scene will, of course, become a commonplace in the detective genre. Gaboriau often presents the discovery of corpses through characters' horrified eyes, as in *Le Crime d'Orcival,* in which two poachers come upon the body of a countess in a river and are struck "half-dead with fright before the spectacle."[12] Poe's influence on Gaboriau is evident in this regard, for Poe had described the rue Morgue murders in a similar manner: "a spectacle presented itself which struck every one present not less with horror than with astonishment."[13] As in *Monsieur Lecoq*, the identification of the murder scene as *spectacle* delays its actual description, so that the word "spectacle," indicative as it is of visual access, functions, ironically, as screen to vision. Arriving as a latecomer to the scene, the reader finds only a description of an "already-seen." The belatedness of our first encounter with the crime spectacle epitomizes our fated role in the *roman policier*, for, like the detective, the reader is called upon to interpret an already done deed. The text of the detective novel can only begin *post* mortem.

Poe's "Murders in the Rue Morgue" furnishes us with the originary example of this (visual) distance between murder and reader. Although the "scene of the crime" (the site where Mlle. L'Espanaye and her mother lie murdered) launches the story's events and Dupin's investigation, the scene itself comes to us many times mediated: the narrator's diaries recount Dupin's recitation of an article in the *Gazette des Tribunaux*, in which a journalist has synthesized the reactions of various witnesses to the wild disorder of a murder site. There are thus four "screens" separating us from the mangled corpses and the blood-soaked room.

These mediations have been understood as symptoms of the detective novel's larger thrust as a genre of the "mind"—of ratiocination and abstract analysis rather than of sensationalism and bodily gore. Martin Priestman, for example, reads the beginning of Poe's tale in terms of Foucault's argument "that the nascent detective genre marks the replacement of the spectacular punishment of the plebeian malefactor by the 'struggle between two pure minds.'"[14] For Priestman, the mediation between corpses and readers enacts the genre's "gap" between brutality and abstraction, between grisly murder and indifferent ratiocination. This argument is suggestive as an explanation of the genre's eventual development into a game of narrative conventions. After all, the *roman policier* did undergo a gradual "purification": from Conan Doyle, who claimed he would perfect Poe and Gaboriau's method by making it an exact science, to the dime detective novels of the 1920s, so mechanistic in their construction that S.S. Van Dine was able to publish a codified list of the "twenty rules" of the genre.[15] These latter examples show almost no traces of the sensationalism and the melodrama that lay in the genre's *feuilleton* roots. Poe and Gaboriau, however, still retain many such traces—so that if their stories enact a "gap" between body and mind, it is not an unambivalent one; I would argue, in fact, that the bodily, *sensory* nature of sensationalism infiltrates even their most abstract and mediated texts.

More specifically, the visual sense and the initial *spectacle* of the "scene of the crime" provide an index of the early genre's ambivalence between physicality and abstraction—and between what I have described as empirical and transcendental ways of knowing. In the citation from Foucault above, with its characteristic theory of history as organized by ruptures, the "spectacular" is relegated to the predetective novel past. By the time the genre has taken root, suggests Foucault, the "action" (murder, crime, punishment) has moved offstage. And indeed, the reader of a detective novel does not see a murder take place, just as in Foucault's historical narrative, spectators are no longer privy to the tortures and punishment of criminals. But if the violent murder does not take place before our eyes, its traces still remain as *spectacle*. For all of the screens erected between the reader and the scene of the crime, including that of the word itself (as suggested above, each time *spectacle* is invoked, it is to recount someone else's horror), a visual connection remains: that of the desire to *see*. In the detective novel, the unseen crime becomes the "scene of the crime," a textual locus with an essentially visual nature.

We are finally afforded a view into *Monsieur Lecoq*'s cabaret only after the violent action and witnessing: we see broken tables and chairs scattered about the room, three dead men stretched out on the floor, a sobbing woman crouched on the stairs, and an old man in mud-covered rags standing in an entryway. But even this description, coming after all the delays to our visual access, is far from satisfying. It is brief and rushed, moving quickly into the narration of subsequent actions: an accusation, an attempted escape, and the arrest of the man in rags. Like the policemen who have rushed to the scene, the reader is denied the comprehension that comes with a slow visual perusal. Compared, for example, to Paquita's bloody boudoir in *La Fille aux yeux d'or*, the cabaret scene lacks visual drama. We can recall the "painterly" effects of Balzac's description: the contrast of colors, red blood on white walls; the imprints of Paquita's hands and feet on cushions and curtains; the appeal to a spectator's eye; the sublime, mythic details of the marquise's wild stance. Gaboriau, by contrast, gives us a quick, facts-only overview of the situation, devoid of blood, of color, of vivid appeals to visual imagination. One could of course attribute this distinction to the aestheticized language of "high" literature versus a more neutral style common in popular literature, but whether due to lack of artistry or to conscious brevity, the effect of Gaboriau's scan of the crime scene remains the same: it eludes visual access.

Whereas Balzac's murder scene ends in mutual visual recognition (between Henri and the marquise), Gaboriau's first chapter ends with a challenge to sight. After cursorily concluding that he's dealing with nothing but a barroom brawl, the inspector in charge, Gévrol, is taken aside by one of his underlings, the young Lecoq. The agent protests that the case may be more involved than he thinks; in response, Gévrol scoffs at Lecoq, ordering him to stay behind to see what he can find: "And if you find anything I didn't see" he adds, "you have my permission to buy me a pair of eyeglasses" (20). This facetious reply, ending the first chapter, indicates that the story will be about trying to see, that it is Lecoq's eye that is being tested, and that for all of the novel's obstacles to sight, it is up to the detective to make up for (Gévrol's, his, and our own) initial blindness.

In Geoffrey Hartman's article on the mystery story, we find a suggestive formulation of the invisibility of the scene of murder and of the "over"-visibility of all that will follow: "No wonder the detective's reconstitution of the scene of pathos has something phantasmagoric about it. So quick that it is always 'out of sight,' the primal scene's existence, real or imagined, can only be mediated by a fabulous structure in which coincidence and convergence play a determining role. . . . The underdetermined or quasi-invisible becomes, by a reversal, so overdetermined and sharply visible that it is once again hard on the eyes."[16] The initial elusion of sight leads to the erection of an extravagant structure that is visual in nature. Hartman's use of the word "phantasmagoric," with its implications of optical illusion and visual destabilization, captures well the spatio-temporal condensations that abound in the *roman policier*. For the purpose of reading *Monsieur Lecoq*, however, let us focus on the end of Hartman's passage, on the "sharply visible," "hard on the eyes" nature of the plot of deduction. For if Balzac's *La Fille aux yeux d'or* is full of the soft-colored veils and misty visual distortions of subjective vision, Gaboriau's novel calls instead upon the sharp points of light, the alternate flashes and blindings of an ophthalmoscopic science. It inhabits, in other words, the more technical, less mystified space of a scientific *fantasmagorie*.

Eblouissements: Blinded by the Light

In the world of the *roman policier*, to see is to know—and if we, like the detective, must slowly recreate the events leading up to the "spectacle" of a crime, it is because that spectacle has momentarily blinded us at the beginning of the narrative. Moreover, the act of seeing can itself be dangerous. In *Monsieur Lecoq*, we receive an early warning that not only can death exist as spectacle, but seeing can lead to death: according to a doctor who arrives at the scene, the victims lying on the floor of the *cabaret* died from witnessing "some totally unforeseen, bizarre, terrifying spectacle" (56). The Greek origin of the word autopsy—*autopsia*: the action of seeing with one's own eyes—reminds us of the close link between seeing and death. When a detective, in this case Lecoq, agrees to "look into" a case, his is not the safe, objective relation of distant observer; he risks his life—or at least his eyes.

In describing Lecoq's visual quest, Gaboriau frequently draws on the conventional post-Enlightenment equation of knowledge with light, mental discovery with illumination. Lecoq plans, for example, to "bring the drama out of the shadows" to elucidate the "tenebrous affair" (52, 60). But as the story progresses, we find that his trajectory from shadow to light is not direct. Nor does Lecoq's vision follow the Cartesian model of sight as innate and immediate. Instead, the young detective seems destined to stumble through his inquiry in a general darkness punctuated by moments of dizzying clarity.

After having written his report on the crime scene, for example, Lecoq awaits the reaction of M. d'Escorval, the *juge d'instruction.* "*Hanging back in the shadows,* pale, jittery, restless, the young policeman scoured the judge's impassive face for any hint of his impressions" (60; my emphasis). In this tale of name and fame, our hero begins in the shadows, literally. From his half-visible vantage point, he hears d'Escorval praise Lecoq's report while mistakenly attributing it to Lecoq's rival, Gévrol. At this, "Lecoq felt something akin to dazzlement [*éblouissement*]" (60). The word *éblouissement* refers commonly to a state of astonishment, but its primary meaning is that of a visual effect: "Condition of sight as affected by an excessively intense burst of light."[17] Gaboriau's usage highlights the optical meaning, for Lecoq experiences "*comme* un éblouissement"—that is, something akin to a momentary breakdown of the eye's physiological functioning. The comparison fits the context, for the report's misplaced credit robs Lecoq of his source of pride and knowledge: his ability to *see* what really happened. His visual mastery is momentarily restored when Gévrol admits to the judge that Lecoq had actually written the report. Relieved, Lecoq walks out of the shadowed part of the room, into the "spotlight" of the judge's attention. Gaboriau's description of the moment implicitly recalls Lecoq's privileged role as observer: "The young policeman moved forward, his lips pursed in the satisfied smile familiarly known as 'la bouche en cœur' [heart-shaped mouth, i.e., a smirk]" (61). Earmarked as conventional, the phrase "bouche en cœur" repeats the image of a heart-shaped hole, reminding the reader of the similarly trite shutter design of La Poivrière's windows, where Lecoq's eye was first to witness the text's primal spectacle. But of course Lecoq's "satisfaction" lasts no longer in this scene than it had at the cabaret, for his visual mode, unlike Gévrol's, is not that of the *coup d'œil.*

In fact, Gaboriau uses Lecoq's rivalrous standoff with Gévrol to contrast two different modes of deduction—and consequently, two different modes of vision: "Gévrol's opinion was based on . . . the evidence that enters one's mind through his eyes. Young Lecoq's hypothesis was based only on a series of subtle observations and deductions whose starting point was a phrase spoken by the murderer" (72). Gévrol's Cartesian reasoning relies on a direct connection between the perceiving eye and the mind. In contrast, Lecoq works empirically, proposing a hypothesis that incorporates sensory perception (his observations) into a series of mental steps of reasoning. So that while Gévrol relies on an a priori, innate capacity to see what is before him, Lecoq initiates a comprehensive search for the most detailed of clues. It is not enough to be a passive seer; Lecoq believes he must look past immediate appearances as potentially illusory ("I think that appearances are deceiving," he says to Gévrol), and that he must use experience to interpret the visible clues (20).

According to the empiricist theory of vision, this is what the human eye does every day. We see blobs and shapes and blurs of color, but we use experience and logic to organize the forms of the world.[18] In short, we constantly overrule what our eye sees, because we (unlike Gévrol) know that appearances can be deceiving. Lecoq's *active* observation, his rejection of an a priori cursory glance, plants him on the side of empiricist vision. As a budding detective, Lecoq constantly revises his hypotheses and modifies his methods according to what he observes. In the empiricist conception of sight as an active, mental process, there is a mistrust of the visible as it appears to the passive eye; similarly, Lecoq is at his best when he remembers to incorporate mental reasoning (based on experience) in order to go beyond what his eye perceives: as he brags to his assistant Absinthe, it is *despite* a suspect's ragged appearance that he has deduced the man's noble origin.

Visual perception's ambiguous nature reappears at another moment of *éblouissement* in the text. In this case, the untrustworthiness of vision is mapped onto a mistrust of women. The proprietress of La Poivrière has been brought in for questioning by the magistrate, who is soon overwhelmed by her lack of cooperation. At one point, he exclaims in exasperation that asking a woman to tell the truth is equivalent to making the devil confess. In order to characterize woman's relationship to truth, he imagines a test of her visual perception of light. "If we show her the light, she shuts her eyes and says, 'It's night.' If we turn her head toward the sun, whose rays dazzle and blind her, she persists, repeating, 'It's night'" (93–94). Light functions here as objective truth, denied by the diabolically perverse woman. In the face of her refusal to acknowledge the light's presence by closing her eyes to it, a stronger light source, the sun, is brought to bear on her perception. At this point, though, she need not close her eyes to refuse the light; the sun's strong rays momentarily blind her. Thus, when she repeats her assertion that it is night, she actually *is* telling the truth, according to her subjective experience. In this way, phenomenological truth is associated with a female form of perversity, while the judge's concept of truth relies on universalized perception, figured as the seeing of light. For him, the light is the truth and the night is an untruth.

This set of oppositions recalls the key terms of the debate in optics at the time, which posed traditional attention to objective sight against a growing interest in subjective visual phenomena. If one reads the magistrate's complaint against Helmholtz's theory, the widow's stubbornness gains in validity. For, as contemporary advances in the theory of visual perception proved, the effects of light on the eye were far from stable. Instead of revelation, they could in fact lead to the perception of "night." In order to understand phenomena such as afterimages, stimulation of the retina, and processes of visual accommodation, nineteenth-century scientists conducted various elaborate experiments involving looking into the sun and shining bright lights into the eye. In 1851, Helmholtz invented the ophthalmoscope, an optical instrument that reflects a bright light on the retina through the use of lenses so that an observer can see into the pupil. This mechanical illumination of the eye is interesting in its reversal of the usual relation between light and vision. Normally, we are able to see precisely because light rays enter our eyes, hitting the retina. In the case of the ophthalmoscope, however, the angle of illumination intercepts the usual functioning of the eye, giving the observer access to visual percepts while in effect blinding the observed eye. The instrument thus effects a transformation of seeing subject into seen object. It also changes conceptions of the relation between subjective and objective perception. When one's eye is being observed through an ophthalmoscope, one is blinded to the external world but one sees all sorts of "blurred starry images" similar to the floating "points" that appear when one's eyes are closed. Helmholtz points out that these images have no relation to exterior objects and refers to them as subjective percepts (2: 12). And yet, not only does he affirm their existence, he dedicates long sections of his treatise to the experiments and experiences that teach us about the nature of such luminous effects; the fact that they are subjective does not mean they are false. The phenomenological truth is that we see neither light nor complete darkness when we look into a bright light or at the sun; we see, as did the woman in the story, La Veuve Chupin, a version of "night"—darkness punctuated by star-like blurs. The magistrate in *Monsieur Lecoq* clings to a conception of objective truth that does not take into account subjective perception. Developments in the field of optics, meanwhile, provide an alternative conception of vision, in which subjective viewpoints are incorporated into a scientific, objective discourse on reality.

I would argue that the early *roman policier* organizes its narrative according to this more fluid, ambiguous philosophy of vision and of man's perceptual relation to the world he wants to understand—and that the character Lecoq in *Monsieur Lecoq* acts as a sort of questing hero as *observer*, trying to orient himself among the complex, shifting categories of perception. Such an active, experiential conception of vision is not purely phenomenological: as evidenced by Helmholtz's extensive catalogue of experiments performed by scientists throughout the mid-century, the careful observation and detailed measurements of subjective visual images are pursued within the scope of a larger attempt to quantify and explain the real workings of the eye. In this way, a visual subjectivity is subsumed within a scientific goal of objectivity.

Indeed, for Helmholtz, experimental truth resides in the combination of perception and experience: "In the preparation of this treatise the chief aim which I have had in view has been to verify all the fairly important facts by the evidence of my own eyes and by my own experience" (1: ix). His own eyes are capable of synthesizing and analyzing visual phenomena, whether they are externally caused ("objective phenomena" such as "extrinsic light") or not ("subjective phenomena" such as the colors, blurred forms, and bursts of light that one sees with one's eyes closed) (2: 228). The split, then, between "objectivity" and "subjectivity" is not located for Helmholtz as we might imagine, between external reality and physiological illusions; both the world and the body produce *real* visual phenomena. What makes a difference to Helmholtz is how these phenomena are studied—the scientific, trustworthy, objective eye is one that puts all these phenomena to rigorous empirical testing while carefully distinguishing between their sources.

In other words, Helmholtz argues for a scientifically based distinction between subjective perception and external percepts. This argument comes in the form of an impassioned passage that is worth examining in the context of nineteenth-century "analytical" fiction, in particular Gaboriau's *Monsieur Lecoq*. While "objective light" is the primary means of stimulating the optic nerve, argues Helmholtz, it is not accountable for *all* such stimulations. Mechanical and electrical actions can also produce the sensation of light (one can verify this by rubbing one's finger across a closed eyelid). Helmholtz's language becomes quite forceful here, as he launches into an explanation of how earlier philosophers and physiologists gave the name "light" to the external causes of a luminous sensation (2: 4). Properly speaking, the word "light" should be used only to denote the sensation itself. This confusion, he says, led philosophers to divide the sun's radiation into two categories: heat rays and light rays. Helmholtz debunks that belief rather vehemently: "As long as man did not ponder over the nature of his sensations, it was natural for him to transfer the qualities of his sensations directly to the external objects, and so to suppose that the rays of the sun were of two kinds corresponding to his two sensations" (2: 4). Let me underline two aspects of this passage: the projection of one's own subjective sensations onto an external source and the subsequent doubling of a single phenomenon.

Helmholtz confidently dismisses such confusion, reminding the reader that studies conducted "in very recent years" have proven that the only difference between the so-called light rays and heat rays of the sun exists in the frequency of their vibrations. His triumphant conclusion: "And thus in this instance at least physics has succeeded in freeing itself from entanglement with the subjective sensations that were so long confused with the objective causes" (2: 5).

Such subjective entanglements affect the detecting eye of various characters in Gaboriau's novels. In *L'Affaire Lerouge*, Tabaret's emotional attachment to Noël, whom he considers as an adoptive son, blinds him to the young man's role in the murder he is investigating. Even beyond moments that clearly indicate Noël's guilt, a certain inelasticity of thought keeps Tabaret from seeing Noël in a different light. Like the men critiqued by Helmholtz, who were unable to distinguish their own sensations from the external rays of the *sun*, Tabaret confuses his own sense of paternity with Noël's real identity as bastard *son* to the rich count whose fortune lies at the heart of the mystery. Until Noel's "dark side" is proven, Tabaret is like a man able to see only one of two possible interpretations of an optical illusion.

Similar hesitations and blind spots plague Lecoq in *Monsieur Lecoq*, impeding his investigation throughout the book's first part. Although the young agent's active observations had put him at an initial advantage over Gévrol, his "vision"—and his confidence—soon falter. In fact, it is precisely because he is an *observer*, in Helmholtz's sense, that sight for him will be a slow process. At times, Lecoq will resemble the confused philosophers that Helmholtz derides, and it is through error that he will learn to see. For the first half of the book, rivalry, pride, and overconfidence in his own powers of deduction hinder Lecoq in his quest for the light of truth—a light that will only appear to him with the aid of Tabaret, in an incarnation worthy of his nickname, Tirauclair (Light-shedder). In the typical detective novel we find an uncomprehending witness, from Dupin's friend-narrator to Holmes's Watson, acting as intradiegetic figure for the reader's state of delayed illumination. In *Monsieur Lecoq*, that figure takes on the central role, as the titular detective combines the Holmes and Watson functions, exhibiting a blindness that seems obstinate in the face of clues, confessions, and even, as we shall see, direct visual evidence.

When Lecoq is left behind at La Poivrière, he is confident that he will find proof that Gévrol was wrong in his quick assessment of the multiple murder as an impromptu, drunken affair. We learn about the visual logics that underlie Lecoq's confidence when he momentarily loses it. This first disappointment of many comes when Lecoq and Absinthe discover women's (instead of the hypothesized men's) footprints outside the tavern: "A single word dashed all his hopes and demolished the ingenious structure his imagination had erected. Gone was the mystery, and with it any chance of a triumphant investigation or overnight celebrity won through a burst of light [*un coup d'éclat*]!" (27). Lecoq had ambitiously counted on a brilliant burst of light, a *coup d'éclat* so bright that all would defer to his luminescent intelligence. Deceived by his hopes of triumph—a quick triumph, figured by a burst of startling light—Lecoq returns to a slower, methodical search of the premises. Soon enough, with the help of a tiny lantern held by Absinthe, he has found enough clues to recommence his deductions. The return of his confidence is also recounted in visual terms, as a beacon of light: "At the end of the path they were traveling along, each saw his own magic beacon shining: one saw the prospect of a decent tip; the other saw the glory of success." (39). Success, for Lecoq, takes the form of "un phare magique," a light whose brilliance would immediately catapult him to fame in the eyes of the world.

But if Lecoq has indeed managed to latch onto a metaphorical *phare* of insights, it is surely an oscillating light, for the agent's investigation into the murders at la Poivrière progresses in fits and bursts. Lecoq stumbles so often in his deductions that a large part of the story consists of letting the reader know whether the hero is in a state of exalted hope or of deflated despair. Lecoq wants the light all at once, through "a dazzling piece of evidence," but the "éclat" [burst of light] eludes him and the mystery remains to be "éclairci" [illuminated]. Lecoq imagines bedazzling all the world's eyes—he himself, however, is the one who ends up dazzled, or *ébloui*.

As indicated earlier, Lecoq's initial police report resulted in a success mitigated by an *éblouissement* of momentary disorientation. It was the magistrate d'Escorval who provoked that vertiginous reaction—we recall that when the officer mistakenly attributes his report to Gévrol, Lecoq loses his composure ("he felt a kind dazzlement" [*il eût comme un éblouissement*] 60). A few chapters later, we find Lecoq bothered again by this particular judge. "M. d'Escorval unsettled him and cast upon him such a chill that he was utterly disconcerted" (62). The extreme reaction, similar to that of the detectives when they first saw the murder scene, alerts the reader to d'Escorval's significance. For, without knowing it, Lecoq is looking directly at the truth he is trying to discover: as we will learn in the second part of the book, d'Escorval had played a central role in the tangled intrigue leading to the night of the murders. It is, in fact, because d'Escorval recognizes his ancient rival the Duke de Sairmeuse in the person of Mai, the ragamuffin suspect, that he withdraws from the case. When the prisoner, calling himself Mai, is told that d'Escorval will no longer hear the case, he turns pale and stumbles, explaining to those who rush to his aid that he is fine—"I felt a bit dizzy just now [*j'ai eu comme un éblouissement*]; I'm fine" (96). Lecoq is witness to this momentary loss of self-control, but he does not understand its significance. Through an *éblouissement,* the text provides a figural burst of blinding light, emanating from a character too close to the truth.

The logic of *éblouissement,* then, provides a wrinkle in the detective novel's trope of truth as light. If the detective's privileged mission is to dispel the shadows of mystery so that truth can shine through, does it not seem strange that Lecoq would be momentarily dazzled, blinded, and dizzied when he actually nears the truth? Perhaps, but maybe Lecoq is learning that truth is not equivalent to light. The term *éblouissement* had a medical meaning that was current in the 1860s: it referred to a momentary blindness provoked by an over-bright burst of light on the retina.[19] Each time Lecoq has an *éblouissement* (including one moment when he discovers the existence of a minor character named Claire—clarity, light), he is spun back into confusion—and the serial narrative continues on its oblique and digressive route to a solution.[20]

If we examine other moments of *éblouissement* in *Monsieur Lecoq,* we note that they continuously tap into larger cultural questions of illusion and falsity. At one point, for example, Lecoq wonders whether a hidden agreement exists between La Veuve Chupin and the suspect Mai: "Why wouldn't the false drunkard have dazzled [*ébloui*] Chupin with all manner of luxurious expectations? Why wouldn't he have promised her money, a lot of it?" (94). Once again, as in the magistrate's complaint of Chupin's obstinacy, a male character imagines the female witness in terms of her optical acuity; once again, truth and falsity enter the visual realm. Here, false hope and the suspect sparkle of gold are the light that blinds her eyes. One is reminded of Balzac, in whose *Facino Cane,* the enigmatic character is literally blinded by gold; in Gaboriau, as in Balzac, gold and ambition are lights that dazzle the eye, shining deceptively. The inherent falsity of the dazzling light is essential to the action of *éblouissement,* a word that once carried the meaning of betrayal, trickery, falseness, speciousness.[21]

Lecoq himself is seduced by the *éclat* of his own imagined success—seduced and tricked into a series of wild goose chases and dead-end investigations. To those who object to his premise (that Mai is not who he seems to be), Lecoq appears a victim of his own delusions. Even Lecoq, in his constant oscillation between hubris and despair, wonders whether his elaborate hypotheses are nothing but illusory projections of his own creation. After failing to disprove the prisoner's alibi, he wonders: "Could the murderer have been telling the truth? . . . If so, he, Lecoq, and Mr. Segmuller were no better than madmen, chasers of chimaera!" And so Lecoq continues his searches of Paris streets, tracking down clues and trying to convince himself that each of his failures is actually a logical success. The alternation between darkness and insight, the renewed chases of possible *chimères,* the clashes between Lecoq's projections and the world's barriers—all these make up the rhythm of "The Investigation," as Gaboriau entitled the first part of *Monsieur Lecoq.* The atmosphere is reminiscent of Helmholtz's version of the visual world, in which flashes of light punctuate darkness and the "phantoms" of subjective phenomena hold as much interest as external facts in the realm of "scientific investigations" (3: 7). The "chimères" of *Monsieur Lecoq,* the moments of possible illusion, punctuate the fictional world of investigation, based as it is on red herrings and false quests; the seductive logic of *éblouissement,* with its bright lights and momentary blindness, defines the *roman policier* process.[22]

Lecoq's Visual Quest

"The only noteworthy thing about him was his eye, which flashed or dimmed at will [*selon sa volonté*] like the on/off beam of a lighthouse" (20). In this early description of Lecoq, we find a corporeal indication of his future oscillations between insight and confusion. As "remarkable" trait, the visual alternation between on/off, bright/dark both signals the young detective's potential for genius and keeps him from settling into a definitive *coup d'éclat* of the sort he ambitiously imagines: "selon sa volonté" [at will]: the pronoun is ambiguous—whose will, Lecoq's or his eye's?—suggesting the possibility of a bodily "pulse," a corporeally grounded visuality whose rhythm determines the detective's ability to see. And as contemporary studies of optical physiology suggested, corporeal vision is often faulty vision.

With a fallible, bodily eye as his guiding light, Gaboriau's young hero lacks the confident, superior sense of vision of a ratiocinating Dupin or Sherlock Holmes. It is true that at the beginning of the story, Lecoq's insightful powers are established in the admiring eyes of old Père Absinthe, in the manner of Dupin and Holmes. And yet, rather than direct the investigation from a privileged position of deductive genius, Lecoq actually gropes around in the dark, grasping at his momentary glimpses of light—of a truth that, like his eyes, "flashed or dimmed at will like the on/off beam of a lighthouse." His murder investigation continues—for hundreds of pages!—without clear signs of progress. Lecoq's false starts are worth examining, for they allow us to read his visual quest as an allegory of sorts for the nineteenth-century tension between Cartesian visuality and the modern, empiricist conception of the observer.

Let me summarize the steps of Lecoq's inquiry into the identity of his main suspect, a ragged and bearded man named Mai. Because of the suspect's learned allusion to Napoleon's troops, Lecoq suspects that Mai is not the penniless street performer he claims to be. Yet, after much questioning, he is unable to crack the suspect's appearance as a commoner. He can theoretically surmise and imagine the man's noble birth, but he is unable to see it himself or to make it visible to others. So Lecoq takes matters into his own hands and has Mai put into prison where he can keep him under constant surveillance. Then, when no confession is forthcoming, Lecoq has the prisoner released and tries to follow him home. Finally, after losing track of Mai, Lecoq turns for advice to an older detective before eventually closing the case. In other words, Lecoq's three main methods of inquiry are these: imprisonment, pursuit, and consultation. Each of these three methods comes with its own textual metaphorics of vision that might be categorized in the following way: (1) the fantasy of omnivision (if you see every action at every moment, you will understand); (2) the faith in precise and stubborn focus (if you look closely enough at your object, you will understand); and (3) the recourse to a seer (if all else fails, appeal to a higher level of vision). Each of these three "false starts" in Lecoq's investigation represents a type of seeing that is doomed to failure—doomed, I would argue, because it adheres to an outmoded conception of vision itself.

Solution 1: Visual Mastery

In despair at Mai's continued act as *saltimbanque* (busker), a role played so convincingly that all but Lecoq and the new magistrate are persuaded, Lecoq decides to enact his own little *coup de théâtre.* He installs himself in a cramped and hidden hole above Mai's cell, where he intends to spend night and day in secret surveillance of the prisoner. His entire identity is reduced to an "œil cachée [hidden eye]," spying continuously on his locked-up quarry. From the chamber that he has fashioned into a hidden "observatoire," Lecoq explains to his colleagues, he will fix his eye to a smaller opening that affords a view of the prisoner's cell.

Such an ambition belongs, clearly, to the visual order of the panopticon, as conceived by Bentham and theorized by Foucault in *Surveiller et punir.* This dream of visual mastery relies on an eye that serves as "the tool of a permanent, exhaustive, omnipresent surveillance that can make everything visible provided that it makes itself invisible."[23] Lecoq's omnivisual project partakes of the same logic, but is doomed to failure—as may be glimpsed by a brief survey of the differences between Gaboriau's detective and the guards in Bentham's hypothetical prison.

The first difference is architectural. Rather than observe the accused from a high, central tower, Lecoq is awkwardly squeezed into the compressed space of an *entonnoir* (a hollow) cut into the prison's wall. More cooped up than the prisoner himself, Lecoq must sleep on a blanket and receive meals in secret from his assistant Absinthe. Lecoq's invisibility, then, comes at the cost of his own freedom. More significant is the fact that Lecoq's view of the cell is incomplete; he sees the door, the bed, a table and chair, but not the cell's window and area near it (162).

Second, Lecoq's goal puts him at an initial disadvantage. Where panoptical prison surveillance need only exist to enforce punishment, Lecoq's spying attempt is based on a lack of knowledge—knowledge that the prisoner has and that he desperately wants to attain. His dream of visual omnipotence, then, is one of discovery, not punishment. It has an epistemological thrust that is not lost on Gévrol, who mocks Lecoq's plan with a comparison familiar to readers of the *roman policier*. "Do you know what you look like, with your eye up against that hole, spying on the prisoner? . . . You look like one of those idiotic naturalists who put little bugs under plates and spend their time looking at them through a big magnifying glass, watching them crawl around" (161). This allusion to the work of naturalists, unlike others we have encountered (in Doyle and Balzac, as well as elsewhere in *Monsieur Lecoq*), ridicules the scientific ideal of discovery through visual observation. Gévrol combines the inefficacity of the magnifying glass with the trivial nature of the object observed to paint the naturalist's patient observation as a complete waste of time. But Lecoq takes up the comparison as a badge of honor: "You guessed right: the idea I'm going to implement comes from the work of those naturalists you speak so ill of. By studying a little bug, as you put it, under a microscope, these clever, patient scientists eventually learn its ways, its habits, its instincts. . . . what they do for an insect, I'll do for a man" (161). The young agent's bravado signals a confidence that prolonged and constant observation from above will lead to significant conclusions. But his confidence relies on a limited understanding of the model of natural science. For Lecoq, the naturalist's microscope figurally affords him the panoptical position of superiority; patient and objective observation, he believes, will reveal the true nature of his object of study. As we have seen, however, a methodological ambivalence underlies the work of naturalists like Cuvier and Saint-Hilaire, an ambivalence suggesting that dogged visual observation is not enough, that empirical science cannot be based solely on "pure" observation (nor, we should remember, on "pure" deduction).

Lecoq's faith in the objective eye of scientific observation is ill-founded, but after many days of patient observation, Lecoq does in fact turn up evidence of communication between the prisoner and the outside world: notes written in a code based on a popular song. Continuing to follow a scientific model of objective mastery, the young detective turns from observation to deduction, from empirical to rational methods of analysis in order to crack the code. Lecoq goes through some unnamed steps of abstract deduction figured as mental illumination; "his face lit up almost right away, and he slapped his forehead, exclaiming: 'Eureka'!" (165). Lecoq's discovery infuriates the prison director, who cannot believe that a prisoner could have foiled his watch-system. Lecoq, reveling in his own success, smugly reminds him: "What an illusion! Hasn't the prisoner's ingenuity always foiled the guard's wiles? Won't it always?" (164). In giving the director this lesson, Lecoq forgets to turn it on himself. For he himself has taken on the role of *surveillant,* watching from above; and by his own rule, the surveillant will be outfoxed by the *surveillé.* That, of course, is what happens next. Lecoq sets out to entrap the prisoner by forging a new note, but Mai foils his plan by calling the guards as though alarmed by this unforeseen message. Lecoq ends up humiliated in front of his colleagues and dashed in his hopes to unmask Mai.

Lecoq's panoptical fantasy fails because, although he remains un*seen* by Mai, his presence is not unknown. While the logic of Bentham's Panopticon consists in the prisoner's awareness of being seen—"a conscious, permanent state of visibility that ensures automatic operation"—in this case that consciousness has backfired (202). If the prisoner is aware he is being watched, he will avoid suspicious activity. Lecoq, however, wants Mai to misbehave. For Lecoq's goal is not punishment but discovery; he wants to know the truth of Mai's identity. His own invisibility to Mai is of paramount importance to his plan. But Lecoq mistakenly assumes that seeing and knowing are equivalent: if Mai does not see Lecoq hiding, he must not know he is there; and if Lecoq sees all Mai's actions, he will know who the man really is. Both hypotheses turn out to be incorrect.

Lecoq's equation of surveillance with knowledge relies on a sense of perceptual mastery, the idea that whatever enters into the visual realm will thereby become comprehensible. Such an attitude may be equated with a scientist's overconfidence in the scope of his objective gaze on the world. But as critics such as Rosalind Krauss and Gillian Beer have recently argued, nineteenth-century Europe witnessed a destabilization of visual epistemology that tended to undermine this confidence.[24] Questions about the eye's dominant power began to surface, even in the scientific discourse of the time. Helmholtz's discussions of subjective visual phenomena, for example, undermine the certainty that what one sees actually exists, objectively, as external truth. An astounding number of nineteenth-century experimental discoveries in the field of visual perception indicate the eye's propensity for illusion, confusion, and self-trickery. With the eye's authority thrown into doubt, there can be no belief in a direct link between surveillance (the positioning the eye above an object) and understanding. Lecoq's failed panoptical plan provides an indication that the new genre of detective fiction draws some of its epistemological suspense from a widespread destabilization of optical power.

The failure of Lecoq's project of visual mastery reveals the uncertainty in a genre that has often been understood in terms of panoptical authority. Drawing on Foucault's well-known image, Dennis Porter, for example, remarks that "by the time of Doyle, the Great Detective of fiction had himself the essential qualities of the unseen seer, who stands at the center of the social Panopticon and employs his 'science' to make all things visible on behalf of the forces of order."[25] While it is true that Lecoq predates Holmes and thus might be considered an inept precursor to this "Great Detective," his failure also signals an important instability in the positivistic science that subtends panoptical order. The text's decentering of the eye is not a conscious literary strategy; in fact, Gaboriau's series will continue to depict the appeal of the police force in terms of its omnipotent, unseen vision. But in *Monsieur Lecoq*, Lecoq's maverick plan of surveillance excludes him from the police system. When Mai outfoxes him, Lecoq's disappointment is matched by his colleagues' anger and suspicion: the director of the prison and his rival Gévrol are both gratified at the failure of Lecoq's departure from the regular norms of surveillance, and the judge himself calls Lecoq's stint in the hiding-place an "outrageous business! . . . and one that I would never have allowed if I hadn't been blinded by my desire to reach the truth" (172). Lecoq's dream of entry into the halls of visual power, then, is temporarily squelched.

The fact that Lecoq's dream of omnivision ejects him temporarily from the node of power may be read as a sign of generic things to come. As D. A. Miller argues in *The Novel and the Police*, the figure of the detective, with his "*super-vision* and the police *supervision* that it embodies," poses a societal threat that results in his relegation (in novels such as Wilkie Collins's *The Moonstone*) to the periphery of actual systems of power.[26] "It is often argued," Miller writes, "that the detective story seeks to totalize its signifiers in a complete and all-encompassing order. On the contrary, it is concerned to restrict and localize the province of meaning: to guarantee large areas of irrelevance" (34). This distinction between a totalizing system of knowledge and one that allows for unintegrated parts seems particularly relevant here, since Miller's presentation of the logic of a classical detective story accords with Helmholtz's account of visual perception. Miller points out that the detective story's economy turns on the necessary elimination by the end of the tale of many of the facts presented for the reader's consideration. "At the moment of truth, the text winnows grain from chaff, separating the relevant signifiers from the much larger number of irrelevant ones, which are now revealed to be . . .

trivial" (33). In this way, the reader's second look at the story is comprehending but not comprehensive. The illumination of the mystery entails a rejection of a large part of the material which had been presented to us.

In his *Treatise*, Helmholtz explains that our daily acts of vision require a similar rejection of many perceptual facts. In order to *observe*, that is, to comprehend actively what we see, we must discard a large quantity of visual percepts as irrelevant; these range from continual "floaters," or *mouches volantes*, to double images caused by binocularity, to changes in lighting which affect appearances in color, to the innumerable external visual percepts that do not further depth perception and object recognition. The experienced reader of the *roman policier* acquires a similar ability to discard any facts irrelevant to the final moment of textual revelation.

This is a lesson to be learned by our young Lecoq. He has tried to see *all*, to acquire visual mastery over Mai through perfect surveillance of the prisoner's space. When his totalizing panoptical fantasy fails, though, he turns to a different visual myth of positivistic science: the observation of an object of study in its own environment. Abandoning the superior position of the panoramic eye, Lecoq decides to come down for a close-up, to focus attention on Mai while eliminating all distracting, seemingly extraneous, material from his field of vision.

Solution 2: Focus

After the surveillance fiasco, Lecoq concocts a new plan: Mai will be allowed to leave prison, and Lecoq will follow the suspect "à l'aveugle" [blindly]. In other words, he will wander through the streets with no premeditated plan other than, ironically, to keep his eyes attentively focused on Mai, to the exclusion of all other informational input. "Lecoq would not have given all the wonders of the universe even a glance or a second's notice" (203). Nothing will distract him from his visual prey. Lecoq's plan is a positivist fantasy of pinpoint vision, focused and unmuddied by the distractions of experience or real life. The "à l'aveugle" suggests that Lecoq's dogged focus is less about optical experience than about some abstract notion of disembodied truth.

And indeed, Lecoq's a priori limitation of his object of study ends up preventing him from seeing and understanding what is before his very eyes. The hypothesis that Lecoq has been trying to confirm is that Mai hides a true nobleman's status behind a beggar's exterior. But when his suspect disappears behind the walls of the Duke de Sairmeuse's elegant chateau, Lecoq cannot fathom the possibility, which the astute reader has by now glimpsed, that Mai in fact *is* the Duke de Sairmeuse. After losing sight of his quarry, Lecoq remains obsessed with the stable visual image of the ruffian whose steps he has followed to the chateau. He orders a thorough police search of the premises, which turns up no sign of the *saltimbanque.* Lecoq himself explores the grounds, coming finally to the duke's bedroom, where he "had the privilege of catching sight of [*d'entrevoir*] the Duke de Sairmeuse through the open door of a small, white-marbled bathroom" (204). The reader who has guessed Mai's secret may be amused at this point by Lecoq's naive reaction to the noble personage in whose home he thinks he is trespassing. The young policeman merely bows and engages in the following short conversation: "'Is the offender still invisible, then?' The duke called out cheerily. 'He still is, your Grace!'" (204). Lecoq's respectful answer plays into the nobleman's confident sally. For the *malfaiteur* is in fact the most invisible precisely at the moment at which he is seen.

Various elements of this visual encounter obscure Lecoq's understanding of what he sees. First of all, his goal had been to set his sights directly, as through a scientist's lens, at his quarry; here, he can only *entre-voir* (catch sight of) the nobleman through an *entre-ouverte* (half-open) door—the image thus slips between his categorical frames of reference. In addition, the respect and honor he feels for nobility is so strong that he is momentarily dazzled, *ébloui* by the glimpse of the duke set off by bright white marble. Like the widow Chupin in Lecoq's imagined scene of blinding gold, Lecoq is unable to discern falseness behind the brilliance. Even though he had approached his search with the certainty that a noble personage was hiding behind the mask of a *saltimbanque,* his eyes cannot adjust their "lens of focalization" to see the *saltimbanque* (an actor, a fake) behind the nobleman.

Lecoq's single-minded focus prevents his understanding precisely because of its singleness. After having left the duke's estate, Lecoq is deflated, disappointed at having lost his quarry. Suddenly, "a bizarre, outrageous, utterly unthinkable idea flashed through the young policeman's mind. . . . What if Mai and the Duke de Sairmeuse were one and the same person?" (208). Although he rejects the idea as too romanesque to be true, what Lecoq has momentarily imagined is the possibility that two different appearances might belong to one single entity. This moment of understanding briefly allows for the empiricist conception of visual perception that was prevalent in the late nineteenth century. If we return to Helmholtz's critique of the traditional understanding of light as the subjective sensation caused by the sun's rays, we note that the error came about by supposing that one thing—solar radiation—was actually two, light and heat. The attribution of two different forms to one object was due to the subjective experience, the different sensory "appearances" of the rays on the body and eye. Similarly, Lecoq has experienced two different forms of a man, whose appearances affect him in manifestly different ways: a ragged, gruff, dirty criminal and an imposing aristocrat in all the sparkling trappings of wealth and nobility. He would have to go beyond appearances, as did Helmholtz and his contemporaries in examining the physical nature of solar rays, to see that the two men are in fact only one. Lecoq's mistake, based as it is on a "single-minded" vision, ignores the physiological reality of shifting appearances. In their studies of the binocularity of vision, the empiricists maintained that it was through experiential training that we learn to ignore two slightly different perspectives in order to perceive what we know to be a single object. In the bildungsroman that is *Monsieur Lecoq*, the young detective has not yet trained his eye to see one man in the double image of Mai/Duke de Sairmeuse. Indeed, Lecoq is far from the visual mastery of Dupin, who recognizes in "the purloined letter" the equivalence of the compromising document and its altered appearance. So he returns to his investigation in despair, having lost the suspect as well as any confidence in his powers to see. Finally, he is compelled to turn to an experienced seer for help in clearing the cobwebs of this *ténébreuse affaire.*

Solution 3: Consult an Oracle

Although Mai's identity as the Duke de Sairmeuse remains a blind spot for Lecoq, he is plagued by the idea that the two men may be one. Unable to let go of the irritating buzz, Lecoq finally goes to consult Tabaret, "someone who will see what I can't, someone who will understand" (208–9). Tabaret, the mentor figure who appears in Gaboriau's books at various moments in his career, is identified as "the oracle" (211). He too has a double nature: to his neighbors, he is Père Tabaret, a sweet and irrelevant aging man; while in his secret identity as consulting detective, he is "Tirauclair," gifted with the ability to see through the most *ténébreuses* of criminal *affaires.* In this character, we find a reworking of the idea of a single entity with a double image that can only be detected by those whose eyes are trained to unite them; "no one had ever imagined that Tirauclair and Tabaret were the same person" (212). His situation is analogous, in fact, to that of Lecoq's suspect, in that what allows him to remain invisible is society's reliance on the external indicators of a man's professional and social role. His unassuming and modestly proper demeanor diverts attention from his nocturnal comings and goings, so that the categories of *retraîté* (retired person) and *détective* remain separate in the minds of those who encounter him. Like Dupin of the "Bi-Part Soul," Tabaret can control images and appearances, enjoying mastery over the visible world. As privileged seer, he may in fact have access to the invisible world as well, for the realm of the visionary is double. He is described by Gaboriau as "the Janus-faced oracle, Tirauclair in rue de Jérusalem, Tabaret in rue St.-Lazare" (212). The religious overtones of the addresses suggest two births, the first as professional detective, the second as resurrected gentleman. And in fact, it was through having experienced and rejected the panoptical fantasy of the police profession, "whose invisible eye is everywhere" (210), that Tabaret has acquired his new sense of sight, one that depends on his peripheral, unofficial relation to the police department. As we shall see, if Tabaret does indeed have any insights to share with Lecoq, it is precisely because his vision, like his position, is peripheral.

Tabaret's status as oracle is problematic, for the text applies the term to various other characters—including a jeweler, Gévrol, and Lecoq himself. There is no one true Oracle; any access to divine authority has been split up, multiplied into minor oracles whose advice does not necessarily result in insight. Oracles "are always wrong, everyone knows that," thinks Lecoq in a moment of doubt about Tabaret. And even as a mature, successful detective in *Le Crime d'Orcival*, Lecoq will renounce any claims to oracular authority. As he explains to Plantat, "Usually . . . I only open my mouth when I'm completely finished with something; then, in a decisive tone, I issue my *oracles*: it's this, or it's that." Today, however, (continues Lecoq), "I am letting others see my uncertain gropings without shame" (78). Throughout *Le Crime d'Orcival*, we hear Lecoq's hypotheses and steps of reasoning, rather than a spectacular pronouncement; this detracts in no way from the character's confidence and final success. Part of Lecoq's professional apprenticeship (and that of the *roman policier* genre) seems, therefore, to involve an acknowledgment that insight comes not from a direct, immediate revelation, but from the hesitant *tâtonnements* (gropings) of one who is learning to see. Such a desacralized conception of vision maps onto Helmholtz's theory in at least three ways: ordinary vision as homologous to the slow acquisition of the resighted; the step-by-step logical process of vision; and the use of touch as an aid to visual contact with the world. It also, of course, decenters the role of oracle, of Tabaret as seer of the Unseen.

Tabaret does, it is true, provide the information that not only fills in Lecoq's gaps of understanding but also furnishes the story that will take up the entire second part of the book—namely, the twisted family relations between the d'Escorvals and the de Sairmeuses. However, it is neither as privileged visionary nor even as rigorous reasoner that Tabaret has acquired the necessary knowledge. Despite the assurances of a "wondrous labor of induction" and an "inductive method" (216), Tabaret's contribution ends up consisting simply of some biographical information that he has looked up in an encyclopedia of contemporary and recent history. It is to this encyclopedia that he directs Lecoq, despite the young detective's desire to get back out on the chase. The information that serves as explanation for the mysterious deaths comes, then, from a peripheral, written source of knowledge, rather than from a direct lead. Lecoq may have begun his investigation by following a trail of footprints to their logical conclusions, but Tabaret's wisdom and experience soon lead him to abandon his direct, focused gaze on his visible target, Mai. In the end, neither the scientific objectivity of a panoptical gaze, nor the single-minded focus of direct observation, nor the abstract faith in an oracular vision lead Lecoq to the truth—indeed, vision must come *indirectly.*

Seeing Stars

At the end of the first part of *Monsieur Lecoq,* Tabaret has shown Lecoq the encyclopedia reference that establishes Mai's identity as the Duke de Sairmeuse. But instead of sending him directly to arrest the duke, Tabaret warns Lecoq against a head-on attack. Lecoq takes this prudent advice, and at this point, the narrative itself refrains from continuing directly to the next logical and chronological step. Instead, *Monsieur Lecoq* takes an enormous detour, sending the reader back to the historical background of the case for hundreds of pages. Lecoq and his investigation disappear for the majority of part 2, "L'Honneur du Nom," leaving us with a whole new cast of characters and the political entanglements of the Restoration—a "tenebrous affair" of a different sort. Taking my cue from Lecoq, I will read part 2 "en diagonale" [obliquely], for to attack it straight on would blind us to the target of this reading: Lecoq's vision. Lecoq's apprenticeship in this novel is visual. His attempts to catch Mai by surveillance and by focused attention both failed; his appeal to an oracle's "direct line of vision" has set him on course, but it has done so precisely by setting him *off* course, by directing his eye away from the center.

Helmholtz announces, "the human eye is not exactly centered," citing various experiments that refute centuries of thought which assumed a central line of light through the pupil into the retina, around which the rays and eye functioned symmetrically and geometrically (1: 116). In fact, given the physiological anomalies of the eye, certain objects can be perceived only if looked at indirectly. This is true of subjective optical phenomena—such as the dark *mouches volantes* that float about in our vitreous humor, like covert spies in rational society (in addition, the word *mouche* referred to privately employed spies in nineteenth-century France). Among such phenomena, Helmholtz describes the "small, star-shaped, blurred image[s]" whose appearance in the eye are due to irregularities of the crystalline lens (1: 190). The presence of such "aberrations" even in normally functioning eyes undermines the idealized, Cartesian conception of the eye's crystalline lens and vitreous humor as clear and transparent; they are caused, explains Helmholtz by the interaction of light with the "imperfect transparency of the ocular media" (1: 193). Such a description goes against Cartesian optics, for the eye's nontransparency makes it impossible to rely on abstract, geometrical models to study vision. The identification of shadowy, starlike phenomena in the field of vision entails the acceptance of indirect perception.

Similarly, Lecoq's acceptance of Tabaret's tactic of indirectness follows its own shadowy logic: "in order to succeed, I must hide. . . . Yes, I'll stay in the shadows until I've lifted the veil from this tenebrous affair" (235). To see, to illuminate the shadowy mystery, Lecoq understands that he must not go straight into the light (for, as we have seen, it can be blinding), but must allow himself to remain in the indistinctness of *l'ombre.* He will allow himself to stay in the shadows, to enter into the tenebrous affair in order to solve it. This is a change from early in the novel, when Lecoq had imagined a brilliant entry into his career through a *coup d'éclat,* a burst of light signaling his innate deductive genius. Such immediate revelation was not to be; instead, Lecoq entered the slow and gradual rhythm of this long visual bildungsroman. Lecoq's final acceptance of *l'ombre* aligns him with a modern conception of vision, taking shadows not as obstacles to illumination but as necessary components of the visual process. As Goethe put it in his *Theory of Colors,* the visible is not defined as presence of light and absence of darkness, but as an ever shifting encounter of light *and* shadow. Eliane Escoubas explicates Goethe's theory in the following way: "Without the contrast between light and dark, only dazzlement [*éblouissement*] is left—which is also blindness."[27]

Monsieur Lecoq, I would argue, tells us the same thing: that the way to see is not by dispelling the shadows but by dwelling within them—and that the reliance on a conception of pure, transparent rationality (figured by an objective, mastering eye) cannot finally guarantee success in the work of detecting crime. Later, in the 1920s, when the detective genre has been codified and purified, it will become the genre of pure intellection, of a neo-Cartesian rationality that sends pure light out to eliminate darkness. But in the 1860s and 1870s, when its roots are still firmly planted in the sensationalistic tradition of the serial novel, the *roman policier* remains a *ténébreuse affaire.*

Even after the formal detour of hundreds of pages, *Monsieur Lecoq* returns to a sequence of muddled, indirect actions. Confident that he knows the truth of the matter, Lecoq leaves Tabaret to continue his investigation, for he still does not have the "material evidence" needed to close the case. So he goes to see M. d'Escorval, the magistrate who had resigned from the case, in an attempt to enlist his aid against the duke. But when he arrives at d'Escorval's home, Lecoq is barred from direct access to him: Monsieur "is in his office with a young man" (595). As he stands waiting, curious and avidly attentive to the sobs he hears coming from the room, the detective's eyes nevertheless stray to an opened letter resting on a table top nearby. The letter reveals that its bearer is d'Escorval's unknown bastard son, born to the Duke de Sairmeuse's sister; upon reading it, "Lecoq felt something akin to dazzlement [*éblouissement*]." And finally, shaken by information happened upon with a sidelong glance, Lecoq is propelled into the visual logics of indirectness, of falsity, of the *éblouissement*. For he then leaves without speaking to d'Escorval and proceeds to take devious, indirect steps to catch de Sairmeuse: he erects another *coup de théâtre*, arriving at the duke's chateau in disguise with a faked letter from d'Escorval. The letter asks for money in return for not having denounced him as Mai. When the duke responds affirmatively, Lecoq triumphantly unmasks himself. At this point, the duke must admit his role to the court, but in consideration of the history behind it, he is absolved of the crime. As for Lecoq, he is granted a coveted post in the police force. He has finally, it seems, learned to "see" in a world of deceiving appearances, of shadows and indirectness.

The indirection of vision in *Monsieur Lecoq* may have its roots in the foundational text of the detective genre, Poe's "Murders in the Rue Morgue." Speaking of Vidocq, the famous former criminal who had turned to law, Dupin announces that, while his intuitive impulses were good, he erred continually by the very intensity of his investigations. He looked too closely, too deep, says Dupin—and truth is most often superficial. Dupin's explanation of the indirect vision necessary for criminal deduction turns to both astronomy and optics:

> The modes and sources of this kind of error are well typified in the contemplation of the heavenly bodies. To look at a star by glances, to view it in a sidelong way, by turning towards it the exterior portions of the *retina* (more susceptible of feeble impressions of light than the interior), is to behold the star distinctly, is to have the best appreciation of its lustre—a lustre which grows dim just in proportion as we turn our vision fully upon it. A greater number of rays actually fall upon the eye in the latter case, but in the former there is the more refined capacity for comprehension. By undue profundity we perplex and enfeeble thought; and it is possible to make even Venus herself vanish from the firmament by a scrutiny too sustained, too concentrated, or too direct. (100)

If we recall that Gaboriau's young detective Lecoq had begun his career as an astronomer's apprentice, and had been dismissed for a mind more compatible with crime solving, we can begin to reconceive his visual quest in *Monsieur Lecoq* as a way to see stars again.

Let me conclude this chapter with a final image from the famous Cheselden case of an adolescent boy's resighting. Before the operation, the boy's blindness had not actually been complete: while his "Ripe Cataracts" prevented him from perceiving shapes, they did allow some oblique light in through his aqueous humor in such a way that he could distinguish some colors in a very strong light.[28] Cheselden equates his very limited sight with the experience of a healthy eye looking "thro' a Glass of broken Jelly, where a great Variety of Surfaces so differently refract the Light, that the several distinct Pencils of Rays cannot be collected by the Eye into their proper *Foci*." This "Glass of broken Jelly" serves as an apt image for the beginning of every *roman policier*. As in a murder, violence has been done to a whole, breaking and scattering it into many parts. The several "Pencils of Rays" can be seen as the clues, the body parts, the suspects, and the contradictory leads which can only be "collected," comprehended, put into logical sense by the detective's Eye. Thus, the whole rest of the text, after the initial discovery of the scene of the crime, must follow the many steps of induction, deduction, hypothesis, and interpretation of scattered facts that go into the daily process of sight. The visual logics that saturate the detective genre position it at the crux of an epistemological ambivalence. It is no wonder, then, that its formulas of delayed understanding replicate the nonsynthesis of corporeal and rational ways of knowing. For the *roman policier* is a genre that invented itself out of the secularized miracle of sensory perception—the continual, repeatable act of "learning to see."

Chapter 7

Sealed Chambers and Open Eyes: Leroux's *Mystère de la chambre jaune*

The 2003 release in France of Bruno Podalydès's film adaptation of Gaston Leroux's *Le Mystère de la chambre jaune* (1907) has brought renewed attention to this classic detective story and to its visual potentiality.[1] Podalydès plays up its scenes of surveillance, blindness, and insight by overlaying tropes of photography with the visual universe of Tintin comic books; in his film, the book's narrator Sainclair becomes a bespectacled photographer whose optical prosthetics identify him as "the man who sees."[2] But while the story's cinematic rebirth may tempt us to read its "optics" in a vague post-Lacanian sense (metaphors of mastery, sins of the filmic gaze), such a reading would elide a scientism specific to Leroux's age.

As with so many late nineteenth- and early twentieth-century detective novels, *Le Mystère de la chambre jaune* embeds its criminal investigation plot in the broader semantic universe of scientific investigation: the initial crime, a nocturnal attack on Mademoiselle Stangerson, occurs in a chamber (the Yellow Room) abutting a scientific laboratory where Miss Stangerson and her father have spent years engaged in physics research—the preradiographic study of the dissociation of matter. The international renown of the Stangersons, described as precursors to Monsieur and Madame Curie, is said to be such that the threatened interruption of their research constitutes an incalculable loss to science.[3] But in Podalydès's film version, laboratory vials give way to quack machinery as Stangerson is recast as a kooky inventor of solar cars and trick gadgets.

In his decision to evacuate the serious scientific content of Leroux's 1907 novel, Podalydès resembles modern critics of the detective fiction genre. In the wake of forceful psychoanalytic and post-structuralist readings of the 1970s and 1980s, critics have generally been loath to invoke the scientific context of detective fiction, perhaps for fear of falling into the simplistic influence model exemplified by one of the genre's earliest studies, Régis Messac's *Le "Detective Novel" et l'influence de la pensée scientifique* (1929).[4] But by foregrounding the tensions inherent to linguistic system and libidinal romance, we risk forgetting that complex streams of ambivalence coursed through the scientific epistemology of detective fiction at its very genesis. These chapters aim to revive the connection between literary detection and scientific deduction, between investigative mode and empirical method in the context of fin-de-siècle positivist thought.

Leroux's *Le Mystère de la chambre jaune*, an acknowledged keystone in the detective genre's emergence, connects explicit musings on physics to a constellation of less obvious allusions to optics—that is, to the science of vision, in the literal, physiological, anatomical sense. This 1907 novel thus emerges as a key to understanding the early detective as private "eye."[5] Indeed, through attention to the optical semantics of the novel's pivotal yellow room (*chambre jaune*/optical chamber) and its elaboration of criminal inquiry, this chapter extends our investigation of the detective genre's visuality as crucially structured by an unresolved epistemological struggle between empirical method and abstract deduction.

The Yellow Room/The Blind Spot

When writing his fiction, erstwhile journalist Gaston Leroux used to follow a peculiar home ritual. He would shut himself up in a small study for the duration of the writing period while his family waited in silence; after days and weeks, he exited the room, announced the completion of his novel with a pistol shot, and was greeted by the jubilant "tintamarre" [din] of his relieved relatives.[6] This anecdote may provide some psychobiographical illumination of themes in *Le Mystère de la chambre jaune*, a novel plotted around pistol shots, enclosed rooms, and a woman silenced by her (former) husband. But more specifically, it evokes precisely what made this popular novel, set in 1892, an instant classic: its "closed room" topos.[7]

Inspired by Poe's "Murders in the Rue Morgue," the "Yellow Room Mystery" takes the theme of crime in an enclosed chamber even further than did the father of the genre. Leroux's narrator mentions as antecedent solutions both Poe's ape and Doyle's serpent (in "The Speckled Band"), but emphasizes that his case involves a hermetically sealed space, with no conceivable or allowed ingress or egress: "But here, any kind of opening whatsoever is totally out of the question. With the door sealed and the shutters closed the way they were, and the window closed, *not even a fly could get in or out*!" (62, emphasis in original). The hyperbolic emphasis leads me to ask, "not even a *mouche volante*?" one of those specks or "flying gnats" that float across the field of vision in a subject at rest? Though seemingly facetious, the question points to a surprisingly trenchant analogy between the fictional topos of the Yellow Room and the scientific concept of the optical chamber—both sites of communication between interior sand exterior, self and other, whose precise functioning raises an epistemological mystery.

Leroux's story revolves around a violent intrusion into a domestic space whose boundaries become the crux of investigation—an investigation triangulated by the narrator Sainclair, the official detective Larsan, and the young journalist Joseph Rouletabille. At Epinay-sur-Orge, the eminent scientist Professor Stangerson lives with his thirty-five-year-old daughter and assistant Mathilde (said to be surprisingly pretty despite her advanced age!) on a large walled property bordering the Sainte-Geneviève forest. In addition to their domestic staff, they are regularly joined by Mathilde's suitor, a fellow scientist named Robert Darzac. But when the mysterious news gets out of a nighttime attack on Miss Stangerson—involving pistol shots, her screams of "Murderer!" and a bloody star-shaped wound on the young lady's forehead—the nearby village's population expands, as judges, police, reporters, and friends flock to the property to help identify the unknown intruder. Although guards have been posted at the property gate to keep out the curious, Rouletabille finds a way to get himself and his friend Sainclair (the story's narrator) both onto the grounds and into the chateau as invited guests. In fact, throughout the investigation, it becomes clear not only that the Yellow Room must have somehow allowed for intrusion, but that Stangerson's entire estate is an unsettlingly porous enclosure. An American visitor, Arthur Rance, for example, is seen coming and going as he pleases, jumping over the park wall without alerting Stangerson's staff. Logically, the initial question posed by investigators is this: was the attacker an insider or an outsider? Based on evidence that the "killer" (as he is called, despite having failed to kill Miss Stangerson) knew the premises well, both Rouletabille and his onsite competition, the detective Larsan, conclude that he was an "insider"—and indeed, the attacker turns out at the end of the story to have been Larsan himself, in disguise to hide his former identity as the criminal Ballmeyer.[8]

In this regard, Leroux's basic plot unexpectedly recalls a scientific question regarding the nature of another "closed chamber": are *mouches volantes,* "intruders" into the optical space or bodies existing within the eye? Like the criminal in Leroux's story, the optical phenomenon of *mouches,* or floaters, had become the focus of an investigation into unknown origin, and by the late nineteenth century their "mystery" was solved by confirmation of an earlier hypothesis that they are "insiders," produced entirely by and within the subject's own body.[9] A *mouche volante* is an insider, but one that is difficult to perceive clearly—for it has the "curious effect," writes Helmholtz, of veering away from the eye's central point of fixation: its "fovea" or "yellow spot."[10] In Leroux's novel, Rouletabille finds it curious that Larsan continually directs attention away from the Yellow Room itself; in the first third of the story, he never sees the older detective at the scene of attack, but rather glimpses him outside, stooped over material evidence found by ponds and paths. Rouletabille's investigations, on the other hand, focus on the physical layout of the Yellow Room and its points of communication with the adjoining laboratory and the outside park and forest. With his map and his questions, the young journalist aims to determine which of the building's windows open onto the property itself (facing the château) and which open out onto the forest outside Stangerson's walls.

In the field of optics, a similar concern with the nature of openings in and out of the eye's chamber led to physiological study of the "yellow spot," or *fovea centralis.* In his 1861 treatise *Physiologie et pathologie fonctionnelle de la vision binoculaire,* Félix Giraud-Teulon defines the yellow spot as "obscure" in both color and nature:

> Central punctum, or yellow spot on the retina. [Thomas] Sœmmering has shown that exactly on the eye's main axis, a few millimeters outside of the optic nerve's point of penetration, there is a small, dark, circular spot measuring roughly one-and-a-half millimeters across; it is surrounded by a wider yellowish border that gradually blends into the contiguous parts of the membrane. This spot was initially described as an opening existing inside the retina. It has been thoroughly discussed by all of the major anatomists, and considerable doubt remains as to its nature. However, it appears evident that this spot does not correspond to a loss of substance of any kind. Nunneley relates it to a cadaverous effect, as do Knox and Bowmann.[11]

There are three elements of this passage that invite extended comparison to Leroux's mystery tale. One, of course, is the yellowish "border" spreading out from the mysterious spot onto the membrane of the eye, which recalls the titular wallpaper in Miss Stangerson's lab-side bedroom. Acting a bit like an optician looking through an ophthalmoscope, Rouletabille announces that he will shed reasoned light onto the mysterious chamber rather than tear out its saffron-colored wallpaper, as do the boorish policemen assigned to the case (93). Skipping to the end of Giraud-Teulon's passage, we might note a second reverberating element, the "cadaverous effect," a morbid trope that seems more at home in a mystery story than in a treatise on optics; in the scientific context, it introduces the threat of death inscribed in the very membranes of our body. Leroux's mystery, with its insistence on the fact that violence occurred in a room that was "closed; indeed, closed *from inside* [à l'intérieur] by the young lady herself" (5, 6; emphasis original) similarly evokes the victim's vulnerability to her own body's effects: not only was it Mathilde's youthful desire that initially allowed Larsan-Ballmeyer into her life (through a secret marriage in America), but the truth is eventually revealed that Miss Stangerson's alarming head wound had been accidentally self-inflicted in the Chambre Jaune. In fact, as Rouletabille explains, the whole screaming scene in the enclosed chamber consisted of a nightmare recreation (or somnambulistic "afterimage") of an earlier attack, so that, alone in the room—at least at the nocturnal moment in question—Mathilde Stangerson had undergone a purely "subjective" somatic experience.

The echo with the "subjective," entoptic phenomena of blind spots, afterimages, and *mouches voulantes* may still seem far-fetched, but let us turn to a third element in Giraud-Teulon's definition of the optical yellow spot, one that pertains more directly to *Le Mystère de la chambre jaune*'s explicit allusions to scientific discourse and disputes. Does the spot's yellow border indicate a hole, an opening in the retinal wall? After debate about the phenomenon's dubious nature, Giraud-Teulon tells us, scientists answer in the negative: there is no "loss of substance" that would indicate egress from the optical chamber. In Leroux's literary mystery, investigators ask whether the Yellow Room contains any hidden openings. The question produces much debate among *juges d'instruction*, witnesses, the detective Larsan, and our journalist-hero, for a response in the negative seems to imply an inconceivable "dematerialization" of the attacker. When Rouetabille explains the actual chronology of earlier intrusion and subsequent closed-room nightmare, he also reaffirms the physical fact that there has been no "perte de substance," no disappearance into thin air of a material being. Moreover, Rouletabille explicitly links his solution to the (Lavoisierian) dictum that "rien ne se perd, rien ne se crée [matter is neither destroyed nor created]"—that is, to the scientific premise that the Stangersons are assiduously trying to overturn in their laboratory (3). Professor and Mathilde Stangerson have been presented to the reader as scientists famous for their inquiries into "la dissociation de la matière," the return of matter to ether by means of electricity, radiography, solar or ultraviolet light (33, 53, 106). The whole world, according to the narrator, is waiting with bated breath for Dr. Stangerson's public presentation at the Academy of Sciences on his theory of the dissociation of matter—"A theory destined," continues Sainclair, "to shake the very foundations of official science, which have for so long been based on the principle: 'matter is neither destroyed nor created'" (3). As forward-thinking scientific revolutionaries, the father-daughter research team had been trying at the time of the crime to prove the existence of "the intermediate substance between ponderable matter and imponderable ether" (106). The theoretical move from material to immaterial subtends the story's narrative oscillation between matter and mystery: when Rouletabille and three other men fail to capture the fleeing attacker in the château's hallway, the narrator dubs this new, seemingly inexplicable episode the "phenomenon of the killer's material disappearance" (142). Rouletabille writes up a "compte rendu" [report] of scientific precision, complete with an accompanying diagram reproduced in the text, in which he explains that the intruder apparently disappeared at the precise moment when the four men converged and crashed at the intersection of two hallways. As with the Chambre Jaune episode, there were no secret passages or discoverable means of egress, and the fact that the attacker has left no trace leads Rouletabille to describe his disappearance as an "strange phenomenon of material dissociation" (155), the same phrase used in the title of Stangerson's scientific treatise. But in fact it turns out that the "killer's matter" had not actually disappeared into thin air, into the ether: as Rouletabille explains in the story's dramatic courtroom dénouement, the "killer" was none other than Larsan, one of the four men who had been posted on watch and had evinced (or feigned, in Larsan's case) amazement at the absence of the criminal in the hall. Perhaps the story's biggest irony resides in the fact that in order to champion Miss Stangerson and her father, Rouletabille undermines the very scientific theory that defines their lifework: the theory of disappearing matter.[12]

Not only do the optical yellow spot and the literary Yellow Room share a narrative of discovery—from mystery to the hypothesis of "lost matter" to the revelation of materiality—they also share a shifting value according to the perspective from which observation takes place. Both can be understood as "blind spots": the "tache obscure" in the optical chamber mars the transparency of the eye, while the Yellow Room fulfills the classic function as site of mystery, as that which cannot be seen. Rouletabille invokes, for example, the typically visual tropes of investigative illumination as he grapples with the "mystère de la chambre jaune": "All of these thoughts flash through my brain like a lightning bolt having no more than shadows to illuminate. Ah! To know . . . Ah! To see and to know" (146). But the Yellow Room is not a site of blindness for everyone involved. In fact, Miss Stangerson, the room's only occupant at the time of the nightmare episode, knows what Rouletabille is trying to discover: the identity and motive of her attacker. What makes the mystery a mystery, in other words, is the external perspective of narration—that of the journalist-investigator, as told to his faithful friend Sainclair. Miss Stangerson's silence (imposed by her conscience, honor, and duty to her father) puts her in the typical position of victim, that of a cadaver unable to tell what it has seen before dying. The fact that *Le Mystère de la chambre jaune*'s victim is not dead may seem perplexing, even maddening, to the reader of classic detective fiction. Why can't the police merely ask her what happened? But such a question apparently misses the point, as Leroux's narrative allows the victim's silence to remind us that some things are meant never to be revealed entirely (thus Rouletabille keeps secret from the court Miss Stangerson's past marriage to the criminal and the narrator keeps secret from us Rouletabille's likely filial relation to the victim).

In fact, the Yellow Room's evocation of the optical yellow spot may point us precisely to something that contemporary studies in physiology were confirming: the ultimate incommunicability of (visual) knowledge between subjects. Even with the advancements of the ophthalmolscope, invented by Helmholtz in 1851, the ability to look directly into another person's eye did not allow the observer access to what that person sees. Paradoxically, the very spot of the optical chamber that appears the most opaque to an observer looking in is the highest point of vision for the subject looking out; the yellow spot—or *fovea* at center of the yellow macula—is the area of greatest sensitivity and visual acuity.[13] It is all, in other words, a question of perspective, of who is looking in (ophthalmologist, investigator: Rouletabille) and who is looking out (living patient, living victim: Miss Stangerson). The optical yellow spot defines the central point of fixation for the subject's gaze, but objects perceived in the periphery of that point appear less clearly. In Leroux's mystery, Miss Stangerson knows who assaulted her in the Yellow Room, but does not see that Larsan, who pursues his investigations peripherally on the grounds, is the same man as her attacker. As "insider looking out," she hopes to keep outsiders looking in from seeing what she does know. "We're not blind!" attests a male family servant, but he—and Rouletabille, drugged so that he is asleep during a key meeting between the victim and her attacker—*is* in fact blinded by his very external position to the crime and the mystery (50).

The context of physiological optics, then, provides a key to the particular dynamics that fuel the mystery of the *Chambre jaune*. Indeed, the optical phenomenon of the yellow spot not only reaffirms, as I have demonstrated, Rouletabille's conviction against loss of (physical) matter, it provides the very tools on which the young journalist relies for solving the mystery of the "disappearing killer" in the château's second-story hallways. Having "determined with near-mathematical precision" that the key "point of fixation" for understanding what occurred is the intersection of the two hallways, Rouletabille reviews in his mind all visual angles of perspective on that point (154). As with the human eye, which was determined to be oriented around not one but two optical axes (the apparent blind spot of the off-center yellow spot and the "actual" blind spot of the central optic nerve), Rouletabille's *mystère des galeries* reveals two angles of perspective: first, the main hallway from which the observers (Rouletabille, Mr. Stangerson, and Père Jacques) were given the false impression of a material disappearance (or blind spot on the killer); and second, Larsan's hallway, which turned out to be the central connection to the truth (of Larsan's "insiderness") as well as the spot from which the killer himself could see most clearly what was going on (Larsan's change of disguise and direction).

In a way, *Le Mystère de la chambre jaune* repeats the "blind spot" logic that Lacan perceptively analyzed in Poe's "The Purloined Letter." In both stories, exhaustive physical searches lead to the mistaken conclusion of missing material evidence; the solution remains "in plain view" but not plainly visible. And in both cases, the "blind spot" is determined less by an inherent unknowability than by the position of the viewer. In Lacan's reading of "The Purloined Letter," the "spot marked by blindness" is determined by the shifting positions of the minister, the queen, and Dupin—who is blind to his own symbolic position within that triad (51).[14] Similarly, in Gaston Leroux's story, Rouletabille's blindness can be understood in structural terms, as the mistaken belief that he occupies one point in a triangulated relation: Rouletabille-Larsan-killer. Only by collapsing the competition (the detective Larsan) and the prey (the killer) into one can he finally "see" the true binary relation that determines the solution. Moreover, there is the Oedipal revelation, which Leroux semi-coyly hides from the reader, of the uncomfortable fact that Larsan-Ballmeyer is Rouletabille's own father; not only are the two "Others"—rival and enemy—one and the same, but that very Other is less "other" than Rouletabille had imagined.[15]

While revealing important structural and formal elements of the detective genre in general and *Le Mystère de la chambre jaune* in particular, however, poststructuralist and psychoanalytic critical methods, if applied exclusively, risk leaving out what Leroux's text insists on keeping in: matter. Written in the latter half of the nineteenth century, an age through which Michel Serres has traced the deep interconnectedness of myth and science, *Le Mystère de la chambre jaune* explicitly filters its Oedipal themes through the matter and methods of his age's scientific inquiry. And it is only by looking into the specifics of Leroux's allusive universe that we can get beyond what all fictional detectives have in common, to see what sets this first Rouletabille mystery apart from the English tradition (Leroux continually cites Poe and Doyle as both precedents and counterexamples) as well as from Gaboriau's *Monsieur Lecoq*. In the broadest of terms, Rouletabille represents a conservative visual epistemology that strains against Lecoq's forward-thinking empiricism, as studied in the previous chapter. One aspect of this conservatism, as I will demonstrate, resides in the young detective's assumption that he alone can see, that he alone sees from the right optical axis and he alone sees straight.

Le Presbyte; or, Bad Guys Can't See Straight

Some of the pleasure in reading *Le Mystère de la chambre jaune* comes from the narrator's ignorant position vis-à-vis his friend Rouletabille. Like

Holmes's Watson, Sainclair observes with stunned incomprehension the results of Rouletabille's ingenious methods, including his dramatic use of a key "Open Sesame" phrase to gain intimate entry into the Stangerson estate. Having previously overheard Miss Stangerson read to her fiancé the phrase, "The presbytery had lost none of its charm, nor had the garden lost any of its beauty," Rouletabille repeats it word for word to the stunned Darzac, who imagines that the young detective knows something about the phrase's threatening origin (39). But of course the cleverness of the investigative gimmick resides in Rouletabille's actual ignorance of the phrase's content and context: he knows nothing either of the phrase's meaning nor of the origin of the letter from which it was taken; he only knows that its use will produce desired effects. As such, the "presbytère" sentence functions as placeholder, or "pure signifier," in the sense that Lacan uses to describe the purloined letter in Poe. One might even see the distance between the phrase and its letter of origin as a further "dematerialization" of the signifier. But as with the charred remnant of the letter—for Miss Stangerson, it turns out, has succeeded only in partially burning evidence of her earlier liaison with the killer (53)—a material trace remains to connect the "presbytère" phrase with the wider network of proof that identifies Larsan as the guilty party: its homophonous echo with the "binocle de presbyte [presbyopic eyeglasses]" that Rouletabille discovers as material evidence of the killer's presence and identity.

Although the "presbytery" of Larsan's letter and the "presbyopia" exposed by his spectacles share no etymological link,[16] they function similarly, through incremental revelation, to identify the guilt of Rouleabille's investigative rival. The "presbytery had lost none of its charm" phrase, as Rouletabille eventually explains to Sainclair, refers to Larsan's secret marriage to Miss Stangerson years earlier in America; almost touchingly, the criminal yearns for a return to ancient affection through a return to the site of that affection. While Rouletabille had long inferred the killer's passionate claim to Mathilde, he remains unable to prove Larsan's guilt until he finds an identifying physical marker: the *binocle* (pair of eyeglasses) that exposes the criminal's visual defect. Upon finding the incriminating object, Rouletabille "literally threw himself on the eyeglasses, his fingers stroking the convexity of the lenses" (139), for it is that convexity that identifies the anomaly of vision that he had already attributed to the criminal: farsightedness. Having witnessed the killer hunched over a writing table, Rouletabille had deduced that the man had trouble seeing close up. Later, when trying to imagine what "tangible mark of his having been there" might compel the killer to return to the scene of his crime, Rouletabille remembers a candle on the floor and the hunched-over posture as key to connecting Larsan, whom he has by now suspected for a while, with the man in Miss Stangerson's room (255). "When I saw this pair of eyeglasses," admits Rouletabille, "I was frightened out of my wits" (256):

> I had never seen Larsan wear eyeglasses. . . . If he didn't wear them, it was because he didn't need them. . . . What did the eyeglasses mean? . . . It was beyond my ken. *Unless the eyeglasses were for a farsighted person* [un presbyte], I suddenly exclaimed inwardly! . . . It was true, I had never seen Larsan write or read. He "might" be farsighted! The Sûreté was sure to know that he was farsighted, "if indeed he were . . ." they would probably recognize his eyeglasses . . . "The eyeglasses of the farsighted Larsan" found in Miss Stangerson's room, after the inexplicable mystery of the hallway, things were certainly looking bad for Larsan! This would explain Larsan's return to the room! . . . And Larsan-Ballmeyer is in fact farsighted, and these eyeglasses, that they "might" recognize at the Sûreté, are indeed his. (256, emphasis original)

The theatricality surrounding Rouletabille's identification of "le presbyte Larsan" highlights the *binocle*'s function in the story as smoking gun and criminal Achilles heel.

For Larsan's imperfect vision is essentially linked by the text to his criminal nature. As a physical marker tracked, like fingerprints, at the Sûreté, his farsightedness perdures through his various disguised identities, from American entrepreneur to international pirate to French detective. The only other character in the *Mystère de la chambre jaune* to wear a *binocle* is the sinister "green man," a working-class lothario who, though innocent of real crime, conveys an ominous presence throughout the book, is disliked by the servants and villagers for his seducing ways, and comes to a violent end (86). In contrast to the louche characters of Larsan and the "green man," Rouletabille asserts his own clear vision as a sign of his ability to use reason over senses by making instrumental use of material evidence: "Yes, yes, I swear it, the tangible traces were never more than my servants. . . . in no way were they my mistresses. . . . In no way did they make *me into this heinous thing, worse even than a man without eyes: a man with poor vision*!" (170; my emphasis). Rouletabille continues his tirade against bad vision with a taunt that transfers the bestial posture of the *presbyte*, "hunched" over his writing table, onto his powers of reasoning: "And that's why I'll get the better of you, with the mistake you made and your animal reasoning, O Frédéric Larsan!" (170). Larsan is an unrefined investigator, a brute criminal, a *presbyte*.

Larsan's particular type of visual pathology was famously analyzed by Félix Giraud-Teulon in his *Physiologie et pathologie fonctionnelle de la vision binoculaire*. In the book's sections on *presbytie*, Giraud-Teulon explains the abnormality as "an accommodation disorder" caused by a foreshortened eyeball and corrected by the use of convex lenses, of the sort that Rouletabille finds at the Stangerson estate (352). Rouletabille's mention of the candle along with Larsan's hunched posture as indicative of farsightedness can be explained by the physiological fact, described by

Giraud-Teulon, that *la presbytie* causes its sufferer to require more reading light than usual (356). Moreover, the very method of deduction used by Rouletabille is confirmed by Giraud-Teulon's text: "the farsighted person may be recognized as such . . . based on his interactions with objects of small size. Simply by seeing how a farsighted person takes up a book to read, his range of vision may be assessed a priori" (355). Beyond confirming a vague sense that Leroux must have had some basic knowledge of physiological optics to hinge his mystery's solution on the deduction and optical correction of Larsan's *presbytie*, Giraud-Teulon's text also suggests a way to read Rouletabille's own vaunted vision, his escape from the "monstrous" fate of seeing badly: as "normal binocularity." As suggested by the title of his treatise, Giraud-Teulon takes binocular vision as the key to understanding both the healthy functions and the anomalies of human sight. While normal sight requires a harmonious alignment of each eye's perception into a unified image, *la presbytie* involves a discordance of images; in order to correct the problem with convex lenses, one must recalibrate the point of convergence for the two optical axes (398–402). As already noted, Rouletabille's solution of the *galerie* mystery involves the convergence of the two optical axes, or angles of visual perspective, of the château's second-story hallways; only after he has accurately aligned those two axes—by "seeing" them together in his mind's eye—can the young journalist solve his puzzle. But even more indicative of the way in which the normal binocularity of physiological vision shapes Rouletabille's investigative "vision" is the very content of that solution: namely, the fact that the killer and Larsan are one and the same man. Having mentally recreated the hallway scene, Rouletabille can merge the two conflicting "images" of criminal and investigator, no longer seeing them as two separate entities, but as two halves of the same person. "Rouletabille knows both halves of the killer" (214), and thenceforth refers to him as Larsan-Ballmeyer. Normal binocular vision necessitates the accurate distinction of single from double images. So it is fitting that when our hero Rouletabille sees double, he is accurately intuiting an actual alliance between two beings: "Through some kind of foreknowledge [*prévision*], the double image of Mr. Robert and Miss Stangerson lingered in my mind throughout the night" (128). This vision makes him unlike Larsan, of course, whose farsightedness blinds him to the investigative danger of the young journalist closest to him in plot, position, and parentage.

Rouletabille Against Empiricism: Ginzburg and the "Galilean" Method

Like so many detective fictions, *Le Mystère de la chambre jaune* presents itself as an allegory of reason's triumph over the senses. Rouletabille's job is to dispel the shadowy superstition and fear-induced confusion that result from the Yellow Room's "supernatural crime" (3); the simple-minded Père Jacques admits that he'd begun to believe in the devil (7), and inhabitants of the estate and its surrounding land all agree that the "Bête du Bon Dieu," a cat belonging to a local witch, screeches diabolically every time Miss Stangerson is attacked (146). When not evoking occult powers, witnesses and investigators alike invoke visual mystery, calling the affair "hallucinating" (25) or an incomprehensible "fantasmagoria" (218), and citing a ghostly shadow (25) and the "strange apparition" (211) of a "black phantom" (147). Rouletabille's rational explanations (the cat's yowl is a signal to poachers, the "phantom" a cloaked woman on her way to a lovers' rendezvous, etc.) counter the unsteadiness of optical illusion by reaffirming a solid mind-eye epistemology. When he is faced, for example, with the seemingly inexplicable disappearance of the killer at the intersection of two hallways, Rouletabille momentarily loses faith in his system; the mystery represents, he says, "The moral destruction of an edifice built on reason, coupled with the actual destruction of physiological vision ["la vision physiologique"] even though my eyes see as clearly as ever, what a dreadful blow to the mind" (160). Mind and eye are meant to work together, with the unfailing certainty of physiological vision in the service of rational thought. Larsan had maddeningly insisted to Rouletabille on the killer's disappearance, "despite what his eyes saw, despite what my eyes saw, despite what everyone's eyes saw" (165), so that when the young journalist finally proves him wrong, the explanation serves not only to establish Larsan's guilt but more generally to reestablish the reliability of (law-abiding, normative) vision. Eyes should not deceive, believes Rouletabille.

Nor, however, should they be taken as anything other than mere instruments of the mind. Eyesight," as Leroux puts it in interestingly scientific jargon) cannot be the dominant tool of investigation; rather, it must provide a posteriori evidence for a priori reason. Asked in the public courtroom how he began to suspect Larsan, Rouletabille responds: "'My mind's better side [*le bon bout de ma raison*]' had clued me in . . . ; so I was keeping my eye on him; . . . Yes, yes, my mind's clever side had shown me! But I needed tangible proof; you might say I needed to see it with my eyes after seeing it with my mind!" (252). The mental eye, figured through Rouletabille's famously quirky "bon bout de la raison," precedes and determines the parameters within which the physical eye will be used. Empirical evidence in this method can only confirm what has already been established by deductive reasoning, as when the *binocle* and the Sûreté's record of Larsan's farsightedness corroborate Rouletabille's thesis: "So you see, sir," explains the young journalist, "what my approach is, . . . I don't ask external signs to lead me to the truth; I merely ask them not to contradict the truth that my mind's better side has told me!" (256).

Indeed, with its reproduction of schematic maps and its presentation of mystery as mathematical "rebus" or "problem" (2), *Le Mystère de la chambre jaune* promotes a purely deductive method, in which the "traces sensibles [tangible traces]" of a crime must enter a posteriori into the boundaries of a conceptual "circle" that Rouletabille has "drawn" between the two "bumps" on his forehead (171). That this method is championed against a more empirical method is made clear by Rouletabille's insistent disdain for Larsan; while he relies on his "bon bout de la raison," Larsan "leans on his cane," the cane that signals infirmity and criminality (it hides his tell-tale hand wound) as well as overreliance on the material world (171).

Rouletabille's clear distinction between an "esprit logique" [logical mind] and an "esprit observateur" [observing mind] (275) fits well with Carlo Ginzburg's claim that the nineteenth century witnessed a paradigmatic tension between two epistemological models. The first, which Ginzburg (following Paul Feyerabend) calls "Galilean," is characterized by physico-mathematical methods that emphasize abstract thought over the material data accessible to the senses.[17] The second, "evidential," or "conjectural" method, is based on observation and the (Cuvier-like) reconstruction of truth based on material traces, symptoms, and clues (96). In *Le Mystère de la chambre jaune*, we find each of these paradigms embodied by an investigator: the "Galilean" Rouletabille subordinates material evidence to a priori reasoning, while the "conjectural" Larsan promotes a reliance on observation and physical clues. In an initial standoff, Larsan accuses Rouletabille of moving directly to conjecture without stopping to observe the evidence; "you're thinking too much" (79), he says, and reacts to one of Rouletabille's (correct) hypotheses with the double exclamation, "lack of observation! . . . lack of observation!" (80).

The visual aspect of this dual epistemology becomes evident if we read Leroux's novel in conjunction with Ginzburg's essay. Larsan, in the novel, had recently risen to great heights on the reputation of his police work; meanwhile his emphasis on observation aligns him with the "conjectural" paradigm that Ginzburg defines as newly dominant in the late nineteenth century. "Sight," writes Ginzburg, "became the privileged function of those disciplines excluded from the suprasensorial eye of mathematics," that is, of the general humanities (113). Validating "insights" that "originated in concrete experience," the conjectural method allowed one to move inductively from what one sees to what one knows (115). By contrast, the Galilean method relied on a conceptual rather than physiological "vision": "only a metaphorical relationship existed between the disembodied 'characters' read by Galileo in the book of nature through the eyes of the brain" (111). Rouletabille, too, privileges the "eyes of the brain" when he allows himself to observe the physical evidence of the crime only "after seeing it with my mind!" (252).

Rouletabille represents, then, a resistance to the newly dominant paradigm of evidential, observation-based logic. By disrupting Larsan's plan and discrediting his method, Rouletabille "fixes" the problems that Ginzburg describes as inherent in the evidentiary paradigm: "its limitation—the inability to make use of the powerful and terrible weapon of abstraction" (115). In a way, *Le Mystère de la chambre jaune* can be read as a long *apologia* of abstraction, and Rouletabille as a conservative hero whose youth belies an attachment to traditional conceptions of truth and how to obtain it. Since Larsan's defense of "observation" belongs to a campaign of criminal deflection, his conjectural paradigm must be taken as tainted. Rouletabille, though not invested in the police work of containment (he purposely allows Larsan to escape punishment), wants to expose the necessary truth of Larsan's guilt and double identity as American criminal and French investigator. Moreover, Rouletabille's philosophical conservatism manifests itself in disdain for the very fluidity of Larsan's identity, a fluidity that Ginzburg ascribes to modernity: with the emergence of new capitalist methods of production and rising population in large European cities, writes Ginzburg, "to cover one's tracks and reemerge with a new identity was child's play" (119). If tracks—whether observed empirically or covered over as symptoms—signal a forward-looking epistemology, Rouletabille's "mathematical idea" (140) represents a backward-thinking epistemology of the mind over the eye.

By distinguishing between two different forms of rational investigation, Ginzburg allows us to add some precision to Geoffrey Hartman's intuition that the detective genre reveals its essentially conservative cast through the containment of the irrational by the rational.[18] But of course, the "rational" can proceed in more than one way: deductively or inductively, from a priori reason or empirical observation. For Ginzburg, the detective genre embodies the latter, Cuvierian and conjectural, paradigm; its success aligned with, even ensured, the ascension of an empiricist epistemology and the "discarding [of] the Galilean model" (115–17). Ginzburg cites Gaboriau's Monsieur Lecoq, "feverishly crossing an expanse of earth, covered with snow" in pursuit of a criminal's tracks, as indicative of the way Poe's, Gaboriau's, and Conan Doyle's detectives share an epistemology with the "conjectural" or "semiotic" sciences of physiognomy and paleontology (118). But Leroux's young investigator, on the other hand, promotes a different model of rationality. As we have seen, Rouletabille wants to distinguish his methods of reasoning from the conjectural propensity "to analyze footprints," writes Ginzburg, "stars, feces, sputum, corneas, pulsations, snow-covered fields, or cigarette ashes" (118). Such attention to the base materiality of physical evidence goes against Rouletabille's sense of reason and propriety; he even goes so far as to admit feeling abject when he bends down over clues like a base and ordinary policeman: "I feel more contemptible, farther down the intelligence scale than the Sûreté agents imagined by modern novelists, agents who have learned their approach by reading books by Edgar Poe or Conan Doyle" (170). With its hero a reporter endowed with "esprit de raison" and its villain a detective bound by "esprit d'observation," *Le Mystère de la chambre jaune* bucks against its *roman policier* predecessors—and should be read, I propose, as a reactionary eddy against the ascension of evidentiary epistemology.

Part of the book's conservatism lies in Rouletabille's attribution of bestial or animal qualities to the typical detective's empiricist mode. The reporter reproaches Larsan for relying on his senses while claiming that he himself only deigns to consider "tangible tracks" if they fit into a preestablished "circle" of reason (170). There is a danger, it seems, in the senses not being anchored by the mind, as when Miss Stangerson goes mad from the shock of her attack: "it was noted that, even as her other senses were returning day by day, she was not recovering her sense of reason" (214).[19] By relying too heavily on his senses and on the observation of the material world, Larsan exposes his criminal nature; his "animal cogitation" is signaled by the doubly bent stature of the *presbyte* hunched over his writing-desk and the investigator hunched over the abject muck of footprints and material clues (170). Rouletabille disdains and resists the animalistic posture and methods of police work: "bent over, looking at the ground and the misleading tangible tracks, I suddenly straightened up, leaning on my mind's clever side, and went up the stairs into the hallway" to solve the mathematical mystery of the killer's apparent disappearance (252). Once again, Rouletabille's characterization meshes with Ginzburg's description of the conjectural method. Ginzburg, having pointed out the primitive roots of an epistemology based on observation, calls it a "low" method based on the senses, one that "binds the human animal closely to other animal species" (125). Rouletabille uses similar language when he states that though he is occasionally forced to search for "tracks" (only after having established a reasoned hypothesis), "I wish to make special note here of the fact that it is not my custom to attach too much importance to the external signs left in the wake of a crime." "This method," he adds, "which consists of deciding who the criminal is based on footprint tracks, is utterly primitive" (169).[20]

Though crime is its subject, *Le Mystère de la chambre jaune* tries to distance its hero from anything that might link the investigator's reason to the criminal mind. Like Vidocq, whose famous memoirs disseminated a "méthode empirique, pas déductive,"[21] Larsan entered the police force after years of criminal activity. The eighteen-year-old Rouletabille, on the other hand, approaches his mysteries as a tabula rasa, applying his two "bosses de la raison" [bumps of reason], rather than experience, to the problems to be solved. Rouletabille's method wins out in the end.

But does *Le Mystère de la chambre jaune* fully escape the epistemological "doublet" that Foucault ascribes to the nineteenth century, its continual reliance on both abstract reason and empiricist observation? No, for as Ginzburg writes, "the flexible rigor . . . of the conjectural paradigm seems impossible to suppress" (124). Although Rouletabille systematically distinguishes himself from, as Ginzburg puts it, "the physician, who hazarded diagnoses by placing his ear on wheezy chests or by sniffing at feces and tasting urine," he is not quite as pure in method as "the Galileian physicist professionally deaf to sounds and insensitive to tastes and odors" (108). After all, not only does he remain wedded to his faith in the accuracy of physiological vision, but Rouletabille also uses his keen sense of hearing and observation to cull useful information like the *presbytère* phrase or the nocturnal habits of the "green man." It is precisely what seems like trivial, minor details—a conversation overheard at a train station, the use of a cane by Larsan—that allows Rouletabille to pursue his investigation and that brings him closer than he admits to Ginzburg's "conjectural" paradigm.

But beyond the inevitable contamination of deductive by inductive method, the very sensationalistic nature of *Le Mystère de la chambre jaune* as narrative dilutes the purity of its avowed rationality. From his introduction as rising reporter star to his theatrical revelations in a public courtroom, complete with audience applause and swoons, Rouletabille appeals to a sensationalistic avidity that the narrator describes as intrinsic to the modern Parisian public. *Le Mystère de la chambre jaune* shares the typical narrative form of detective fiction, with its hermeneutical delays and serialization (Rouletabille will become Chéri-Bibi in future installments), so that even as a story, based as it is on a metonymical rather than metaphorical logic, it partakes in the "conjectural" mode; for, as Ginzburg puts it, "Perhaps the actual idea of narration (as distinct from charms, exorcisms, or invocation) may have originated in a hunting society, relating the experience of deciphering tracks" (103). Indeed, when the narrator presents his tale to the reader, he appeals not to our "mind's eye," but to our visual senses: a description provides "the atmosphere needed for the dramas about to unfold before the reader's eyes" (30), and the whole tale is introduced as both spectacle and sensation: "I am going to set before your eyes the problem of the 'Yellow Room,' as it was set before the eyes of the whole world shortly after the drama at the chateau of Glandier" (2). So that after all, even with his mathematical methods, what Rouletabille proves throughout the *Mystère de la chambre jaune*—and for the novel of inquiry in general—is that matter still matters.

Part III
Villiers, Verne, and Claretie: Toward a Fin-de-Siècle "Optogrammatology"

Chapter 8

Death and the Retina: *Claire Lenoir, L'Accusateur,* and *Les Frères Kip*

While the burgeoning detective genre strained to locate solutions to mystery in the ratiocinating mind, one literary topos at the fin de siècle proposed an astoundingly literal discovery of truth in the body—namely, in the retinal membrane of a corpse's eye. Recent scientific findings that images are photochemically imprinted in the eye directly inspired three French authors to imagine the dramatic implications to the recovery of those images. What if a corpse could reveal its own murderer's identity? Or, as a character in Jules Claretie's *L'Accusateur* puts it, "what if the final image seen, that of the murderer himself, were permanently fixed on the retina of his victim?" What might we learn by retrieving that image? How might our very bodily matter serve as witness and proof of what has been?

Villiers de l'Isle-Adam's fantastic philosophical tale *Claire Lenoir* (1867/1887), Jules Claretie's little-known detective story *L'Accusateur* (1897), and Jules Verne's science-fiction sea adventure *Les Frères Kip* (1902) answer these questions with varying degrees of fantastic imagination and philosophical reflection, but all three texts revolve around the conceit of the *optogram*: a photograph of a dead body's eye.

The simplest, Verne's *Les Frères Kip*, is the story of Harry Gibson, a sea captain who is stabbed to death by two of his men on a remote island in the tropical South Pacific. Two of his passengers, the titular Dutch Brothers Kip, are falsely accused of the murder and imprisoned, until the captain's son happens to look closely with a magnifying glass at an enlarged photograph of his dead father's eye. The retinal image he sees is blurry, but distinct enough to identify the faces of the two actual killers. In light of this new evidence, the brothers Kip are exculpated and set free.

In *L'Accusateur*, by Jules Claretie, a retired foreign consul is stabbed to death in his Paris apartment and the typically eccentric detective Monsieur Bernardet is called in to investigate. Bolstered by an amateur interest in optical science and photography, Bernardet convinces a magistrate to photograph the dissected retina of the murdered man's eye. The resulting image, reasons Bernardet, may well reveal the identity of the last person seen by the murder victim, presumably his killer. The detective's plan works up to a point: the photo reveals a hazy retinal image recognizable as the face of the victim's close friend, who is subsequently jailed and accused of the murder. But in fact the photo turns out to be a red herring, for the last image seen by the victim, Monsieur Rovère, had not been his murderer's face, but a portrait of his close friend (the man who would be thus unjustly accused). At the end of the novel, the truth is revealed—not by the optogram, as it is in *Les Frères Kip*, but by circumstance and confession.

Finally, the earliest and best known of the three texts is Villiers' fantastic and philosophical *Claire Lenoir.* In this tale, the unreliable eccentric Tribulat Bonhomet reports on his philosophical debates with the married couple Claire and Césaire Lenoir. Claire, who is blind, has had a secret affair with a naval officer. Claire's husband knows nothing about it until his untimely death, but he wreaks posthumous revenge on the adulterous couple by coming back in the form of a savage South Sea pirate who brutally murders his wife's lover. The story's fantastic dénouement finds Tribulat Bonhomet at Claire's deathbed, about a year later. After watching Claire die in a state of visionary horror, Bonhomet performs an unwieldy examination of her eyeball with an ophthalmoscope (not, one should note, a camera, as in the other two texts). Through the eyepiece of the ophthalmoscope—or as he calls it, the keyhole to infinity—Tribulat sees a horrifying retinal image: a vampiric savage holding high in triumph the bloody head of his victim, identifiable as Claire Lenoir's sea captain lover. This vision of Monsieur Lenoir's supernatural revenge shakes Tribulat's belief in materialism and the tale ends with a reflection on the impenetrable mysteries of death.

In all three of these fictions, then, the observation of a newly dead person's retina reveals the last image seen by that person, thereby apparently communicating to an observer the mysterious circumstances of the victim's death. Although the imaginative appeal of such a morbid conjunction of technology and revelation may seem self-evident, it is worth exploring its figural and philosophical effects. For the topos of the optogram in *L'Accusateur, Claire Lenoir,* and *Les Frères Kip* owes its resonance not only to the context of burgeoning photographic technology, but also—indeed, primarily—to the underlying scientific discovery of the retinal image as a site of troubled epistemology.

Here we have a material, visceral literalization of the long-standing *chambre obscure* metaphor for vision. By calling on the deepening details of optical physiology, optogram fiction has located knowledge, whether judicial or metaphysical, in bodily matter itself. Indeed, the optogram trope literalizes a nineteenth-century visual empiricism that locates data in the organ of perception rather than in the mind of the perceiver. This does not imply a simple "physiologization" of reality, however; on the contrary, studies of subjective vision open up, by the end of the century, a potentially radical *mise en question* of the objective reality of the material world. As the chapters in this section will reflect, the classic question of whether we see with our eyes or our minds is given a new valence at the fin de siècle by studies in psychopathology, in which the troubled perceptual boundaries of madmen, hysterics, and hypnotized subjects reveal the threatening horizon of "subjective vision," its loosening from the anchor of the physical world.

Indeed the theme of muddled boundaries may well serve as the key to understanding what made the optogram so compelling at this particular fin-de-siècle moment. For one thing, the 1880s and 1890s in France combined future-thinking positivism with revived interest in supernatural phenomena. While we now dissociate scientific progress from the spirit-rapping, table-tapping mysteries of the beyond, late nineteenth-century science rubbed elbows continuously with the occult: empiricism joined with magnetism, scientific method with arcane magic, technology with esoteric technique. As a motif that mediates between living knowledge and deathly mystery, the retinal optogram confirms Garrett Stewart's intuition about the nineteenth century: that it is an age where "science intersects art with particular urgency at the horizon of mortality."[1] Optical physiology gave a precise anatomical location, the retina, to the slipping point between life and death, the physical world and the beyond. As a fictional motif, the optogram preserves the fin-de-siècle nexus of science and spiritism by cutting across generic categories like naturalism (associated with positivism primarily through Zola's self-proclaimed affinity with Claude Bernard) and the fantastic (associated with anti-scientism through its otherworldly themes and decadent tropes). By reading Villiers, Verne, and Claretie together, this book proposes an "optogram moment" of troubled epistemology for fin-de-siècle France, characterized by an obsessive interest in the boundaries between subjectivity and objectivity, the self and the beyond.

Retinal Violet and the Photo in the Eye

One cannot study optogram fiction without considering the context of photographic technology, which crops up as a contemporary amateur craze in these stories of dead-eye images. In Verne's *Les Frères Kip*, the key identification of Captain Gibson's murderers comes about through his son's hobby: "During his free time, Nat Gibson was an avid practitioner of photography, this quickly evolving art"[2] Likewise, Claretie's *L'Accusateur* owes its central revelation to the detective Bernardet's laconically noted avocation: "Photography. His passion."[3] When praised for his keen spirit of observation, Bernardet modestly attributes it to "The photographer's eye [*coup d'œil*] . . . a knack with the Kodak!" (17). Even *Claire Lenoir*, first written in 1867, a moment not yet imbued with the casual familiarity of "a knack with the Kodak," alludes to the mechanics of photography when the walls of Claire's sick-room remind Tribulat Bonhomet of the metal plates "used in studios by Daguerre's worthy competitors."[4]

Naturally, the synchronism of French optogram fiction with the advent of photography has already inspired compelling commentary on these little-known texts.[5] It is important to keep in mind, however, that photographic logic takes on a particularly physiological cast in *Claire Lenoir*, *L'Accusateur*, and *Les Frères Kip*, stories whose plots revolve not so much around a photograph of the eye—or even the metaphor of the camera *as* an eye, but around a more literal conceit, the photo-graph *in* the eye.[6] The fictional optogram found its realist anchor in Franz Boll's 1876 discovery of retinal rhodopsin ("retinal violet" or "visual purple") and Willy Kühne's subsequent experiments on the eye's photochemistry—discoveries that became internationally known through mentions in both scientific and mass-circulation journals of the time.[7] It was Kühne who in 1877 first captured an "optogram" (a term first used to denote the retinal image itself and not a photograph taken to document it),[8] using a method both grisly and precise:

> An albino rabbit was fastened with its head facing a barred window. . . . The animal's head was covered for several minutes with a cloth to adapt its eyes to the dark, that is to let rhodopsin accumulate in its rods. Then the animal was exposed for three minutes to the light. It was immediately decapitated, the eye removed and cut open along the equator, and the rear half of the eyeball containing the retina laid in a solution of alum for fixation. The next day Kühne saw, printed upon the retina in bleached and unaltered rhodopsin, a picture of the window with the clear pattern of its bars.[9]

It should come as no surprise that such experiments on the eyes of newly dead rabbits and dogs and, occasionally, human cadavers fired the imagination of amateurs and fiction writers, for not only did they point to potential forensic uses, they also—I want to emphasize this—exposed camera photography as a technical double of what had always already been happening physiologically. They fundamentally and quite suddenly rendered more precise the centuries-old camera obscura analogy by showing how light actually imprints images on the eye's own "screen" or "plate," the retina. In terms of a purely historical study, one might see photographic advances and optical discoveries as running along parallel tracks of rapid acceleration in the late nineteenth century; but in the fictive imaginary of optogram stories, these tracks converge in complex and startling ways. To take a picture of an optogram, as Gibson and Bernardet do in *Les Frères Kip* and *L'Accusateur*, is to capture an image that has already been captured, to repeat—in *mise en abyme* manner—the photochemical process of a "print."

It is this doubling that allows Philippe Bonnefis, in his essay "Clair-obscur," to formulate the relation between photographic technology and physiological optics in Verne's novel as essentially specular: "The laws of vision overlap with . . . the principles of photography. A natural activity and a mimetic technique shed light on and fortify each other."[10] Moreover, continues Bonnefis, a third term is introduced by the fact that this reciprocal relation of representation is itself represented through the novel's fictional discourse:

> This reflection would be ideologically useful, since it kills two birds with one stone, proving vision through photography and photography through vision, if the reciprocity underpinning it were not, in turn, the subject of a representation. Indeed, the enlargement obtained through the process that J. Verne has just complicated beyond all measure is located at the intersection of two optical systems, one of which translates the other. The final test sends back to the image-taking device the image of its own operation, demonstrating in particular that the lens is like this eye whose befouled appearance transfigures stagnant water [*les eaux mortes*]. (19)

A triple *mimesis*, then, whose very functioning reveals the nontranslucence of representation—and of physiology. If the camera lens is muddied water, it is because the eye is literally a "mottled screen."[11] The very choice of that screen as central plot catalyst signals a break in the optogram fictions of Villiers, Verne, and Claretie from both realist reflection (mirror) and romantic transcendence (lamp or clear lens), positing instead a textuality figured as reciprocal refraction of the imaginary and the real.

Indeed, one may well hypothesize that mid-century science enabled fin-de-siècle fiction's uncanny bent by giving a specificity—even a color (violet)—to the age-old suspicion that the eye interacts with the world rather than merely transferring passively (and transparently) its images to the mind. At the most basic level, we find explicit allusions in optogram fictions to the science that enabled them, as in *Les Frères Kip*'s somewhat ponderous gloss on the image retrieved from Captain Gibson's dead eyeball:

> For some time now, ever since the peculiar ophthalmological experiments performed by ingenious scientists, observers of great talent, it has been demonstrated that external objects that produce an image on the eye's retina may remain there indefinitely. The organ of vision contains a particular substance, *retinal violet*, onto which these images become fixed. They can even be seen there, perfectly clearly, when the eye is removed after death and placed in an alum bath. (250, my emphasis)

The "particular substance," retinal violet, is invoked by Verne to anchor his story in the realm of scientific veracity. Villiers's cribbing of scientific language, on the other hand, does little to counteract his story's farfetchedness; when *Claire Lenoir*'s narrator, Tribulat Bonhomet, first encounters the optogram in the newspaper, it is sandwiched between a news scandal and a quack medical advertisement, reading thus:

> The Académie des Sciences in Paris recently confirmed the authenticity of an astonishing fact. It is evidently the case that animals used for our sustenance, such as sheep, cattle, lambs, horses, and cats, retain in their eyes, after the butcher's final blow, the imprint of the objects found under their dying gaze. It is a veritable *photograph* of paving stones, butcher stalls, gutters, and shadowy figures, which almost always include that of the man giving the blow. (43)

In the original report on which this passage is based, the image of a slaughterhouse appears only within one cow's eye;[12] Villiers's fanciful inclusion of cats in an expanded list of animals destined for human consumption hints at the irony that underlines his use of scientific discourse.

Claretie's *L'Accusateur*, meanwhile, goes into far more detail than either of the other two stories in its encyclopedic presentation of cases and documents related to the optogram. When asked to justify his request for a retinal photograph to be taken of the cadaver, Bernardet cites the historical precedents, including an 1860 American newspaper account of a murdered man's optogram, as well as the key scientific document from the Société de médecine légale in 1869, wherein a Dr. Vernois presents a "Photographie prise sur la rétine d'une femme assassinée le 14 juin 1848" (51–52).[13] After a brief debate with his superior officer Ginory about the Vernois photo's validity, Bernardet continues his overview, emphasizing Kühne's 1877 experiments with dogs and rabbits (56). There is no shying away from medical detail, as evidenced by the improbably well-informed Ginory's disputatious coda to Bernardet's account: "Well! Professor Kühne only managed to act upon the retina during the following experiment: subsequent to the death of dogs or rabbits, he removed the inner part of the eye, turned over the rear part, placed it under bright light, and placed a screen made of small iron strips between the light and the eye" (56).

Ginory's reluctance sends Bernardet, described throughout the novel as a *bibliophile*, to his book-cluttered study, where he pores over the many scientific journal articles devoted to optogram cases; passing a magnifying glass (*une loupe*) over documentary evidence, Bernardet brings the detective's tools to bear not on his murder victim's body, but on the scientific body of research that suggests a possible solution to the novel's mystery (or perhaps, in this positivist age, to *all* mystery) (69). I will not reproduce the entire scene, as it goes on for seven pages, but it is interesting to note that Claretie, through lighting details and the indirect narration of Bernardet's reactions, creates a sense of narrative suspense out of archival research, so that bibliophilia combines with the impulsive charge of the scoptophilic drive.[14] As though to highlight the epistemological desire underlying any detective's work, Claretie imbues Bernardet's study of recent scientific documents with the same dramatic and emotional suspense that we find in later scenes of tracking a criminal through the night streets of Paris. Moreover, the detective's motivated perusal of the scientific debate's documents allows Claretie to reanimate that debate in the fictional realm while reproducing directly the scientific hypotheses and technical language of ophthalmological treatises.

In a similar though more public mise-en-scène of the optogram debate, the narrator presents a discussion by doctors assembled around the body of the tale's victim at the morgue. Each physician puts in his skeptical two cents, as though this moment were crystallizing a quarter-century of scientific progress and hesitations. Finally, Bernardet acquires an accomplice in optimism, the young Danish doctor Erwin, who claims to have seen the image of a wolf's toothy maw in the eye of a man killed by the beast. Dr. Erwin's explanation for this amazing fact directs the discussion to the substance of retinal violet:

> in the retina, there is a red-colored substance, *retinal violet,* that can be acted upon by light. On the red background of this membrane, objects appear in white. And the image of them can be fixed. Mr. Edmond Perrier, professor at the Muséum d'histoire naturelle, reports . . . on an experiment he performed wherein, after removing an eye from a rabbit that had been placed in darkness, . . .—the eye is placed in a camera obscura in order to yield, on the retina, the image of a given object, a window for example, . . . by immediately immersing the eye in an alum solution, any decomposition of the retinal violet is prevented, and the window can be seen, fixed on the fundus of the eye. So this camera obscura we all have under our eyelashes, inside the eye socket, stores up images and can retain them, just as the gaze of my old great Dane, devoured by a wolf, retained the muzzle and teeth of the wild beast. And who knows? It may be possible to ask the eye of a dead man to give up the secret it saw when he was alive. (101–2)

The italicized emphasis on "retinal violet" is Claretie's, and it calls attention not only to the term's newly established legitimacy, but also to the key role played by this photochemical pigment in Erwin's impassioned defense of Bernardet's audacious plan. In this passage, the discovery of retinal violet not only anchors the *chambre noire* analogy of the eye, it is also precisely what opens up—rhetorically as well as experimentally—the astounding possibility of uncovering truth in a dead man's eye.

Metaphysical potentiality, in other words, is impelled by physiological fact. If I have been citing at length Claretie's direct discursive use of physiological optics, it is partly to reorient readings of optogram fiction toward the bodily side of the physiology/photography equation mentioned earlier—or at least to propose that the camera-eye analogy is motivated in the late nineteenth century not merely by an abstract technological mode, but more essentially by a new understanding of the primal, visceral workings of vision.

One need only read Claretie's description of the cadaver's surgical enucleation to see that the *chambre obscure* metaphor—which still retained for Balzac a transcendent abstraction—has, by century's end, been given a tactile and nervy materiality:

> what a masterpiece it was, this human eye, taken apart by the demonstrator, into the sclera, the transparent cornea, the aqueous humor, the crystalline humor, and the retina, which is like a Daguerre's plate of this camera obscura where, as the light rays move along it, perceived images are reflected upside-down. And Mr. Morin, holding the organ under study between his fingers, spoke of the membrane formed by the fibers and terminal elements of the optic nerve as an art and sculpture professor would have spoken of a jewel cut by Benvenuto. (106–7)

Anatomy is raised to the level of art, as the doctor's aesthetic admiration for the visual organ escalates into an enthusiastic—if rather graphic—paean to its constituent parts:

> Shaking the vitreous humor, which was running out like an egg white from the hyaloid membrane, Mr. Morin exclaimed, "It's the wonder of the human body, gentlemen! It's life itself, radiation, the thing that produces masterpieces, discoveries, gives man genius. We see here eight layers of fibers or nerve cells, granular or radiated, which start at the protective membrane and end at the limiting membrane; how astonishing they are, with their admirable design and these radiating fibers, these ramified processes, these rods and cones, these granules and filaments, these rods only a few thousands of a millimeter in diameter that are like the source of all light; an object made to elicit cries of admiration. (107)

Not all observers share in this connoisseur's enthusiasm; Bernardet, for example, is itching to leave the dissection room for the photo lab. But even negative reactions to the eye are rendered in visceral detail, so that the reader cannot forget the bodily origins of the optogram-photograph conceit. The nauseated Ginory, for example, glimpses the eyeball: "And this eye, like a glistening, flaccid, black-flecked ball, with its flat, cloudy crystalline humor, looked as though it was floating in the midst of an oily tissue of orbicular muscles or nerve pieces; and this inert thing, this glassy, lightless eyeball, was like a huge pupil looking back at life from the depths of death" (108). What both descriptions—the delighted and the disgusted—have in common is an expansive metaphysical rhetoric (source of light and genius, life in the depths of death, etc.) inextricable from the physicality of the eye: its nerves and fatty tissue, its fibers and crystalline cones.

While such flourishes may seem typical of a fiction writer's imaginative elaborations on the dry language of anatomy, the rhetorical difference between Claretie and his scientific sources is not as great as one might imagine. Indeed, flights of fanciful optimism about potential applications for the discovery of retinal violet were not limited to newspaper sensationalism; even the top scientific expert of physiological optics in France, Félix Giraud-Teulon, showed relatively little reserve in his 1881 discussion of these fecund anatomical studies: "We should hope for, rather than deny the possibility of, being able to one day recognize the final optograms inscribed onto a human retina, as we currently are attempting to discover them ophthalmoscopically on the living retina."[15] The optogram here literally bridges life and death, offering the possibility of retrieving a human's final percepts. While the tone of an earlier discussion of the persistence of retinal impressions (in *Physiologie et pathologie fonctionnelle de la vision binoculaire*, published in 1861) had been staid and somewhat arid, enthusiasm creeps into Giraud-Teulon's breakdown of optical anatomy in the comprehensive treatise *La Vision et ses anomalies* when he turns to Boll's discovery of retinal violet, the precise "seat" of the eye's long-suspected photochemical properties: "It is widely known that, in early 1877, science benefited from a veritable revelation concerning the retina's innermost constitution and operation. Professor Boll, at the University of Rome, had just recognized and demonstrated that retinal images were not mere physical, vibrational effects, directly transmitted from light waves to primitive nerve elements, but were actual photographic images involving prior alteration to the tissue; in other words, a chemical action" (272). A "veritable revelation" that is also a veritable revolution, for Boll's discovery fundamentally changed the way visual relations between subject and world are understood.

As I demonstrated in an earlier chapter on Balzac, the phenomenon of the afterimage had particularly captured the imagination of empiricist thinkers in the nineteenth century by calling into question the distinction between objective and subjective vision: after all, the perceived image exists outside our bodies, but the afterimage it produces can no longer be understood to have an immediate cause or referent in the objective world. Somehow, the bodily eye has interacted with an external stimulus to produce its own interior, blurred, and spectral image. The question of where the afterimage originates, in the objective world or in the observer's organ of sight, tapped into the larger question of where one locates knowledge outside of or within the perceiving subject, while its haziness underscores the uncertain status of entoptic phenomena. As supplement or trace "left over" from the primary, mimetic image-making system, the afterimage troubles the dichotomies of world/self, object/subject, known/unknown (in a way localizing, temporally and spatially, the broader Derridean sense of representational *supplément*).

It was the study of afterimages that led to Boll's discovery of retinal violet, the layer of reddish-violet pigmentation on the back surface of the retina. The afterimage question was answered by Boll's discovery, but not in a way that gave priority to either side of the subject/object equation. In fact, the retinal membrane was now taken to be the very threshold between light and body. In a key formulation, Giraud-Teulon writes that retinal violet could now be understood to constitute "an unknown, unsuspected intermediary, [that] therefore makes its appearance between pure physics and physiology."[16] In other words, retinal violet embodies the threshold between objective world and subjective perception. What had theretofore been understood as two separate realms of scientific inquiry (and, by extension, two epistemological modes)—"pure physics" and "physiology," in Giraud-Teulon's formulation—could no longer be kept separate.

Giraud-Teulon's work, then, points to the discovery of retinal violet as an epistemological switchpoint—not, that is, as just one more incremental addition to the anatomical plate, nor merely as an analogy for the camera.[17] As a motivating trope for Verne, Claretie, and Villiers, the retina emerges as an embodied space of interaction (rather than static liminal barrier) for the mysteries of life and death, subject and world. It is not enough to imagine the retinal membrane as figural murky border between these dichotomous realms, for the word "between" can only inadequately express a relation that allows the physiological alteration of bodily tissue to unsettle the dichotomies themselves. We begin to get a sense of what is at stake when Claretie's fictional doctor holds up the eye's "limiting membrane," proclaiming, "what an object made to elicit cries of admiration!" (107). Admiration, yes, but anxiety as well, for while the discovery of retinal violet contributed to a positivist sense of untapped potential and progress, it also carried some unsettling, even uncanny, implications. In subsequent sections, I will discuss further the figural links between the science of retinal violet and the fictional discourse it informs—between morbid details of retinal experimentation and metaphysical musings on life and death, between the epistemological ambiguity of the retinal image and the hallucinatory logics of fin-de-siècle fiction, and between the retina's susceptibility to alteration and thematic signs of unease about borders, barriers, and limits for nation and self. For now, let us begin with Villiers' *Claire Lenoir,* a text that cannot be matched for its rich obsession with the eye as liminal site.

Claire Lenoir and the Purpled Windows of the Eye

From the *clair-obscur* embedded in its title, through its heroine's blindness, to the final, italicized words "ces Yeux" [*these Eyes*], the strange story of *Claire Lenoir* dwells in vision as the *unheimlich* home for Villiers's fictionalized feuds between materialism and idealism, science and the occult. The story's unreliable narrator, Tribulat Bonhomet, announces that "the Nose is the expression of man's ability to reason" (27), but of course the comedy of his physiognomical pronouncement lies in its reattribution of reason from the noblest sense to the basest—and quickly enough, Tribulat reorients us to his true passion: optics. A devotee of the eighteenth-century Italian microbiologist Spallanzani, Bonhomet is so enamored of the optical sciences that he happens to carry an ophthalmoscope in his pocket, handily present for the story's dénouement. Tribulat's pompous style threatens to render his obsession ridiculous, and we can only laugh at the priorities of this wannabe scientist, as he spends his inheritance on microscopic study:

> the spirit of *analysis*, of *magnification*, of *minute examination*, is the essence of my nature to such an extent that my enjoyment of life is entirely confined within the precise classification of tiny mealworms, . . . within the phenomenon of foreshortened horizons, which remain vast based on the proportions of the retina in which they are reflected! . . . Reality then becomes visionary—and I have the feeling that, microscope in hand, I'm heading straight into the domain of Dreams! (29)

The emphasis on minutiae renders Bonhomet's endeavors risible, but for all of its spoofery of scientific method, this passage establishes the centrality of optics in the story's nexus of positivist inquiry and metaphysical mystery. Most readers of Villiers rightly exempt from irony the passage's main point: that microscopic observation leads to visionary revelation. As Ross Chambers puts it in his article on the alliance of "scientific gaze" with "occult vision," *Claire Lenoir* allows science to become "a technique of second sight [*voyance*]"; there is a metaphysical audacity in Bonhomet's science that is not to be scoffed at, as it acts as the breach through which one passes from the material to the spiritual realm.[18] Indeed, it is *through* the field of optics and its machinery that Bonhomet becomes a visionary: "The optical instruments with which the scientific researcher arms himself—microscopes, telescopes, ophthalmoscopes . . . —endow him with an artificial gaze comparable to the sixth sense or inner eye used by all who know how to pass through the veil of appearances."[19] Villiers combines, in this story, the two modes of sight and vision so vigorously that their alliance pierces through the tale's irony. More significantly, the retina here is named as the very site of the spatial (proportional, perspectival) distortion that allows the limitless expanse of Infinity to interact with human finitude: "my enjoyment of life is entirely confined . . . within the phenomenon of foreshortened horizons, which remain vast based on the proportions of the retina in which they are reflected!" (29). Of course, Bonhomet is toeing, as usual, the line between comic self-delusion and metaphysical reflection, for his joy is "confined," a word that somewhat undermines his rhapsodic vision by calling attention to his amateur small-mindedness. But my point remains the same: that unlike a more abstracted Balzacian or Hugolian visionary moment, the slip from physical world to otherworldly is given by Villiers a precise anatomical location in the eye.

In fact, what *Claire Lenoir* may most have in common with other optogram fiction is its attention to anatomical detail. Despite Villiers's flair for the fantastic, the eye exists in this story not just as symbol of visionary expansion, but as a material organ organized by a complex and particular working logic. For example, the epigraph to part 3 of *Claire Lenoir,* a citation of Lysiane d'Aubelleyne, imagines an uncanny seer inhabiting our visual organ: "That which SEES, inside our eyes, keeps watch and lurks at the back *of our pupils of clay*" (40, my emphasis).[20] Clay is altered by dust in the description for which this epigraph seems to serve as preview: Claire Lenoir's loss of sight, as the heroine's pale green eyes—"her pupils—her large pupils!"—are damaged by a "burning, grit-laden wind" (40–41). Bodilyness continues to mark visuality in the section on Claire's eyeglasses, with its title both antiquated and poetic, "Azure-Toned Spectacles." Here, Bonhomet seems first astonished by Mme. Lenoir's blue lenses, then physically assaulted by what lies behind them. "See! See!" she says as she raises the eyeglasses to expose her (italicized and capitalized) "*Eyes*"; "They were so glassy-bright, so inward-looking, that her gaze was stone-cold; they were hurtful to behold" (47). Bonhomet's hyperbole literalizes the cliché of the "penetrating gaze," of Claire's "penetrating and inquisitorial pupils" (81), so effectively that when he claims, for example, that "like all tactful people, I have two eyes in the back of my head," the reader hesitates, begins to envision two ocular globes attached to the back of the strange man's head, before falling back onto the less fanciful, more figural sense of the phrase (50).[21] The reanimation of dead metaphors (or, in a Derridean sense, "white metaphors") in Bonhomet's language points both to his stylistic eccentricity (a trademark "galimatias" [gibberish], 67) and, in a way, to his very materialism, to his fervent (and soon-to-be-toppled) denials of a "beyond" to Matter. In debating Dr. Lenoir, Bonhomet fights superior intellect first with his own "philosophical hodgepodge"; but when he cannot "éblouir" the doctor with the razzle-dazzle of disjointed language and vague anti-Hegelianism, he resorts to a literal "éblouissement" [dazzlement/blinding]—of Lenoir's eyes: "And to fully confuse the good doctor, I flashed the facets of my diamond at his eyes" (67). An amusing gesture, the "hah!" of the jester at the end of his tricks, but also an attempt to alter the doctor's ideas through an alteration of his matter, as though Bonhomet expects to induce a state of stupor like the one that Flaubert's Pécuchet endures, in a similarly humorous scene of optical confusion, when the metal on his visor reflects the sun's rays into his eyes.[22] Bonhomet's diamond is designed to muddle Lenoir's sight—and thereby to resist his theories of spiritual/spiritualist vision. Eyes, for Bonhomet, must not be limpid pools, but "pupils of clay," clay-matter as real as the *bûche* (log) whose substantiality Lenoir tries to deny. And if—as turns out to be the case—an uncanny vision lurks within or behind the material eye, it is only by "looking into the matter" that Bonhomet will discover it.

Of course, the most obvious example of a physiological precision attributed to this slide from "scientific gaze" to "occult vision" is *Claire Lenoir*'s final scene, in which Bonhomet unlocks Infinity's *trou de serrure* (keyhole) not with a key, but with an ophthalmoscope. Claire Lenoir has just died, and after frantically searching through his handy-bag of instruments, Bonhomet first pulls out a magnifying glass, which allows him to verify her death; propelled by a commanding inner voice ("Look!"), he looks "*à la loupe*" [through the magnifying glass] at the "opacity covering her tenebrous pupils" and notices in her eye some curious "dots that looked like holes made by shadows" (116–17). In his desire to observe the eye (and its *shadows*) more closely, Bonhomet runs through and rejects two alternative scientific modes—an electrical jolt to the optical nerve and a chemical dilation of the pupil—before hitting on the solution that thrills him: he will use an ophthalmoscope.[23] As usual, the scene falls quickly into farce, with our foolish protagonist pulling Claire's body into a series of grotesque positions justified absurdly by appeals to the science of vision:

> Gritting my teeth a little, I took the corpse in my arms, . . . and stood it up against the wall beneath a large nail. I was going to support it with a rope passed under her armpits, suspended on the nail by its knotted ends. . . . But a thought came to me that changed my mind. *Whatever may have remained behind inside those eyes would appear upside-down to me, with the cavity behind the iris forming a camera obscura.* There was a way around this: . . . taking great care, I placed the body of Mme. Lenoir right back onto her deathbed, but put it there *crossways*,—so that her neck and head, facing up, projected out past the edge of the bed, as if suspended above the floor. (117–18, my emphasis)

Physiology of the eye has been invoked to absurd purpose: the question of the inverted retinal image, though a topic of discussion for Descartes and others, had been fully put to rest well before Villiers's time, so Bonhomet is both misusing and mischoosing his facts in this topsy-turvy scene. And with Bonhomet's use of the ophthalmoscope, Villiers' text continues to work on the double register of inflation and deflation, scientific impressiveness and buffoonish humor. Bonhomet's experiment is quite unwieldy: "I adjusted an enormous lens inside the lens holder opposite the reflector and prepared to direct the beam of light into the depths of Mme. Lenoir's eyes" (118). (This would be the equivalent today, I suppose, of bringing a bulky, newly outmoded MRI machine to one's bedroom at home.) Villiers emphasizes the instrument's awe-inspiring nature with theatrical hesitations as Bonhomet approaches the instrument, but in the end, the silliness gives way to the undeniable charge of the story's most famous line, the proclamation that sets the stage for the final, fantastic scene: "And I fixed my eye on the lighted opening. I thought that, alone among the living, I would be the first to peer into the Infinite *through the keyhole*" (119).

"Alone among the living," treading the mysterious entry to the other world, with ophthalmoscope in hand, Bonhomet looks into a human eye whose retina is given primordial status as the liminal membrane that opens up onto the infinite. Its profound liminality is not just a product of Bonhomet's—or Villiers's—febrile imagination, but had already started to define scientific understanding of the physiology of vision. For what Giraud-Teulon's exhaustive treatise tells us is that Boll's discovery of retinal violet radically changed the symbolic function of the retina.

From our perspective today, the optogram—that is, the photochemical image in the eye—might be taken as a literalization of the post-Lockean empiricist theory that knowledge is to be found within the organ of perception rather than through abstract deduction or external laws. This is a tempting interpretation, as it creates a sort of historical bridge between abstract idealism and phenomenology by tilting vision toward the experience of the observer, by grounding it, literally, in the bodily organ of vision. But as compelling as that diachronic interpretation might be, it does not reflect the scientific responses to retinal violet in the fin de siècle (well past the shift toward subjective vision that Jonathan Crary locates in 1830), which invest the retina with a more complex role: as noted above, the retinal membrane, rather than locating vision primarily in the body, creates a continual interchange of outside and inside, objective and subjective vision.[24]

Identified no longer as a transparent screen through which light rays pass to the brain, the retina has become less window than "frame," in the Derridean sense of *parergon*: through its liminal status and representational function—that is, by "printing" or "being imprinted with" (the agency is precisely at question) images—the retina confuses any stable sense of what constitutes the spatial limits of the human body.[25] As we have seen, the windowframe's strong light/dark contrast made it the typically evoked object in all discussions of afterimages—for the same reason it became central to Kühne's optogram experiments. In other words, not only is the retina not a transparent window; it actually reproduces (and alters) the negative-outline shape of a window, creating a specular relation between outer room and inner chamber.

With this in view, we can return with more historical and interpretive clarity to Bonhomet's postmortem examination of Claire Lenoir's body in the penultimate scene of *Claire Lenoir.* The attentive reader of this chapter may have noticed that in the passages I have cited thus far, both Verne and Claretie explicitly mention retinal violet, whereas Villiers does not refer to the *pourpre rétinien.* Since the first version of Villiers's tale was written in 1867, between the invention of the ophthalmoscope and the discovery of retinal violet, this apparent omission makes perfect sense. But in fact, although retinal violet itself is not mentioned in any scientific context in *Claire Lenoir,* Villiers' revised 1887 version of the tale intriguingly inserts into the scene of Bonhomet's ophthalmoscopic preparations of Claire's body scattered references to the color purple. The first addition comes right after the narrator has leaned down to look into the cadaver's eye:

> But after my first look into those eyes through the hole of the ophthalmoscope, I stepped back, not knowing—not wanting to know—what I had caught sight of! I stayed motionless for a moment; as for the ideas that then sprang to my mind, I believe that Hell itself has not reflected any more hair-raising. With a shudder I saw, *through the empurpled windowpanes,* the fireworks marking the national holiday explode over the exultant city in the distance, to the cheers of a bisexual multitude. (119, my emphasis)

A horror wends its way through this passage, following a strange path from the ophthalmoscope's hole to the hellish reflection of internal ideas, to the external lighting of fireworks outside of Claire's room's window.[26] From inside the eye but outside the (dead) body, to outside the eye but inside the mind, then jolted outside the mind into the room by what is outside the room . . . these confusing warps of an outside/inside boundary line seem governed by the logic of a purpled windowpane, itself a kind of exteriorized "retinal violet." Borders, vision, horror, and violet combine again, just after Bonhomet readies himself to "peer into the Infinite *through the keyhole,*" but before he gives a detailed description of the "tableau" in Claire's eye: "Then,—oh! It was the fright of my life, the vision that changed the world into a tomb for me, that ushered Madness into my soul!—As I examined this dead woman's eyes, *I first saw, distinctly, the border of violet paper running along the top of the wall.* And, inside this frame, thus reflected, I saw a tableau that no language . . . could ever express" (120, my emphasis). The "border of violet paper" becomes both literal and narrative *frame* to the uncanny and spectral vision that will dominate the final pages of the story. As with the fireworks passage, the violet border here constantly troubles inside/outside distinctions: it is outside Claire's body (as wallpaper of her room), but inside her eye (as afterimage), while impossibly framing the strange vision seen by Bonhomet.

Like retinal violet, the purple fireworks outside Claire's window and the violet border to her wallpaper both inhabit and create an uncanny specular space between the room (*chambre*) of a hotel and the chamber of the eye.

Claire Lenoir's room has been read as a figural evocation of the occult workings of light and dark in the camera obscura of photographic technique. Daniel Grojnowski, for example, writes, "This 'border of violet paper' represents, in negative fashion, the background upon which the apparition is imprinted. We should recall that Claire's room had been repainted in a 'silvery white' reminiscent of metal plates."[27] And Bonnefis cites Villiers's reference to Daguerre in order to trace, dazzlingly, a slide in Villiers' text from *chambre noire* to *chambre claire*, connecting the "photographic operation" of Claire's chamber to Gautier 's "camera obscura of dreams."[28] But neither Bonnefis nor Grojnowski remarks on the specificity of color in the "empurpled windowpanes" and "violet border" that creates an implicit link to the very substance that motivates the camera obscura analogy. Villiers' use of retinal violet is more subtle, more figurally daring than the irony-free allusions in Verne and Claretie, but in all three stories, the retina articulates and embodies the unsettling effects of the border-space.

If I have tried in this chapter to reorient readings of *Claire Lenoir, L'Accusateur,* and *Les Frères Kip* from the externalized, mediated camera obscura of photographic technology to the internal, bodily chamber of the eye, it is because I want to reverse the terms of an analogy: the retina is not interesting because it is like a camera; rather, photographic technique compels and motivates both fictional and nonfictional discourse because it reproduces what is already happening within our very bodies. In other words, the many sorts of epistemological ambivalences that we find in discussions of early photography—the liminal life/death status, the temporal instability of a fixed image, the ambiguity of indexical relations to a referent—are already in place in the human eye. Nineteenth-century discourses of physiological optics allow us to understand that optogram fiction expresses a forceful anxiety about the porous relations between body and world. As a liminal site of knowing (think of Bonhomet's step back, "not knowing—not wanting to know—what I had caught sight of!"), the retina embodies an epistemology of desire and hesitation, of progress and mystery, that constitutes a particular characteristic of the fin-de-siècle moment and its new fictional genres.

Temporality and the Optical Threshold

Like many of its contemporary texts, *L'Accusateur* signals a self-awareness of being poised at a temporal threshold: "Today's dream, tomorrow's reality!"[29] Published three years before the end of the nineteenth century, Claretie's novel defines its own moment as the fulcrum point between ignorance and illumination. Bernardet's musings on the application of photography to criminal justice, for example, compare past hesitancy to the exciting and unknown advances of the future (79).[30] More than just generally reflecting the progressivist optimism of the moment, though, *L'Accusateur* situates its future-oriented manifestoes squarely and specifically in the realm of visuality:

> But look at the progress made in photography over the past twenty-six years! What advances! What intense beams of light cast onto the infinite, the unknowable, the mysterious! The human skeleton seen through the flesh! The movement of a crowd captured as it passes and eternally fixed onto a ribbon that, when rotated, brings it back to life! The human voice, this soul of sorts, recorded for all time on a phonograph roll! Mystery dragged out into the full light of day! So many secrets turned into unremarkable realities! The invisible itself, the invisible, the occult, brought before the gaze of all humankind, like a theatrical performance.—We still don't know, Bernardet thought to himself, everything that a Kodak lens can reveal! (77–78)

Even the phonograph takes its place here among technological advancements of the visual—photography, early cinema, the X-ray—as a medium by which mystery is "dragged out into the full light of day." When it comes to the visual techniques themselves, the metaphor of progress—bringing the occult to light—joins with the actual optical effect: "the invisible . . . brought before the gaze of all humankind." To see what has been hidden, in other words, becomes both trope and content of fin-de-siècle progress. At one moment, the official corpse photographer in *L'Accusateur* expresses admiration at the potentially miraculous discovery of a murderer in the dead man's eye; Bernardet responds that this would be "No more improbable . . . than what we read in the papers: Edison plans to restore sight to the blind by acting on the retina with Rœntgen rays. There's a miracle for you!" (111). Miraculous, indeed, this update of the healing-the-blind parable through the application of X-ray technology; as the ultimate agents in a progressive rendering visible of the invisible, the rays would not only reveal inner workings of the human body to those who can see, but would "de-occult" vision itself for the formerly blind. As in Villiers's *L'Eve future, fiat lux* has been given both a temporal and a technological specificity in the secularized domain of human science.

Perhaps predictably, the promise of science, in the symbolically meaningful moment of a century's end, brings with it trepidation and concern about its proper role and future powers. Claretie emplots the potential misuse of technology by having the novel's central optogram misidentify the murdered man's killer; the photographic process itself has successfully revealed the face of the last man seen by Rovère, but the premise that this man must necessarily have been his killer proves faulty. Even after the confusion has been lifted and the wrongly accused man freed, Bernardet feels deep misgivings: "He had very nearly harmed an unlucky fellow instead of the guilty party by wielding a weapon, namely Dr. Bourion's famous discovery, which he, Bernardet, had taken to its logical conclusion; yes, it was the very same experiment performed on the eye of the dead man that resulted in this possibility of error.—So is man fallible, pondered the policeman, even in his most wondrous discoveries? A terrifying prospect!" (311) Optogram technology stands here for the very apex of human endeavor, but its execution makes possible alarming error.

Of course, scientific advancements (well into the twentieth and twenty-first centuries) always teeter in this way between inspiration and fallacy, but the optogram in particular captures the compulsions of late nineteenth-century thought both through its uncannily literal placement on the threshold of death and through its logic of interaction between light and darkness. Never before and never since the nineteenth-century fin de siècle has the *clair* of positivist scientific thought grappled so intimately with the *obscur* of occult mysteries.[31]

Much more explicit and polarized than the Bernardet/Ginory debates in *L'Accusateur* are *Claire Lenoir*'s battles between the rational, materialist Bonhomet and the Lenoirs, whose receptivity to the spiritual realm Bonhomet dismisses as "abracadabrant" follies. We all know that the crotchety pedant will get his comeuppance in the end, when he is forced to confront the shadowy unknowability of the occult *au-delà*. The optogram's fascination, in fact, may be traced to the fact that it functions centrally on *both* sides of the positivist/occult equation in *Claire Lenoir*. When Bonhomet first encounters the newspaper account of optogram technology, he responds with satisfied confidence in the power of positivist science to propel his century's progress (43). But the optogram beheld by Bonhomet in Claire's dead eye reveals the astounding, fundamental error of man's reliance on Reason. In the eye of another, Bonhomet's myopic scientism is exposed as blindness to the powers of the other world. Through the lens of the nineteenth century, science and mystery, progress and confusion collide in the space of the retina, where light rays meet chambered darkness.

"Lumière des siècles" and "siècle de lumières" is Claire's way of distinguishing between Bonhomet's positivist investment in nineteenth-century progress and her Christian belief in an Eternal God (85); her husband adds shadow to the mix, affirming his belief in the afterlife return of phantom voices "from the depths of the SHADOW" (90). What comes through in these discussions is a troubled temporality that haunts, as it were, the interplay of light and dark: the now of science, the always of the divine, and the before and after of death create crossings of time unclearly mapped onto figures of light and shadow. In all three of the stories considered here, the science of vision is enlisted in the narration of an eternal quest—the quest to recover knowledge from the mysterious realm of death.

As noted earlier, the other nineteenth-century technology most associated with such crossings of light and life, shadow and death, is photography.[32] But if, as Milner writes, "photography . . . remains the primary point of intersection between optics and temporality,"[33] I want to emphasize that this is even more true of photography *within* the eye than of its second-order technique, the camera. Already in the primal bodily chamber, the optogram creates a temporal gap, an overlapping lag, between the continual light/retina interaction and the fixed image of what the subject (or the subject's observer) can see.[34] Moreover, the observation of an optogram, whether through the lens of a camera or, as in *Claire Lenoir*, an ophthalmoscope, implies an unstable temporality located at the intersection of life and death (remember that retinal images cannot appear to an observer on a living eye, nor do they last more than a few seconds after death). While the universal morbidity of camera photography is, in the end, either metaphorical (every picture based on past presence and present absence) or belated (pictures of a dead corpse), the optogram literally inhabits the precise temporal moment of death. To put it in the bluntest of terms, in order to access the picture *in* an eye, a living being actually has to die! "[Y]es, there's cruelty in science," says Dr. Erwin in *L'Accusateur*, when he describes the process of excising an eye from a live rabbit to observe its retinal violet (102). He continues, in a passage I cited earlier, to describe the experimental process in terms of time-stoppage, of the halting of decomposition of the freshly killed organ, of the fixing of an image that allows for communication of a secret across the threshold of life and death: "by immediately immersing the eye in an alum solution, any decomposition of the retinal violet is prevented, and the window can be seen, fixed on the fundus of the eye. . . . And who knows? It may be possible to ask the eye of a dead man to give up the secret it saw when he was alive" (102). The scientific discourses and methods surrounding the retinal image thus carry already within them the motif of life/death liminality that later gets associated with technical (rather than bodily) photography. This is why I propose reading the scientific context not merely as cultural "substructure" to fictional flights of fancy in the writings of Villiers, Verne, and Claretie, but as integral shaper of the metaphorical nexus of time, light, and body that propels these literary texts. It may seem like a stretch to compare musings on the mysteries of death to the nonmetaphysical register of physiological optics (*oculistes occultistes*?), but as we can see in the works of Giraud-Teulon, Helmholtz, and others, the nineteenth-century discovery of retinal violet revealed a fundamentally ambiguous relation between temporality and light. For all of the studies on optical physiology, the precise clocking of the eye's photographic processes remained out of reach, thus inscribing mystery within the very fabric of science.

In both the field of physiological optics and our optogram fictions, what is at stake is the *fixing* of a fleeting image, the pinning down of a revelatory moment before it slips into an unknowable past. In Ginory's statement cited above, the external image of a window is fixed on the fundus of the eye by an anti-decomposing chemical, and indeed this interruption of passing time is what makes Boll's discovery so promising; from now on, we will be able to glimpse and freeze a moment in the continual interaction of light and the eye that constitutes vision. To fix an image from the past, to give it the incontrovertibility of material evidence is what also propels the *roman policier*'s interest in the optogram, in which the science of vision is enlisted in a juridical quest to retrieve knowledge. But if "fixing" an image creates epistemological possibility, it also carries the risks of timelessness: namely, the paralysis of death. In all three of the novels, themes of ocular witnessing are insistently associated with the term *fixité*—"yeux fixes," "regard fixe," and so on—as though to emphasize the optogram's unsettled position between the intensity of life and the morbid stiffness of a cadaver. When Captain Gibson is murdered in *Les Frères Kip*, for example, his eyes "fixed onto his killers for one last time" (97)—a hint to the reader of the "fixing" of their image taking place inside the eye; but the immobility also crosses over to the realm of the living as the cadaver's accusing gaze stiffens the very perpetrators of the murderous act (98). Similarly, in the following passage from *L'Accusateur*, an exchange between the eyes of a living man and dead man create a chiasmus (living fixity/dead animation) that underlines the paradox of propelling plot and discovery through an inert body: "the magistrate stood there at the corpse's feet and *gazed with a near-savage fixity* not at the open wound that Mr. Jacqulin des Aubrays had told him about, *but at those eyes, those fixed eyes, those eyes that no opacity had yet entered* and that, wide-open, terrifying, blazing with rage, threatening, somehow heavy with accusations, and quickened with vengeance, *met his gaze with an immobile, powerfully vigorous gaze of their own*" (62, my emphasis).

The physiological detail of these eyes "that no opacity had yet entered" both invokes scientific fact and plays with its parameters, for far too much time has passed since the murder for the judge to see clearly into the dead man's eyes; and, of course, the story's central autopsy occurs after an even less plausible delay. Still, Claretie emphasizes this particular post-death moment as a key window of opportunity for clearing up opaque mystery: "'The retina, which is highly translucent during life, quickly grows opaque after death,' said Vernois. 'Yes,' Bernardet added, 'but what if the image is taken between these two conditions!'" (77). Between translucence and opacity, between throbbing life and still death, only in that short moment of the in-between can knowledge be communicated across the final frontier. Despite discouraging setbacks, Bernardet reminds himself of the stakes involved in fixing the image within the dead man's eye: "I don't know! . . . I don't know! But the dead man knew, all right! And the Kodak knows, too! . . . It isn't subject to passion or rage. It takes things down, it reflects, it denounces—impassively, without hatred, because it has recorded what is transitory, fixed what is fleeting" [*fixé ce qui est fugitif*] (211).

Bernardet's phrase "fixé ce qui est fugitif" (in addition to condensing nicely criminality with temporality) points to what made the original discovery of the retinal optogram both promising and problematic. When the scientists Boll and Kühne began dissecting the eyes of dead animals in order to photograph the retinal image, they were stymied by its fleeting nature. As Giraud-Teulon puts it, "retinal violet is an extremely short-lived [*fugace*] property."[35] Lasting only seconds in its most brilliant stage of chemical alteration, the retinal layer of violet must be accessed immediately after the subject's death in order to be observed, for although the retinal image is initially caused by light, it is also destroyed by light and conserved by darkness.[36] This fact is what enables the photographic darkroom analogy. But more significant is the fact that death, or darkness, can halt both the living processes of vision and the post-death process of decomposition, so that there is a sort of intermediate death zone in which conservation of a still image is possible. This is the liminal moment, I suggest, that characterizes the fin-de-siècle mentality, one that strains toward a retrieval of a past understood to be passing, as the future symbolically approaches in the form of a new century. In a way, then, the novels metaphorize and meditate on their own epochal moment through the resonant figure of the optogram.[37] Through its refusal of clear boundaries between past, present, and future, the retinal image literalizes the temporality of overlap that defines the mythos of the fin de siècle as threshold moment.

Chapter 9

Optogram Fiction: Communication, Doubt, and the Fantastic

In his introduction to the 1881 treatise *La Vision et ses anomalies*, Félix Giraud-Teulon compares the laws of optics to the laws that regulate the transfer of knowledge from one subject's mind to another's: "The laws governing how daylight strikes our eye are less complicated but no more infallible than the laws governing how light from another person's thought enters one's mind and illuminates it."[1] Communicability—between world and subject as between other and self—is identified as the common "fault line," the area of ongoing fallibility. This is a rather unconfident tone to strike at the outset of a long scientific treatise on the "state of the art," but it echoes Helmholtz's similar avowal of limits to knowledge in physiological optics. As the scientific discourse of vision in the late nineteenth century confronts the occult, the mysterious, that which eludes the grasp of knowledge, the eye becomes the physical and metaphorical locus of communicability's promise as well as its limits—for how can another see what I see?

Like Giraud-Teulon, Helmholtz apparently takes the question of sight's communicability to be central in the study of vision, as he addresses it in the most cited theoretical section of his *Treatise on Physiological Optics*, "The Theory of the Sensations of Vision." Here, he proposes that *subjective* vision can exist even without the stimulus of *objective* light, as when mechanical stimulation of the eye (for example, that of a sudden blow) produces the sensation of light. Adds Helmholtz, "it may be pointed out here that when this happens in the dark, no trace of light in the injured eye can be seen by another person; no matter how strong the subjective flash may be. And it is impossible to discern any real object in the outside world by virtue of this subjective illumination of the dark field."[2] Helmholtz's denial of the transferability of subjective perception rests on the premise that vision can occur without light, but that *shared* vision cannot. For a visual percept to be communicated, there needs to be a "medium" between subject and observer. And this is where, I would argue, the optogram comes in: by the 1880s, the photochemical thesis has been proved by Boll's discovery, offering the needed link from solipsism to shared reality—the registration of light on the retinal membrane.

In other words, mechanically induced subjective perception may not be transferable, but once the photochemical reaction of the retina is understood, it opens up a whole new realm of communicability. The discovery of retinal violet literalized the analogy made in this section's epigraph, between laws of optics and laws of intersubjective communication. For it identified as physiologically traceable the steps between a subject's perception and an observer's eye. This is truly, as suggested earlier, a major breakthrough; previous physiologists had known that the retinal image is sent to the brain, but now it could also be communicated to another observer! For centuries, the eye had been compared to the camera obscura, but with the discovery of its photochemical processes, the *chambre noire* of the eye was no longer a purely hermetic chamber, a vault of secret and fleeting images trapped within the subject's incommunicable experience.

What does this scientific opening of a previously unknown passage between self and world imply for our study of fin-de-siècle fiction? For one thing, the idea that a subjective image can become objective reality creates a new epistemological mode based not on observation of external physical laws, but on a far more slippery grasp of the interactions between the self and the world. If the body can create its own reality, one may no longer discount the senses to get at an underlying, ideal, objective truth. Undoubtedly, this point had already been made by earlier empiricists, but there is a specificity to the retinal image's new epistemology (which posits a combined physiologico-physical order of truth) that resonates with the particular fin-de-siècle concerns of contact between science and the occult. For it is not only, as I will suggest in the following readings of Villiers, Verne, and Claretie, that fictionality itself becomes a question once the real/illusory divide gets blurred. It is also that these three authors, among others in late nineteenth-century Europe, found the discourse of optics compelling because the eye had become a site for the ever more porous relation between subjective and objective reality—as evidenced by the age's obsession with hallucinations, Mesmerism, hypnosis, and all manner of fantasmagoria. Empiricist theories of vision in the field of optics occupied an interesting and ultimately untenable position at this moment, straddling the divide between physiological subjectivity (which in its radical form, puts the knowledge of any reality into question) and the positivist myth of objective observation. This is the doubleness that drives *Claire Lenoir*, *L'Accusateur*, and *Les Frères Kip*, all stories in which the eye holds the key to the retrieval of knowledge from the realm of the unknown, but in which, too, the promise of communicability is always shadowed by its failure.

Les Frères Kip

Let us begin with Verne's story of seafaring adventurer and mercenary murder, for though its optogram conceit may appear to be a mere plot device, *Les Frères Kip* manages nonetheless to touch implicitly on some of the philosophical questions generated by the new science of sight. Even a sensationalistic tale meant for twelve-year-old boys cannot escape, it seems, the troubling implications of the retinal image.

Like many other Verne novels, *Les Frères Kip* confines its heroes and villains to a small, isolated space of boundary-crossing adventure, in this case the English brig *James-Cook,* captained by Harry Gibson with the help of his son, Nat. Out at sea, the men are often surrounded by "heavy mist" and "thick fog,"[3] language that establishes a current of visual and epistemological confusion: even aided by a *longue-vue,* the men cannot be sure they know what they are seeing. Nature reinforces the moral blindness of the Gibsons to the "ecueils" [snags] (in the sense of dangers, obstacles) of their ill-intentioned crew, the band of ne'er-do-wells led by the sinister pair Vin Mod and Flig Balt.

The protagonists' reliance on the very sense that is limited by the sea's optical effects is underlined when the crew of the *James-Cook* discover the shipwrecked brothers Kip. It is Nat Gibson who first thinks he can dimly make out a human shape as he surveys the hazy seas early one evening: "Since he was roughly a mile away, and sunset was just beginning to darken the horizon, he wondered if he might be mistaken. Was it a man that the dinghy's arrival had drawn to the shore? . . . Was he waving his arms to call for help? It was nearly impossible to tell for certain" (48). With his subjective perception fundamentally in question, Nat turns to his fellow sailors for objective verification, but they fail to discern a human shape ("I didn't see anything") and the young Gibson's vision is explained as possible illusion. A sailor named Hobbes, for example, suggests that a seal raising its head might well be mistaken, by the light of a sunset, for a man in the water.[4] Their questions continue, until the decision to wait until morning, at which point they will be able to scan the coast with a telescope. But the *longue-vue* is not what supplies visual certainty—and it is only in deep night that the men finally perceive a fire signal. To communicate with the shipwrecked men, they rely on auditory rather than visual communication as verification of presence: a volley of rifle shots. And in the morning, when a dense, vaporous fog, crossed by the early sun's rays, limits all vision, the men comfort themselves with the sound-communication with the castaways: "Even though the brig was still invisible, hadn't they heard and seen its signals during the night?" (53). Finally, the telescope allows them to distinguish the men, then the fog lifts and they see them with their naked eyes, but all this had to follow the long night of visual confusion and questioning of the very presence of other men—a mise-en-abyme for the story's entire structure of confusion and final revelation. The scene's signal-fires and fog will remind today's readers of Michel Serres, who tells us that "in Verne's writings, all of technology's strivings are grounded on means of communication" and its interruptions;[5] certainly here the telescope partakes of an epistemological crisis in which the extended and supplemented eye tries—largely unsuccessfully—to pierce through the fog, to communicate and receive knowledge across *écueils* of all sorts.

Almost every decisive plot change in this novel is preceded by the captain and crew peering through a telescope at a blurred image that may turn out to be anything from attacking pirates to mere flotsam and jetsam. Sun rays by day, darkness by night, even sea storms have blinding effects—"their eyes were dazzled by the flashing electrical discharges" (109)—and a catastrophic shipwreck is ascribed to atmospheric conditions of invisibility (62). And though visual uncertainty here is not explicitly linked to referential doubt either philosophically or linguistically, as in Villiers or Claretie, it does seem to rub elbows with fictive possibilities, as when the Kip brothers' account of their shipwreck ends and the narrator tells us that "of course, no one considered questioning its veracity" (64). Certainly, veracity and eye-witnessing will be central to the story's judicial plot, and darkness provides cover for the nefarious villains, who take advantage of the atmosphere of visual confusion by shooting at the captain under cover of fog and by planting false evidence. Optical blurrings usher in the very possibility of error in all its forms.

Though set in tropical seas, *Les Frères Kip* evokes in small measure the more dramatic visual disturbances typical of Verne's polar exploration novels.[6] In *Le Sphinx des glaces*, the blinding optical effects of the white polarscape give Jeorling the illusion of a shared subjective perception, as the visions of his predecessor are communicated to him in an unusual manner, both optic and psychic:

> Fog everywhere. . . even more mist was gathering . . . And it was then that I found myself in the grip of a kind of hallucination —one of those odd hallucinations that must have clouded the mind of Arthur Pym. . . . I thought that I was melting into his remarkable personality! . . . *I thought that I was at last seeing what he had seen! . . . This impenetrable fog was the curtain of mist drawn across the horizon before his maddened eyes*![7]

The thick curtain of fog both blocks the travelers' perception of their immediate real ("Not once did the curtain open before our gaze," adds Jeorling) and serves as metaphysical passage to the eyes of a madman. This passage echoes a topos that appears in both Villiers's and Claretie's optogram fiction: an optical *clair-obscur* that suggests the possible exteriorization of hallucinatory vision, a communication between seeing subjects that overshadows scientific observation with the supernatural troublings of the eye. This is not to say that science falls away, as Jeorling's repetition of "I was looking for. . ." gives his exploratory (mind-) trip the cast of an epistemological quest, similar to that of Captain Hatteras, who sets off to conquer the extreme endpoint of the human and geographical known. But in both cases, madness supplants reason—Hatteras goes insane as he nears the Pole—and the visual confusion of the polarscape (sky and snow melding into a horizonless, blinding white) makes its mark on the bodies and minds of its human explorers. Marie-Hélène Huet persuasively links such optical effects to the journal writing that constitutes the text of Verne's polar adventures; here, she discusses *Les Aventures du Capitaine Hatteras*:

> Writing has its price; while the trace of the *Forward* is immediately erased by the combined efforts of ice and sun, the text of the trip itself is painfully written onto the bodies of the travelers. To the same extent that nature remains untouched and that ice resists inscription, the bodies bear within themselves the marks of each degree that brings them closer to the pole. It's a disorder of vision that displays iridescent colors and exotic scenes. The optical illusions make up for the seascape's emptiness and produce lovely falsehoods; here, an oriental alley with its minarets and gothic arches; there, the ruins of an enormous city with its felled obelisks and palaces laid waste. The finest seascapes of the crossing are the result of this optical disorder, which degenerates into dizziness: "Here, our ears are unsound and our eyes see what is untrue," the doctor notes.[8]

Bodies and books carry their own fragile traces, blurred and intermittent as they are, back from the vast regions of perceptual error. With its emphasis on trace and inscription, Huet's reading usefully signals to us a Vernian interest in what gets left behind when the human body and mind enter the realm of shadow. In the polar tales, the textual inscriptions of written journals mirror the bodily marks of optical illusion, while in *Les Frères Kip*, the optogram reveals a literal inscription in the body of Harry Gibson of the dangers inherent in the exploration of another region of perceptual error: the sea.

What characterizes this particular inscription, the optogram, is its function as antidote to the visual uncertainty that runs as an undercurrent through the seas of *Les Frères Kip*. Before Captain Gibson's retinal image is discovered, conventional photography has been invoked in the courtroom as testimony against the brothers Kip. The photo provides what seems conclusive evidence as "preuve matérielle" and "indubitable" demonstration that a Malaysian kris was the murder weapon (153); and yet, it leads to the erroneous conviction of the innocent brothers Kip. But this first-order photography will give way to a truly conclusive document when Nat Gibson discovers, with the aid of a magnifying glass, the retinal photograph within the mechanical one: "Them!. . . them!" he cries, "my father's killers!" And at the back of Captain Gibson's eyes, on the enlarged retina, appeared the figures of Flig Balt and Vin Mod, in all of their ferocity!" (250). It is at this moment that Verne gives the scientific background of the phenomenon, the discovery of "retinal violet," and it is here, too, that clear vision can finally be invoked: Nat "took up a magnifying glass and distinctly saw and recognized the face" (251). Promising a higher order of verifiable truth than even photography, the optogram constitutes, according to the judge in the case, "material proof beyond dispute" (251). The new evidence leads to a "revision" of the Kip brothers' conviction: an overturned judgment, but also a "re-vision," a new optical image to supplant the previous, erroneous one.

As absolute guarantor of truth, the retinal image provides *Les Frères Kip* with an easy solution that restores, after Villiers's and Claretie's more ambivalent tales, the positivist promise of retinal violet's discovery. The optogram in Verne's novel seems not to carry the same uneasy implications for ambiguity and manipulation; if the tale has sailed through the visually unstable high seas, it ends on the ground of solid truth and clear optical evidence. And yet the shadow-realm cannot be conclusively eliminated, for, in good suspense-series form, Verne ends his tale not with the exculpation of the innocent, but with the mysterious presence of the guilty, not with clear knowledge but with an avowal of its absence. While one of the murderers has been killed, the other remains at large—"As for Vin Mod, he had reached one of the islands in the archipelago along with a few others, and no one knew what had become of him" (253). These final words of the text recall an earlier admission of the difficulty of tracking down the guilty criminals: "At that time, neither the boatswain nor Vin Mod was in Hobart-Town; how could anyone track them down now?" (199). "At that time," it is still difficult to pin down traces, to fix communication, to see, once and for all, what the other has seen.

L'Accusateur

As with *Les Frères Kip*, Claretie's *L'Accusateur* holds out the promise of indisputable optical evidence, but far more forcefully than Verne, Claretie troubles his representation of the optogram with the persistent theme of uncertain doubt—about what is real and what is not, what we can know and what we cannot, what can be communicated and what will always remain locked in the chambers of mystery.

The eyes in Claretie's tale are keepers of the truth: "the dead man's eyes have, on their retinas, the reflection of the last person seen by the killer before dying. They are still looking at it . . . and they hold onto it."[9] Knowledge lies encased in the body, ready to be extracted by the "savants" if they know where to look. The possibility of accessing the definitive image, of prying it from the locked vault of the optical chambers, thrills the hero, Bernardet, and propels Claretie's entire narrative, a detective story whose mystery and solution are both literally located inside, within the cadaver. To conduct an autopsy means to see for oneself, to see with one's own eyes; but here, in order to get at the truth, it is necessary to see into—and thereby through—the eyes of another. But of course what the dead man saw while living is now doubled by what he sees once dead, so that the eye both encapsulates an afterimage of the death scene and suggests to those of us still living the possible mysteries beyond our ken. The body lies "Stiff on its marble slab . . . , its fixed gaze peering out into infinity, into the once-unknowable, which it now knows," reminding Bernardet and his colleagues that the communication of knowledge back from and across the blurred and ultimate barrier of death is what is at stake in the photo of a dead man's eye (104).

The scientific discovery and new technology that make this communicability imaginable infuse Bernardet with palpable optimism, as he predicts with certainty that the opening of this optical vault will lead to definitive knowledge. It is quite fitting that what Max Milner calls the "incriminating device" of the optogram is applied to the *énigme policier*, for both *romans policiers* and *romans judiciaires* had turned frequently to the notion of ocular proof as a remedy for epistemological doubt.[10] In court, physical evidence rarely carried the undeniability of an eyewitness account, but what could one do with a dead witness? Now, with the possibility of exteriorizing sight, the cadaver itself could furnish ocular proof. The notion is so compelling that even the doubting judge Ginory eventually takes the photographed retinal image in *L'Accusateur* as absolute evidence of guilt. When he questions the suspect Dantin, Ginory holds the optogram as an irrefutable sign that Dantin had been at the victim's house at the time of his death. "You cannot deny it!" yells the infuriated Ginory, and when Dantin asks why not, the judge responds: "Because the vision—even if fleeting and unclear—remained on the retina, because this photograph, in which you recognized yourself, denounces you, denotes, if you will, your presence at the moment of death" (168).The image denounces and denotes, or rather, it denounces inasmuch as it denotes, for the photochemical imprint of the retina guarantees an indexical relation between the external world and a documented image. The optogram represents the judicial and epistemological ideal of a one-to-one correspondence between the crime and the trace it leaves behind, between the referent and the sign.

But as in Villiers, this ideal of one-to-one correspondence is continuously undermined in *L'Accusateur*—or to put it into the Serres-inflected terms of communication: static interferes. At the most literal level of plot, the retinal photograph leads to error, the imprisonment of an innocent man. The optogram causes so much epistemological confusion that even the accused Dantin, sure as he is of his own innocence, is forced to acknowledge an inexplicable resemblance between his own face and the image taken from his dead friend's eye. What Dantin, Ginory, and Bernardet do not know—that is, the true facts about the killer's identity and the source of Dantin's image—will come not from the material evidence of the optogram, but from the vagaries of chance, as Bernardet's *flânerie* allows him to stumble on both Dantin's portrait and the true killer himself. And so the optogram, Bernardet's main piece of evidence and the story's central motivation, becomes a red herring. As I have already noted, although *L'Accusateur* seems to herald with enthusiasm the practical applications of retinal photography to the fighting of crime, the story itself mitigates the optogram's promise by reflecting on the potential dangers of its misuse.

It is not, however, merely the misuses and misinterpretations of the image that render the optogram ambiguous, it is the image itself. From its first iterations in Heinrich Böll's laboratory on, the optogram has been haunted by the blurriness of the afterimage. When discussing the scientific precedents for the current case, Ginory points out that Dr. Vernois' photograph was "so unclear that no one saw in it what Bourion claimed to have seen there" (53). This is subjective perception in its essence, for two different people have seen two unlike things when observing the same image. In making his case, Bernardet can only have further recourse to subjective perspective, as he calls upon his own eye, extended by the magnifying glass, as confirming witness. Despite Dr. Vernois' inability to discern the optogram image, Bernardet affirms, he has been able to see it:

> I saw, yes, your honor, I saw with a magnifying glass [*une loupe*], while carefully studying the print submitted to the Société de médecine légale and reproduced in the Bulletin of Volume 1, Section 2, of 1870, I saw, noted, deciphered the image that Mr. Bourion had seen and that Mr. Vernois did not see. The print is indeed unclear! I grant you that it is scarcely readable! But there are cloudy mirrors that nevertheless reflect one's shadow, if not one's face. And I saw, saw, anyone would say that I saw, your honor, the specter of the murderer that the Vosges physician had seen and that had escaped the notice of the member of the Académie de médecine and the Conseil d'hygiène, the honorary physician at the Hôtel-Dieu, no less. (54–55)

Bernardet's testimony insistently emphasizes the act of seeing, as though repetition will invest the subjective perception with an authority usually reserved for objective fact. Indeed, the dispute becomes a question of which perceiving eye is invested with authority, as Ginory objects with a snicker that "following this logic, the famous physician's knowledge ceded to the provincial doctor's instinct and foresight, and it becomes too easy to declare that academicians are wrong and that independent physicians are right" (55). Bernardet's stubborn optimism comes from the fact that photographic technology has advanced in the intervening years, giving him the hope of a clearer result. But when his optogram is developed, it is just as blurred and hazy; when Bernardet and the magistrate peer at the photo's shadowy forms, they sound like men lost at sea: "But I don't see a thing! Some mist, some fog; then what?" (112).

The interpretation of the visual image becomes an exercise in learning how to see, as the viewers grope toward an interpretation of its shadowy, imprecise forms. More unsettling than interpretive error—drawing the wrong conclusions from a correct image—is the fact that the image itself may never resolve into clarity, that it may point not to knowledge but to fundamental doubt. Ginory offers step-by-step instructions on *how to see* the optogram image, echoing the Cheselden case and its implications of gradual sight. Claretie's story at large provides a similar narrative overcoming of visual/mental confusion. Let us recall that the young boy in Cheselden's case mistakes a painting of a house for a real, though miniature, house; as visual percept, the image can afford him no information on its status as reality or representation. Similarly, the face in *L'Accusateur*'s optogram registers an image, but the representational/ontological status of that image itself cannot be resolved through recourse to sight. For as Bernardet learns from the actual killer, Monsieur Rovère had turned to look at a painting of his friend's face at the moment of his death—and so it is a visual representation of Dantin that falsely suggests his presence at the victim's house. Long before Barthes's *La Chambre claire,* Claretie undermines the indexical function of (retinal) photography, its testimony to past presence, by interposing a mediating form of (painted) representation between living referent and optical sign. Already at one remove from its original referent (the real Dantin), the painted portrait offers a false solution to the story's enigma, while relocating truth from the scientific to the hazier aesthetic realm. Even after the story's satisfactory judicial conclusion (based on the killer's confession, Dantin is released), Bernardet must repeatedly turn to external authorities to confirm that the optogram had indeed registered a recognizable image. In the end, even though the optogram in Claretie's novel seems to have lived up to its fundamental promise of recording a real image (if not of a real referent), the story evades *resolution* in both senses of the term. *L'Accusateur* is typical of the detective genre in that it stages the momentary triumph of knowledge over epistemological doubt, but the shadowy tint of its central optogram conceit keeps it from fully eradicating mystery.

As though to indicate its affinity with the occult, *L'Accusateur* presents

Bernardet's actual discovery of truth not within the laboratory—or even the morgue, which had been described as the guarantor of objective inquiry ("Only there could a definitive, scientific examination be performed" 63)—but within a typically fin-de-siècle scene of fantasmagoria: the Cabaret du Squelette into which Bernardet has wandered during his Parisian peregrinations. Like the fantasmagoria discussed earlier in this book, Claretie's scene aligns lighting effects and optical illusion with the tropes of death to create an uncanny site of epistemological ambiguity. This intermediate zone, an urban bar decked out as morbid spectacle, sends its inhabitants on a voyage of continual alternation between life and death, light and shadow: as one enters the black-painted corridor, one first encounters pleasant scenes of *bals masqués*, gondola riders, serenades under balconies, couples in pastoral calm; but when the gaslights (mounted on tibias) go out, the painted scenes shift into sinister mode and rosy cheeks become ghastly skulls, velvet-clad limbs give way to skeleton bones (218–19).[11] Then the lights return and the clients regain their initial gaiety as they are guided by waiters in undertaker uniforms to their coffin-shaped tables and "poisonous" drinks. The alternation of light and shadow, celebration and morbid reflection does not rattle Bernardet, familiar as he is with the "macabre spectacle" of such "fantasmagoria": "Bernardet knew it well, and he knew the lighting effects, the clever projections by which the public was given the sinister illusion of a cadaver's decomposition within the narrow wooden coffin" (222). But even though the public "knows" that its senses are being deceived, the optical effects put the crowd into a state of cinematic suggestibility as it watches with nervous giggles, and it is the "jeu des lumières" [lighting effects] (227) that reveal to Bernardet the story's actual killer, who has been made nervous by the ocular evocation of death.

What I want to point out about the way this revelation occurs is that the fantasmagoric realm exists not in contrast to but in homologic parallel to optogrammatic science, for it repeats both its *clair-obscur* logic and its interrogation of an unmediated referent-sign bond. When Claretie describes Bernardet's discovery of the new suspect's face among the cabaret crowd, he does so in the same terms of visual emergence and hazy readability as Ginory had used when he showed the optogram to Dantin: "Out of the half-light where the spectators sat huddled together, the pallor of the unknown person came into view, creating a white patch" (224). Highlighting the fact that this is a gradual process of learning to see, of visual deciphering, is its identified location in the anatomical eye: "The officer's clear eyes [*prunelles claires*] were riveted on this face" (224). The logic of *clair-obscur* runs Claretie's narrative as much as it does Villiers', for as Bernardet watches his suspect, the fantasmagoric spectacle around them reverses through morbid parody the visual process of bringing a face into clarity; here, the spectacle of death takes it back into shadow, gradually decomposing its lines and contours into murky confusion (227).

The optogram, which raised questions in the field of optics about the interaction between objective reality and subjective perception, tilts the narrative toward the general epistemological problem of visual reality by evoking not only fantasmagoria but the same possibility that troubles Tribulat Bonhomet in *Claire Lenoir,* as we shall see: the reality of a madman's hallucinations. When *L'Accusateur*'s Danish doctor describes to Bernardet optogram accounts in the *Archives de Psychiatrie* and the *Annales d'Anthropologie Criminelle,* he reports an incredible fact: that an Englishman named Rogus had published in *Nature* the photographed reproduction of "the image of a postage stamp, stared at intently, on the retina of a madman." He continues:

> But there's more. Professor Ottolonghi claims that we may eventually be able to photograph thought. Don't laugh. *Psychophotography* already exists as a name, if not as a reality. The famous Lombroso . . . did not immediately reject this notion of psychic photography. He attempted to photograph, in the eyes of a madman, the vision that obsessed this poor unfortunate. In his delirium, the man believed he was being chased by a tiger. He saw the tiger everywhere. Lombroso hoped to discover it by photographing it in this vision-beset gaze. The experiment failed, but who knows? Psychophotography may one day work miracles. (103)

The notion of psychophotography takes the optogram premise to its logical extreme. If the photochemical imprint can exteriorize subjective perception, and if subjective perception combines the psychic with the physiological, then images can be registered and communicated regardless of their origin (external stimulus or insane fantasy). For centuries, objective truth had been understood as existing in opposition to subjective perception; now a new order, one based on the objective verification of subjective truth, has unhinged the distinctions between essence and appearance, truth and error. The optogram has opened up a new, but anxiety-provoking, space of communicability, one that drives *L'Accusateur*'s entire plot.

Claire Lenoir

Claire Lenoir is, ultimately, a story about how to define reality. Tribulat's materialist definition—"What I see, what I feel, what I touch"[12]—is countered by both Claire's idealism—"The IDEA is therefore the highest form of Reality" (72)—and Dr. Lenoir's belief that "Reality" lies beyond the purview of the senses (64). In Tribulat's inimitable way, he recounts his role in these verbal disputes with pride, all the while letting his argumentative ineptitude shine through to undermine his materialist theses. Even Tribulat's beloved optical instruments are turned against his wide-eyed positivism, as Lenoir cites them as proof that man is condemned to perpetual error: "The first microscope we happen across will prove to us that our senses deceive us and that *we cannot* see things as they are" (64). Rather than extend, transparently, the powers of vision and comprehension of the world, the microscope for Lenoir opens up epistemological doubt. And although Bonhomet will stubbornly stick to his guns, later asserting, "I can conclude by affirming that, since I neither touch nor see ideas, I prefer to denote as real only that which is perceptible" (72), he is unsettled by Lenoir's attack on science, the senses, and his beloved mealworms, the microscopic beings whose new visibility had seemed to attest to a widening scope of human mastery. He is most taken aback by this startling parry by Lenoir: "So, . . . if the real is in fact what we see, I don't understand why the hallucinations of a madman can't be called realities."

This hypothesis about the reality status of visual hallucinations has rightly been taken seriously by readers of Villiers, not only because it foretokens the story's final scene, but because it apparently reflects the author's musings on the matter. Drougard's 1931 study asserts the likely influence of Brierre de Boismont's 1845 *Des hallucinations* on Villiers's thought;[13] as I will explore further in Chapter 11, the materiality of visual hallucination remained a living issue for both science and fiction throughout the latter half of the century. And Raitt, after having established Villiers' interest in the occult sciences, reminds us that *Claire Lenoir* has less to do, essentially, with spiritist mumbo-jumbo than with the idealist thesis at play in Lenoir's after-dinner debate, concluding, "The plot revolves primarily around the need to prove that visions have an objective reality."[14] For Jacques Noiray as well, the reality status of visual hallucinations represents *Claire Lenoir*'s "*idée-force*, its foundational theme," whose validity will be proven to both Bonhomet and the reader by the final ophthalmoscope scene.[15] Moreover, writes Noiray, it is as authorial spokesman that Césaire Lenoir proclaims, "The things seen by a visionary are, at heart, *material* for him in as real a sense as, for example, the Sun itself" (12). But before we jump too quickly to the conclusion (supported by the italicized word "material") that Villiers wants Claire's husband to prove the thesis that visions have objective reality, we should note the potential loophole in Lenoir's phrasing of "for him." As images of subjective perception, these *choses vues* may or may not be communicable to an outside observer. It is conceivable, in other words, that these images may exist as optical phenomena while still remaining within the enclosed chamber of one subject's mind-eye—and therefore that their "materiality" is subjective rather than objective.

The relevance of this point will become clearer if we look again at the twists and turns of Lenoir's postprandial debate with Bonhomet. The argument starts with a discussion of the visions not of a "visionary" but of a madman, as Bonhomet facetiously poses a question "on an issue of physiology": "have health officials who work in lunatic asylums ever thought of measuring, to an approximate extent, the degree of *reality* that their patients' hallucinations may have?" (64). If vision is matter, it must be quantifiable, goes the logic of Bonhomet's baiting question (and we might further note that by being posed under the sign of "physiologie," the question embeds its philosophical content in the structures of the body). Lenoir, with his superior intellect, undermines Bonhomet's logic while pretending to play into it, by forcing the bumbling narrator to recognize the limits of a materialist definition of reality; it is to Bonhomet's query that Lenoir replies with the phrase we have seen before: "*if* the real is in fact what we see, I don't understand why the hallucinations of a madman can't be called realities." I have italicized the "if" this time to emphasize the sometimes overlooked hypothetical structure of Lenoir's statement, for it relies on a rather large conditional designed to hoist Bonhomet on his own petard, rather than to make a particularly forceful case for the objective materiality of hallucinated images. And in fact Lenoir goes on to warn Bonhomet against the kind of solipsism that would come of projecting subjective perception or intuition onto the external world. In theological terms, this is put as the possibility of adoring oneself under the guise of adoring God, an act of narcissistic projection: "When I imagine God, I project my mind out as far away from myself as possible, . . . but it's still within my own mind; I never reach God. I don't get outside myself" (65). Extreme subjectivity (which in philosophical terms, Bonhomet points out, is called "objectivity") is then linked to hallucination: "Once outside the realm of what most people think, I'd be no better than a madman hallucinating heaven and earth" (66). Here, hallucination is associated with error, so that Lenoir seems to have backtracked away from the hypothesis of hallucinated images as real. It is only if we remember the *subjective* nature of that reality that the two statements jibe both with each other and with the Lenoirs' broader Hegelianism or "illusionnisme," which Raitt defines in subjective terms: "what a man thinks has actual existence for him alone."[16] For Lenoir, this subjective reality is not the ultimate one; it belongs still to the contingent world, beyond which lies the highest form of the real, the "Idea."

This still leaves some questions unresolved, especially when Claire's own visions are given material form at the tale's conclusion. Raitt, for example, points out that the final objectification of the reincarnated Lenoir as Ottysor is "hard to reconcile with Villiers's illusionism" (191); one might add to this the irony of the tale's need for *sensory* proof of Lenoir's thesis that the real exists beyond the deceptive senses. But before I turn more closely to the story's ending, let me add a point or two about

Lenoir's arguments cited above. For one thing, we should remember that Lenoir's ideas are presented in this playful text less as systematic treatise than as befuddlement for Bonhomet; despite the many pages that have been devoted to untangling Villiers's own thoughts from Claire's and Césaire's statements, most readers agree that that it would be untrue to Villiers's tone to insist on a coherency throughout. But while it is hard to know exactly when Lenoir is playing devil's advocate to Bonhomet's petty demon, we can still note a few characteristics that connect the fictional debate to broader contextual discourses beyond the explicit Hegelian allusions.

It is significant that the status of hallucinations is brought to bear so centrally on the question of Reality, for studies in pathology had recently brought them to the fore; furthermore, Lenoir's implicit connection between hallucination and subjective projection resonates with physiological debates of the time. Though we might now distinguish among the visions of a "visionary," a madman, and a normally sighted subject, the three lay along a continuum for Villiers and his contemporaries. It was not only people interested in psychic pathology or paranormal phenomena who studied hallucinations, but the scientists of the eye, physiologists and treatise writers for whom hallucinatory phenomena had as much to do with vision as did the anatomy of the eye. Madness may have been posed at the time as the extreme limit of subjectivity,[17] but already normally occurring visual phenomena (like afterimages, etc.) were opening up new epistemological ambivalences, so that visual perception could slide—as I see it doing in Lenoir's discussion—down the slippery slope to pure solipsism. A corollary to this point is that although Lenoir's point is that the essential "ideal real" exists beyond the contingencies of physics and physiology, his own philosophical musings follows the forms of reflection typical not only of Hegelians and metaphysicians, but also of physicians and physiologists. To put it simply, Lenoir's spiritualism, occultism, and idealism bring him to the same questions that defined studies in physiological optics from Descartes (whose suspicion of the senses Lenoir carries on) to Giraud-Teulon and Helmholtz (who devoted sections of their optical treatises to hallucinatory phenomena): that is, questions about the interrelations between spirit and body; about appearance versus essence; about the status of material properties like form, color, and weight; and about the role of subjective perception in the apprehension of the objective world.[18] And if befuddlement (Bonhomet's, the reader's) is part of the point in this debate, it is not only because of Villiers' story form, but because the very "optogrammatic" questions raised by *Claire Lenoir* are born of—and obsessed with—epistemological uncertainty, the impossibility of conclusive verification, and the possibility of communicability between subject and (human or supernatural) other.

This, of course, is why the end of *Claire Lenoir* is so unsettling. Certainly, the image that Bonhomet witnesses in Claire's eye is in itself horrifying: an open-mouthed, knife-wielding, rage-filled monster holding high the bloody head of Sir Henry Clifton. But the real horror is epistemological; it has to do with brains, not guts. The identification of the "Ottysor-vampire" as reincarnation of the vengeful husband Césaire Lenoir forces Bonhomet to acknowledge an otherworldly afterlife—but even this, the irruption of the supernatural into the world of the living, does less to trouble Bonhomet than do the violent disruptions of his beloved optical laws, his visual field of scientific comfort. In his earlier description of optical instruments, he had talked of "the phenomenon of foreshortened horizons, which remain vast based on the proportions of the retina in which they are reflected" (29), but here in Claire's eye, no boundaries or proportion are at play: "the horizon appeared limitless to me" (121). In his horrified reaction, Bonhomet tropes Science as woman, giving her one significant physical attribute: "Staggering, arms outstretched, quaking in fear like a child, I reeled backwards. My ability to reason fled from me; a jumble of dreadful conjectures sent me into a daze. . . . And Science, the smiling, *clear-eyed* old woman whose logic is a bit too *disinterested*, snickered in my ear, saying that she, too, was no more than a decoy for the Unknown that lies in wait for us" (121, my emphasis). Bonhomet drops his ophthalmoscope, that instrument of clear-eyed observation, in horror, as the irrational implications of the retinal image muddy and muddle the "clear eyes" of his materialist guide, Science. What shocks him the most is the physical impossibility of the image, its defiance of all rational laws of space and time: "But, in defiance of the old lies about Extension and Duration . . . the APPARITION had to be *actually* external, to some imponderable degree, *perhaps in the form of a living fluid,* in order to refract upon your seeing eyes [*voyantes prunelles*] as it did . . . !" (121). Extension and Duration are rendered obsolete as rational categories, as Bonhomet grasps still at a scientific explanation for the apparently necessary objective exteriority of the image. As answer to Lenoir and Bonhomet's initial debates on the reality of hallucinated images, this scene is far from conclusive, mostly because no matter how hard Bonhomet tries to reconcile the perceived image with the laws of refraction, he cannot, for what he sees in Claire's eye is multiply removed from any possible external referent. For one thing, Claire is blind, so her eye's physiological capacity for registering light is in question. Secondly, the image is hallucinated (the memory of a dream): a bloody murder scene that, if real, had taken place weeks earlier and thousands of miles away (by, moreover, an agent in his afterlife).

But while this is all understandable as Villiers's mise-en-scène of the undeniability of the uncanny and infinite mysteries of the beyond, with the supernatural as oppositional foil to science, what has not been adequately noted is that along with phenomena like hallucinations, the retinal afterimage itself had already opened up the passage between the known (clear-eyed science) and the unknowable (shadows of incommunicability).[19] Remember that the uncertain status of the retinal afterimage—that is, the fact that it is cut off from an immediate external referent—created the theoretical possibility of a self-producing, subjective reality with objective, physiological results. The central topos of the optogram, then, has just as much to do with Lenoir's musings on hallucination as it does with exposing the folly of Bonhomet's reliance on scientific technique; in other words, Villiers is not using the discourse of the optogram as mere strawman of materialist positivism, but as a motivating topos for a most radical questioning of the material relations between image and reality. Yes, the ophthalmoscope slips away from the newly aware Bonhomet (whose confrontation with the shadow-world reverses the usual trope of realization as newly clear sight), but as death veils Claire's eyes in the final words of the story, the italicized *Yeux* remind the reader that images and eyes—and images of/to/in the eye—remain the fulcrum for the entire tale's reflection on our knowledge about the real.

What's more, the optogrammatic disjunctions between image and external referent destabilize not only philosophical, but also narrative, realism. The separation of the retinal afterimage from a scientifically plausible referent is coupled in Villiers's text by a gleeful fictionality that breaks with realist convention from the start: Bonhomet introduces his story by saying that he need make no definitive claim to its veracity, "For even by admitting that the following facts are absolutely false, the mere idea that *they are possible at all* is just as terrifying as their demonstrated and acknowledged authenticity might be" (26, emphasis original). I find this audacious claim to have less to do with the fantastic genre's affinity with the supernatural than with an ironic extension of the very positivism that the story undermines; it finds its motor, its literal, physiological figure, in the optogrammatic disjunction of light and retina, cause and effect, external image and imprinted body. It has recently been argued that nineteenth-century discourse surrounding visual hallucinations opened up a narrative space between realism and the fantastic: citing Hippolyte Taine's 1870 concept of an antagonistic relation between sensation and image, Paolo Tortonese writes that "in the vista opened up by Taine, the distinction between a literature of realist representation and a literature of fantastic invention is lost. It disappears in the face of a new problematics and a new set of issues at stake, based on the image's growing ability to challenge the real on an equal footing."[20] Through its own destabilization of the relation between external world and subjective image, the optogram provides a literal, physiological location for this new visual epistemology and its narrative implications.

If Villiers's audacious fictionality in *Claire Lenoir* seems to break with the narrative contract of suspended disbelief, the very disjunction between truth and literary sign can be understood to have found its figural possibility in the epistemological ambivalence of the retinal image itself. Let me propose taking literally, then, Ernest Hello's statement, "The fantastic is not in the object, it is always in the eye."[21]

Chapter 10

Tropical Piercings: Nationalism, Atavism, and the Eye of the Corpse

a group of Polynesian pirates, the Ottysors, on the lookout for shipwrecks, hide there . . . awaiting their prey. . . . Behind him, he furtively sharpened a crude stone cutlass.

—Claire Lenoir *(104, 114)*

On the wall were paintings, china, and full sets of precious weapons, Japanese sabers or Malaysian kris. Bernardet gave them a quick glance as he passed by.

—L'Accusateur *(21)*

It was then that, under the lower bunk in this cabin, inside a drawer, [Vin Mod] found an object that Karl and Pieter Kip had overlooked. It was a Malaysian dagger, a saw-toothed kris, that had fallen into a gap between two disjointed planks.

—Les Frères Kip *(70)*

The Kris and the Optogram Fantastic

Beyond their central optogram motif, these three texts—Villiers's *Claire Lenoir*, Claretie's *L'Accusateur*, and Verne's *Les Frères Kip*—have something else striking in common: the theme of domestic space violently troubled by the invasion of foreign, exotic elements. In *Les Frères Kip*, the murder weapon that comes between English father and son is a Malaysian kris, and the scene of the crime is a tropical island near New Caledonia populated by suspicious primitives. The killer in Claretie's novel, identified by the foreign cut of his hat, hails from Buenos Aires, but has come to Paris to track down his victim, a former French ambassador; in the antechamber of the murdered man's salon, the detective Bernardet notes a Malaysian kris among a collection of exotica. And in the most troubling displacement of all, Claire Lenoir's European husband wreaks revenge on her seagoing lover by atavistically inhabiting the form of an "Ottysor," described as an exotic combination of primitive beast and Polynesian pirate. In short, all three of these novels figure the invasion by the Other of a known body through geographical dislocation—of weapons, hats, savages, and diplomats from across the South Seas.

This thematic convergence is made evident in the epigraphs above, in which a primitive Polynesian cutlass and the surprising intertextual detail of two Malaysian kris knives remind us that these are tales not only of metaphysical inquiry, judicial mystery, and scientific plot, but also of colonial crossings and bloody murder. Why a knife? I have discussed ways in which the retinal optogram blurs and crosses boundaries, creating an unstable relation between exterior and interior, world and self; let me further propose that the South Seas knives—instruments made for piercing, puncturing membranes, violating the contours of a bounded body—bring out the latent violence of a particular colonial moment, which is itself linked to a whole cluster of anxieties plaguing late nineteenth-century France.[1] One way to define this cluster is as what Françoise Gaillard has called the late nineteenth century's "hantise de l'autre en moi" [obsession with the other inside the self], its haunting fear of a foreign element's irruption into one's own (bodily, psychic, or even national) space. This is, after all, the moment in France when Louis Pasteur's microbiological studies and Alphonse Bertillon's criminal anthropometry have turned attention to the idea of containment, of the protection of a corporeal or domestic sphere from the external threat of invasion.[2] Irruption and invasion also served as metaphors for psychic and supernatural hauntings: pre-Freudian atavistic theories portrayed uncontrollable violent impulses as a threat to modern order, while Mesmerist dabblings in the occult posited the existence of otherworldly forces at work in the here and now.

But not only do tropes of irruption and invasion inhabit the historical discourse surrounding these texts; they also serve as metaphors for the *literary* mode that I will call the "optogram fantastic." Although Villiers's, Claretie's, and Verne's stories belong to different generic categories—fantastic tale, *roman policier*, and science-adventure fiction—in this fin-de-siècle moment of contaminated membranes we might do well to ignore such boundaries and suggest that if *Claire Lenoir*, *L'Accusateur*, and *Les Frères Kip* share the theme of violent encroachment on private space, they share as well a particular textual quality that has traditionally marked the category of the fantastic as "irruptive" in its very form. From Pierre-Georges Castex's classical definition of the fantastic genre as "abrupt intrusion of mystery into the context of real life," to Roger Caillois's statement that "The fantastic is characterized . . . by the irruption of the unthinkable within everyday, unvarying lawfulness," the genre's inherent ambiguities are figured as a piercing confrontation between two disjunctive spheres or planes.[3] The imaginary and the real, the irrational and the rational, the queer and the quotidian—these are not two balanced, parallel realms mediated by a static barrier, but clashing forces whose interpenetration results in the uncanniness of the fantastic. Writing about *Claire Lenoir,* Jacques Noiray proposes that "The ophthalmoscope . . . makes it possible to measure scientifically the irruption of a visionary reality into the universe of objective reality."[4] Indeed, in all three optogram fictions discussed here, optical technology blurs boundaries between two distinct realms (life and death, inside and outside) to reveal the uncanny gap created by their clashing.

Geographical Displacement and National Boundaries

In the epigraph above from *Les Frères Kip*, the Malaysian kris "had fallen into a gap between two disjointed planks," as though a space for the penetration or invasion by a foreign object had been opened up by the misalignment of two planes. The gap of wooden planks in the Dutch brothers' ship cabin, a gap that allows the interloper knife to be displaced to nefarious ends by the criminals Vin Mod and Flig Balt, repeats in miniature the much larger "gap" opened up by colonial exchange between nations. For in the South Seas setting of Verne's novel, the misalliance (the "disjointed planks") of distinct cultures creates an opening for savage encroachments on civilized, rational, national order.

Verne sets his tale in 1885, identifying the date as forty-six years after Great Britain's occupation of New South Wales and thirty-two years after the colonization of New Zealand, a place, he writes, devoured by gold fever and dangerously affected by the promiscuity of nations.[5] As Australians, Chinese, Americans, and Europeans descend like birds of prey on the rich territories, criminals driven by cross-boundary gold lust take advantage of an unpoliced space opened up by colonial expansion: the seas and the islands. Throughout the novel, in fact, oceanic territories, unmoored by single and stable national affiliation, are presented as a dangerous place of mixing, of unchecked circulation (open, like a post-Pasteurian body, to infection and contamination by blood-thirsty or gold-hungry visitors).[6]

It is noteworthy that colonial expansion, with its attendant clashes, provides a setting not only for the French optogram fictions I am primarily discussing, but also for Rudyard Kipling's 1891 short story "At the End of the Passage," in which a group of civil servants face death in a lonely Indian outpost of the British empire. This fin-de-siècle story, too, features an optogram: the photograph of a dead man's retina that may or may not reveal the terrifying circumstances of his death. But what is striking is the conjunction of colonial threat with optical boundaries, as one character (Mottram of the Indian Survey) complains that in this "tawny" land, he must continually "wash . . . my eyes to avoid ophthalmia, which I shall certainly get," and another civil servant (the engineer Hummil) suffers nightmarish visions that dissolve into "swimming specks within the eyeball" before literally inscribing themselves as death into his terrified eyes.[7]

Like Kipling's tale, Claretie's *L'Accusateur* links its optogram premise to the political scene: in both texts, the victim is a civil servant whose circulation in the expanded colonial sphere has rendered him vulnerable to attack.[8] Witnesses in Claretie's novel tinge their comments with xenophobic anxiety and distaste for colonial crossings, as, for example, when a suspect is described as follows:

> "Felt hat, tanned cheek, peculiar accent. From far away. Most likely a Spaniard."
> "Some beggar or other. Some poor bastard that the consul knew in America, the colonies, Lord knows where."
> "I don't like the looks of him," thought Moniche. (87–88)

But well before Kipling and Claretie, Villiers had combined the motif of the retinal afterimage with the theme of dangerous travel, in the particularly brutal murder of Sir Henry Clifton, naval officer and lover of Claire Lenoir. The ill-fated marine lieutenant is an *aventurier*, in both French senses, exploring the seas and engaging in adultery, itself a form of intrusion by a foreign body into a domestic sphere. Clifton is killed by the Ottysor-pirate-cum-avenging-husband in the island dunes of "extreme Oceania," at the latitude and longitude of the Marquesas, "ahead of the sinister group of the Pomotou Islands" (104). Given the violent outcomes of marine exploration for characters in Verne, Villiers, and Claretie, it becomes evident that the sea is coded as a site of confusion—not only perceptual, but also moral and territorial.

In the case of Jules Verne, it is perhaps his external perspective on British imperial rule that allows him free play with the colonial tropes of this moral and territorial confusion. One of *Les Frères Kip*'s two central villains is the Irishman Flig Balt, a dishonorable wanderer of suspect national allegiance. Seafaring in this novel is not a condemnable activity in and of itself—after all, the heroes (Gibson, Hawkins, and the Kips) represent upright participants in the international exchange of merchandise—but an unmoored wanderlust never fails to signal rogue intentions. While tavern-hopping criminals, for example, look forward to cutting ties with their origins, the "good guys" never forget their homeland. Pieter and Karl Kip, though brave and dedicated temporary citizens of the English sailing vessel, announce to the captain their ultimate desire to return to their homeland (64). Even after death, repatriation represents the way of honor: when Harry Gibson's postmortem photo is conveyed to his good friend Hawkins, the latter sends it to his native England as ritual service of respect (102). In other words, boundaries matter. And British imperial expansion disrespects traditional boundaries, geographical and political. The pro-Fenian excursus at the end of *Les Frères Kip,* invoked to distinguish honorable Irish rebels from the unsavory population of a Tasmanian prison, gives voice to Verne's support of self-rule, that is, of a nationalist resistance to cross-boundary incursions. It is as though each nation, for Verne, were a seed pod that, when opened (by a puncturing intruder-state), would disperse its bad seeds into the world to wreak havoc against the vulnerable organisms.

The patriotic chauvinism associated with British imperial rule allows criminal elements to take cover, as xenophobia guarantees that the first suspicions after a violent crime (in this case, Captain Gibson's murder) will be cast on the "indigènes" (144), who are understood as barely policeable and uncontained—"how could we find them in the midst of this Melanesian population, scattered from one end of the territory to the other?" (190). With the multiple crossings of nationalities, races, and motives enabled by maritime exchange, Flig Balt's sedition and deflection of blame find fertile ground in nationalist sentiment; for the citizens of Hobart-town, the guilt of the Dutch brothers Kip is overdetermined by "the egotism so often seen in the Saxon races," as Gibson's British identity is continually contrasted with that of the "foreigners" (172). The floating "Other," whether European or indigenous to the South Seas, becomes a repository in this novel for all sense of threat to civic order and moral rectitude; that both the Kips and the "natives" are innocent of crime may be Verne's undercurrent lesson to his twelve-year-old male readers (although, of course, his own exploitation of exotic tropes and seafaring titillations allows him both to invoke the glamour of imperial wanderlust and to warn of its dangers).

Moreover, geographical displacement in *Les Frères Kip* is marked by linguistic intermixing, as when Verne provides both European and native names for the tropical islands of the Pacific: "Dunedin is located along the southwest coast of the South Island, separated by Cook Strait from the North Island—in the native language, Tawai-Pounamou and Ika-na-Maoui, which make up New Zealand" (8). One might compare these linguistic borrowings, which mobilize an exoticizing anthropological discourse, with the stupefying babble of *Claire Lenoir*'s Tribulat Bonhomet, as he chats up the Lenoirs before dinner: "I spoke . . . about witch doctor sects in Africa that dance with lit sulphur sticks under their arms,—about the passport tattooed onto my back, which was given to me as a sign of esteem by Zoué-zoué-Anandésoué-Rakartapakoué-Boué-Anazenopati-Abdoulrakam-Penanntogômo V, king of the Honolulu and Moo-Loo-Loo islands."[9] Though mere afflatus, Bonhomet's invocation of savage sorcery and tongue-twisting foreignness in the calm of Claire Lenoir's staid salon presages the much more violent and intimate irruption that will end the tale. The comical disjunction between "Moo-Loo-Loo" and Hegelian philosophy points to a way in which Villiers' fictional universe differs from Verne's, for in *Claire Lenoir*, intercultural exchange is neither rational nor economic; it brings together completely separate spheres without the mediating space of the seas, without the space-time logic of human travel. Still, Bonhomet's tattooed passport introduces, in a symbolic register, the themes of circulation and foreign imprint that will motivate Verne's (and Kipling's and Claretie's) optogram fiction.

In Verne's text, the language of anthropological science is harnessed by the Europeans to describe Maori natives as physiological types; "this type of native having average height, mulatto complexion, a sturdy, muscular, and lithe build, with woolly hair, that generally makes up the common people among the Maoris" (22). As we shall see with Claretie, the fictional uses of physiological discourse of the 1880s and 1890s acquire a post-Balzacian inflection of surveillance and containment from the context of police anthropometry. *Les Frères Kip* follows this trend, as it takes visible traits as indicators not of inner essence or social standing (as in Balzac), but of racial type and character profile—as in this description of a Papuan native: "The native who had just come aboard embodied the distinctive type of this Papua-Malay race that occupies the coastal section of New Guinea: average height, stocky build, strong constitution, with a coarse, flat nose, a wide, thick-lipped mouth, angular features, rough, straight hair, skin of a light dirty-yellow color, and a physiognomy that, while insensitive, is not devoid of intelligence and even guile" (73). The ethnographic tone of cultural objectivity, however, can only be an ineffectual prophylactic, like the ring of coral that protects the islands "as an outer wall defends a fortified city" (45). Things—arrows, bullets, knives, foreignness—breach the bounded spaces of civilized life. As do people. The criminals Flig Balt and Vin Mod, who first "invaded" the ship under cover of falsified documentation, constantly penetrate the Kip Brothers' chambers, both on and off the ship. But what allows them to do so with such ease is the preexisting porosity of these spaces; when Vin Mod comes to the Kips' hotel room to plant the incriminating kris, he is aided by a window opening and his previous visual "invasions": "He entered the brothers' lodgings without even having to break a single windowpane, as the window had been left half-open [*entrouverte*]. He knew the room's layout well from having peered inside countless times, . . . into it, he slipped the papers, the piastres, and the dagger, then closed the window behind him" (137). As with the two "planks" in the epigraph above, a gap has already been opened in *Les Frères Kip*—opened by colonialism, by the promiscuity of nations and races, by xenophobic fears and linguistic incomprehension. Within this space, no chamber's membrane (and not least, that of the optical chamber) remains impervious to invasion by external forces. At this new moment of understanding that the external world actually imprints itself on—and modifies—the inner chamber of the eye, communication and exchange at the international level are fraught with anxieties about the cohesion and protection of the self.

Circulation and Infection Within the Punctured (Urban) Space

Jules Claretie's *L'Accusateur* is dedicated to Cesare Lombroso, the famous criminal anthropologist whose work influenced French fin-de-siècle thought on criminality, race, physiology, and hallucination.[10] And though Claretie's admiration for his dedicatee centers on an openmindedness regarding science and occult mysteries, it is the anthropometric side of Lombroso, with its fantasy of control of foreign and native elements through photography, categorization, and classification, that runs most explicitly in *L'Accusateur*. The police agent Bernardet brings the contemporary methods of "la police scientifique" to his own fictional investigation, as he studies, like Bertillon, the morphological traits in a photograph from the "service d'anthropométrie" with a view to find "not only an indication, but a detailed description" of his suspect's identity.[11] Claretie fuses anthropometric photography with optogram biology in order to urge the application of new technologies to the field of criminal justice. He catalogues at length, for example, the objects that may usefully be photographed in the service of criminal justice: suspects in and out of disguise, the shape and size of wounds, the weapons used in crime, the leaves of plants ingested in poisoning cases, the shape of the victim's clothing, the foot- and handprints left at the scene of the crime, the interior of a writer's study, the characteristic nervous tics of certain suspects, and, finally, body and bone fragments. The retinal photograph is presented as a natural extension of these now commonplace forensic procedures, in which "the *snapshot* nearly replaced the policeman's report" (79–80).

Of course, as we have seen, the optogram carries its own ambivalence, one that manages to cast a shadow on even this most positivist of applications, the Lombroso-type identification of criminals through the methods of Bertillon. When *L'Accusateur*'s judge Ginory lays eyes on Dantin (the initial suspect identified through resemblance to the optogram), he "reads" his features according to the physiological indicators of criminality, confirmed by the anthropometric service's measurements: hard eyes, bristly eyebrows, fierce-looking maxillaries, and a strangely protruding lower jaw all indicate a "latent brutality" (141–42). But Ginory's reading of the innocent Dantin's physical traits is wrong, so that the very methods of the *police scientifique* that fill Bernardet and Ginory with such confidence are susceptible to misapplication.[12] Still, when the true killer is discovered and booked for the crime, Claretie affords his readers a glamorous glimpse into the bureaucracies of contemporary criminal justice by typographically miming the official form of *signalement* as found at the actual *service anthropométrique.* Without identifying details, the list of categories is reproduced vertically in the novel's text:

Height (meter, centimeters)
Forehead:
Nose:
Eyes:
Mouth:
Chin:
Eyebrows:
Hair:
Face: (260)

The physical categorization of criminals by ethnic type was a primary mode of policing circulation within the city limits of Paris at the time of *L'Accusateur,* and though Claretie's novel is set in Paris rather than the high seas and Pacific islands, it has in common with *Les Frères Kip* the representation of xenophobic profiling and anxieties about the undetected circulation of invading bodies. In this case, the threat is to the civil order of an urban space, whose boundaries have been pierced in two directions: by the victim, whose diplomatic duties have taken him to the southern hemisphere; and by the killer, brought back, like a delayed virus, to the European continent. It is the killer's foreignness—though displaced from visage to accessory—that identifies him from the start, as a cooperative witness describes to Bernardet the stranger's only evident distinguishing trait: a sombrero. Bernardet hypothesizes from this fact that the man is a stranger: "His Spanish headgear showed that he had not had time to cast off the fashion of the country he came from, aimlessly seeking adventure" (214). The man must be an adventurer, a wanderer (Bernardet later adds the epithet "errant" to his description), unmoored and unfixed to his place of origin, like the criminals in *Les Frères Kip.* This makes him a threat within the very logic of the story's underlying motivation, the optogram technology that hopes to pin down, to fix once and for all, a fleeting image in the eye. When Bernardet finally sees the man at the Cabaret du Squelette, he is struck immediately by the tell-tale hat, but also by an optical fixity that signals, paradoxically, the wandering impulse that makes him a dangerous suspect: "His eye had a fixed gaze like that of pursuers of the unknown who scan the horizon, watch water flow, contemplate the sea, as if asking the infinite to set them onto good fortune [*bonne aventure*]" (222).[13]

This suspicious wanderer, named Charles Pradès, claims to have recently arrived from Australia but lets drop a reference to Buenos Aires, the city where the murder victim, Rovère, had filled a diplomatic post. As in *Les Frères Kip*, the southern hemisphere's new contacts with Europe touch off anxieties about circulation and exchange. Moreover, *L'Accusateur* shares with Verne's novel the displacement and condensation of criminal threat onto objects marked as foreign: objects of penetration, like the Malaysian kris or the "short-bladed Spanish knife" that Pradès carries in his pocket (244); objects of *signalement* for the surveilling eye, like the Spanish-style hat worn by Pradès; and objects that call attention to liminality, like the missing frame that ends up playing a central role in the story's plot. This frame, "encrusted with Mexican stones, cabochons of some kind that he [Rovère] had brought back from America long ago" (206), embodies an insertion of the foreign into domestic space, one that reverberates with meaning for Pradès as he, an intruder in Rovère's home, plunges his knife into the victim's body. As the murderer explains to Bernardet, he had become distracted by his victim's intense stare at a painted portrait on the wall, "a portrait surrounded by a type of storied frame in which Pradès thought he saw precious stones, pearls set inside the ornamental scrolls (he later learned that they were only attractive minerals in a sculpted frame that had been decorated by some goldsmith in the Argentine Republic and brought back from Buenos Aires)" (301–2). Motivated by both avarice and uneasy guilt (he senses the painted friend as witness of his misdeed), Pradès rips the portrait from his victim's hands, steals the frame, and sells the painting; this is what allows the painted "witness" to become a living red herring—the frame (a sort of fetish *parergon*), whose imported and inlaid stones mark exoticism, wealth, travel, all that made Rovère vulnerable to attack.

In her book *Membranes: Metaphors of Invasion in Nineteenth-Century Literature, Science, and Politics,* Laura Otis connects the policing of national and urban boundaries to the microbial theories propounded by Louis Pasteur and his contemporaries.

> As European nations incorporated more and more foreign territory into their empires, they opened themselves to new people, new cultures, and new diseases. Koch's and Cajal's scientific writings show how the new science of bacteriology in the 1880's is inseparable not only from the desire to conquer new territory but also from the fear that natives of these lands, in a quest for revenge, would ultimately infiltrate and infect the imperial "nerve centers."[14]

Although her book focuses on the Anglo-German context, Otis's characterization of a British "imperial immune system" can be productively applied to France. Christian Phéline tells us that in French thought of the 1880s, the racial classification systems of Bertillon and Tarde, with their attempts to visualize criminal threat through racial features, were understood as analogous to Pasteur's work; the containment of criminal "contagion" became a sort of "social macro-biology."[15] In the decades of Villiers', Claretie's, and Verne's optogram fiction, as Bruno Latour puts it in the English title of his book, France was "Pasteurized."[16] The "irruption of the microbe" created a sense of external threat and infection to the no-longer-integral body, but already hygienist concerns had localized life and death anxieties on the corporeal boundaries between outside and inside (17). The confluence of themes with those I have been discussing in optogram fiction should by now be obvious, but Claretie adds another implicit connection in an analogy used to describe Bernardet's avid study of Vernois' optogram research: the detective pores over the archival documents with "the zeal of a paleographer decoding a palimpsest or of a Pasteurian bent over his petri dish" (70). Here, the scientific desire to conquer new territory is combined not only with the theme of microbial irruption, but also—through the figure of paleographic palimpsest—with the theme of temporal irruption, a topos that equally haunts the "optogram fantastic."

Atavistic Hauntings: Irruptions of Past into Present

In *Jouvences sur Jules Verne,* Michel Serres writes: "The impure has only one meaning, and Pasteur makes us wash our hands with the fervor of Levites. The age of germs and disease recalls us to an archaic ritual."[17] At the risk of robbing Serres's statement of its evocative grace, let me point out its characterization of fin-de-siècle France as a place of modernity inhabited by ancient impulses. This paradigm holds sway not only in the realm of Pasteur and microbiology, but, as we saw in regard to the optogram's temporal disjunctions, in various forms of visual science as well. When a character in *Les Frères Kip* proclaims that "we're both possessed by the demon of photography," he is lightheartedly mocking his own modern technophilia while invoking the archaic trope of possession, of the loss of control associated with an invaded body (40). And it is, paradoxically, the very modernity of the fin-de-siècle moment that seems to awaken atavistic impulses, as Dr. Erwin of *L'Accusateur* implies in his description of the new century's threshold: "This is a time of miracles. But for them to come true, they must, like those found in primitive religions, be believed in consistently and forever" (310). Primitive faith, primitive rituals—and primitive savagery—crop up in the literary, scientific, and theoretical works of the late nineteenth century with notable frequency; from Zola's *La Bête humaine* to Morel's and Tarde's degeneration theories, the French stage is set for Freud's work in *Totem and Taboo* on the "phylogenetic fantasy" and primitivist reversions.

The idea of a savage impulse as threat to the modern civilized order rests upon the trope of xenophobia and criminality discussed in the previous section. Lombroso, for example, incorporated atavistic theories into his 1880s studies on violence, defining the criminal as "an atavistic creature who reproduces in his physical person the ferocious instincts of primitive man and of the lower animals."[18] According to his "recapitulation" thesis, both crime and insanity constitute brutal regressions to a primitive state, "humankind's simian ancestral past"; moreover, this state of regression characterizes entire "savage" races, primitive peoples understood as blocked in an anterior phase of biological progress.[19] In our optogram fictions, savage and foreign incursions of violence into the spaces of civility and civilization carry with them the threat of contagion, that is, the capacity to render modern European subjects brutal and bestial. When *L'Accusateur*'s "crime du boulevard" is discovered and announced in the Parisian press, crowds follow its details with avidity: "All of man's vulgar curiosity comes alive, as atavistic bestialities are spurred by the smell of blood" (85). The whiff of foreign-primitive contagion permeates *L'Accusateur*'s descriptions of its South American murderer, identified by a sombrero whose exotic cut transforms the man into something rather eerie: "a return of something from far away" (195). One hears echoes here of another fin-de-siècle text, Maupassant's *Le Horlà*, where that which possesses the narrator—ghost? demon? disease?—seems to have arrived by boat from South America, part of an "an epidemic madness from Rio." As the narrator explains, "'That' [*Le ça*] always comes from somewhere far away. But now it's inside me."[20] What Claretie's text suggests is that the "elsewhere" that haunts late nineteenth-century Europe is both spatial and temporal, for the "return from afar" responsible for the diplomat Rovère's brutal murder in a Parisian parlor refers both to a geographical displacement (South America to France) and an atavistic episode of primitive savagery in modern civilization.

Both suspects in *L'Accusateur* carry the physical markings of this double troubling of foreigness and pastness. Jacques Dantin, the murder victim's innocent friend, appears in the optogram image as a ghost, rising up from a past both personal (his own earlier youth) and civilizational (an earlier century): "A ghost, perhaps, but the ghost of a man who must still have been young and who, with his wedge-shaped beard, resembled some sixteenth-century rascal, like the phantom of a lord painted by Clouet" (111). The atavistic theme continues, as Dantin's resemblance to a nobleman of earlier epochs allows Bernardet to connect optogram image to painted portrait to the man himself: "This man . . . was like some nobleman from Henri III's time" (120); his beard and redingote give him "the undeniable appearance of a crafty fellow, a Clouet-era swordsman from Guise" (188). Might we take liberties with a vowel and hear "d'antan [yesteryear]" in Dantin? Certainly something is arising from the past, in this detective story, which, like so many mysteries, hinges on a haunting secret that connects a victim's former life with his present killer. If the innocent and honorable Dantin refuses to come his own defense, it is because he is guarding his friend's secret: an illegitimate daughter whose financial welfare is in question. And the murder itself, like the killings in *La Bête humaine*, is ascribed to base animal instinct rather than reasoned revenge: "Although he had come with entreaties or threats in mind, Pradès now thought only of one hideous, savage thing: killing. Reason had no hold on him. He was nothing more than an instinct that had broken loose" (300). This instinct is not only primitive, but foreign, honed in a geographical "elsewhere," the "là-bas" of South America: when the killer slashes his victim's throat with a knife, he does it, writes Claretie, like the gauchos of Argentina as they slaughter their beef.

The atavistic motif returns in *Claire Lenoir* even more dramatically, as each of the story's three central characters is affected by a savage Other irrupting into psychic or bodily inner space. The theme of invading alterity appears early on, in the context of the salon debate; when Bonhomet is confronted with Césaire Lenoir's reasoning, "foreign" to him, he is reduced to inarticulate exclamations (a rare and short-lived speechlessness on the part of our loquacious narrator): "Oh! Oh! . . . I exclaimed with a nervous twitch, feeling as if a crocodile had just leapt inside me" (93). Penetrated by another's thought, he feels possessed by a South American crocodile, whose bestial nature hints of what is to come when Césaire Lenoir will return in the form of an island savage. Césaire's own discourse and physiology adumbrate the violent conclusion's themes; arguing that civilized humans "are still caught in the inferior bonds of Instinct, are invisible beasts," Lenoir laughs "open-mouthed, showing two fine rows of teeth rivaling those of any Carib" (94). And it is Lenoir himself, well before he inhabits the form of the savage Ottysor, who casts the *bête humaine* thesis within the multiple displacements of geography, time, and culture: "And I, and my very self, . . . I feel voracious instincts within myself! I feel beset by shadows, furious passions! . . . Savage hatreds, an untamed, unslaked thirst for blood, *as if I were being haunted by a cannibal!*" (95, emphasis original). After Lenoir's death and reincarnation in the South Seas, it is Claire who is haunted, atavistically possessed by the very image of her savage husband. "Oh!" she cries, as she recounts the vision that torments her, "through what sequence of thoughts, *what ancient impressions*, did I come to imagine him . . . in that way, so formless, so different?" (114, my emphasis). And in a final destabilization of intersubjective barriers, the troping of Claire's vision as bodily possession ("Ah! Vampire! Demon! . . . Leave my feeble eyes!) gets transferred onto Bonhomet: "A Demon seized my arm, pushed down on my old head, pressed upon my eye and, nearly by force, showed me, into the depths of my soul, the dead woman's eyes with its powerful magnifying glass; deafening my horror, it shouted into my ear:—Look!" (116). Thus the story's astounding conclusion is explained not in terms of optical science but as the work of a demonic invader.

With this conjunction of demon-possession and looking into the dead woman's eye, we come back to our earlier question: why does each of these tales combine the scientific topos of the retinal image with scenes of brutal savagery? One answer lies in the applications of optogram science to policework, which itself taps into broader social anxieties about contagion, crime, and colonies. But it is not just the practical applications of retinal imagery that raise the issue of troubled boundaries; rather, something in the very nature of the object being studied, the anatomy of the eye, affects our most primal sense of self in relation to outside world. As noted earlier, the nineteenth century is commonly read in light of a broad shift in the study of optics from physics to physiology, with the retinal image straddling the abstraction of the former and the subjective nature of the latter. But as we near the twentieth century and the age of burgeoning psychoanalysis, renewed scientific interest in phenomena like visual hallucinations raises further issues about the boundaries between the body and the mind, with the mind now understood not as clear center of pure reason but as a roiling, mysterious site of potential pathology and illusion. Interactions between outside world and inner self become all the more charged, with domestic and national spaces increasingly figured as vulnerable to invasion by disease, criminals, foreigners, and occult supernatural forces—each able to leave a troubling trace, a mark of violence or a haunting ghost. At the most intimate level of the individual's body, the optogram literalizes this trace. It registers an inscription of external light on the optical chamber's inner membrane in such a way as to trouble our sense of the membrane's role: Is it window? Mirror? Mottled screen? By the end of the nineteenth century, the retinal afterimage has come to be understood as destabilizing: temporally (delay and fleetingness), spatially (unanchored mobility), and epistemologically (confused double origin and reality status). Undoing boundaries between positivist knowledge and metaphysical mystery, the retinal image leaves its own haunting traces of displacement and disjunction on the popular fictions of fin-de-siècle France.

Chapter 11

The Fin-de-Siècle Logic of the Afterimage: Hysteria, Hallucination, and Villiers's *L'Eve future*

The optogram fictions discussed in the three previous chapters reveal the ways in which the scientific discovery of retinal violet wrote the philosophical problems of subjectivity and objectivity into the membrane of the eye. While subjective vision posits a radical disjunction between truth and perception, the physiological inscription of that vision allows for a new order of objective verification that realigns perception and truth. If one were to extend the referential implications of this ambivalence, one might suggest that the very disjunction between truth and literary sign that Villiers plays with in *Claire Lenoir* finds its figural possibility in the retinal afterimage itself.

Because the afterimage seems to exist cut off from any immediate external referent, it opens up the possibility of a self-producing reality. The implications of such a disjunction between image and referent are many. Perhaps foremost in our post-Saussurean minds is the arbitrary relation between signifier and signified—and it is tempting to think of the afterimage phenomenon as a catalyst for literary poststructuralism *avant la lettre*. Indeed, my reading in Chapter 9 of *Claire Lenoir* veers in that direction. Nonetheless, I believe it to be more productive to resituate the literary "afterimage effect" in its own time, to imagine the network of epistemes within which Villiers—and his contemporaries—wrote. Certainly no one would call Verne or Claretie self-consciously antireferential. Nor, on the other hand, do their optogram fictions participate in the esoteric spiritism or Hegelian mysticism that fascinated Villiers. And yet, as we have seen, something beyond the mere scientific fact of retinal photography links these three stories to each other and to their broader cultural and philosophical context. In the most general sense, that "something" constitutes the breakdown of the outside/inside boundary, troped in various ways (temporal, metaphysical, geographical). It remains for us to develop, however, the philosophical implications of the fact that the afterimage and its tropological "aftereffects" are neither purely subjective nor purely objective phenomena. If we are to take, as

I propose, the retinal afterimage as a localizing and literalizing metaphor, or "iconotope," of the fin-de-siècle mentality, it must be with attention paid to its own poised location in a central zone between (but tinged and threatened by) two conceptual horizons: extreme (objective) idealism and extreme (subjective) solipsism.[1]

Extending beyond the fictions that explicitly revolve around the optogram conceit, then, let us examine three other fin-de-siècle "scenes" in which the retinal afterimage plays a central role in redefining reality. Situated in three different contexts—psychopathology (Charcot's "theater"), physiology (Wundt's hallucination studies), and fantastic fiction (Villiers's *L'Eve future*)—these scenes signal a network of cultural and philosophical associations that contribute to our understanding of the fin-de-siècle moment as threshold to the modern conception of the subject as "split" or "fragmented." Indeed, the retinal afterimage functions in this constellation of texts to disjoin the real from the unreal and the body from the self. In general, new scientific attention paid to liminal psycho-corporeal phenomena like dreams, trances, drug-induced states, and hallucinations had replaced a Cartesian "mind/body" split with a murkier, uncannier sense of the self's doubleness. More specifically, the afterimage captures the overlapping, optical trace-logic that makes that very doubleness so unsettling and compelling in the fictional realm of the fin-de-siècle.

The Hysterical Afterimage: Charcot's Blank Card

Jean-Martin Charcot's psychopathological research of the 1880s prepared the terrain directly for Freud's theory of the unconscious not only by exploring bodily and mental behaviors beyond the (hysteric) subject's control, but also by identifying visual distortion as a symptomatic key to psychic disturbance. Head doctor of La Salpêtrière hospital in Paris from 1878 to 1893, Charcot embarked on a systematic study of the neurophysiological effects of hysteria—that is, on the bodily manifestations of the disease and its delusions.[2] Alongside other charged sites—the skin, the womb, the genitals, the voice—the eye takes its place as object of a literal inscription of mental disorder.[3] In addition to the hospital's photographic laboratory and wax-modeling studio, Charcot established at La Salpêtrière an ophthalmological lab that allowed him to examine the visual characteristics of hysteria and its fits.[4] Georges Didi-Huberman's much-cited study of La Salpêtrière's *iconographie photographique*, concerned as it is with Charcot's construction of hysterics as objects of a scientific gaze rather than as seeing subjects themselves, reminds us that these female patients were understood to be marked by pathological vision: a contorted gaze ("le regard tors de l'hystérique"), an abnormal dilation of the pupil, and a chromatic asymmetry of the iris were considered the typical "stigmata," or corporeal marks, of the hysterical state.[5] The deep connections between ophthalmological pathology and psychic (mis)functioning were to be drawn out by Freud and, even later, Lacan, as Emily Apter recounts in her essay "The Garden of Scopic Perversion from Monet to Mirbeau." Apter traces succinctly the genealogy from Charcot's "scotomization" (partial or distorted vision) to Freudian repression and Lacanian "méconnaissance"; she convincingly argues, moreover, that the ambiguous oscillation between visual investment and optical repression that underwrites modern psychoanalytical conceptions of the subject was already at work in Charcot's articulation of hysteria.[6]

But where Freud's formulation of optico-psychic ambivalence posited *internal* conflictual drives, Charcot's was less clear about the origins of mastery and its loss. As we know, Charcot routinely subjected his patients to hypnosis in order to control, observe, and redirect, through suggestion, the behaviors that seemed already to escape the hysterics' control. Extrapolating backward, then, he imagined those behaviors in terms of the hypnagogic state; hysterical blindness, for example, was identified with "spontaneous autosuggestion, a kind of mirror of hypnosis."[7] In other words, Charcot postulated a sort of internalization (though he does not use this term) of the controlling subject, without attempting to define (as would Freud) its relation to the externalization of mental suggestions onto the surface of the body—that is, to the corporeal symptoms that make manifest underlying disturbance.

Nor was the visual pathology of Charcot's hysterical patients limited to the nervous eyelid tics, orbital spasms, and off-kilter pupils documented at his ophthalmological laboratory. Such aberrations of the eye were tracked as indicators of onset and duration of hysterical fits and seizures, but a less noticeably anatomical disturbance of sight—namely, delusional visions, or hallucinations—signaled a more essential problem in the hysterical subject: her conceptual inability to distinguish the real from the imagined. The hysteric's eye not only looks askew (to the instrument-laden scientific observer), but it *sees* askew. It sees what we know not to be.

Let me elaborate on this point by evoking the following "afterimage scene."[8] In his semipublic lessons, Charcot presented a completely blank deck of cards to a hypnotized, hysteric patient, telling her that on one of the cards was represented a specific image (the head of Marie Antoinette, perhaps, or a vase of flowers).[9] After hearing his patient confirm that she saw the image clearly, Charcot reshuffled the (discreetly marked) card into the deck, spread the cards out and—Voilà!—the hysteric was able to pick out that card among all the blank ones, identifying it out loud by its (hallucinated) image. "Moreover, the image continued indefinitely, after the hysteric had revived from the hypnotic trance under which she had originally 'seen' it."[10] The image, suggested by Charcot's mere words, thus persisted as a sort of hysterical afterimage, inscribed somehow in the hysteric's mind and attached to that particular blank card. Like the optical afterimage, the hysterical image consists of a visual percept existing independently from an original external stimulus or referent—but in this case the primary image has never existed: the hysteric's blank card bears an *after*image without an objective "before." Unanchored to its (mentally suggested) referent, the hysterical afterimage persists well beyond the physiological term limit. In fact, one Blanche Wittman, the so-called "Queen of the Hysterics," kept an entire collection of such blank cards in a drawer, taking them out from time to time, to gaze with pleasure at her favorite ones.[11] In this curious case, a suggested mental image had been transferred onto a specific external location, perceivable repeatedly but only to a single viewer.

Although we are talking here of a visual image, the physiological processes of visual perception seem to have been completely bypassed by the conjunction of hypnosis and hysteria: no external percept has been transmitted to the retina by rays of light, so that the photochemical alteration necessary to produce persistent retinal images cannot have occurred. How to explain such a thing: perception without the body? In part, this case, which I am calling the "hysterical afterimage," can be assimilated to the other extrasensory phenomena that scientists and occultists of the nineteenth century associated with the hypnotized state. These phenomena might be divided into two categories in which a subject "sees" without eyes: "second sight" and "altered perception."

The first, second sight, refers to the purported clairvoyance of hypnotized subjects, their ability to discern objects, events, and even conversations occurring outside of their "eyeshot." From the early experiments of Mesmer and James Braid, to the later "confirmations" by Sir William Crookes and Charcot, psychic perception was understood to flourish in the hypnotized state; "sleepwalkers," their observers claimed, were able to distinguish the color and value of playing cards with eyes firmly shut, to play dominoes while blindfolded, or to read letters still enclosed in their envelopes.[12] In his popularizing (and self-serving) *Le Nouvel hypnotisme* of 1887, the fashionable hypnotizer Moutin traces a brief history of Mesmerism and its descendants, citing many cases of "Sight without the help of eyes."[13] One such case, in which a young woman "sees" the precise movements of a doctor two rooms away, recalls the similar "second sight" of Ursule Mirouet in Balzac's novel of 1841.[14] But of course, as I have argued in this book's earlier chapters on Balzac, second sight and afterimages work according to two very different logics: simultaneous inspiration and bodily-temporal perception. I want to distinguish, then, between clairvoyance and the persistent images perceived by Blanche

Wittman and Charcot's other hysterics. At the most basic level, we can recall that Charcot's patients were neither blindfolded nor physically distant from the cards held to their open eyes. They looked, they saw, and they continued to see even after hypnosis. But what they saw was suggested by the imagistic words of Charcot himself, so that their experience has less in common with "second sight" than with the second extrasensory category, "altered perception."

"Altered perception" refers to the sensory illusions produced by suggestion under hypnosis. A well-known example, observed by experimenters from Faria to Charcot, involves telling a hypnotized subject to drink a glass of water described as a tasty cordial; the subject believes he or she is drinking a delicious beverage and testifies to its flavor, aroma, and even, at times, its intoxicating effects. Other suggested perceptions might include taking a dog to be a dragon, or a rag to be a filigreed garment. In these cases, an externally verifiable object exists; it is its interpretation, not its presence or even location, that falls under the rubric of subjective illusion. It is within the rubric of hypnotic suggestion that Gilles de la Tourette classifies the "hysterical afterimage" seen by Blanche Wittman and others; here is Tourette's account of the experiment I described above:

> We take (in an experiment often performed at La Salpêtrière) ten sheets of white paper that are so alike that, unbeknownst to C., we must mark one of them with a sign that she cannot see; this helps us recognize it. As we show her this sheet, we tell her: "Here is the portrait of Mr. X.," whom she knows; "he is dressed in such-and-such a manner; I am giving it to you, and once you are awake, you will still recognize it." We then stress the illusion's persistence upon awakening, for the suggestions may only be intrahypnotic; we shuffle the ten squares of paper; we awaken C.: she never errs, and, out of these ten sheets that are exactly alike, she always finds the one that represents the portrait of Mr. X. *for her.*[15]

The "for her," italicized in the text, emphasizes the subjective nature of the image, while Tourette's next point brings in the elastic temporality of the feat: "We hasten to add that this illusion may persist almost indefinitely. W., for example, an easily hypnotized hysteric from M. Charcot's department, has collected a series of portraits in this way that she takes great pleasure in looking at from time to time" (125). So far, Tourette's description fits within the more general claims of hypnotic suggestibility; although extrasensory perception seems to touch, as Hustvedt rightly suggests, on the inexplicable regions of the occult, its occurrence within hypnotized and hysteric patients allows observers to relegate it to the category of mental delusion, thereby erasing its potential destabilization of the categories of real and unreal. "We" know, despite the hysteric's belief, that no image exists on the blank card; her subjective perception is merely apparent. As with the optical afterimage, though, the question of external verification is a thorny one. How can we know with certainty what the hysteric actually sees? Is it merely a mental image, projected onto a blank card, whose consistent identification smacks of magic trickery rather than objective existence? Is the bodily organ of the eye even needed for a conceptual image to exist and to persist? It seems not, until one reads the next passage in Tourette's text, which makes an astounding claim that reinserts optical physiology into the "hysterical afterimage" phenomenon: "Better still (a phenomenon stressed repeatedly by M. Féré and M. Binet), if, as C. looks at the fictitious portrait, a prism is placed between her eye and the paper, she will immediately exclaim, 'How odd, I see two portraits now.' She herself objectifies her illusion." Tourette does not seem bothered by the optical process described (he still calls the portrait an illusion), but the fact that the hysterical image abides by the optical laws of physics and physiology should give one pause. Why would a suggested, purely mental image be affected by a prism—the instrument that, since Newton, has been used to reveal and confirm the existence of objective physical laws? Why would "extrasensory" perception be so sensory? If hysterical delusion can be seen as the threatening horizon of subjective perception, its fall away from objective reality, then this prismatic event pulls it back into a corporeal realm of potential verification. Charcot's hysterics both internalize his suggestions and externalize their mental images, but once the eye—through the interpolation of the prism—is identified as the active, corporeal locus for this double exchange, the process by which the hysteric "objectifies her illusion" cannot be seen merely as psychic or delusional. The perceptual image is embodied, objectified, made "real"—and thereby threatens to leave the realm of delusion and to enter the general realm of subjective vision, experienced by all and verifiable through observations of the eye's physiology. Charcot's study, in other words, exposes some of the gaps in the scientific and philosophical comprehension of the mind/eye relation. Freud, of course, was to draw out explicitly the psychosomatic repercussions of Charcot's work, by generalizing from the pathological cases of hysteria to the experience of the everyday. But if we look at Charcot's contemporaries—colleagues and competitors, scientists and charlatans alike—we find various rearticulations of the question underlying Villiers' *Claire Lenoir*: what is the ontological status of a madman's hallucinations? Or, by extension: are subjective visual perceptions "real"? Let me turn now to a second "afterimage scene" that extends the prismatic doubleness of Blanche Wittman's hysterical image even further into the realm of optical physiology.

The Hallucinated Afterimage: Wundt's Red Cross

In *Hypnotisme et suggestion* (1893), the German physiologist Wilhelm Wundt describes the positive and negative hallucinations experienced by subjects under hypnotic suggestion.[16] In a positive hallucination, one sees what is not there; Wundt describes, for example, a man who recoils in fear when told that a rabid dog is approaching. Correspondingly, a negative hallucination involves blindness to what is present; a subject in a room full of observers, for example, perceives only his or her hypnotist-suggestor.[17] Obviously, such hallucinations must be determined by the mind, which bypasses the eye by either projecting or blocking visual percepts. And yet positive hallucinations apparently behave as though subject to the same optical laws as real images: "For example, we suggest to the hypnotic that, on the white wall in front of him, there is a red cross: he replies that he sees it. If we then order him to look at the ground, he declares that he sees the portrait of this cross, in green" (28). This is astounding! Here we have, literally, an afterimage—a persistent image that shifts with the direction of the eye's gaze and that appears in the color complementary to that of the original image. But the original image was merely suggested. To use Helmholtz's physiological terms, the "reacting light" or "secondary stimulus" exists without any "primary light" to cause a photochemical impression on the retina. As in Charcot's scene of hypnotized hysteria, a case of (mental) subjective perception defies logic precisely by following the objective physical laws of (optical) subjective perception. Wundt matter-of-factly describes the ways in which hallucinations born of suggestion follow the optical rules of projection, binocularity, color complementarity, and prismatic refraction:

> the hallucinations prompted by suggestion and localized within a specific site in space appear to be subject to the laws of external projection that govern images originating from visual impressions. When, by fixing one's gaze on a red cross, its green-colored binocular copy is produced, it is possible, as is known, to divide this image into double images either by strabism or by interposing a refractory prism between one of the eyes and the image; this assumes, however, that the eye follows the displacement of the objects through space. An analogous division may be brought about by the same means during visual hallucinations by patients under hypnosis. (28)

The double vision of normal physiology is mimicked exactly by the hallucinating "eye," so that even when set free from the limits of reality's corporeal registration, perception functions within a bodily logic. In this age of heightened interest in physiological optics (Giraud-Teulon's *Physiologie et pathologie fonctionnelle de la vision binoculaire* had appeared in France in 1861), the binocularity of vision acquires its own uncanny double in the realm of illusion, where even mental suggestion is imprinted by the eye's anatomy.

In his 1910 book on hypnotism and spiritism, Cesare Lombroso recalls a series of empirical studies that similarly prove that "the suggested image behaves as a real image would." In one such experiment, sixty-three of sixty-five hallucinated images provoke pupil dilation and are susceptible to distortion by optical lenses. "It should be noted," writes Lombroso, "that the hallucination behaves, in almost all subjects, like a real image. It enlarges under a magnifying lens: the pupil dilates when the image of a distant object is suggested; in the opposite case, it contracts."[18] But he has no answer to the question this phenomenon raises: "How are we to explain that suggested images behave like real ones, that the hallucinatory image obeys the laws of optics?" (41). How indeed?

If we go back to Wundt, we get a proto-Freudian answer to this question. Reflecting on the positive hallucinations that must take the place of a blind spot in the hypnotized subject's vision, Wundt hypothesizes the existence of a second state of consciousness, an "unconscious consciousness," that somehow causes, through the vivid impressions of memory, an excitation of the physiological organ; it is this effect, he writes, that produces in a deluded subject the intensity associated with real perceptions (58). Wundt does not really explore the implications of such a hypothesis—not only for psychoanalytical conceptions of the incoherent self, but for the more basic philosophical question of perception's role in defining reality. And yet his entire book has been set up by a polemical introduction in which he contrasts a known universe of stable scientific laws with an imperceptible alternate reality whose unsettling existence might be indicated by the unsavory Occultist practices of his contemporaries. To indulge in the latter, he writes, would be tantamount to acknowledging two separate and incompatible worlds at once: the first would be "the type espoused by Copernicus, Galileo, and Newton, along with Leibniz and Kant, involving a universe subject to immutable and eternal laws," while the second, inhabited by "hobgoblins and poltergeists, witches and mediums," would turn all of the first world's laws upside-down for the benefit of vulgarizers and hysterics (16). Wundt jabs with catty verve at the topsy-turvy world of spiritism: "Gravitation, *optical effects*, even the laws of our psychophysical constitution *give way* once Madame Léonie from Poughkeepsie [*du Havre*] falls into a magnetic sleep" (17, my emphasis). Given Wundt's underlying desire to shore up the physical laws of objective reality against occultist threats, his evocation of the less explicable hypnotic phenomena may seem surprising, until one realizes that it is precisely what strikes us as least believable—that a hallucinated red cross would produce pupil dilation and a complementary green afterimage—that allows him to reconcile physiological science with the unsettling powers of the mind. In the apparently mysterious realm of extrasensory perception, "optical effects" do not "give way"! Stable Newtonian laws hold out against Madame Léonie's mesmerism and the physiology of subjective perception, paradoxically, has come in to anchor objective perception itself.[19]

Villiers, on the other hand, will not back away in his fictions from the occulted implications of psycho-sensorial delusion and double vision that the afterimage provokes. Troubled perceptual boundaries between mind and eye inhabit not only *Claire Lenoir* but his best-known work, the long novel *L'Eve future* (1886). Although this whole text plays with the sensorial modes of acoustic and optic, I will focus here on one "afterimage scene" that combines visual technology with a decadent imaginary to reflect on perception, projection, and the real.

The Afterimage as Woman/Spectacle: Edison's "Picture Show" in *L'Eve future*

In his long decadent novel *L'Eve future*, Villiers de l'Isle-Adam borrows heavily from the psychopathological discourse of Charcot and his contemporaries, referring to cateleptic hypnotism, hysterical neurosis, somnambulist clairvoyance, metallotherapy, and magnetism.[20] The novel's protagonist, Edison, embodies the fin-de-siècle's unholy alliance between science and spiritism: as a character, he is based on the American Thomas Alva Edison, whose practical innovations—the microphone, the phonograph—brought science to the masses; but when applied to the novel's central conceit, a perfectly constructed artificial woman (the Andréide, or android, Hadaly), the fictional Edison's scientific genius surpasses the technical realm and enters into that of the occult. "Le Sorcier de Menlo Park" presides over a space that is at once scientific laboratory and séance salon, as he tampers with the mysteries of life and death and introduces Lord Ewald to up-to-date technologies and the inexplicable phenomena of clairvoyance, spirit-communication, and telekinesis. Edison uses, for instance, Mesmerist techniques of suggestion to hypnotize the novel's female characters, Alicia Clary and Mistress Any Anderson; meanwhile, his explanations of the Andréide Hadaly's clairvoyance and the mysterious Sowana's psychic telepathy as the transmitted effects of magnetic and neuro-electric fluids remain inadequate to their eerie effects.

A spectrum of visual disturbances and anomalies marks the female characters in *L'Eve future*: Sowana's clairvoyance, Hadaly's artificial vision, Alicia's "tearful . . . pupil" and artificial gaze (260). But the text's women exist far less as seeing subjects than as objects of the male gaze; in fact, in many ways in this text, "woman" becomes equivalent to "image." While philosophico-optical debates of the time asked, "are images (essentially, primarily) material or mental?" *L'Eve future* asks, "are women (essentially, primarily) physical or spiritual?" In both cases, the mixed answer seems to lie in the male eye of the subjective perceiver. Anne Greenfield describes some of the many ways in which *L'Eve future*'s female characters disappear into the specular realm of the male protagonists; even Alicia

Clary, seemingly the most "real" of the women, takes form as reflection of Lord Ewald's narcissistic gaze. Greenfield cleverly suggests that women in Villiers exist as *faute d'œil* or optical illusion.[21] Indeed, when Lord Ewald first falls for Alicia Clary, the effect is both optical and de-realizing: "I was dazzled [*ébloui*]," he later explains.[22] The opticality of the moment continues to resonate, as Alicia's paradoxically banal character eventually leaves its mark, literally, on Lord Ewald's eyes: to Edison's concerned query about his apparent sadness, Ewald responds, "There's nothing physical about it, I assure you. Odd as it sounds, it's a type of unending sorrow that, over time, has made my gaze a bit careworn" (70). Despite Ewald's disavowal of a physical problem, Edison picks up on the *chagrin*'s bodily effect: "Indeed, you just alluded to a sorrow of which your gaze bears the mark" (71). The male gaze has been "ébloui," then *imprinted* by a female image, just as an eye is hit with light, then imprinted with the photochemical trace of an image. The psychic slips into the physiological, in this morality tale about the dangers of letting Woman into one's (male) scope. The text's problematic gap between feminine Ideal and female real is stated clearly in Alicia's case as a troubling doubleness: her "noncorrespondence of the physical and the intellectual" (85), which recalls both the hysterical rift between body and mind and, more generally, the uncertain sensorial/mental status of a visual image.

Hadaly is often called a "mirror image" of Alicia Clary, but there is a lack of perfect symmetry between the two, as well as a blurry reverberation of feminine artifice onto the novel's other female characters—Sowana, Mistress Any Anderson, even Evelyn Habal—that lead me to suggest that all the women in *L'Eve future* might better be understood as "afterimages" of an originally projected ("hallucinated," unreal) image of Woman.[23] They are, in other words, a lot like the green cross on the floor of Wundt's patient's room: negative versions of a positive image whose reality itself is in question.[24] Lord Ewald's specular narcissism, in the psychological register, might be called solipsism in the philosophical register; both involve radical self-enclosure and the creation of an artificial other—and both, according to the logic of the text's visual scenes, follow the complex physiological dictates of the eye. When Hadaly is described as a "metaphysical fantasmagoria" (211), the phrase should be taken to retain its visual force, for Woman in *L'Eve future* belongs to a doubled plane that combines the two aspects of fantasmagoria that Terry Castle has identified: optical (spectral, spectacular) and subjective (mental, projected).[25] These two orders are linked by the field of physiological optics, whose study of subjective vision opens up the radical possibility of solipsistic reality, a possibility that haunts *L'Eve future* and the French fin de siècle.

Within this context, I want to focus on one scene that particularly captures the afterimage logic of Villiers' philosophical antirealism. It is the

"Danse macabre" scene of protocinematic projection, in which Edison exposes to Lord Ewald the truth about Evelyn Habal, a courtesan whose corruption of Edison's close friend Anderson motivates the inventor's entire Andréide project. This fallen Eve(lyn), who has led Anderson to suicide, embodies feminine evil in the eyes of Edison; she belongs, he says, to the class of seductresses, contaminated carriers of hysteria and ultimate "artificieuses," who blind, sully, and bewitch their male victims "by the lingering hysteria emanating from them" (191). Edison's virulent, misogynistic rant ends with the conclusion that all prostitutes are vampiric vipers deserving of death—primarily because they are false. Creatures of artifice, they depend on fake hair, fake teeth, fake makeup, fake lashes, fake nails, fake smiles, and fake looks for fake love. But what I find remarkable in this passage is the optical effect that this fakery has on the seduced male: "They accustom his vision," says Edison, "through subtle graduations of hues, to a softened light that starves his moral and physical retina"—an interesting merger of the ethical and the anatomical, the moral and the pathological in the man's receptive organ of vision (189).

To prove his point about the source of such depravation, Edison presents to Lord Ewald a moving picture show.[26] Using reflectors, lamps, and successive photography, he projects onto a large screen first the lovely image of Miss Evelyn Habal as a dancing beauty. Decked out in exotic finery, her ravishing body stands out in every commented detail: the russet-golden locks, the gentle curve of the hip, the moist and rosy glisten of the well-shaped lips . . . and just as Lord Ewald is sinking into erotic delight, Edison pulls a switch and superimposes a new image, this time of the same woman doing the same dance, but now exposed in the hideous reality of her ugly true self. Gone are the prosthetic breasts, the wigs, and the false teeth, and now, dancing her *danse macabre*, is an aging, balding, toothless whore. Screen number 1: the Image of Beauty; Screen number 2: its horrible *after*image. In a way, the screens of the "Danse macabre" scene might be understood as Edison's externalization through technology of what is already happening in the eye, in the *chambre obscure* of the male subject—that is, the projection of an illusory image of woman.[27]

Like a retinal afterimage, Villiers's scene works according to a binary logic. But where the retinal image shifts a single form from light to dark or from red to its complementary green, Villiers's screens carry this logic into the moral and aesthetic registers. His play of projected images switches—in the blink of Ewald's eye—from beauty and youth to hideous age, from goodness to evil. Here, in the realm of "the moral and physical retina," we find not only a mise-en-scène of the gap between ideal and real, but a fundamental questioning of reality itself. For Edison has projected these two images of Evelyn Habal in order to justify his creation of a female android by the fact that women always already lack in authenticity. As he puts it, since woman is already artificial, Edison might as well replace her with an artificial woman, one with no pretense to reality: "instead of the real, since one chimera is worth another, why not the Andréide herself? Since it is impossible, in passions of this type, to extricate oneself from an *entirely subjective illusion*; since they *all*, without exception, are artificial in nature; since, in a word, Woman herself offers us the example of replacing herself with the Artificial, let us spare her . . . this task" (209, my emphasis). Part of the deparavity of one's "moral retina," then, consists in being imprisoned in an illusory subjectivity, defined here by the corrupting force of female seduction and yet connected more universally to the solipsistic horizon of Villiers's illusionism, his "impasse solipsiste."[28]

In *Villiers de l'Isle-Adam et le mouvement symboliste*, A. W. Raitt explains that Villiers veered away from Hegel's objective idealism toward a more radically subjective idealism, one that takes the inadequacy of our senses not as a spur to seek a higher objective truth but as evidence that we create our own realities. "Not only are our senses unable to reveal the world to us as it is in reality, but matter itself is no more than an intellectual convention, a mere subjective invention" (227). Raitt continues, later: "Elsewhere, Villiers does not stop at this relatively simple idea; he goes so far as to wonder whether an objective test exists for what we choose to view as the outer world. Since only thoughts that we ourselves think are real to us, and since our senses deceive us, Villiers concludes that we are free to create a personal truth for ourselves by choosing what we prefer to view as real" (248). This radical subjectivity is demonstrated in Villiers' fiction by the externally verifiable materiality of Claire Lenoir's hallucinated vision and throughout *L'Eve future*, not only by Edison's discourses on the illusions of the sensory world, but by the mises-en-scène of masculine creations of the feminine other, from Ewald's narcissistic projections onto Alicia Clary to Edison's invention of Hadaly.[29] These latter seem, paradoxically, to extend the impossibility of escaping from the "entirely subjective illusion" that Edison ascribes to Evelyn Habal's seductive corruption—and yet, of course, Sowana's mysterious consciousness points to the limits of the subjective, even solipsistic, endeavors of the story's male protagonists. At the moment, then, that Edison's projective power is understood to fail, a redemptive nonsolipsistic reality asserts itself. What is not clear is whether that reality is material or spiritual, a logical extension of Hadaly's constructed nature or an occult being, mediated by Mistress Any Anderson's *voyance*. This ambivalence between material and spiritual is vital, as it undergirds the story's philosophical charge.

One recent critic has rethought, suggestively, the materialist/illusionist rift of Villiers' text in terms of computers, artificial intelligence, and twentieth-century philosophical strains. Carol de Dobay Rifelj argues that Villiers's subjective illusionism in *L'Eve future*, which in radical form would deny objective reality, is in constant tension with a materialism that Edison also professes.[30] As opposed to Raitt's characterization of Villiers as moving chronologically in his career away from materialism and toward a subjectivism represented by *L'Eve future*, Rifelj identifies a continued strain between the two poles within the same novel. While Raitt's reading is more positivist/historicist and Rifelj's more poststructuralist, however, the two have in common the identification of a dualism in Villiers' philosophical thought. Both see a radically subjective illusionism as having its materialist counterpart; but where Raitt identifies the latter as Hegelian objective idealism, Rifelj sees illusionism's tug-of-war partner as akin to a modern philosophy of "reductionism," that is, the belief that there is no reality beyond the physical. Contemporary reductionism, writes Rifelj, denies any mental component, including consciousness. *L'Eve future*'s Edison seems to be working within this reductionist vein when he asserts that the human body is nothing but a machine and that consciousness of others is nothing but a construction.[31] But at other moments—most clearly in the famous "grave squirrel" passage—Edison veers back toward a radical illusionism that is incompatible with reductionism because it asserts that consciousness is all we have: "we create the world out of our subjective experience" (134). The introduction in *L'Eve future* of Sowana's soul, concludes Rifelj, resolves the textual strain between materialist reductionism and subjective illusionism by revealing "a metaphysical dualism that is anathema to contemporary philosophers" (139).

I am interested in pursuing further the form, the figural shape, that this metaphysical dualism takes. Rather than imagine it as either a two-sided dialectic or a bipolar opposition, I propose that Villiers' philosophical dualism acts itself according to the logic of the optical afterimage. This idea was suggested to me by the fact that the two parts of Rifelj's distinction—materialist "reductionism" and radical illusionism—are so difficult to distinguish from each other. The first, reductionism, explains Rifelj, puts consciousness itself into question because "the consciousness of other people is nothing but a construction of our own minds, our projection on the other" (132). The second category of subjective illusionism, which Rifelj presents as a second step in the fictional text's strategy of resistance, reasserts consciousness by saying that all we have is the world that we create out of our subjective experience (134). In other words, both categories are based on some form of subjective projection. The first denies that such projection implies the existence of the "mental"—and yet, it defines consciousness as "something in the *mind* of the beholder" (131, my emphasis), thereby seeming to slip into the very terms of the second category. Rifelj's distinction usefully explains the dualistic tension in Villiers, yet both the materialist assertions *and* the illusionist reactions of the text have the same projective form (or "shape"), even though the latter reverses the essential valence of the former, from objective to subjective—as though materialist philosophy were an objective "image" and illusionism its subjective "afterimage."

As a critical figure, the afterimage brings out the blurrings and overlappings in the very philosophical ambivalence of Villiers's text. It is not, after all, as though Edison were consciously arguing against himself by proposing alternate definitions of reality; in fact, from his subjective (though fictional) perspective, his proclamations about sensory illusion and his assertions of essential materiality are all of a piece. The afterimage logic reveals these two aspects of Edison's (and Villiers's) philosophical stance not as combatants that vie against each other but as projected conceptions whose blurred reverberations emphasize their very reliance on each other. In this way, the materialist/illusionist tension reformulates on the abstract, conceptual level the various tensions—between other and self, mind and eye, spirit and body—that I have traced in the afterimage phenomenon throughout this book's chapters on optogram fiction. If contemporary reductionism is an attempt, per Rifelj, "to redefine consciousness as something in the mind of the beholder," then perhaps the more complex "metaphysical dualism" of Villiers redefines consciousness as something—literally—in the eye of the beholder. After all, Edison's famous profession of illusionist subjectivity—"And, grave squirrel, Man vainly thrashes about within the mobile jail of his SELF, unable to escape Illusion, where his pitiable senses hold him prisoner!"—appears within a specifically optical context, one that explores the role of the eye in "seeing" the truth. Both Rifelj and Raitt cite this phrase as evidence of the extreme solipsistic horizon of Villiers's illusionism, but neither emphasizes the fact that in the sentences preceding and following this statement, visual perception stands in for all of the "pitiable senses" beyond which an occult reality is said to exist. Paradoxically, it is by the instruments of optical science that one can "glimpse" what precisely is not perceivable to the human eye, "the undefinedness of hidden realities":

> Tell me, you think that you can see, clearly, this drop of water, don't you? But if I place it between these two sheets of crystal, opposite the reflector of this solar microscope, and if I project its exact reflection onto this white silk, over there, where a moment ago the bewitching Alicia appeared before you, won't your eyes reject what they first saw in favor of the more intimate spectacle revealed to them by this drop of water? . . . Therefore, always remember that all we see of things is what our eyes alone *suggest* of them; we only form an idea of them based on what they allow us to glimpse of their mysterious entities. (129)

As in *Claire Lenoir*, the optical creates a passage to the suprasensory, so that even within a statement of the eye's limitations, the eye is not entirely bypassed. In the citation above, the eye's relation to spectacle is one of suggestion (Villiers's emphasis); in this presentation of optical projection, we should also hear the echo of hypnotic suggestion, the introjection of an Other's will in the creation of perception. For if the relation between eye and mind in Villiers can be seen as, on the one hand, an iteration of the materialism/idealism debate that (as we saw earlier in this study) subtends the Balzacian text, it has been given a new, more troubling form, one that takes into account the potential rifts, torques, and gaps exposed by pathological studies in hysteria, hypnosis, and hallucination.[32]

Let me return now to the "beauty-hag" scene, in which Edison sets before our eyes, as it were, the projective subjectivity that (as I have been arguing) undergirds both parts of Villiers's philosophical dualism. As John Anzalone observes, this scene's essential message lies in "the lack of correspondence between appearance and reality."[33] Lord Ewald's stupefaction at the idea that "these two visions reproduce only a sole, identical woman" stems from the incongruity of the two projected images—one of ravishing, youthful beauty and the other of hollow, horrible decay (202). The latter, asserts Edison, is "the real one," and he proceeds to detail in the section entitled "Exhumation" the prosthetic aids by which Evelyn Habal artificially transforms her appearance. But as cinematic projections within the narrative, both versions of the woman in Edison's *son et lumière* are second-order images, cut off from an authentic referent. Even the second image, "la vraie," can be said to have been manipulated, for it was only by hypnotizing Evelyn—by putting her into an altered state of consciousness and taking control of her projected image—that Edison had been able to photograph her ugly nudity: "Only through the persistence of fixed Suggestion was I able to obtain this pose" (202). As the hypnotist projecting his will onto a passive object, Edison reverses Evelyn's self-projection and reveals both the unreality of her beautiful image and—as he strives to convince Ewald—the underlying, essential artifice of feminine nature itself. Remember that Edison uses this double-screen spectacle to justify his creation of Hadaly, an artificial women who differs from a "real" woman only in the lack of pretence about her very artificiality. His play of projected scenes unfolds not only into an explicit moral about the dangers of female (hysterical, sexual) corruption, but also a philosophical reflection on the solipsistic horizon, the slip toward an unanchored projection of reality based on no authentic, stable referent.

As with the hallucinated red cross and green afterimage in Wundt's hypnotized patient, Edison's two-part screening replaces one image (thought to be real but revealed to be an illusion of subjective perception) with another (patently artificial, unlinked even to "suggested" or "projected" reality). In this way, *L'Eve future* joins with *Claire Lenoir* and the optogram fictions of Verne and Claretie in exploring the radical implications of subjective visual perception. Whether shadowed by visual technology or left to reveal its own visceral ambivalence, the retinal membrane—as revived site of inquiry at the fin de siècle—becomes a crucial switchpoint between reality and the unreal. While scientific and pseudoscientific studies of hysteria, hallucination, and hypnosis touch upon some of the retina's "afterimage logic," it is the fiction of the time that most effectively combines visual fact with optical mystery. In fact, both *L'Eve future* and the optogram fictions of Verne, Villiers, and Claretie allow us to propose that the fin-de-siècle moment was marked by a mixed, "hallucinatory" visuality that bridges the "objective vision" of nineteenth-century realism (in its most straightforward attempts to reflect the world) and the newer "subjective vision" of twentieth-century forms of phenomenology and self-referentiality.

Indeed, without the nineteenth-century's study of subjective optical phenomena and the resultant *mise en question* of an external realm of objective truth (an *au-delà* to perceptual experience), the notion of textual self-referentiality may well have remained inconceivable. For it was the conceptual gap between objective reality and perceptual experience that allowed later thinkers and writers—from Merleau-Ponty and Lacan to Robbe-Grillet and Claude Simon—to imagine a radical disjunction between seeing and knowing, between the eye and the mind.

Epilogue
The Afterimage of Reference: Optics and the *nouveau roman*

Through this book's readings of nineteenth-century novels and short stories in the context of optics, the retinal *afterimage* has emerged as a key topos whose fictional deployment crystallizes both shifting notions of visual perception and evolving forms of narrative in the modern age.

In Balzac's *La Comédie humaine*, afterimage effects signal an embodied temporality that exists in tension with the camera obscura model of visionary purity. Objective and subjective vision vie for precedence in a narrative quest for knowledge—knowledge of the ineffable beyond of the "absolute" as well as of the ins and outs of glittering society and its shadowy underworld, its "tenebrous affairs." On the one hand, Balzac's text remains residually rooted in an idealist conception of vision as transparent window onto an objective, external realm. But on the other hand, *La Comédie humaine* incorporates the subjective thrust of empiricist vision into its realist project through an accumulative, temporal, narrative logic. The afterimage in Balzac thus propels his fiction beyond nostalgia for visionary "second sight" and toward the "second" sight of bodies in the world.

The *roman policier*, a popular genre that grew, partly, out of Balzac's serialization of scientific themes, extends realism's empiricist logic into the realm of detection. But as privileged figure for the acquisition of knowledge through sight, the fictional detective has generally been coded as a figure for pure, abstract rationality in ways that ignore the genre's "afterimage effects" of hermeneutic delay, temporal red herrings, and subjective vision. By resituating the early *roman policier* in the context of empiricist visuality, this book has revealed its structural, epistemological double bind of a priori deduction and a posteriori reconstitution of facts.

And finally, if the detective genre represents the empiricist outgrowth of the Balzacian "tree," fin-de-siècle fantastic fiction would seem to constitute its other branch, its escape from realist observation into an occult and extrasensory universe. But as we have seen in Part III of this book, the fantastic genre remains materially anchored to worldly vision. From the explicit optogram fiction of Villiers, Verne, and Claretie to the uncanny iterations of the "afterimage" in psychopathological, scientific, and fictional discourse of the fin de siècle, the late nineteenth century inhabits a liminal space, where blurred boundaries are captured in the anatomical figure of retinal violet. By continually registering external forms in the inner chamber of the eye, through the photochemical alteration of bodily tissue, retinal violet literalizes the interaction between objective world and subjective perception. It absorbs into one locus both objective light *and* blood-pulsed perception—and thus complicates the binaries (objectivity/subjectivity, idealism/materialism, abstraction/physicality) that have marked discourses of and about science and fiction in nineteenth-century France.

But of course the history of modern narrative and visuality does not end here. In the final pages of this Epilogue, I want very briefly to sketch out some possible directions for exploring the statement that ends Chapter 12: namely, the argument that the gap between real and unreal in the "optogrammatic" fiction of the fin de siècle prepares the terrain for an eventual twentieth-century move toward textual self-referentiality and phenomenologies of vision—features of the *nouveau roman* of the 1950s through 1970s.

First of all, one might trace the scientific and philosophical shifts entailed by the crucial notion of "subjective vision," a term that emerged in the eighteenth and early nineteenth centuries as referring to literal and bodily perception (in contradistinction to the "objective" physical laws of sight). As the study of optical phenomena like afterimages undermined the distinction between perceptual appearance and objective truth, nineteenth-century empiricists negotiated that gap by taking the "optical truth" of subjective phenomena as their new object of study, with its own identifiable and quantifiable laws. Their study of subjective vision changed the terms of discourse around visual perception, allowing theorists to posit a "modern observer" whose visual relation to the world is structured by physiology and temporality, by the body in time. Indeed, the subject-centered epistemology of nineteenth-century empiricism paved the way for a phenomenological theory of vision that went even further, calling into question the theoretical foundations of scientific inquiry itself. Merleau-Ponty disputed the theoretical confidence in the subject's ability to gain access—whether through abstract reason or empirical observation—to a stable realm of objective truth. Once one understands the subject as a body *in* the world, Merleau-Ponty writes, it becomes "impossible to conceive of vision as a thought process that calls to mind a tableau or representation of the world, a world of immanence and ideality."[1] The visible world can no longer be understood as a transparent window onto an ideal realm of truth; nor can visual perception be conceived as a conscious relation of mastery between subject and reality.

Lacan extended this critique of traditional optics with his formulation of the gaze as that which escapes control in the visual field. The theories of Merleau-Ponty and Lacan may constitute a radical break with the philosophical structures that underlie the science of optics, but their authors could not have conceived of that break without the careful study of optical history—and particularly, I suggest, without attention to the epistemological implications of subjective vision.

The nineteenth century, in other words, set the stage for the phenomenological and psychoanalytical theories of vision that underwrote twentieth-century forms of the novel, from Proustian subjectivity through the Sartrean "gaze." But even beyond those direct influences, we can find traces of the nineteenth-century split between objective and subjective vision in the *nouveau roman*, a novelistic school that presented itself, at least in its heyday of self-definition, as rejecting all previous forms of narrative visuality: the omniscient gaze of so-called classical realism, the psycho-subjective perspective of post-Freudian fiction, and the (de-)politicized gaze of the existential project. By proposing a purely textual or "narrative" subject, the *nouveau roman*—as well as the structuralist and post-structuralist theories that constellated around it—strove to escape the anthropomorphizing consequences of visual perception. (Jacques Derrida famously announced in 1972 that perception does not exist.)[2] But I would argue that the terms of this rejection were only conceivable, paradoxically, *because of* visual perception: that is, because the study of optics had already, a century earlier, toppled the epistemological mastery of the visual subject over an objective world.

Let me conclude briefly, then, with the example of another fictional *afterimage*, one whose internal logic will at least suggest some of the ways in which even the most antireferential narrative projects of the twentieth century owed their structure to the unsettling gaps of modern *optiques*.

The afterimage appears in Claude Simon's 1973 *Triptyque*, a novel written with a consciously antimimetic goal; its self-reflexive textuality, based on multiple and discoherent *mises en abyme*, aimed to purge the novelistic form of both (nineteenth-century) representational realism and (early twentieth-century) psychological referentiality. Among the techniques used by Simon to eliminate extratextual reference is the organization of *Triptyque*'s descriptions around a focal point (ascribed only to an unspecified "on" rather than to a human subject of perception) whose optical locatedness is meant to undermine perspectival mastery. In fact, *Triptyque*'s references to physiological phenomena of vision continuously cut into the conception of transparent visuality that sustained mimetic theories of representation, as in this passage describing a trout in a river: the trout, arrowlike, darts off and disappears upstream into the zone occulted by the sun's blinding reflection, leaving behind [*laissant persister*] on the retina the trace of its elongated, rigid form, propelled simply by the quick movements of its tail."[3] Although this passage identifies no subject of perception, it posits a hypothetical eye whose relation and reaction to the scene are physiologically circumscribed. As in many of Simon's descriptions, a gap in the field of vision is described—in this case, the blind spot underwater caused by a reflection of light on the river's surface. The fish is no longer visible when it enters into that zone. Moreover, the interaction of light with the dark form of the fish has caused a second "blind spot," this time in the perceiving eye's own retina: the blind spot of an *afterimage*.[4] The initial perception of an illuminated object creates a retinal image that persists even after that object is no longer there. The persistent image interferes with the normal perception of the external world at this second moment, limiting the new field of vision through a kind of temporary screen or fish-shaped "blind spot." Here, the afterimage effect partakes of a larger waning of confidence in the power of the eye; vision can no longer be understood as a transparent relation between viewing subject and objective world when the eye's own physiognomy can create objects of perception known not to exist externally. In *Triptyque*'s description of trout and river, there are two "occulted zones": the part of the water that is reflected back to the perceiver and the section of the perceiving eye's retina that has been imprinted with the trout's afterimage. Light in this passage inserts the perceiving eye into a relation of reciprocal and blinding specularity—a far cry from Light's traditional illuminating function as metaphorical guarantor of knowledge. Through the play of reciprocal reflection, Simon destabilizes the primacy of the seeing subject over perceived reality. He creates a textual universe in which eye and object exist at the same level of representation (boh screened by blind spots, neither is more "real" than the other), so that optical physiology is brought into the service of linguistic nonreferentiality.[5]

The retinal *afterimage*, then, has allowed us to trace narrative visuality from the Cartesian *chambre obscure* to Lacanian gaps in the scopic field, from Balzac's nostalgic second sight to Simon's *nouveau* antimimesis. While twentieth-century writers like Simon and Alain Robbe-Grillet saw themselves as radically breaking the rules of realist visuality, *Optiques* reveals the trajectory that not only made such a break possible but actually structured its figural logic. By recovering the ways in which physiological optics and the French novel joined forces to shape our notion of the modern subject, this book reveals the lambent traces—or afterimages—of a nineteenth-century visual epistemology in the discursive and literary networks of our own time.

Notes

Introduction. The Epistemology of Optics: Seeing Subjects, Modern Minds

1. Gustave Flaubert, *Bouvard et Pécuchet* (Paris: Garnier-Flammarion, 1966), 245. (All translations of French citations, from primary and secondary texts, are by Margaret Jean Flynn, with occasional changes by the author.)

2. Cited in an optical treatise published the same year as *Bouvard et Pécuchet*: Félix Giraud-Teulon, *La Vision et ses anomalies* (Paris: J.-B. Baillière et Fils, 1881), 250.

3. With its parodic encyclopedism, *Bouvard et Pécuchet* (which Flaubert wrote to expose the "L'immense bêtise moderne [qui] me donne la rage" [the modern world's vast stupidity (that) infuriates me] has been read as a novel of epistemological crisis, as postmodern *avant la lettre*. Such readings turn especially to self-referential passages like the absurdist biography of the duc d'Angoulême, emphasizing linguistic indeterminability, fragmentation, and discontinuity. See, for example, Françoise Gaillard, "Une inerrable histoire," in Pierre Cogny et al., *Flaubert et le comble de l'art: Nouvelles recherches sur Bouvard et Pécuchet: actes du colloque tenu au Collège de France les 22 et 23 mars 1980* (Paris: Société d'Edition d'Enseignement Supérieur, 1981).

4. Representative contributions to this emerging "history of vision" include the following: Hal Foster, ed., *Vision and Visuality* (Seattle: Bay Press, 1988); David Michael Levin, *Modernity and the Hegemony of Vision* (Berkeley: University of California Press, 1993); Stephen Melville and Bill Readings, eds., *Vision and Textuality* (Durham, N.C.: Duke University Press, 1995); and Teresa Brennan and Martin Jay, eds., *Vision in Context: Historical and Contemporary Perspectives on Sight* (New York: Routledge, 1996).

5. In *Picture Theory: Essays on Verbal and Visual Representation* (Chicago: University of Chicago Press, 1995), W. J. T. Mitchell describes a "pictorial turn" in intellectual and academic discourse, whose visual paradigms may supplant the textual paradigms that characterized the "linguistic turn" of theoretical studies after structuralism. He defines this "pictorial turn" as "a postlinguistic, postsemiotic rediscovery of the picture as a complex interplay between visuality, apparatus, institutions, discourse, bodies, and figurality" (16).

6. Jonathan Crary, *Suspensions of Perception: Attention, Spectacle, and Modern Culture* (Cambridge, Mass.: MIT Press, 2000), 3.

7. See Corbin's olfactory history of France, *Le Miasme et la jonquille: l'odorat et l'imaginaire social XVIII–XIX siècles* (Paris: Aubier Montaigne, 1982).

8. See, for example, the *Journal of Visual Culture*. Other recent additions to the field include Nicholas Mirzoeff, ed., *The Visual Culture Reader* (London: Routledge, 1998); Nicholas Mirzoeff, *An Introduction to Visual Culture* (London: Routledge, 1999); Marita Sturken and Lisa Cartwright, *Practices of Looking: An Introduction to Visual Culture* (Oxford: Oxford University Press, 2001).

9. Jonathan Crary, *Techniques of the Observer: On Vision and Modernity in the Nineteenth Century* (Cambridge, Mass.: MIT Press, 1990), 3; Lorraine Daston and Peter Galison, "The Image of Objectivity," *Representations* 40 (Fall 1992): 81. In a later piece, Galison argues that the term *objectivity* is "deeply, ineradicably, a nineteenth-century category" and identifies a shift "after about 1830" toward philosophy as a self-denying objectivity. "Judgment Against Objectivity," in *Picturing Science, Producing Art*, ed. Caroline A. Jones and Peter Galison (New York: Routledge, 1998), 327–28.

10. *Picturing Science*, Introduction, 17–18.

11. Some touchpoints: in all his work, Michel Serres importantly emphasizes the mutual imbrication of myth, science, and literature. See *Hermes: Literature, Science, Philosophy*, ed. Josué Harari and David F. Bell (Baltimore: Johns Hopkins University Press, 1982). George Levine's edited volume *One Culture: Essays in Science and Literature* (Madison: University of Wisconsin Press, 1987) contests Charles Percy Snow's classical distinction between the "Two Cultures" of science and literature as strictly divergent. See also George Levine, ed., *Realism and Representation: Essays on the Problem of Realism in Relation to Science, Literature, and Culture* (Madison: University of Wisconsin Press, 1993). In his study of chance and causality in modern French fiction, David F. Bell warns against the reductionism of taking science to "influence" literature, with the latter understood as merely borrowing or reflecting knowledge from the former's stabler domain. *Circumstances: Chance in the Literary Text* (Lincoln: University of Nebraska Press, 1993). More recently, Allan Thiher proposes that not only did literature share in science's epistemic quest, but that in the nineteenth century particularly, novelists believed they could rival science in the pursuit and proposal of knowledge. Thiher, *Fiction Rivals Science: The French Novel from Balzac to Proust* (Columbia: University of Missouri Press, 2001).

12. See especially Michel Foucault, *Les Mots et les choses: une archéologie des sciences humaines* (Paris: Gallimard, 1966) and Jacques Derrida, *Mémoires d'aveugle: l'autoportrait et autres ruines* (Paris: Editions de la Réunion des musées nationaux, 1990).

13. In the field of art history, as in literary studies, mutual interactions between scientific discourse and visual culture are receiving wider attention. On art's relation to the realm of optics in particular, see, for example, Michael Baxandall's reflections on Chardin and Locke in *Patterns of Intention: On the Historical Explanation of Pictures* (New Haven, Conn.: Yale University Press, 1985) and Rachael Delue's book-length study, *George Inness and the Science of Landscape* (Chicago: University of Chicago Press, 2004).

14. Henri Mitterand, *L'Illusion réaliste: de Balzac à Aragon* (Paris: Presses Universitaires de France, 1994).

15. On the history of optics, I have primarily used the following sources: A. C. Crombie, *Science, Art and Nature in Medieval and Modern Thought* (London: Hambledon Press, 1996); William N. Dember, *Visual Perception: The Nineteenth Century* (New York: John Wiley, 1964); Richard L. Gregory, *Eye and Brain: The Psychology of Seeing* (New York: McGraw-Hill, 1966); Hermann von Helmholtz, *Helmholtz's Treatise on Physiological Optics*, ed. James P. C. Southall, 3 vols. (New York: Dover, 1962); David C. Lindberg, *Theories of Vision from Al-Kindi to Kepler* (Chicago:

University of Chicago Press, 1976); Peter K. Machamer and Robert G. Turnbull, eds., *Studies in Perception: Interrelations in the History of Philosophy and Science* (Columbus: Ohio State University Press, 1978); Nicholas Pastore, *Selective History of Theories of Visual Perception: 1650–1950* (New York: Oxford University Press, 1971); Gérard Simon, *Sciences et savoirs aux XVIe et XVIIe siècles* (Paris: Presses Universitaires du Septentrion, 1996); René Taton, ed., *Histoire générale des sciences* (Paris: Presses Universitaires de France, 1958); and Nicholas J. Wade and Michael Swanston, *Visual Perception: An Introduction* (London: Routledge, 1991).

16. See, in addition to Lindberg: David E. Hahm, "Early Hellenistic Theories of Vision and the Perception of Color," in Machamer and Turnbull, *Studies in Perception*, 60–95.

17. Simon, *Sciences et savoirs*, 81. See also Gérard Simon, *Le Regard, l'être et l'apparence dans l'optique de l'antiquité* (Paris: Editions du Seuil, 1988). In this earlier study, Simon was already emphasizing the epistemological implications of discoveries in the field of optics: vision, he writes, has always served as metaphor for theoretical knowledge: "if one takes seriously this archetypal function of vision, one must conclude that each major optical mutation brought about a transformation in the theory of knowledge" (17).

18. Simon, *Sciences et savoirs*, 83.

19. Crombie, *Science, Art and Nature*, 336.

20. René Descartes, *De la Dioptrique*, in *Oeuvres philosophiques*, vol. 1, *1618–37* (Paris: Garnier Frères, 1963), 651–76, 681–82. On the "disincarnated" Descartes, see Karsten Harries, "Descartes, Perspective, and the Angelic Eye," *Yale French Studies* 49 (1973): 28–42, and Dalia Judovitz, "Vision, Representation, and Technology in Descartes," in *Modernity and the Hegemony of Vision*, ed. David Michael Levin (Berkeley: University of California Press, 1993).

21. Martin Jay, *Downcast Eyes: The Denigration of Vision in Twentieth-Century French Thought* (Berkeley: University of California Press, 1994).

22. Merleau-Ponty and Jacques Lacan, for example, were responsible in twentieth-century French thought for setting Descartes up as the strawman-king of pure abstract reason and geometric perspectival order.

23. Lyle Massey, "Anamorphosis Through Descartes or Perspective Gone Awry," *Renaissance Quarterly* 50 (Winter 1997): 1148–89. Another recent contestation of Descartes's "pure abstraction" can be found in "Descartes' Empirical Epistemology," in which Charles Larmore argues that the philosopher appealed as much to the physiology of perception as to "a theory of the mechanical nature of light which he found himself forced to justify empirically." In *Descartes: Philosophy, Mathematics, and Physics*, ed. Stephen Gaukrager (Sussex: Harvester Press, 1980), 9.

24. David Summers, "Representation," in *Critical Terms for Art History*, ed. Robert S. Nelson and Richard Shiff (Chicago: University of Chicago Press, 1996), 10–11.

25. See, for example, *Histoire générale des sciences*, ed. René Taton (Paris: Presses Universitaires de France, 1958), 2: 200.

26. For more, see Alan Donagan, "Berkeley's Theory of the Immediate Objects of Vision," in Machamer and Turnbull, *Studies in Perception*. See also Pastore, *Selective History of Theories of Visual Perception*; and Wade and Swanston, *Visual Perception*.

27. *Histoire générale des sciences*, 2: 502.

28. The distinctions made in Helmholtz's 1867 magisterial history of optics have allowed modern scholars to characterize eighteenth- and nineteenth-century theorists of vision as either "nativists" (believers in Descartes's innate ideas) or "empiricists" (followers of a Lockean model of vision as experientially acquired).

29. See, for example, Merleau-Ponty, *L'Œil et l'esprit* (Paris: Gallimard, 1964), 25.

30. *L'Etre et le néant: essai d'ontologie phénoménologique* (Paris: Gallimard, 1943), esp. 310–64.

31. For a clear discussion of the ways in which Sartre and Lacan deconstruct "[the eye's] fantasy of mastery and transcendence," see Kaja Silverman, *The Threshold of the Visible World* (New York: Routledge, 1996), chap. 5, "The Look."

32. Martin Jay, *Downcast Eyes: The Denigration of Vision in Twentieth-Century French Thought* (Berkeley: University of California Press, 1994), provides a thorough and important overview of twentieth-century reactions against "ocularcentrism," or the privileging of vision. Jay's book, which traces the crisis of Cartesian perspectivalism back into the nineteenth century, is an invaluable resource for work on twentieth-century visual thought and the history of visuality.

33. Jacques Lacan, "Le Séminaire: du regard comme objet petit a," in *Les Quatre concepts fondamentaux de la psychanalyse* (Paris: Editions du Seuil, 1973), 79.

34. Stephen Melville, "Division of the Gaze; or, Remarks on the Color and Tenor of Contemporary 'Theory'," in *Vision in Context: Historical and Contemporary Perspectives on Sight*, ed. Teresa Brennan and Martin Jay (New York: Routledge, 1996), 110.

35. Crary, *Techniques of the Observer*, 7.

Chapter 1. Second Sight and the Authorial chambre noire: Les Chouans, Louis Lambert

1. Victor Brombert, *Victor Hugo and the Visionary Novel* (Cambridge, Mass.: Harvard University Press, 1984). Another of the most suggestive studies of Hugolian visuality—and, more particularly, visual epistemology—is Guy Rosa's article "Voir aveuglément." Rosa begins by saying that Hugo, who famously categorized experience as "Choses vues," seems to rely on a clear link between visual perception and knowability. Such a link, claims Rosa, derives from a particular notion of visual perception: the "hypothèse cartésienne" that sight and understanding are coextensive (20). In contrast to such an ancien régime idea, Rosa poses the modern optics of Stendhal, "in whose writings the text and occasionally the plot are built upon a series of visual incidents—inattention, obstructed or out-of-focus vision," and Flaubert, "wherein the narrative's almost-excessive attentiveness constantly rests its gaze upon the fascinating opacity of objects" (21). But, he continues, the seeming "tyranny" of Hugolian vision is in fact troubled by a fascination with its effacement, as Hugo's texts tend toward the disincarnation of the visual field in their reach for verticality, infinity, and metaphysical "vision." Indeed, as the ultimate poet of "lumière aveuglante" [blinding light] and "ombre éblouissante" [dazzling shadow], Hugo ends up situating his narrative subject not within the regime of quotidian perception, but on one side or the other of sight: in the realm of blindness or the reach for divine panoptism (34). Guy Rosa, "Voir aveuglément," in *Du visible à l'invisible: pour Max Milner*, ed. Stéphane Michaud (Paris: Librairie José Corti, 1988). See also Jacques Neefs, "Marges d'Ombre," in *Hugo dans les marges*, ed. Lucien Dällenbach and Laurent Jenny (Geneva: Zoé, 1985), on Hugo's *L'homme qui rit* and *Notre-Dame de Paris*, in which he distinguishes between "regard" and "vision," linking the first to the describable reality of the world and the latter to infinity, mystery, and the invisible. And finally, for a seminal study of literary blindness in Hugo, Diderot, and others in the context of philosophies of vision, see William Paulson, *Enlightenment, Romanticism, and the Blind in France* (Princeton, N.J.: Princeton University Press, 1987).

2. William J. Berg, *The Visual Novel: Emile Zola and the Art of His Times* (University Park: Pennsylvania State University Press, 1992).

3. In 1850 St.-Beuve and Baudelaire took the antirealist side in the debate, declaring Balzac to be a *visionnaire* or *voyant,* while Zola, not surprisingly, claims him as precursor of naturalist observation. On the history of this "quarrel," starting with St.-Beuve's and Baudelaire's interventions in 1850, see Pierre Barbéris, *Balzac: une mythologie réaliste* (Paris: Librairie Larousse, 1971); another now-classic locus is the section on "Balzac-*visionnaire,*" in Albert Béguin, *Balzac lu et relu* (Paris: Editions du Seuil), 1965.

4. *Avant-propos,* in Honoré de Balzac, *La Comédie humaine,* 12 vols., ed. Pierre-George Castex, Bibliothèque de la Pléiade (Paris: Gallimard, 1976–81), vol. 1.

5. Gwendolyn Bays, "Balzac as Seer," *Yale French Studies* 13 (Spring-Summer 1954): 83–92, 83.

6. Not only does Balzac give equal due to practitioners of naturalist science (Cuvier, Saint-Hilaire, Buffon, Gall, Lavater) and of philosophical mysticism (Swedenborg, Saint-Martin, Leibniz) in his *Avant-propos de la Comédie humaine,* he also explicitly combats the adherence to a matter/spirit divide that characterizes some of his critics. Defending against the charges of materialist atheism leveled against his proposals that light and the mind are not immaterial entities, Balzac invokes the once controversial theories of Galileo and Columbus in order to argue the compatibility of empirical rationality with metaphysical concerns (*AP,* 16–17). Balzac restates this argument as a hypothetical question posed by Théophile (note the name, "God-lover") in *Les Martyrs ignorés*: "Even were we to discover that thought is as material as light, perfume, and electricity, would this disprove the existence of God?" "No," answers the chemist Grodninsky (735). *Les Martyrs ignorés,* in *La Comédie humaine,* vol. 12. With this response, and with the passage from the *Avant-propos,* Balzac reconciles the progress of science with the pursuit of spiritual truth.

7. The nineteenth-century sciences have been categorized according to discipline as either empirical and "inductive" (biology, natural history) or abstract and "deductive" (physics, mathematics). See, for example, William Whewell, *History of the Inductive Sciences* (New York: Olms Verlag), 1976. Nonetheless, Michel Foucault's formulation of modern (post-1800) epistemology as caught in an "empirico-transcendental doublet" better reflects the methodological and theoretical intersections of induction and deduction that pertained across scientific thought and within particular disciplines. *Les Mots et les choses: une archéologie des sciences humaines* (Paris: Gallimard, 1966), 330–31.

8. In addition to having certain contact with optics through mainstream philosophy, Balzac cultivated direct knowledge of optical treatises through his private library. In his collection are found various works on visual perception, including a general *Traité d'optique* and writings by Monge, d'Hassenfratz, and l'Abbé Nollet (*La Comédie humaine,* 1: 1137 n). Balzac also apparently read Diderot's *Lettre sur les aveugles* and had access to the complete works of Buffon through his friend Villiers La Faye (*La Comédie humaine,* 1: 1111–12). Mentioned frequently by Balzac for his work as a naturalist on animals, Georges-Louis Buffon also made contributions to the field of experimental optics. See "Du sens de la vue," in *De l'Homme: histoire naturelle* (Paris: Vialetay, 1971). What might Balzac have learned from such treatises? A glance at the *Encyclopédie méthodique,* a three-volume alphabetized compendium of scientific knowledge of the time, suggests a tangled conjunction of Cartesian theories, Newtonian physics, and empiricist discoveries by post-Lockeans like Buffon, Scherffer, Meusnier, and Prieur. Edited by members

of the Académie des Sciences (Monge, Cassini, Bertholon, Hassenfratz, "&c") and also called *Dictionnaire de physique*, this reference work, with its encyclopedic form and hodgepodge inclusion of sometimes conflicting theories, is reminiscent of the *Comédie humaine* itself. More particularly, though, the many entries from the field of optics (including "Vue," "Vision," "Chambre claire," "Chambre obscure," "Perspective," "Couleurs," "Couleurs accidentelles"—and especially "Lumière") reflect a double outlook that provides a suggestive context for Balzac's own double visuality: their authors are at once looking back at objective idealism and looking forward to empirical subjectivity. *Encyclopédie méthodique*, 3 vols. (Paris: Académie des Sciences, 1793).

9. Barbéris writes that Balzac was a "matérialiste convaincu" in his early youth, an adept of Locke rather than Descartes. "He also meditated on the lessons of Cousin, who led him to Thomas Reid and his philosophy of innate perception and 'second sight'" (Barbéris, *Balzac*, 56).

10. In *Reid and His French Disciples: Aesthetics and Metaphysics* (Leiden: E.J. Brill, 1994), James W. Manns describes the broad dissemination of Reid's theories in France by Victor Cousin (whose lectures in 1828 caused "a stir . . . on the left bank the likes of which had not been witnessed since the days of Abelard") and Théodore Jouffroy (4). Although we might, post-Helmholtz, distinguish Cartesian objectivity from Lockean subjectivity, Reid was reacting to Descartes and Locke jointly: as Manns explains, both of these philosophers' ideas were recast by Hume's and Berkeley's skepticism as supporting a radical subjectivity that neither Descartes nor Locke fully intended (14–15); Reid's strong critique of this radical subjectivity retained certain elements of Descartes's and Locke's work while rejecting others (30–31).

11. Thomas Reid, *An Inquiry into the Human Mind on the Principles of Common Sense*, ed. Derek R. Brookes (Edinburgh: Edinburgh University Press, 1997), 95–98. See also the French translation, "De la vue," *Œuvres complètes*, vol. 2, *Recherches sur l'entendement humain d'après les principes du sens commun* (Paris: Sautelet et Cie, 1828). For my reading of Reid's relation to Balzac, I relied primarily on the French translation, assuming its more likely influence on the French intellectual scene. One key problem arises, however: the French *seconde vue* does not uphold the English distinction between (physical) "double vision" and (metaphysical) "second sight." The resulting slippage would, I imagine, trouble a philosopher like Reid, but I think that its ambiguity signals, significantly, Balzac's interest in the intimate homologies between literal and metaphorical vision.

12. "All of the deceptions inherent to the telescope, microscope, camera obscura, and magic lantern are of the same stripe: they may deceive the ignorant spectator, but for the philosopher trained in the principles of optics, they are the most accurate sources of information." *Œuvres*, vol. 4, *Essais sur les facultés intellectuelles de l'homme*, 48.

13. This is primarily evident in the French translation, not the English original.

14. Marie-Claude Amblard distinguishes between *les voyants* and *les initiés* in *L'Œuvre fantastique de Balzac: Sources et philosophie* (Paris: Didier, 1972).

15. Balzac's "Préface" to *La Peau de chagrin* is reprinted in the Livre de Poche edition with annotations by Pierre Barbéris (Paris: Librairie Générale Française, 1984), 3–13, 9.

16. *Les Chouans* (Paris: Garnier-Flammarion, 1988), 56.

17. Introduction to Garnier-Flammarion edition, 23.

18. Suzanne J. Bérard, "Une énigme Balzacienne: la 'Spécialité,'" *L'Année Balzacienne* (1965): 61–82 (63).

19. Hermann von Helmholtz, *Optique physiologique* (Sceaux: Jacques Gabay, 1989), vol. 2, §26, "Historique de la théorie des perceptions," 593.

20. The existence of innate ideas remained a point of contention in optics well into the nineteenth century. Both Hume and Kant critiqued this Cartesian principle for its a priori positing of objective knowledge as unrelated to the experience of reality, and the Young-Helmholtz empiricist theory of vision continued to take the innate theory to task, citing experiments in which comprehensive sight is only gradually acquired.

21. "De la vue," *Œuvres,* 1: 145–46.

22. "De la perception," *Œuvres,* 3: 126.

23. Elsewhere, Reid makes the point that we do not perceive inexistent objects (even though we can conceive of, for example, a winged horse); it is possible, therefore, to have conception without perception but not the other way around. *Œuvres,* vol. 3, *Essais sur les facultés de l'esprit humain,* 23–24.

24. One should note, however, that for all its abstraction, Victor's *mental* imaging does not strictly eliminate the material world. His "imagination fantasmagorique" (419) communicates a particular "shade of colors he knows well" (422). The young genius makes images so vivid that they add up to an alternate reality. And that reality is not, after all, the stuff of typically mystical visions—the *voyant* sees sparkling balls and beautiful women, lavish silks and colored tapestries, elegant horses and sensuous jewels. Given the *génie*'s ascetic lifestyle, one might have expected his inner eye (a concept that emerged from a mystical, religious tradition) to be focused on spiritual truths. But instead it accesses a social realm of truth mediated through the material world. Like Balzac, who applied his self-ordained faculties of "voyance" to Society, Victor uses his second sight to perceive a world of material images rather than an unrepresentable divine sphere. The material world is recuperated as the very object of Victor's abstract and idealized imagination, so that his is not a purely mystic revelation. In this way as well, Victor's second sight fits the secularized idealism of the Cartesian age, in which the scientific gaze—figured as abstract and disembodied—is cast onto the physical (and in Balzac, social) world.

25. Honoré de Balzac, *Louis Lambert,* in *La Comédie humaine,* 11: 595 (hereafter, *LL*).

26. See, for example, Louise Vinge, *The Five Senses: Studies in a Literary Tradition* (Lund: Liber Läromedel, 1975), and Constance Classen, *Worlds of Sense: Exploring the Senses in History and Across Cultures* (London: Routledge, 1993).

27. As many critics have explained, this antimaterialist notion of second sight can be traced to a Swedenborgian mysticism. See, for example, Bays, "Balzac as Seer"; Bérard, "Une énigme Balzacienne"; Henri Evans, *Louis Lambert et la philosophie de Balzac* (Paris: Librairie José Corti, 1951); and Juliette Frolich, "L'ange au pays des neiges: Séraphîta," *L'Année Balzacienne* 13 (1992): 319–31. But read in the context of scientific notions of sight and second sight, Lambert's "grande perfection de vue" shares with Cartesian optics its conception of physical sensation as an obstacle to real knowledge. In Descartes' famous formulation, "c'est l'âme qui sent, et non le corps [the soul is what feels, not the body]," reality and truth are assured by Reason, and not by the evidence of the senses. Descartes, *De la Dioptrique, Œuvres philosophiques,* vol. 1, *1618–1637* (Paris: Garnier Frères, 1963), 681–82. Let me note, however, that I use the term "Cartesian optics" in these chapters to refer to conventional interpretations of Descartes rather than to his own text, which in fact often deviates from the mode of abstraction (see Introduction).

28. Jonathan Crary takes the figure of the camera obscura as paradigmatic of the status of the observer in the seventeenth and eighteenth centuries in Europe. *Techniques of the Observer: On Vision and Modernity in the Nineteenth Century* (Cambridge, Mass.: MIT Press, 1990); see especially chap. 2. Martin Jay also refers to the "Cartesian perspectivalism" figured by the camera obscura as the "dominant scopic regime of the modern era." *Downcast Eyes: The Denigration of Vision in Twentieth-Century French Thought* (Berkeley: University of California Press, 1994), 69–70.

29. Hermann von Helmholtz, for example, writing in the late nineteenth century in defense of the empiricist theory of vision, uses the image to explain the physiological phenomenon of the inverted retinal image: "In its optical behaviour the eye is essentially like a *camera obscura.*" *Helmholtz's Treatise on Physiological Optics*, ed. James P. C. Southall, 3 vols. (New York: Dover, 1962), 1: 91 ("Optical System of the Eye"). The comparison had been made centuries earlier by J. B. Porta (1545–1615), but Helmholtz's use is anti-"Cartesian" in that it shifts the figure's connotation from transparency to anatomy.

30. In "La Révélation de la société invisible chez Balzac," Per Nykrog distinguishes Balzac's *voyance* from an occultist *clairvoyance*, citing an Apollinaire poem. Nykrog suggests that the Balzacian type of prophetic vision has less to do with religion, occultism, or superstition than with "une façon d'observer la nature / Et d'interpréter la nature [a way of observing nature / And interpreting nature]" (12). In *Balzac et les parents pauvres*, ed. Françoise van Rossum-Guyon and Michel van Brederode (Paris: Société d'Edition d'Enseignement Supérieur, 1981), 11–19.

31. As Peter Brooks writes, the Balzacian text continually slips from *vue* (physical sight) to *vision* (symbolic significance), but while the realm of meaning associated with *vision* remains the telos of the Balzacian text, it cannot be accessed without "the 'pressure' applied to the surfaces of the real, the insistence of the recording glance." *The Melodramatic Imagination: Balzac, Henry James, Melodrama, and the Mode of Excess* (New Haven, Conn.: Yale University Press, 1976), 125.

Chapter 2. "Tomber dans le phénomène": Afterimages in La Maison Nucingen *and* Le Bal de Sceaux

1. Helmholtz, in his *Treatise of Physiological Optics*, tells of a seventeenth-century wager in which Bonacursius bet a Jesuit scholar named Kircher that he could make a person see just as well in the dark as in the light. He won the bet by making Kircher look steadily at a drawing displayed in a window and then darkening the room and having him look at a blank piece of paper, on which Kircher plainly perceived the same drawing. *Helmholtz's Treatise on Physiological Optics*, ed. James P. C. Southall, 3 vols. (New York: Dover, 1924), 2: §23, 261.

2. Jonathan Crary, *Techniques of the Observer: On Vision and Modernity in the Nineteenth Century* (Cambridge, Mass.: MIT Press, 1990), 69.

3. *Helmholtz's Treatise on Physiological Optics*, 2: 229.

4. In *Techniques of the Observer*, Jonathan Crary writes, "First, . . . the privileging of the afterimage allowed one to conceive of sensory perception as cut from any necessary link with an external referent. The afterimage—the presence of sensation in the absence of a stimulus— . . . posed a theoretical and empirical demonstration of autonomous vision, of an optical experience that was produced by and within the subject. Second, and equally important, is the introduction of temporality as an inescapable component of observation" (98).

5. *La Maison Nucingen*, in Balzac, *La Comédie humaine*, 12 vols. ed. Pierre-George Castex, Bibliothèque de la Pléiade (Paris: Gallimard, 1976–81), vol. 6. Hereafter *MN*.

6. Remember that the *camera obscura* model elides not only corporeality (by reducing the body to one abstract point of perspective) but also temporality (by representing the act of seeing as virtually instantaneous).

7. Their tale belongs to Balzac's attempt to represent a moment of transition—from one form of capitalism (still anchored in precapitalist value systems) to another, more modern form: "From nascent capitalism to capitalism's glory days, from shame-faced wealth to insolent wealth, from monetary scarcity to monetary abundance, such is the evolution that, from *Gobseck* to *La Maison Nucingen*, Balzac forces us to probe." Pierre Citron, Introduction to *MN*, 326. Note that Citron's formulation, in addition to explaining the economic transition, also suggests an appeal to the senses in Balzac's representational mode: to the direct material witnessing of probing ("toucher du doigt").

8. On literary visualization as a phenomenological experience, see Ellen J. Esrock, *The Reader's Eye: Visual Imaging as Reader Response* (Baltimore: Johns Hopkins University Press, 1994).

9. Balzac, *Bal de Sceaux*, in *La Comédie humaine*, vol. 1, Anne-Meininger, Introduction, 1: 103 Hereafter *BS*. Fontaine's character is based on a real count, Ferrand, who followed his king's politics of compromise.

10. On the historic and literary connotations of fantasmagoria, see Max Milner, *La Fantasmagorie* (Paris: Presses Universitaires de France, 1982); and Terry Castle, "Phantasmagoria: Spectral Technology and the Metaphorics of Modern Reverie," *Critical Inquiry* 15 (Autumn 1988): 26–61.

11. On the mastering logic of the "tableau," see Michel Foucault, *Les Mots et les choses: une archéologie des sciences humaines* (Paris: Gallimard, 1966). On perspectival vision, see Norman Bryson, *Vision and Painting: The Logic of the Gaze* (New Haven, Conn.: Yale University Press, 1983); and Hubert Damisch, *L'Origine de la perspective* (Paris: Flammarion, 1988). See also Jann Matlock's work on depictions of women looking (often aided by lorgnons or other extensions of visual power), which suggests the existence in the early nineteenth century of a certain subjectivity that has often been denied to women of that historical period. Matlock identifies the early nineteenth century as "an era in which, rather than simply being 'forbidden' . . . , the woman's gaze is elicited, evoked, and problematized." "Censoring the Realist Gaze," in *Spectacles of Realism: Gender, Body, Genre*, ed. Margaret Cohen and Christopher Prendergast (Minneapolis: University of Minnesota Press, 1995), 35. See, too, Matlock, "The Invisible Woman and Her Secrets Unveiled," *Yale Journal of Criticism* 9, 2 (1996): 175–221, 184. Matlock's work provides a suggestive context for my argument here that Emilie's visual space, in 1815, was losing its coherence after a period of relative mastery.

12. Emilie's conservatism is perhaps textually figured by the stasis in this passage, which starts with *père* and ends with *pair*; despite the story's Austen-like telos of marriage, its heroine does not propel her family name forward through attachment to a young suitor, but ends up in a state of family retrenchment by marrying her great-uncle.

13. Jean-Joseph Goux's article "Descartes et la perspective," *L'Esprit Créateur* 15, 1 (Spring 1985): 10–20, examines the way the perspectival logic of Descartes' philosophical writings is "at once monarchical and democratic" in its positing of a central viewpoint from which a single subject (in the king position, whether actually king or not) sees the world: "This is what perspective postulates as a *cogito:*

absolute subjectivity does not contradict, indeed makes possible, perfect objectivity" (19). Commenting on this article, Virginia Swain writes: "The new emphasis on viewpoint both gave power and took it away—gave it, by placing the viewer at the optimum point of control, and refused it, by making this place open, democratically, to everyone." Virginia E. Swain, "*Lumières et Vision*: Reflections on Sight and Seeing in Seventeenth- and Eighteenth-Century France," *L'Esprit Créateur* 28, 4 (1988): 7.

14. In the end, I am proposing that *La Comédie humaine*, the material production of what started as an envisioned ideal, moves into a mode of visuality that incorporates the phenomenal world. This is in contrast to readers of Balzac who emphasize the symbolic, referential function of material objects in his texts—the ways in which vision for him is conceptual rather than perceptual. Fredric Jameson, for example, describes objects in the Balzacian text as primarily existing as signs rather than as percepts (given to bodily apprehension). Fredric Jameson, "Balzac et le problème du sujet," in *Le Roman de Balzac: recherches critiques, méthodes, lectures*, ed. Roland Le Huenen and Paul Perron (Ottawa: Marcel Didier, 1980), 65–76.

Chapter 3. Alternative Optics: Séraphîta, La Recherche de l'absolu, *and* La Peau de chagrin

1. Alain Robbe-Grillet, *Pour un nouveau roman* (Paris: Editions de Minuit, 1963); Roland Barthes, *Essais critiques* (Paris: Editions du Seuil, 1964).

2. Dällenbach wrote a series of articles in the early 1980s in which he called *La Comédie humaine* a "patchwork, a *bricolage*, a bundle of bits and pieces [*tout en morceaux*]": "Du fragment au cosmos." *Poétique* 40 (1979): 420–31; "Le Tout en morceaux," *Poétique* 42 (1980): 156–69; and "Le *Pas-tout* de *La Comédie*," *Modern Language Notes* 98 (1983): 702–11. And in his 1996 *La Canne de Balzac* (Paris: José Corti, 1996), a spirited meditation on the liberated play of the signifier, Dällenbach goes so far as to call Balzac a "'nouveau romancier' avant la lettre" (165).

3. Lucien Dällenbach, *Claude Simon* (Paris: Editions du Seuil, 1988), 48.

4. Note that Dällenbach calls the desire to see "beyond" unfulfillable, never satisfied. Peter Brooks has also rightly emphasized the perpetual frustration in Balzac of a scopophilic impulse: in *Reading for the Plot* and the more recent *Body Work*, he connects the epistemophilic propulsion of the realist novel to sexual desire ("vision in Balzac . . . almost always is 'scopophilia.'" *Body Work: Objects of Desire in Modern Narrative* (Cambridge, Mass.: Harvard University Press, 1993), 84. In keeping with the psychoanalytic and narrative implications of desire—whether formulated by Lacan as the unattainability of the "objet petit *a*" or by Barthes as the suspension of hermeneutic closure—the scopophilic drive in Balzac can never attain its end.

5. *La Peau de chagrin*, in *La Comédie humaine*, ed. Pierre-George Castex, 12 vols., Bibliothèque de la Pléiade (Paris: Gallimard, 1976–81), vol. 10.

6. Cited in André Maurois, *Prométhée; ou, la vie de Balzac* (Paris: Editions Robert Laffont, 1993), 174.

7. Among the contemporary *opticiens*' warning against being "blinded by the light," we find, for example, Reid and Buffon, both of whose work was known to Balzac. Reid tells of having experienced temporary "blindness" (in the form of a long-lasting "sparkling spot" or "luminous apparition" in the eye) due to looking directly at the sun through a telescope and warns his readers to avoid

similar retinal damage. French version in "De la vue," *Œuvres complètes* (Paris: Santelet et Cie, 1828), 1: 237. Similarly, Buffon writes of the dangers of "(an) overly bright impression of light: one disorder involves always seeing colored spots, white circles, or black dots that flit about like flies." Georges-Louis Buffon, "Observations sur les couleurs accidentelles et sur les ombres colorées," *Œuvres complètes* (Paris: Furne et Cie, 1853), 1: 655–662, 660.

8. *La Recherche de l'absolu,* in *La Comédie humaine,* 10: 743.

9. Similarly, the unworldly and fragile young lovers in *L'Enfant maudit,* Etienne and Gabrielle, flourish not in the sunlight—associated with a world of avarice and ambition from which they are protected—but in the soothing glow of the moon: "It was perhaps appropriate that these two beings first saw each other bathed in the mellow light of the moon, so as not to be immediately blinded by Love's radiance." *La Comédie humaine,* 10: 942.

10. *Facino Cane,* in *La Comédie humaine,* 6: 1030. See Janet Beizer, *Family Plots: Balzac's Narrative Generations* (New Haven, Conn.: Yale University Press, 1986), 24–25: "It is evident that Facino Cane's loss of sight, as retribution for excessive visual activity, translates the narrator's fear of madness (losing his senses) as punishment for the abuse of his powers of second sight." What the context of physiological optics adds is the underlying, literal danger of sight, not just "second sight," for the perceptual faculties already render the seer vulnerable before he becomes a blind visionary punished symbolically for the scopic/sexual transgressions that Beizer so suggestively traces. In the text, Balzac gives a blunt and literal explanation for Facino Cane's blindness: when asked how it happened, the blind man quickly responds, "By accident, . . . an accursed *goutte sereine*" (6: 1023) A note in the Pléiade edition explains that this term refers to a "Form of blindness wherein the eye remains transparent (amaurosis)" (1539) Interestingly, then, this is a form of blindness due not to opacity (as with a cataract), but to transparency, so that it accords with the logic of blinding light, not shadow.

11. *Séraphîta,* in *La Comédie humaine,* 11: 822.

12. Throughout the nineteenth century, scientists continued to debate the question raised in *Séraphîta* of whether color exists as a quality of an objective body or as an effect of light. As late as the 1870s, Helmholtz (in "Progress of Vision") still avoided a conclusive judgment, stating that some color qualities reside in the body of the object, while some reside in luminous effects. In an appended chapter to the 1924 edition of Helmholtz's *Treatise on Physiological Optics,* Christine Ladd-Franklin Southall writes, "Our ancestors thought that redness resides in the rose. They had, very naturally, no conception of the fact—now a commonplace of science (save for the physicists)—that there is no redness until specific light-frequencies have passed through the alchemy of the retina." Hermann von Helmholtz, *Helmholtz's Treatise on Physiological Optics,* ed. James P. C. Southall, 3 vols. in 2 (New York: Dover, 1924), 2: 457. Her parenthetical comment hints at the continuing polemics in the discussion of color theory.

13. Emanuel Swedenborg, *The Universal Human and Soul-Body Interaction* (New York: Paulist Press, 1984), 125.

14. The antique dealer is traditionally understood, as by Henri Evans, as less a "real character" than a symbol of the (unattainable) ideal. *Louis Lambert et la philosophie de Balzac* (Paris: Librairie José Corti, 1951), 64.

15. Helmholtz, *Treatise* (1924), 2: 296–97.

16. In 1760, Melville and Bouguer tried to account for shifting color appearances by invoking Newton's theory, which held that shadow colors were objective; Beguelin supported this in 1767 and was followed by Paula Schrank (1811),

Zschokke, Osann, and Pohlmann. Meanwhile, Rumford proposed the subjective nature of shadow color and his view was adopted by Goethe, Grotthuss, Brandes, and Tourtual. Helmholtz writes that it was Fechner who chiefly proved the subjective nature of these phenomena in the 1830s, to be further supported by the studies of Plateau and Chevreul, whose "Sur l'influence que deux couleurs peuvent avoir l'une sur l'autre, quand on les voit simultanément" appeared in 1832 in Paris, before "De la loi du contraste simultané des couleurs" (Strasbourg, 1839).

17. See Robert G. Weyant's introduction to Etienne Bonnot de Condillac, "An Essay on the Origin of Human Knowledge" (1756), in *Condillac's Treatise on the Sensations,* trans. Geraldine Carr (Los Angeles: University of Southern California School of Philosophy, 1930), xiii.

18. Donata Pesenti Campagnoni, "Les Machines d'optique comme métaphores de l'esprit," in *Les Arts de l'hallucination,* ed. Donata Pesenti Campagnoni and Paolo Tortonese (Paris: Presses de la Sorbonne Nouvelle, 2001), 133. Campagnoni traces, with interesting results, some of the literal and metaphorical references to camera obscura, kaleidoscopes, magic lanterns, panoramas, and fantasmagoria in nineteenth-century French literature. She notes that in Balzac's work the term *fantasmagorie* can range in connotation from mere magic trick to illusory spectacle (126). For a compelling discussion of the socio-historic phenomenon of the panorama in relation to the Balzacian project, see Maurice Samuels, "Realizing the Past: History and Spectacle in Balzac's *Adieu,*" *Representations* 79 (Summer 2002): 82–99.

19. Terry Castle's suggestive article on fantasmagoria describes a nineteenth-century shift in meaning from public light show to psychological illusion, from (technical) exterior to (psychic) interior, from spectacle to hallucination. "Phantasmagoria: Spectral Technology and the Metaphorics of Modern Reverie," *Critical Inquiry* 15 (Autumn 1988): 26–61. Campagnoni also describes the accretion of a hallucinatory sense onto the term *fantasmagoria,* as it becomes a metaphor for *une réalité seconde* impossible to distinguish from true reality (128). See also Max Milner, *La Fantasmagorie* (Paris: Presses Universitaires de France, 1982), which—along with his equally fascinating *On est prié de fermer les yeux: le regard interdit* (Paris: Gallimard, 1991)—remains a crucial reference on visuality in modern French fiction.

20. In a way, this reading goes against the interesting narratological analysis of Henri Mitterand, for whom the pell-mell order of the antique shop's objects represents an accumulatory "chosisme" that displaces Raphaël's "originary gaze." *L'Illusion réaliste* (Paris: Presses Universitaires de France, 1994), 19. As opposed to Zola's novelistic descriptions, in which multiple reminders of subjective perspective confirm to the reader that "perceptual contact has not ceased between the described object and the gaze's agent," Mitterand claims that *La Peau de chagrin*'s passage allows "the materiality of bric-à-brac" to "overwhelm the gaze of the person looking at it" (19). In his view, the very accumulation of objects undermines—or overwhelms—the formal rules of description that would assign a coherent point of view to an intratextual observer. With "the character" momentarily "lost in the overburdened description," the antique shop passage allows material objects to eclipse the seeing subject (20). I would argue, however, that Raphaël's perceptual experience in the shop does assert itself through sensory references and, moreover, that the opposition that Mitterand sets up between visual perception (aligned with subjective point of view) and descriptive materiality (signaling the real as independent of human observation) misses the tangled and necessary cooperation of perceiver and perceived that this "philosophical compost heap" allegorizes.

21. The earliest (1831) version of the text articulates this either/or subject/object logic even more explicitly: "these optical phenomena caused *either* by fatigue *or* by the tension of ocular forces, *or* by the vagaries of twilight." *La Peau de chagrin*, ed. Pierre Barbéris, Livre de Poche (Paris: Librairie Générale Française, 1984), 44, my emphasis.

22. Buffon, "Observations sur les couleurs accidentelles," 44.

23. M. H. Abrams, *Natural Supernaturalism: Tradition and Revolution in Romantic Literature* (New York: Norton, 1971), 414.

24. Tony James, *Dream, Creativity, and Madness in Nineteenth-Century France* (Oxford: Clarendon Press, 1995), 81.

Chapter 4. "Effets de lumière," or, A "Second" Second Sight: La Fille aux yeux d'or

1. Honoré de Balzac, *Le Père Goriot* (Paris: Editions Garnier Frères, 1960), 72.

2. A passing reference in *Les Secrets de la Princesse Cadignan* to a "moral" second sight suggests that worldly love can inspire such visual intuition: as the poet d'Arthez falls in love with the Princess Cadignan, "he noted the surprising phenomenon of moral second sight that a lovestruck man discovers within himself." *Les Secrets de la Princesse Cadignan*, in *La Comédie humaine*, ed. Pierre-George Castex, 12 vols., Bibliothèque de la Pléiade (Paris: Gallimard, 1976–81), 6: 438. For Scott Sprenger, the moral second sight is central to the idea of an "moral archaeology" in Balzac's work; see his "Balzac, archéologue de la conscience," in *La Mémoire en Ruines*, ed. Valérie-Angélique Deshoulières and Pascal Vacher (Clermont-Ferrand: CRIMC, 2000).

3. Balzac, *La Fille aux yeux d'or*, in *La Comédie humaine*, 5: 1039. Hereafter cited in text.

4. Christopher Prendergast, *Paris and the Nineteenth Century* (Oxford: Blackwell, 1992), 52–59. I will return to Prendergast's cogent analysis of the Paris passage in *La Fille aux yeux d'or*, but let me first mention here a bit of critical context for discussing Balzac's narration as "panoramic." In most cases of a nonlocalized narrator, interpreters have tended to figure the textual perspective as an omniscient, "angelic" gaze from above. Pierre Barbéris, for example, contrasts the passage we are discussing with other Balzacian descriptions of Paris that are "views from down below, wandering along the streets." *La Fille aux yeux d'or*'s Paris, he writes, is "seen from above." *Balzac: une mythologie réaliste* (Paris: Librairie Larousse, 1971), 104. Structuralist theorists of the 1970s strove to identify with more technical precision the narrative "point of view" implicit in various textual strategies. In narratological terms, *La Fille aux yeux d'or*'s description of Paris unfolds through a "focalisation sujet non délégué," that is, without any identified hypothetical observer, and a "focalisation objet externe"—that is, without entering into the thoughts or perceptions of the characters discussed. Beginning with Gérard Genette's *Figures III*, the problem of narrative perspective had been posed in terms of "focalisation." The terms I have used here come from Pierre Vitoux's reworking of Mieke Bal's efforts to define with even more precision than had early formalists the narrative modes of point of view. To Genette's categories of "récit à focalisation-zéro (non focalisé)," "focalisation interne," and "focalisation externe" have been added distinctions between the subject and the object of focalization. Vitoux's categories allow one to distinguish *La Fille aux yeux d'or*'s Paris description from its second section, which follows the adventures of Henri de Marsay. Both sections would fall under Genette's "focalisation-zéro"

mode, since the narrator of both parts imparts knowledge that surpasses the limits of any particular character's consciousness; both parts of the story partake, therefore, of a "focalisation sujet non-delégué." But as regards the *object* of focalization, the Paris section remains "externe" (the narrator does not impart the thoughts of particular characters), whereas the story of de Marsay includes indirect discourse on his and other characters' internal musings ("focalisation objet interne"). See Pierre Vitoux, "Le Jeu de la focalisation," *Poétique* 51 (September 1982): 359–68. While this language may now seem overtechnical, it is worth noting that even in the most abstracted narratological studies of textual procedures, the human subject of visual perception remains—if only through the optical metaphor of focalization—the crucial axis of distinction.

5. As Madeleine Fargeaud points out in her notes to the *Avant-propos,* Goethe's well-known analysis of the conflict characterized Cuvier as exclusively occupied by "the *description* of everything that happens within his sight," and Saint-Hilaire as attached primarily "to the search for the *analogies* and *obscure affinities between beings*" (*AP,* 1112). The distinction might be assimilated to what Claude Lévi-Strauss was later to call "the empirical" versus "the deductive." Claude Lévi-Strauss, introduction to *Anthropologie structurale* (Paris: Librairie Plon, 1958), 3–33. but as I discuss in Chapter 5, Cuvier's own writing, for its part, reveals more ambivalence about empiricism and induction than this dichotomy would suggest.

6. Françoise Gaillard, "La Science: modèle ou vérité? réflexions sur l'*Avant-propos à La Comédie humaine,*" in *Balzac: l'invention du roman,* ed. Claude Duchet and Jacques Neefs (Paris: Pierre Belfond, 1982), 57–83, 73.

7. Fargeaud notes that Balzac concedes victory to Saint-Hilaire on only the particular, limited point of *unité de composition,* while continuing to praise Cuvier throughout his writing—in *La Peau de chagrin* and *La Recherche de l'absolu,* for example. In *Illusions perdues,* Balzac calls Cuvier and Saint-Hilaire "two men of equal genius" (*AP,* 1117). See also Madeleine Ambriere, "Balzac homme de science(s): Savoir scientifique, discours scientifique et système balzacien dans *La recherche de l'absolu,*" in which she similarly concludes: "So it isn't Cuvier *or,* but rather *and* Geoffroy Saint-Hilaire; the former's method, the latter's system" (54), in *Balzac: L'invention du roman: colloques de Cerisy-la-Salle,* ed. Claude Duchet and Jacques Neefs (Paris: Belfond, 1982).

8. Michel Eugène Chevreul, "De la différence et de l'analogie de la méthode *a posteriori* expérimentale, dans ses applications aux sciences du concret et aux sciences morales et politiques" (Paris: Geuthier-Villars, 1871) (excerpt from *Comptes rendus des séances de l'Académie des Sciences,* vol. 71, meeting of October 17, 1870).

9. Roland Le Huenen and Paul Perron, "Balzac et la représentation," *Poétique* 61 (February 1985): 75–90, 90.

10. Shoshana Felman, "Rereading Femininity," *Yale French Studies* 62 (1981): 19–44, 37–38.

11. Roland Barthes, *S/Z* (Paris: Editions du Seuil, 1970), 61.

12. Balzac's valorization of particularly European ideas is echoed in his description of de Marsay, which starts out conforming to the tale's orientalist aura but ends with a paean to the Cartesian mind of rational thought: "De Marsay wielded the autocratic power of an Oriental despot. But this power, so poorly implemented in Asia by fools, was multiplied tenfold by European intelligence, by French wit, the liveliest and keenest of intelligence's devices" (1084–85).

13. Jean Starobinski, *Jean-Jacques Rousseau: la transparence et l'obstacle* (Paris: Gallimard, 1957), 104 (hereafter, *Transp.*); *L'Œil vivant* (Paris: Gallimard, 1961).

14. See chapter 2, "Dialectic of EnLIGHTenment," in Martin Jay, *Downcast Eyes:*

The Denigration of Vision in Twentieth-Century French Thought (Berkeley: University of California Press, 1994). Citing Derrida's extension of Starobinski's argument, Jay writes that the model of pure transparency casts aside actual sensorial perception, experience of human, living body: "In Rousseau, the Enlightenment's apotheosis of sight . . . paradoxically turns into its opposite" (93).

15. Peter Brooks, *Body Work: Objects of Desire in Modern Narrative* (Cambridge, Mass: Harvard University Press, 1993), 84.

16. Jean-Jacques Rousseau, *Julie; ou, La Nouvelle Héloïse* (Paris: Bordas, 1988), 604.

17. Jonathan Crary, *Techniques of the Observer: On Vision and Modernity in the Nineteenth Century* (Cambridge, Mass.: MIT Press, 1990), 91.

18. Geneviève Delattre, "De *Séraphîta* à *La Fille aux yeux d'or*," *L'Année Balzacienne* (1970): 183–226, 210.

19. Raymond Trousson, *Balzac disciple et juge de Jean-Jacques Rousseau* (Geneva: Droz, 1983), 95.

20. Béguin and Bonard both focus on this scene as the height of *picturalisation*, a "feast for the eye" and "actual visual orgy." Olivier Bonard, *La Peinture dans la création balzacienne: Invention et vision picturales de* La Maison du Chat-qui-pelote *au* Père Goriot (Geneva: Droz, 1969), 159. Rose Fortassier also notes the visual link between the scene and Delacroix's dramatic paintings, (preface to *La Fille aux yeux d'or* (Paris: Folio, 1976), 38.

21. On Paquita's double nature as related to the text's own heterogeneity, see Doris Y. Kadish, "Hybrids in Balzac's *La Fille aux yeux d'or*," *Nineteenth Century French Studies* 16 (Spring-Summer 1988): 270–78. Kadish suggestively links the characters' mixed nationality and mixed sexuality to the social impurities and "deviant politics" of Restoration society (271). See also Pierre Saint-Amand, "Balzac Oriental: *La Fille aux yeux d'or*," *Romanic Review* 79, 2 (March 1988): 329–40.

22. Séraphîta's second sight, "a kind of inner sight that penetrates everything" (794), is defined according to Swedenborg's *Exposition du sens interne*.

23. *Séraphîta*, 822.

24. Cited in Leyla Perrone-Moisés, "Le Récit euphémique," *Poétique* 17 (1980): 27–38, 30.

25. Condillac's *Traîté des sensations* of 1754 modifies his 1746 critique (in the *Essai sur l'origine des connaissances humaines*) of Locke's *Essay Concerning Human Understanding* (1690).

26. William Paulson, *Enlightenment, Romanticism, and the Blind in France* (Princeton, N.J.: Princeton University Press, 1987), 34–35.

27. "At the core of Leibniz's thought was the goal of reconciling the validity of universal truths with the inescapable fact of a world consisting of multiple points of view. The monad became, for Leibniz, an expression of a fragmented and decentered world, of the absence of an omniscient point of view, of the fact that every position implied a fundamental relativity that was never a problem for Descartes. At the same time, however, Leibniz insisted that each monad had the capacity to reflect in itself the whole universe from its own finite viewpoint." Crary, *Techniques of the Observer*, 50.

Chapter 5. Cuvier, Helmholtz, and the Visual Logics of Deduction: Poe, Doyle, Gaboriau

1. I use a culturally specific definition of the *roman policier* as a genre whose conventions emerged in Europe in the nineteenth century. Other critics have

expanded the boundaries of the term to include any "enigma-tales," such as Sophocles' *Oedipus*. For histories of the development of the detective novel, see Boileau-Narcejac, *Le Roman policier,* Que sais-je? (Paris: Presses Universitaires de France, 1975); Uri Eisenzweig, "L'Invention du genre," in Eisenzweig, *Le Récit impossible: forme et sens du roman policier* (Paris: Christian Bourgois, 1986); Fereydoun Hoveyda, *Histoire du roman policier* (Paris: Editions du Pavillon, 1965); Régis Messac, *Le "Detective Novel" et l'influence de la pensée scientifique* (Paris: Honoré Champion, 1929).

2. Sir Arthur Conan Doyle, *Adventures of Sherlock Holmes* (New York: Quality Paperback Book Club, 1994), 66.

3. I will return later in this chapter to Foucault's elaboration of the "empirico-transcendental doublet" as he articulates it in *Les Mots et les choses.*

4. See Michel Foucault, *Les Mots et les choses: une Archéologie des sciences humaines* (Paris: Gallimard, 1966). In Foucault's broad periodization, the modern (nineteenth and twentieth centuries) interest in the invisible contrasts with the "classical age" (seventeenth and eighteenth centuries) and its epistemological reliance on a primarily visual model: the taxonomical tableau ("taxonomy establishes the tableau of visible differences," 88). Foucault defines natural history in the classical age as "the naming of the *visible*" (144), a phrase that claims priority of sight over the other senses and, more basically, that posits a physiological sense as the basis for epistemological enquiry ("As of the seventeenth century, observation is a form of sense-based knowledge" 144); the microscope acts here as the dominant figure for the exclusion of other senses: "observing, then, only requires seeing" (145).

5. Ibid., 150.

6. Georges Baron Cuvier, *Recherches sur les ossemens fossiles de quadrupèdes,* vol. 1, *Discours préliminaire* (Paris: Deterville, 1812), 1–116.

7. To Cuvier, it is this "generalizing" capacity that makes the naturalist's work so compelling. William Coleman, *Georges Cuvier, Zoologist: A Study in the History of Evolution Theory* (Cambridge, Mass.: Harvard University Press, 1964), 96.

8. Sigmund Freud, *Civilization and Its Discontents,* ed. James Strachey (New York: Norton, 1961), 41–43.

9. Jacques Derrida's discussion of the logic of supplementarity—as both excessive addition and compensation for a lack—appears in *De la grammatologie* (Paris: Editions de Minuit, 1967), among other texts. In *Memoirs of the Blind: The Self-Portrait and Other Ruins,* trans. Pascale-Anne Brault and Michael Naas (Chicago: University of Chicago Press, 1993), Derrida extends the logic to the figure of the visual prosthetic—that is, to "technical objects intended, like prostheses, to supplement sight, . . . such as mirrors, telescopes, eyeglasses, binoculars, monocles" (70). Such instruments, being both connected to and detachable from the body, inhabit a liminal space between the subject and the world. This relation is relevant to my project not only as background for a local reading of Cuvier's language, but as a key to the larger question of empiricism versus abstraction, in which the figure of prosthesis functions as a mechanized compensation for the limitations of both purely sensory processing and purely cognitive reach.

10. Even within *Les Mots et les choses,* many "ambivalences in the terms of visuality" can be found. See Martin Jay, *Downcast Eyes: The Denigration of Vision in Twentieth-Century French Thought* (Berkeley: University of California Press, 1994), esp. 404–6.

11. Dorothy Sayers, "The Omnibus of Crime," in *Detective Fiction: A Collection of Critical Essays,* ed. Robin W. Winks (Englewood Cliffs, N.J.: Prentice-Hall, 1980).

12. Boileau-Narcejac, *Le Roman policier.*

13. Eisenzweig, *Le Recit impossible*, 8–9.

14. Messac, *Le "Detective Novel" et l'influence de la pensée scientifique*, 396. Unlike Messac, I will be using the term *roman policier* interchangeably with "detective novel," precisely because I want to blur the generic distinction between pure analysis and romanesque fiction.

15. See William Whewell, *History of the Inductive Sciences*, vols. 1 and 2 (1857; reprint New York: Olms Verlag, 1976).

16. See *Compact Oxford English Dictionary*, 2nd ed. (Oxford: Clarendon Press, 1987), s.v. "deduction."

17. Emile Gaboriau, *Monsieur Lecoq* (Paris: Liana Levi, 1992), 215–16. In *L'Affaire Lerouge* (1866), too, Tabaret exults in the "triomphe de [l]a méthode d'induction" in criminal justice.

18. Hermann von Helmholtz, *Helmholtz's Treatise on Physiological Optics*, ed. James P. C. Southall (New York: Dover, 1962), 2: 36.

19. Foucault, *Les Mots et les choses*, 330.

20. Although Dupin himself rejects a "purity" of mathematical thought, the abstraction of his reasoning motivated, partly, Lacan's and Derrida's readings of "The Purloined Letter" in terms of function and nonreferential relationality. See John P. Muller and William J. Richardson, *The Purloined Poe* (Baltimore: Johns Hopkins University Press, 1988), for the now classic exchange, along with other psychoanalytic and deconstructionist readings of Poe. For a fascinating (and mathematical) extension of the debate, see John T. Irwin, "Mysteries We Reread, Mysteries of Rereading: Poe, Borges, and the Analytic Detective Story. Also Lacan, Derrida, and Johnson," *Modern Language Notes* 101, 5 (December 1986): 1168–1215.

21. Edgar Allan Poe, *The Purloined Letter* (London: J.M. Dent, 1928), 18.

22. Doyle, *Adventures of Sherlock Holmes*, 117; my emphasis.

23. It is perhaps worth noting that Doyle was himself a failed ophthalmologist. See Sir Arthur Conan Doyle, *A Study in Scarlet* (Oxford: Oxford University Press, 1993), 7.

24. Ibid., 18–19.

25. Cuvier, *Recherches sur les ossemens fossiles de quadrupèdes,* 61.

26. William Coleman, *Georges Cuvier, Zoologist: A Study in the History of Evolution Theory* (Cambridge, Mass.: Harvard University Press, 1964), 44.

27. See ibid., 73.

28. Ibid., 107.

29. Ibid., 120.

30. Cited in Rosemary Jann, *The Adventures of Sherlock Holmes: Detecting Social Order* (New York: Twayne, 1995), 41.

31. See Coleman, *Georges Cuvier, Zoologist*, 116, on these two terms.

32. Honoré de Balzac, *Louis Lambert*, in *La Comédie humaine*, ed. Pierre-Georges Castex, Bibliothèque de la Pléiade (Paris: Gallimard, 1976–81), 11: 615.

33. See the Cerisy-la-Salle colloquium on the French detective novel, with contributions by Jean Tortel and Charles Grivel, among others: Noël Arnaud, Francis Lacassin, and Jean Tortel, eds., *Entretiens sur la paralittérature,* Centre culturel international de Cerisy-la-Salle (Paris: Plon, 1970).

34. *Helmholtz's, Treatise on Physiological Optics* (1924), 3: 228–30.

35. Ibid., 292.

36. A well-known example is Helmholtz's story of having mistaken, as a child, people in a far-off belfry for dolls. An understanding of scale, size, and distance was needed to interpret the scene correctly.

37. James Sully, *Outlines of Psychology* (1884), cited in Nicholas J. Wade and Michael Swanston, *Visual Perception: an Introduction* (London: Routledge, 1991), 186.

38. Massimo A. Bonfantini and Giampaolo Proni, "To Guess or Not To Guess?" in *The Sign of Three: Dupin, Holmes, Peirce,* ed. Umberto Eco and Thomas A. Sebeok (Bloomington: Indiana University Press, 1983), 119–34, 123. Eco and Sebeok's book examines the detective novel in terms of semiotics and "the logic of scientific discovery"; it identifies a primary structure of reasoning in detective fiction as *abduction,* a form of conjectural logic elaborated by C. S. Peirce that consists of reasoning from effect to probable cause.

39. Ibid., 122.

Chapter 6. Learning to See: Monsieur Lecoq *and Empiricist Theories of Vision*

1. For an extended discussion of the topic, see Michael J. Morgan, *Molyneux's Question: Vision, Touch and the Philosophy of Perception* (Cambridge: Cambridge University Press, 1977).

2. John Stuart Mill, quoted in Nicholas Pastore, *Selective History of Theories of Visual Perception: 1650–1950* (New York: Oxford University Press, 1971), 72.

3. During the nineteenth century, a small number of other cases of restored vision were documented, including "Franz's Case (1841)," written up by Abbott in 1864, and "Nunneley's Case" of 1858, but it was the Cheselden case that remained the most frequently cited source, ranking "as the most celebrated case study in the history of science until the early case studies of Freud came along" (Pastore, *Selective History,* 99).

4. William Paulson has described the French Enlightenment's general *desacralization* of blindness as a cultural theme and construct. *Enlightenment, Romanticism, and the Blind in France* (Princeton, N.J.: Princeton University Press, 1987), 5. This book remains a key touchpoint on the cultural legacies of the Molyneux problem in France.

5. Hermann von Helmholtz, *Helmholtz's Treatise on Physiological Optics,* ed. James P. C. Southall, 3 vols. (New York: Dover, 1962).

6. For Jean Tortel, for example, the genre is defined by its mythic "univers dichotomique." Jean Tortel, "Qu'est-ce que la paralittérature," in *Entretiens sur la paralittérature,* ed. Noël Arnaud, Francis Lacassin, and Jean Tortel, in association with the Centre culturel international de Cerisy-la-Salle (Paris: Plon, 1970).

7. Honoré de Balzac, *Une Ténébreuse affaire, La Comédie humaine,* ed. Pierre-Georges Castex, Bibliothèque de la Pléiade, vol. 8 (Paris: Gallimard, 1977), 513; Michel Foucault, *Surveiller et punir: naissance de la prison* (Paris: Gallimard, 1975), 214.

8. Notably, Doyle chose the colorful title of his first Sherlock Holmes mystery, *A Study in Scarlet* (1887), in direct homage to Gaboriau's *L'Affaire Lerouge.*

9. Emile Gaboriau, *Monsieur Lecoq* (Paris: Liana Levi, 1992), 14. Hereafter, cited in text.

10. Roland Barthes's definition of the hermeneutic function in *S/Z* has been imported into *roman policier* studies as a description of the genre's narrative structural "skeleton" of delays and deciphering. An excerpt from *S/Z,* "Delay and the Hermeneutic Sentence," for example, appears in the anthology of critical work on detective fiction, *The Poetics of Murder: Detective Fiction and Literary Theory,* ed. Glenn W. Most and William W. Stowe (San Diego: Harcourt Brace, 1983). Peter

Brooks brings structures of narrative desire to bear on Barthes's categories of suspense with his readings of detective fiction, especially Conan Doyle's "The Musgrave Ritual," in Brooks, *Reading for the Plot: Design and Intention in Narrative* (Cambridge, Mass.: Harvard University Press, 1992), 23–28.

11. By the time the genre has been fully codified and conventionalized, the detective novel will no longer represent any form of individual *Bildung*, or development. As Franco Moretti puts it, the detective novel is an anti-bildungsroman: "detective fiction's characters are inert indeed: they do not grow. In this way, detective fiction is radically anti-novelistic: the aim of the narration is no longer the character's development into autonomy, or a change from the initial situation, or the presentation of plot as a conflict and an evolutionary spiral, image of a developing world that it is difficult to draw to a close." Franco Moretti, *Signs Taken for Wonders: Essays in the Sociology of Literary Forms* (London: Verso, 1988), 137.

12. Emile Gaboriau, *Le Crime d'Orcival* (Paris: E. Dentu, 1868), 2.

13. Edgar Allan Poe, *Tales of Mystery and Imagination* (London: Grant Richard, 1902), 92.

14. Martin Priestman, *Detective Fiction and Literature: The Figure on the Carpet* (London: Macmillan, 1990), 6.

15. For Van Dine's rules, see Boileau-Narcejac, *Le Roman policier*, Que Sais-je? (Paris: Presses Universitaires de France, 1975), 51–55.

16. Geoffrey H. Hartman, "Literature High and Low: The Case of the Mystery Story," in Hartman, *The Fate of Reading and Other Essays* (Chicago: University of Chicago Press, 1975), 203–22, 207–8.

17. Robert Le Grand, *Dictionnaire de la langue française* 9 vols. (Paris: Dictionnaires Robert, 1985), 3: s.v. "éblouissement."

18. Helmholtz argues that the actual percepts available to us (lights, colors) are overruled by our experience (of solidity, space, distance) and by the "inductive conclusions" that allow us to identify particular configurations as objects (see especially vol. 3, §26, "Concerning the Perceptions in General"). We are for the most part unaware, as Helmholtz reminds us, of the mental processes at work in our perception: despite our active efforts, the association of ideas seems to be communicated to us directly and immediately, "without any effort of will or conscious activity on our part" (2: 293). Similarly, Lecoq is under the impression that he sees the truth through "hunches"; when Gévrol asks for an explanation of his theory, Lecoq gives an answer that assumes innate perception: "How do you explain a hunting dog's sense of smell [*flair*]?" (20).

19. See, for example, "éblouissement" in the 1793 *Encyclopédie méthodique*, ed. Monge, Bertholon Cassini, and other members of the Académie des Sciences (Paris, 1793).

20. The word *éblouissement,* with its melodramatic and medical connections to fainting spells and vertigo, seems to have sparked the imagination of many popular fiction writers in the later nineteenth century, from Balzac (e.g., *Une Ténébreuse affaire,* 50) to Ponson de Terail, *Les Exploits de Rocambole* (Paris: E. Dentu, 1868),2: 3). Ponson de Terail's writing, as overblown and sloppy as it might be, provides the modern reader insight into the "hot" words and best-selling plot twists of the time.

21. From *Le Petit Robert*: *éblouir*: (1) To disturb (sight, or a person's sight) through an over-bright burst of light. *See* "to blind." (2) Fig. (archaic). To trick through a deceptive burst of light [*éclat trompeur*], by something specious. *See* "to fascinate; to seduce; to deceive."

22. As Charles Grivel observed, the detective novel is "un jeu truqué" [a setup];

with its tricks of suspension and suspense, the *roman policier* spends its whole time hiding what it claims to reveal. Constantly putting off the reader's moment of revelation, it enacts not "an investigation," but "*the pretense* of an investigation." "Observation du roman policier," in *Entretiens sur la paralittérature* (Paris: Plon, 1970), 229–47, 235. In "Le Récit impossible," Uri Eisenzweig explains this speciousness of the genre as an insurmountable tension between "mystery and elucidation" *Le Recit impossible*, 55).

23. Foucault, *Surveiller et punir*, 215.

24. Gillian Beer, "'Authentic Tidings of Invisible Things': Vision and the Invisible in the Later Nineteenth Century," in *Vision in Context: Historical and Contemporary Perspectives on Sight*, ed. Terese Brennan and Martin Jay (New York: Routledge, 1996), 84–98; Rosalind E. Kraus, *The Originality of the Avant-Garde and Other Modernist Myths* (Cambridge, Mass.: MIT Press, 1985).

25. Dennis Porter, *The Pursuit of Crime: Art and Ideology in Detective Fiction* (New Haven, Conn.: Yale University Press, 1981), 124–25; cited in Priestman, *Detective Fiction and Literature*, 10.

26. D. A. Miller, *The Novel and the Police* (Berkeley: University of California Press, 1988), 35.

27. Eliane Escoubas, "L'Œil (du) teinturier," *Critique* 37, 418 (March 1982): 231–42, 233.

28. William Cheseldon, "An Account of Some Observations made by a Young Gentleman, who was born blind, or lost his Sight so early, that he had no Remembrance of ever having Seen, and was couch'd between 13 and 14 Years of Age," cited in Nicholas Pastore, *Selective History of Theories of Visual Perception: 1650–1950* (New York: Oxford University Press, 1971), 413.

Chapter 7. Sealed Chambers and Open Eyes: Leroux's Mystère de la chambre jaune

1. Other movie versions of the novel had been made by Maurice Tourneur (1913), Emile Chautard (1919), Marcel L'Herbier (1930), and Henri Aisner (1948).

2. Interview with Bruno Podalydès, in Gaston Leroux, *Le Mystère de la chambre jaune* (Paris: Garnier-Flammarion, 2003), 352.

3. Gaston Leroux, *Le Mystère de la chambre jaune*, Premiers Exploits de Rouletabille. (Paris: Editions Robert Laffont, 1961). Hereafter, cited in text.

4. Régis Messac, *Le "Detective Novel" et l'influence de la pensée scientifique* (Paris: Honoré Champion, 1929). One current and useful exception to theoretical antiscientism is David F. Bell, whose Serres-inflected work traces networks of meaning shared by nineteenth-century detective fiction and probability science. See, for example, his "Pensée probabiliste et récit policier: le cas de Poe," *Alliage* 37–38 (Winter 1998-Spring 1999): 100–122.

5. As early as 1908, private detectives advertised their services under the logo of an eye, thus linking the promise of omniscience ("You will know all") to the visual act; one French agency, comprised of detectives "of both sexes," was actually named "L'Œil." See Dominique Kalifa, *Naissance de la police privée: détectives et agences de recherches en France 1832–1942* (Paris: Plon, 2000), a riveting historical account of the birth of detective agencies. In Kalifa's taxonomy, Leroux's fictional detective counts merely as an amateur, but his primary function as journalist marks him as central to what Kalifa calls France's age of "investigation" or "enquête." See Kalifa, "Crimes et enquêtes criminelles en France à la fin du dix-neuvième

siècle," *Cahiers Victoriens et Edouardiens* 6 (April 2005), ed. Nathalie VanFasse and Anne-Marie Kilday, special issue, *La Déviance sociale en Angleterre et en France (1830–1900)*. I find the historical analogy between detection and journalism persuasive, but want to extend it further to an overarching model of inquiry, that of scientific investigation.

6. Related in Fereydoun Hoveyda, *Histoire du roman policier* (Paris: Editions du Pavillon, 1965).

7. The "closed room" quickly became a popular convention of the genre, starting with the upper room in Poe's "Murders in the Rue Morgue." For Uri Eisenzweig, the "lieu clos" reflects the particular historical concerns of modern French society and should be considered "the ultimate detective enigma." Uri Eisenzweig, "L'Instance du policier dans le romanesque: Balzac, Poe et le mystère de la chambre close," *Poétique* 51 (September 1982): 282.

8. The blurring of boundaries in detective fiction between interior and exterior is intriguingly explored from a Benjaminian perspective by Tom Gunning in "The Exterior as *Intérieur*: Benjamin's Optical Detective," *boundary 2* 30–31 (Spring 2003): 105. While his approach emphasizes the suggestive psycho-politics of bourgeois architectural space, my study points to an even more intimate site of interior/exterior porosity, the eye.

9. Called in optical treatises "flying gnats," *mouches volantes*, or *muscae volitantes*, these "entoptic" phenomena are caused by the cast shadow of small opaque particles suspended in the vitreous or aqueous humors or in the crystalline lens. Hermann von Helmholtz, *Helmholtz's Treatise on Physiological Optics*, ed. James P. C. Southall, 3 vols (New York: Dover, 1962), 1: 208–9, 218–21. Starting in the seventeenth century, when a Jesuit named Dechales attributed the origin of the *mouches volantes* correctly to shadows of little particles suspended in the eye in the retinal region, there were debates about whether the *mouches* are confined to the retina or in the transparent media; advances in the study of such entoptic phenomena led to Purkinje's and Burow's observations in the nineteenth century of the "yellow spot" in the center of the field of view that affected the movements of the *mouches*.

10. *Helmholtz's Treatise on Physiological Optics*, 1: 209.

11. Félix Giraud-Teulon, *Physiologie et pathologie fonctionnelle de la vision binoculaire* (Paris: J.-B. Baillière, 1861), 92.

12. That the Stangersons represent a "science of the future" (30), destined to lead to the Curie's discovery of radium, implies conversely that Rouletabille clings to a more conservative (in both senses, as he believes in the conservation of matter) theory; indeed, I will return later in the chapter to Rouletabille's reactionary scientific thrust.

13. Yves Le Grand, *Physiological Optics*, trans. Sami G. El Hage (Berlin: Springer-Verlag, 1980), 35; *Helmholtz's Treatise on Physiological Optics*, 2: 301.

14. Muller and Richardson's *The Purloined Poe* bring together key essays—by Derrida, Barbara Johnson, and others—responding to and extending the poststructuralist and psychoanalytic implications of Lacan's study of "The Purloined Letter." Johnson's essay is particularly interesting for its discussion of the "mathematics" of deduction.

15. The textual clues include an evocative "scent of the lady in black" (55), the "maternal" interest taken in Rouletabille (126), the young journalist's physical resemblance to Larsan (the physiognomic "bosses," that "sautaient aux yeux" [jump right out at you], 142). Even at the end, Leroux teases out the mystery; Miss Stangerson and the criminal had had a son years earlier, whereabouts unknown,

whose story is to be continued in the sequel, *Mystère de la dame en noir.* Through the occulted blood relation, Rouletabille comes to inhabit the "insider" position that allows his to see from the perspective of the Yellow Room/yellow spot, moving thus from subterranean Oedipal misprision to partial revelation.

16. *Presbytère* comes from ecclesiastical Latin for priest; *presbyte* from Greek "old man" (*Le Petit Robert*). (A link of sorts can be found in the *Shorter Oxford* entry for *presbyter*, an elder of the church.)

17. Carlo Ginzburg, "Clues: Roots of an Evidential Paradigm," in *Clues, Myths, and the Historical Method,* trans. John Tedeschi and Anne C. Tedeschi (Baltimore: Johns Hopkins University Press, 1989), 111. Hereafter, cited in text.

18. Geoffrey H. Hartman, "Literature High and Low: The Case of the Mystery Story," in Hartman, *The Fate of Reading and Other Essays* (Chicago: University of Chicago Press, 1975).

19. Miss Stangerson's disturbing silence and narrative marginalization might be compared with the heroine of Charlotte Perkins Gilman's *The Yellow Wallpaper,* a turn-of-the-century American text in which insanity results from enclosure in a domestic space.

20. In *Reading in Detail,* Naomi Schor points out that Ginzburg links the conjectural method not only to the animalistic primitive but also to the feminine. The feminine aspect of an "epistemology of detail" might suggest that Rouletabille's excessive pride in using deductive reasoning rather than evidentiary, material, visible clues indicates a desire to distinguish himself from the criminal Larsan, as the link to the maternal Miss Stangerson, as well as a denial of his own feminine impulses (such as the awkward kiss he plants on the narrator).

21. See Hoveyda, *Histoire du roman policier,* on this point.

Chapter 8. Death and the Retina: Claire Lenoir, L'Accusateur, *and* Les Frères Kip

1. Garrett Stewart, "Introduction," *PMLA* (May 2002): 429. The comment comes in Stewart's introduction to a cluster of three essays on science and literature in the nineteenth century; they treat, respectively, Keats and vitalism, Tennyson and thermodynamics, decadent fiction and positivism.

2. Jules Verne, *Les Frères Kip* (Paris: Hachette, 1972), 40. Hereafter cited in text.

3. Jules Claretie, *L'Accusateur* (Paris: Bibliothèque Charpentier, 1897), 6. Hereafter cited in text.

4. Villiers de l'Isle-Adam, *Claire Lenoir et autres contes insolites* (Paris: Garnier-Flammarion, 1984), 106. Hereafter cited in text.

5. Max Milner mentions optogram fiction in the context of "photography, which remains the primary point of intersection between optics and temporality, because in it the image sheds its burden of present-ness and the instant is transformed into image." *On est prié de fermer les yeux: le regard interdit,* Collection Connaissance de l'Inconscient (Paris: Gallimard, 1991), 191. More recently, Daniel Grojnowski has suggestively linked the spectral, alchemical effects of photography in Villiers, Verne, Claretie, Hello, and Bloy to the occult sciences of late nineteenth-century France. "Sortilèges photographiques, de Villiers à Strindberg," *Romantisme* 105 (1999): 71–83. And, of course, Philippe Bonnefis had already discussed *Les Frères Kip* in his essay "Clair obscur," *Littérature* 26 (May 1977): 10–23, which probes the figural, metaphysical, ideological, and psychoanalytical implications of early photography.

6. One might add that the development of photographic technology was itself

already closely linked to optical science: among the earliest producers of daguerrotypes in the 1830s were the opticians Chevalier, Bianchi, Philippe, Gaiffe, Bloch, and Dörfell; and it was thanks to progress in the study of optical light and chemistry that the photographic process was improved in the 1840s. See Jean-Claude Lemagny and André Rouillé, *A History of Photography*, trans. Janet Lloyd (Cambridge: Cambridge University Press, 1987) , 23–24.

7. See Arthur Evans, "Optograms and Fiction: Photo in a Dead Man's Eye," *Science-Fiction Studies* 20, 3 (1993): 341–61. In this wide-ranging overview of the novel's roots in the scientific experiments of ocular physiology in the 1870s, Evans traces the optogram topos to cultural contexts as varied as Scotland Yard's Jack the Ripper investigation notes, Rudyard Kipling's imperialist *At the End of the Passage* (1891), post-Civil War fiction in America, and twentieth-century science fiction novels and films that employ high-tech brain scanners as imaginary variants of retinal photography.

8. See Hermann von Helmholtz, *Helmholtz's Treatise on Physiological Optics*, ed. James P. C. Southall, 3 vols. (New York: Dover, 1962), 2: 52.

9. George Wald, "Eye and Camera" (1953), cited in Evans, "Optograms and Fiction," 342.

10. Bonnefis, "Clair-obscur," 19.

11. The latter is a term highlighted by Mieke Bal's 1997 book on Proust, translated as *The Mottled Screen: Reading Proust Visually*, trans. Anna-Louise Milne (Stanford, Calif.: Stanford University Press, 1997). Bal takes it from an early scene in *A la recherche du temps perdu* in which the visual similarly interposes itself into the representational realm (in this case, reading) and contrasts its conjunction of imagination and eye with Zola's "translucent" naturalist poetics (18).

12. E. Drougard writes that he was unable to find any mention of the optogram in the "Comptes-rendus des séances de l'Académie des Sciences de Paris" between 1850 and 1867, but cites the 1876 Larousse dictionary entries on "optogramme" and "optographie" and an 1876 issue of the *Gazette Médicale*, in which Boll's and Kühne's experiments are mentioned. Villiers de l'Isle-Adam, *Les Trois premiers contes: Claire Lenoir, L'Intersigne, L'Annonciateur*, ed. E. Drougard, critical ed. (Paris: Presses Universitaires de France, 1931), 78–80. Drougard's inability to find earlier reports on the retinal image leads him to conclude that Villiers' imagination had anticipated science (81–82); we now know that optical physiologists (and not only journalistic writers of *puffs* and *canards*) had already made inroads into the study of this afterimage effect.

13. Dr. Vernois's retinal photograph has recently been reprinted in Daniel Grojnowski's article "Sortilèges photographiques." The image, recovered from a murdered woman's eye, looks hopelessly blurred to us (as it had to many 1860s readers of the journal). Dr. Vernois, however, claimed to see in it the triple image of the woman's murderer, her child, and the family dog! Not surprisingly, given the image's illegibility, the technique of retinal photography turned out to be entirely impractical in the judicial world.

14. In his 1935 "The Scoptophilic Instinct and Identification," Otto Fenichel assimilates bibliophilia to the Freudian theory of scoptophilia. The passion for books—and scientific inquiry in particular—is understood as a visual drive that sublimates a sexual, primordial, or bestial impulse by displacing it onto the abstract, intellectual realm. In a way, any detective's investigation might be read in this light, as the *roman policier* genre itself functions according to a decorporealizing or sublimating formal impulse that displaces a blood-splattering moment of violence onto the extended plotline of abstract ratiocination. But while other

detectives are rarely seen actually doing their research (their *acquisition* of relevant knowledge takes place offstage), Claretie's Bernardet fits the scoptophilic profile more directly, as he is presented to the reader in the full throes of bibliophilic pleasure. See my "Curiosity's Killer Instinct: Bibliophilia and the Myth of the Rational Detective," *Yale French Studies*, special issue on crime fiction, ed. Andrea Goulet and Susanna Lee (Fall-Winter 2005): 48–59.

15. Félix Giraud-Teulon, *La Vision et ses anomalies* (Paris: J.-B. Baillière, 1881), 287–88.

16. Ibid., 273.

17. Giraud-Teulon includes a section in his treatise "Réserves à faire encore sur le caractère photographique des images rétiniennes" (277–79), in which he cites physiological evidence (like the existence of a small nonpigmented section of the retina) to caution against a too hasty reduction of vision to "a sort of retinal photography."

18. Ross Chambers, "'De grands yeux dans l'obscurité': regard scientifique et vision occulte dans *Claire Lenoir* et l'*Eve Future*," *Australian Journal of French Studies* 9, 3 (September-December 1972): 308–25, 309.

19. Ibid., 309.

20. This epigraph, appearing in the 1887 version, replaces the following Baudelaire quotation of the earlier version: "My child has dark eyes, deep and vast/ Like you, great night! Like you, they are alight!" (Villiers de l'Isle-Adam, *Les Trois premiers contes*, 51). The Hugolian *clair/obscur* of the 1867 quote, with its evocation of a visionary affinity between self and space, gives way to a more uncanny sense of otherness in the self—the "that which sees" lurking within the eye—in the d'Aubelleyne citation; as I will argue in later sections of this chapter, the "hantise de l'autre en moi" [obsession of the other within the self], as Françoise Gaillard has put it, is characteristic of the later, fin-de-siècle moment in France. Villiers' epigraph alteration combines this new split (between self and hidden other) with an emphasis on the clay-ey nature, the thick materiality, of the human eye.

21. In fact, it may be a paradoxical quality of the fantastic that in its very flights of fancy, it is more literalizing—of both science and metaphor—than is the realist mode.

22. Gustave Flaubert, *Bouvard et Pécuchet* (Paris: Garnier-Flammarion, 1966), 72. In this humorous scene, which combines physiological optics and hypnotism, a doctor finally explains the weird trances that Pécuchet has been experiencing as he wanders outside wearing a visored hat.

23. The very enumeration of these modes of observing the eye creates narrative out of science and its advancements.

24. In some ways, the conception of vision has always, at each moment, oscillated between opacity and transparency. At this fin-de-siècle moment, however, a new understanding of physiology switches from oscillation or coexistence to interrelated imprint. Certainly, after the 1870s, the visual relation between subject and world cannot imply the clarity, the translucence associated—rightly or wrongly—with the Cartesian age. Bonnefis is right to distinguish (while inserting it into its genealogy) the optogram from an earlier Cartesian moment of the famous "l'œil d'un homme fraîchement mort [the eye of a newly dead man]"; "Une variante d'importance est . . . introduite: l'image, ici, est non seulement révélée, elle est en outre conservée" [An important variation is . . . introduced: here, the image is not merely revealed, it is also preserved] (Bonnefis, "Clair obscur," 18).

25. "We think we know what properly belongs or does not belong to the human body, what is detached or not detached from it—even though the parergon is precisely an ill-detachable detachment." Jacques Derrida, *The Truth in Painting*, trans. Geoff Bennington and Ian McLeod (Chicago: University of Chicago Press, 1987), 59). (Derrida's concept gives a twist to our idea of floaters or *mouches volantes* as both normal phenomena of subjective vision and pathological symptoms of retinal detachment.)

26. The story's three references to "feux d'artifice [fireworks]" were added into the 1887 version (Villiers de l'Isle-Adam, *Les Trois premiers contes*, 139, 154, 159).

27. Grojnowski, "Sortilèges photographiques," 77n.

28. Bonnefis, "Clair obscur," 20.

29. With characteristic overstatement, Claretie repeats the point throughout the novel: "folie hier, vérité demain [yesterday's folly, tomorrow's truth]!" (55); "C'est l'heure des miracles. . . . Le vingtième siècle en verra bien d'autres [This is the era for miracles. . . . The twentieth century will witness many more of them]" (310).

30. As witnessed by his multiple articles collected in the multivolume *La Vie à Paris*, Claretie was an avid observer of his era, as well as being fully engaged in the Parisian scene himself. He directed the Comédie française and shows up as an audience member, for example, in the famous image by André Brouillet, in "A Clinical Lesson of Dr. Charcot at the Salpêtrière" (1887).

31. There has been ample study of the combination in fin-de-siècle European literature and thought of positivist scientism with inquiry into the mysteries of death and the afterlife. Perhaps one of the simplest formulations of why such an obsession would coalesce at the end of a century is to be found in Asti Hustvedt's Introduction to *The Decadent Reader*: "Simply by measuring time in hundred year cycles, we create the inevitable metaphors of birth and death. At the end of the nineteenth century in France, this metaphor of a dying century became a veritable obsession in popular culture." Asti Hustvedt, ed., *The Decadent Reader: Fiction, Fantasy, and Perversion from Fin-de-Siècle France* (New York: Zone Books, 1998), 10.

32. Death and photography have been linked literally (the sociological context of morgue photographs; the "vernacular" photo-mementos of the dead that Geoffrey Batchen has recently studied) and metaphorically ("Death is the *eidos* of the Photograph," writes Barthes in *Camera Lucida*, 15) since well before the advent of the camera: Bonnefis' essay writes a "long history" of photography, showing that its origins in the eighteenth-century camera obscura, in Nicephore Niepce's 1826 *bitume* proof, and even in the Shroud of Turin have always primally, deeply linked photography to death, mourning, and memory, "as if the camera had in a single step taken up a position between the evidence of death and the forgetting of it" ("Clair obscur," 13).

33. Milner, *On est prié de fermer les yeux*, 191.

34. In Kries's appendix to Helmholtz, he states that "The *temporal relations* of the processes of stimulation are much more complicated than was formerly supposed" (2: 443, "Temporal Effects of Stimulations") and describes the observation of successive stages of sensation following short-lived stimuli on the retina, with "dark gaps" occurring between the secondary image (called "afterimage" by Purkinje, "recurrent vision" by Young and Davis, "pursuant image" by Kries, "ghost" by Bidwell, and "satellite" by Hamaker) and a blurred tertiary image, subsequently followed by a phase of "darkening" (444).

35. Giraud-Teulon, *La Vision et ses anomalies*, 273.

36. Ibid., 273–74.

37. The retinal image acts, in all senses of the word, as a medium: a way to access, through troubled temporality, an uncanny and ultimately unknowable realm. Even more concretely, in this age so concerned with the hauntings, revenants, and the occult afterlife of the spirit world, the optogram literally brings the dead back to life: in Heidelberg in 1877, Kühne reactivated the photochemical plate of the retina minutes after a subject's death through a process that Giraud-Teulon calls the "revivification of matter" (275).

Chapter 9. Optogram Fiction: Communication, Doubt, and the Fantastic

1. Félix Giraud-Teulon, *La Vision et ses anomalies* (Paris: J.-B. Baillière, 1881), viii (citing X. Doudan, Eloge de Villemarin).

2. Hermann von Helmholtz, *Helmholtz's Treatise on Physiological Optics*, ed. James P. C. Southall, 3 vols. (New York: Dover, 1962), 2: 5.

3. Jules Verne, *Les Frères Kip* (Paris: Hachette, 1972), 62. Hereafter cited in text.

4. In the mid-century, Esquirol established a distinction between "illusion," the misidentification of an existing object (like the seal in this Verne passage), and "hallucination," a purely subjective vision with no external stimulus. The distinction is upheld by various writers and thinkers at mid-century. See Tony James in *Les Arts de l'hallucination*, ed. Donata Pesenti Campagnoni and Paolo Tortonese (Paris: Presses de la Sorbonne Nouvelle, 2001), 15–32. But by the time that Verne is writing, these distinctions break down in various contexts, including in physiological optics. Giraud-Teulon writes, for example, of an intermediate category of visual hallucination, the "ragle" of the desert, in which the desert traveler's visions are often based on existing forms, but whose new shapes are culturally determined.

5. Michel Serres, *Jouvences sur Jules Verne* (Paris: Editions de Minuit, 1974), 13.

6. For his part, Helmholtz wrote in his physiological treatise on the phenomenon of snow blindness and was particularly interested in polar scapes as the ideal images for stereoscopic viewing.

7. Cited in Marie-Hélène Huet, "Itinéraire du texte," in *Jules Verne et les sciences humaines*, ed. François Raymond and Simone Vierne (Centre culturel international de Cerisy-la-Salle: Union Générale d'éditions, 1979), 9–26, 18, my emphasis.

8. Ibid., 22–23.

9. Jules Claretie, *L'Accusateur* (Paris: Bibliothèque Charpentier, 1897), 58. Hereafter cited in text.

10. Max Milner, *La Fantasmagorie* (Paris: Presses Universitaires de France, 1982), 195.

11. In a way, this spectacle represents precisely the underside of the futuristic optimism of the whole book's premise summed up in its epigraph, "Today's dream, Tomorrow's reality!"; the club's emcee, "dressed in mourning" announces with raillery: "This shows you the rot awaiting you tomorrow, rotten Parisians of today!" (219).

12. Villiers de l'Isle-Adam, *Claire Lenoir et autres contes insolites* (Paris: Garnier-Flammarion, 1984), 64. Hereafter, cited in text.

13. Villiers de l'Isle-Adam, *Les Trois premiers contes: Claire Lenoir, L'Intersigne, L'Annonciateur*, ed. E. Drougard, critical ed. (Paris: Presses Universitaires de France, 1931), 54–55.

14. A. W. Raitt, *Villiers de l'Isle-Adam et le mouvement symboliste* (Paris: Librairie José Corti, 1965), 191.

15. Jacques Noiray, introduction to Villiers de l'Isle-Adam, *Claire Lenoir et autres contes insolites* (Paris: Garnier Flammarion, 1984), 12.

16. Raitt, *Villiers de l'Isle-Adam,* 191.

17. Gwenhaël Ponnau describes the fin-de-siècle fear of solipsism, with madness as the extreme limit of subjectivity realigning with idealism (an idea that brings Lenoir's own musings full circle. *La Folie dans la littérature fantastique* (Paris: CNRS, 1987), 246.

18. As though to highlight the discourse of optics as a sneaky, snaky intertext for this story, Villiers frames his characters' high-minded debates with comically physical effects on their eyes. I have already mentioned the diamond that Bonhomet dangles in front of Lenoir's eyes in order to confound him, with the undesired result that Lenoir "opened his eyes as wide as he could" (67) rather than shut his eyes protectively—a sign that he has retained mastery in this comic debate. Bonhomet's eyes, on the other hand, register defeat, as one of Claire's metaphysical questions about the mystery of the *au-delà* makes him "blush to the whites of his eyes" (66); once again, we are tempted to take the amusing phrase literally, as a recognition of human folly that irrupts into a realm that had been kept artificially transparent, the realm of mastering knowledge and totalizing vision.

19. Milner makes a similar point when he writes of "the chance to both ridicule scientists' presumptuousness and to beat them on their own turf by requiring them to act as agents for this experimental verification of the spiritual, the dream of many fin-de-siècle believers who were more contaminated by materialism than they realized." *La Fantasmagorie,* 199.

20. Campagnoni and Tortonese, *Les Arts de l'hallucination,* 47.

21. Ernest Hello, *Du genre fantastique* (1858), cited in Ponnau, *La folie,* 36.

Chapter 10. Tropical Piercings: Nationalism, Atavism, and the Eye of the Corpse

1. Chris Bongie's *Exotic Memories: Literature, Colonialism, and the Fin de Siècle* (Stanford, Calif.: Stanford University Press, 1991) describes a shift from mid-century high colonialism to a fin-de-siècle exoticist discourse characterized by the very "end of the exotic," that is, by a confrontation—spurred by ever-increasing European geopolitical expansion—with the inevitable breakdown of civilized/barbarous dichotomies (17). The final decades of the nineteenth century mark the advent of a global modernity that "inevitably, and irreparably, puts into question the Other's autonomy, absorbing this Other into the body of the Same and thereby effacing the very ground of exoticism" (18). Bongie's use of the "body" metaphor to describe this geopolitical effect confirms the (metaphysical, physiological, and narrative) boundary blurring that marks what I have been calling a fin-de-siècle optogram logic.

2. The ur-example of a South Sea violent intruder into European urban space is, as Larry Schehr reminds me, the orangutan in Poe's "Murders in the Rue Morgue."

3. Pierre-Georges Castex, *Le Conte fantastique en France de Nodier à Maupassant* (Paris: Librairie José Corti, 1951), 8; Roger Caillois, *Au coeur du Fantastique* (1965), cited in Gwenhaël Ponnau, *La Folie dans la littérature fantastique* (Paris: CNRS, 1987), 4.

4. Jacques Noiray, Introduction to Villiers de l'Isle-Adam, *Claire Lenoir et autres contes insolites* (Paris: Garnier-Flammarion, 1984), 12.

5. Jules Verne, *Les Frères Kip* (Paris: Hachette, 1972), 7. Hereafter, cited in text.

6. Based on a reading of *Les 100 millions de la Bégum*, Bruno Latour identifies Jules Verne as a "pre-Pasteurian hygienist": Verne, he writes, "contrasts Hygié, the healthy French town, with Noson, the unhealthy 'Boche' town, without the slightest mention of a microbe." Bruno Latour, *The Pasteurization of France*, trans. Alan Sheridan and John Law (Cambridge, Mass.: Harvard University Press, 1988), 23. Whether or not Verne incorporated the bacteriological theory into his thinking, however, his work reflects a generalized European obsession with defense against contagion that Latour describes thus: "The vague words 'contagion,' 'miasma,' and even 'dirt' were enough to put Europe in a state of siege, and it defended itself by cordons sanitaires against the infectious diseases" (25). By the time Verne wrote *Les Frères Kip*, the colonial project had joined forces with the Pasteurizing movement, as tropical medicine and the control of infectious diseases became flourishing fields (140 et passim).

7. Rudyard Kipling, "At the End of the Passage," in *The Collected Works of Rudyard Kipling* (New York: Doubleday, 1941), 154.

8. Claretie playfully invokes Kipling in *L'Accusateur* through a character's skepticism regarding the book's ophthalmological premise: "It's as diverting as one of Edgar Poe's tales . . . ," says a morgue doctor, "But finding the specter of the killer in those eyes, come now! Leave that to the likes of Rudyard Kipling" (98).

9. Villiers, *Claire Lenoir*, 48–49. Hereafter, cited in text.

10. For more on Lombroso's mark on crime fighting in fin-de-siècle France, see Robert Nye, *Crime, Madness, and Politics in Modern France* (Princeton, N.J.: Princeton University Press, 1984); and Pierre Darmon, *Médecins et assassins à la Belle Epoque: la Médicalisation du crime* (Paris: Editions du Seuil, 1989).

11. Jules Claretie, *L'Accusateur* (Paris: Bibliothèque Charpentier, 1897), 109–10. Hereafter, cited in text. See Christian Phéline, *L'Image accusatrice*, Cahiers de la Photographie 17 (Laplume: ACCP, 1985), on the late nineteenth-century rise and eclipse (by fingerprinting) of Bertillon's application of anthropometry and photography to the police work of criminal identification.

12. Early doubters of the Bertillon system pointed out imprecisions with the photographic identification method applied to imprisoned criminals; physical traits, they noted, were not always objectively readable—and interestingly, the central locus of possible confusion was the eye: "we open their eyes and discuss the color of their eyes, a subject of some disagreement" (37).

13. This description, though seemingly unconnected to the epistemological repercussions of the retinal optogram, touches on its themes of two-sided fixity (the glaze of death and the anchoring by light), of knowability and the occult ("pursuers of the unknown"), and of liminality and unstable boundaries ("scan the horizon").

14. Laura Otis, *Membranes: Metaphors of Invasion in Nineteenth-Century Literature, Science, and Politics* (Baltimore: Johns Hopkins University Press, 1999), 90.

15. Phéline, *L'Image accusatrice*, 55.

16. Latour, *The Pasteurization of France*. One of the key elements of Latour's argument is that the "Pasteurization" of France came about through a constellation of social forces, whose flux and resistance prepared the terrain for contagion theory, rather than as a clearly marked epistemological rupture marked by Pasteur's sheep inoculations of 1881 (49–50).

17. Michel Serres, *Jouvences sur Jules Verne* (Paris: Editions de Minuit, 1974), 259.

18. Phéline, *L'Image accusatrice*, 47.

19. Ibid., 45.

20. Like the optogram fiction I am discussing in this chapter, Guy de Maupassant's *Le Horlà* combines optical effects of epistemological uncertainty (e.g., the mirror scene) with the theme of contagion through geographical crossings (South America/Europe). Maupassant, *Contes et nouvelles,* ed. Louis Forrestier, Bibliothèque de la Pléiade (Paris: Gallimard, 1979), 2: 935. I am indebted to Françoise Gaillard for bringing to my attention these interconnected mind frames of the late nineteenth century: Freud, Pasteur, and the hauntings of *La Bête humaine* and *Le Horlà.* In her seminars at the 1999 French Cultural Studies Institute held at Dartmouth College, Gaillard related the "stranger coming from afar" in *Le Horlà* to the Freudian "phylogenetic phantasy: "the distant ancestor who returns within him, an indelible imprint of a past beyond recollection," thus suggestively setting up the late nineteenth century as a "prehistory" of a modern decentering of the subject.

Chapter 11. The Fin-de-Siècle Logic of the Afterimage: Hysteria, Hallucination, and Villiers's L'Eve future

1. The term "iconotope" is taken from Hamon's 2001 book *Imageries,* in which he identifies nineteenth-century literature's characteristic tendency "to localize images, to embody the issue of the image within a specific topography." Continues Hamon: "These sites are organized in literature according to a particular logic, which forms a system, creating what might be referred to as the century's *iconotope.*" *Imageries: littérature et image au XIXe siècle* (Paris: Librairie José Corti, 2001), 31. I am suggesting such a localization not just in the eye—(Hamon writes of the *chambre obscure* as an iconotope of the century), but in the retinal membrane. The afterimage phenomenon is more than a metaphor for knowledge at the fin de siècle; it restructures the relation of knowledge to the unknown.

2. Mark Micale's *Approaching Hysteria: Disease and Its Interpretations* (Princeton, N.J.: Princeton University Press, 1995) is a useful resource for multidisciplinary writings on hysteria. Micale cites a shift from gynecological and demonological models to the neurological studies of the late nineteenth century, to be followed in the Freudian age by psychological theories of the disease. Important interventions on the topic have also been made by Janet Beizer, *Ventriloquized Bodies: Narratives of Hysteria in Nineteenth-Century France* (Ithaca, N.Y.: Cornell University Press, 1994), Elaine Showalter, "On Hysterical Narrative," *Narrative* 1 (January 1993): 24–35, and *The Female Malady: Woman, Madness, and English Culture, 1830–1980* (New York: Pantheon, 1985); Charles Bernheimer and Claire Kahane, eds., *In Dora's Case: Freud-Hysteria-Feminism* (New York: Columbia University Press, 1985); and the art historian Georges Didi-Huberman, *Invention de l'hysterie: Charcot et l'iconographie photographique de La Salpêtrière* (Paris: Macula, 1982). Jann Matlock reminds us that hysteria has primarily been understood through a sexual-pathological lens. *Scenes of Seduction: Prostitution, Hysteria, and Reading Difference in Nineteenth-Century France* (New York: Columbia University Press, 1993). See also on this, Marcel Gauchet and Gladys Swain, *Le Vrai Charcot: les chemins imprévus de l'inconscient* (Paris: Calmann-Lévy, 1997), esp. 141–42.

3. In discussing the visual manifestations of hysteria, it is important to recall that while Freud would later pay close attention to the complex relations between the scopic and the sexual, nineteenth-century clinicians still considered optical symptoms as secondary to the diagnosis of an underlying nervous pathology. For

Charcot, hysteria is not a "maladie imaginaire," but a real disease of neurological (rather than primarily psychological) etiology that imprints the body with pathological symptoms. Among the most important of these, he writes, are lesions of the optic nerve, which lead to partial and full blindness; Charcot also emphasizes the importance for diagnosis and study of using "le miroir d'Helmholtz" (53), that is, the ophthalmoscope. J.-M. Charcot, *Leçons sur les maladies du système nerveux faites à La Salpêtrière*, 2 vols. (Paris: Delahaye, 1877).

4. Georges Guillain and P. Mathieu, *La Salpêtrière* (Paris: Masson et Cie, 1925), 60. Charcot's writings indicate a certain level of expertise in the field of physiological optics, as when, for example, the physician observes such effects as a "marked contraction of the visual field" and a "contracture of the orbiculares of both eyes" in patients suffering petit mal seizures. J.-M. Charcot, *Critical Lectures on Certain Diseases of the Nervous System*, trans. E. P. Hurd (Detroit: George S. Davis), 1888), 9–10.

5. Didi-Huberman, *Invention de l'hysterie*, 127–28.

6. Emily Apter, "The Garden of Scopic Perversion from Monet to Mirbeau," *October* 47 (Winter 1988): 91–115. For more on the links and disjunctions between optics and psyche in Freud's and Lacan's use of the term "scotomization," see also Martin Jay, *Downcast Eyes: The Denigration of Vision in Twentieth-Century French Thought* (Berkeley: University of California Press, 1994), 353–56.

7. Apter, "The Garden of Scopic Perversion from Monet to Mirbeau," 113.

8. The scene is recounted in Asti Hustvedt, ed., *The Decadent Reader: Fiction, Fantasy, and Perversion from Fin-de-Siècle France* (New York: Zone Books, 1998), 17.

9. The fact that Charcot's celebrated *leçons du mardi*, public lectures given at La Salpêtrière, were attended by men of letters like Maupassant, Jules Claretie, and Villiers de l'Isle-Adam underlines, of course, the connections between the literary texts these chapters discuss and the psychopathological work of the age.

10. Hustvedt, *The Decadent Reader*, 17.

11. Ibid., 29.

12. Some explanations of the time were curiously resistant to a "visionary" hypothesis that would completely bypass the bodily organs. In *Hypnotisme et spiritisme* (1916) Lombroso writes, for example, of the transposition of the senses onto other parts of the body: a fourteen-year-old female hysteric loses sight in her eyes but it is replaced by clear vision in the tip of her nose and left earlobe; her sense of smell, it seems, has similarly moved—to her heel! *Hypnotisme et spiritisme*, trans. Charles Rossigneux (Paris: Flammarion, 1916), 10.

13. L. Moutin, *Le Nouvel hypnotisme* (Paris: Perrin et Cie, 1887), 27.

14. Balzac's description of his young heroine's clairvoyance under hypnosis reveals less an interest in the psychopathological sciences that were to dominate fin-de-siècle treatments of the theme than a continued fascination with the visionary mode; the scene is filled with familiar Swedenborgian allusions and uses the same metaphor of organs as "constricting corsets" as was used in *Louis Lambert* to evoke transcendent illumination: "Sight and hearing then occur more perfectly than in the so-called *wakeful* state, and possibly without the involvement of the organs that are mere sheaths [*gaines*] for these luminous swords called sight and hearing!" Honoré de Balzac, "Ursule Mirouet," in *La Comédie Humaine*, ed. Pierre-Georges Castex, Bibliothèque de la Pléiade (Paris: Gallimard, 1976), 3: 829.

15. Gilles de la Tourette, *L'Hypnotisme et les états analogues au point de vue médico-légal* (Paris: Librairie Plon, 1887), 124–25.

16. Wilhelm Wundt, *Hypnotisme et suggestion: étude critique* (Paris: Félix Alcan, 1893). Wundt's study of hypnotism belongs to a field that ranged from Mesmerist

quackery to serious academic study and that intersected with studies of hallucination as both physiological and mental state. Among the influential contributions to the latter, we find Baillarger, whose reports to the Royal Academy of Medicine in the 1840s introduced the term "psycho-sensorial hallucinations," and Brierre de Boismont, who wrote "Des Hallucinations; ou, Histoire raisonnée des apparitions, des visions, des songes de l'extase, du magnétisme et du somnambulisme" in 1845. In the 1880s, Charcot's critics at the Ecole de Nancy showed continued interest in hallucinatory phenomena as related to the therapeutic uses of hypnotism and the psychopathology of hysteria. For more on the history of hallucination studies, see Tony James, *Dreams, Creativity, and Madness in Nineteenth-Century France* (Oxford: Clarendon Press, 1995). James's book traces the ways in which use of the term "hallucination" acquired visual connotations in the eighteenth century (70), veered away after 1830 from connotations of religious ecstasy as nineteenth-century science began to influence fiction (81), and contributed to conceptions of "double personality" by the fin-de-siècle period (184).

17. Giraud-Teulon and Helmholtz also study positive and negative hallucinations as optical phenomena.

18. Lombroso, *Hypnotisme et spiritisme*, 40.

19. Tony James describes an avid debate about whether hallucinations were "continuous or discontinuous with ordinary perception" (*Dream, Creativity, and Madness*, 148). In this debate, "physiological" was taken to be synonymous with "normal"; this is an interesting point for my broader argument, as physiology has actually come to stand in for perception itself. As for Wundt, he wants to restrict the use of hypnosis and his discussions of suggested hallucinations to the realm of medical therapy. By affirming, however, that images hallucinated under hypnosis can actually produce the same effects on the pupil and retina as do real images, Wundt reinscribes hallucinatory phenomena as physiological—rather than pathological.

20. On the connections among Charcot's psychopathological studies, Lombroso's decadent theories, and Villiers' novel, see Asti Hustvedt, "The Pathology of Eve: Villiers de l'Isle-Adam and *Fin de Siècle* Medical Discourse," in *Jeering Dreamers: Essays on L'Eve future*, ed. John Anzalone (Amsterdam: Rodopi, 1996), 25–46. This collection of essays on *L'Eve future* remains the most valuable resource on modern critical responses to the novel and its themes.

21. Anne Greenfield, "The Shield of Perseus and the Absent Woman," in Anzalone, *Jeering Dreamers*, 76.

22. Villiers de l'Isle-Adam, *L'Eve future* (Paris: Gallimard, 1993), 77. Hereafter cited in text, with the abbreviation *EF* where necessary for clarity.

23. Edison proposes the recreation of Woman "with the sublime assistance of Light!": "Within this vision, I will force the Ideal itself to show itself, for the first time, to your senses, PALPABLE, AUDIBLE, AND IN MATERIAL FORM" (125).

24. The question asked by Lombroso in relation to the delusional images perceived by hypnotized subjects, "How do we explain that suggested images behave like real ones?" can be reposed in the context of *L'Eve future* as "How do we explain that Hadaly, an artificial woman, behaves like a real one?"

25. Terry Castle, "Phantasmagoria: Spectral Technology and the metaphorics of Modern Reverie," *Critical Inquiry* 15 (Autumn 1988): 26–61.Of course, in Villiers's fiction as well as in Charcot's studies, women's bodies trouble the epistemological certainty even of subjective projection, as their screened (in the sense of covered over, repressed) agency returns in a way that surpasses the controlling,

rational male discourse: examples include Claire's retinal image, Hadaly/Sowana's garden monologue, and Blanche Wittman's private card collection.

26. The scene's anticipation of the invention of cinema in 1895 has been explored by, for example, Marie Lathers and Raymond Bellour. For Lathers, the scene puts into play the two sides of the scopophilic coin, fetishism and voyeurism: as cinema, it extends the fetishizing function of photography and as a show put on by a man for a male spectator, it enters into the male voyeuristic modality. *The Aesthetics of Artifice: Villiers's L'Eve future* (Chapel Hill: North Carolina Studies in the Romance Languages and Literatures, University of North Carolina, 1996), 107. For more on the representations and constructions of the feminine in *L'Eve future*, see Mary Ann Doane, "Technophilia: Technology, Representation and the Feminine," in *Body Politics: Women and the Discourses of Science*, ed. Mary Jacobus et al. (New York: Routledge, 1990), and Marie-Hélène Huet, *Monstrous Imagination* (Cambridge, Mass.: Harvard University Press, 1993).

27. One might recall here that cinema's effectiveness as illusion of motion is technically reliant on the afterimage effect in the observer's eye.

28. A. W. Raitt, *Villiers de l'Isle-Adam et le mouvement symboliste* (Paris: Librairie José Corti, 1965), 232.

29. Villiers's story "Véra" also presents a supernatural vision imbued with a reality that can be independently confirmed: "The analogy with *Claire Lenoir* is obvious: once again at stake is a subjective illusion that can be objectively proven." Raitt, *Villiers de l'Isle-Adam et le mouvement symboliste*, 249.

30. Carol de Dobay Rifelj, "Minds, Computers, and Hadaly," in Anzalone, *Jeering Dreamers*, 127–39.

31. Ibid., 132.

32. Asti Hustvedt, in "The Pathology of Eve," explains the way in which the hysterical "split" implies a broader, troubling philosophical gap: "Unlike other disorders, grounded in the body, hysteria was characterized by its peculiar ability to mimic symptoms of other diseases without having a physiological source. . . . This rupture between symptom and source that is played out on the female body is a drama of disconnection between outside and inside, or body and 'soul'—a gap that lies at the very heart of *L'Eve future*" (*Jeering Dreamers*, 37).

33. John Anzalone, "Danse macabre, ou le pas de deux Baudelaire-Villiers: essai sure un chapitre de *L'Eve future*, in Anzalone, *Jeering Dreamers*, 117–25, 124.

Epilogue. The Afterimage of Reference: Optics and the Nouveau roman

1. Maurice Merleau-Ponty, *L'Œil et l'esprit* (Paris: Gallimard, 1964), 17.

2. Quoted in Martin Jay, *Downcast Eyes: The Denigration of Vision in Twentieth-Century French Thought* (Berkeley: University of California Press, 1994), 497.

3. Claude Simon, *Triptyque* (Paris: Editions de Minuit, 1973), 18.

4. Helmholtz explains that afterimages—or "persistent luminous impressions"—momentarily affect a certain number of retinal cells, thereby interfering with the observer's ability to perceive external objects in the world: "after light acts on the retina, the nervous mechanism of vision continues in the state of excitation for a long time still. . . . there is [a] very noticeable effect after bright light has been acting on any part of the retina. To new light falling on it from outside, this place now responds differently from those other parts of the retina that were not affected previously. In other words, the sensitivity of the visual organ to external stimuli has been altered here by the action of light." Hermann

von Helmholtz, *Helmholtz's Treatise on Physiological Optics*, ed. James P. C. Southall, 3 vols. (New York: Dover, 1962), "Variations of Sensitivity," 2: §23, 228.

5. In an extended discussion of narrative blind spots and the limits to Simon's antihumanist project, I link the afterimage passage in *Triptyque* to the psychoanalytical concepts of *forclusion* and *scotomization.* See my "Blind Spots and Afterimages: The Narrative Optics of Claude Simon's *Triptyque*," *Romanic Review* 91, 3 (May 2000): 289–311.

Index

a priori/posteriori reasoning debate, 95–97, 103, 104
Abrams, M. H., 58, 239n23
absolutism, 47
L'Accusateur (Claretie), 155, 158, 170–75, 177, 181–86, 193–95, 196, 203, 252n11; atavistic theme in, 203–4; Charles Pradès character in, 201; communication/communicability themes, 182; Dantin character in, 182, 183, 199, 203–4; Ginory character in, 172, 174, 182–84, 199–200; Monsieur Bernardet character in, 155–56, 162, 171–72, 175, 183–84, 185, 200, 202; —, as bibliophile, 160–61, 249n14; the occult and, 184–85; plot, 155–56; potential misuse of science theme, 171–72
"The Adventure of the Blue Carbuncle" (Doyle), 86
L'Affaire Lerouge (Gaboriau), 112, 121, 244n8
afterimages ("afterimage effect"). *See* retinal afterimages
Amblard, Marie-Claude, 232n14
Ambrière, Madeleine, 240n7
"Les Amours de Milord Bomston" (Rousseau), 74, 76–77
anthropometry, 194, 198; photography and, 199
Anzalone, John, 220, 257n20, 258n33
Apter, Emily, 208, 256n6
Aristotle, 53
art history, 5–6, 8, 228n13
"At the End of the Passage" (Kipling), 195–96
atavistic themes, in nineteenth-century fiction and culture, 202–5
autopsy (*autopsia*), 116
Avant-propos de la Comédie humaine (Balzac), 20, 21, 24, 30–31, 61, 88; science and, 63, 64, 231n6
Les Aventures du Capitaine Hatteras (Verne), 180
"Avertissement du Gars" (Balzac), 23, 26, 28

bacteriology, 201
Bal, Mieke, 239n4, 249n9
Le Bal de Sceaux, 41–47; Emilie in, 41–46, 67, 69, 235n12; plot of, 41–42
Balzac, Honoré de, 2, 4, 7, 15, 123, 209, 222, 225, 231n6, 232n9, 233n24, 240n7, 256n14; Balzac-*observateur* versus Balzac-*visionnaire*, 19–20, 231n3; on capitalism, 235n7; communication of images in, 23; concept of vision, 30; defense of materialism, 21, 30–31; knowledge of optics, 231n8; nineteenth-century naturalists and, 63; scoptophilic impulses, 236n4; theory of second sight (*la seconde vue*, *La Spécialite*, *voyance*), 20–22, 24, 25; valorization of European ideas, 240n12; visual epistemology, 48–49, 58. *See also* specific works
Barbéris, Pierre, 231n3, 232n9, 239n4
Barthes, Roland, 48, 68, 184, 236n1, 240n11, 251n32; on hermeneutic function, 244n10
Baudelaire, Charles, 231n3, 250n20
Baxandall, Michael, 228n13

Bays, Gwendolyn, 231n5, 233n27
Béatrix (Balzac), 60
Beer, Gillian, 127, 246n24
Béguin, Albert, 231n3, 241n20
Beizer, Janet, 237n10, 255n2
Bell, David F., 228n11, 246n4
Bentham, Jeremy, 125
Bérard, Suzanne, 24, 232n18, 233n27
Berg, William, 19, 231n2
Berkeley, George, 9; visual perception theories, 110–11
Bernheimer, Charles, 255n2
Bertillon, Alphonse, 93, 194, 199; racial classification systems, 201–2, 254n12
La Bête humaine (Zola), 202, 204
bibliophilia, 160–61, 249n14
blindness, 50, 52, 123, 230n1, 236n7, 237n10, 244n4; hysterical, 208; snow, 252n6. *See also* vision, restored
Boileau, Pierre (Boileau-Narcejac), 92, 241n1, 242n12, 245n15
Boismont, Brierre de, 187
Boll, Franz, 158, 163–64, 168, 174, 175, 177, 183
Bonard, Olivier, 241n20
Bonfantini, Massimo A., 109, 244n38
Bongie, Chris, 253n1
Bonnefis, Philippe, 159, 170, 248n5, 250n24, 251n32; "Clair-obscur" and, 159
Bouguer, Pierre, 237n16
Bouvard et Pécuchet (Flaubert), 1–3, 166–67, 227n3, 250nn22, 23
Braid, James, 209
Brennan, Teresa, 227n4
Brombert, Victor, 19, 230n1
Brooks, Peter, 234n31, 236n4, 241n15, 244n10
Bryson, Norman, 235n11
Buffon, Georges-Louis de, 2, 33–34, 57, 231n8, 236n7

Caillois, Roger, 194
camera obscura, 7, 28–29, 35, 36, 158, 177, 234n28, 235nn6, 13, 251n32; of dreams, 170. See also *chambre obscure*
Campagnoni, Donata, 56, 238nn18, 19
capitalism, 235n7
"Cartesian perspectivalism," 5, 8, 35, 60, 230n32
Cartesianism, 8–9, 12, 24, 29, 34, 44
Castex, Pierre-Georges, 194
Castle, Terry, 215, 235n10, 238n19
L'Œil vivant (Starobinski), 70
Chambers, Ross, 165, 250n18
La Chambre claire (Barthes), 184
chambre noire, 36, 39, 57, 161, 177
chambre obscure, 29, 35, 36, 156, 162, 225, 255n1. *See also* camera obscura
Charcot, Jean-Martin, 207–11, 255n3, 256n4; critics of, 256n16; public lectures, 256n9
La Chartreuse de Parme (Stendhal), 60
Cheselden, William (Cheselden case), 110, 111, 135–36, 184, 244n3, 246n28
Chevreul, Michel-Eugène, 10, 64, 237n16, 240n8
Les Chouans (Balzac), 20, 22–23, 39, 41; second sight (*seconde vue*) concept in, 24; Victor Morillon character in, 22–29, 32, 37, 39, 47
cinema, 258nn26, 27
Citron, Pierre, 235n7
Civilization (Buckle), 94
Civilization and Its Discontents (Freud), 90
Claire Lenoir (Villiers de l'Isle-Adam), 155, 158, 164–70, 177, 185–95, 197–98, 206, 211, 220, 221; atavistic theme in, 204–5; attention to anatomical detail in, 166; Bonhomet/Dr. Lenoir debates in, 187–90; Claire Lenoir character in, 156, 166, 167, 169, 204–5, 217; definition of reality theme, 186–87; discourse of optics and, 253n18; Dr. Césaire Lenoir character in, 156, 187–90, 204; "Ottysor" figure in, 188, 193–94, 196, 204; plot, 156; science versus occult theme, 165, 172–73; Sir Henry Clifton character in, 196; Tribulat Bonhomet character in, 156, 165–68, 172, 186–87. *See also* visual hallucinations
clair-obscur, 179–80, 185
clairvoyance, 209–10, 234n30
Claretie, Jules, 4, 15, 155, 184, 199, 200, 202, 206, 221, 251n30, 254n8
Classen, Constance, 233n26
Coleman, William, 102, 242n7, 243nn26–31
colonial expansion, 195, 253n1
color, 77, 237n12; theory of, 9–10, 53–54
La Comédie humaine (Balzac), 10, 15, 19–22, 27, 39, 53, 60, 63, 87–88, 222,

236n14; blindness theme in, 50–51; link of seeing and knowing in, 48–49. See also *voyance* (second sight)
Comptes rendus de l'Académie des sciences (Robert-Houdin), 1
Condillac, Itienne, 2, 9, 20, 80, 238n17, 241n25
Corbin, Alain, 3, 227n7
Cousin, Victor, 232n10, 233n24
Crary, Jonathan, 3, 4, 10, 14, 168, 227n6, 228n9, 230n35, 234nn28, 4, 241n27
Le Crime d'Orcival (Gaboriau), 113–14, 132
criminals, categorization of by ethnic type, 200
Crombie, A. C., 228n15, 229n19
Crooks, Sir William, 209
Cuvier, Georges Baron, 63, 86–91, 93, 94, 100, 108, 109, 242nn6, 7; on reasoning, 89–90, 101; reconstruction principles, 102; on relation between observation and theory, 90–91

Dällenbach, Lucien, 48–49, 236nn2, 3, 4
Damisch, Hubert, 235n11
Darmon, Pierre, 254n10
Daston, Lorraine, 4, 228n9
De la Dioptrique (Descartes), 7, 8, 12, 14
De la loi du contraste simultané des couleurs (Chevreul), 10
deduction/deductive reasoning, 93–98, 101, 103, 104, 107, 126–27, 149, 240n5; a priori, 112; mathematical, 247n14; pure, 108. *See also* vision, "slow vision" (*vision lente*)
Delattre, Geneviève, 241n18
Delue, Rachael, 228n13
Dember, William N., 228n15
Derrida, Jacques, 5–6, 90, 228n12, 243n20, 251n25; on the logic of supplementarity, 242n9
Des hallucinations (Boismont), 187
Descartes, René, 2, 14, 31, 77, 78, 80, 167, 189, 229nn20, 22, 232n10, 233n27, 241n27; optic theories of, 7–9, 43, 134; —, geometrical, 12–13; pure abstract reason and, 229nn22, 23; theory of direct vision, 25. *See also* "Cartesian perspectivalism"
Le "Detective Novel" et l'influence de la pensée scientifique (Messac), 93, 137
detective novels, 128–29, 134, 144, 150, 155, 222, 243n14, 244n38, 245n22, 247n8; as an anti-bildungsroman, 245n11; "Bi-Part Soul" of, 99; narrative form of, 152, 244–45n10; nineteenth-century, 93, 111, 112, 246n4; scientific epistemology of, 137–38; and "trickle-down" science, 97. See also *roman policier*
detectives. *See* private detectives ("private eyes")
Diderot, Denis, 12–13, 20, 79
Didi-Huberman, Georges, 207–8, 255n2
"Dissertation sur les couleurs accidentelles" (Buffon), 34
Dobay Rifelj, Carol de, 218–20
Donagan, Alan, 229n26
Downcast Eyes (Jay), 8
Doyle, Sir Arthur Canon, 87, 93, 94, 102–3, 114, 243n23, 244n8
Dreams, Creativity, and Madness in Nineteenth-Century France (James), 256n16
Drougard, E., 187, 249n12

éblouissement, 117–18, 122, 135, 166, 245nn19, 20; definition, 245n21; logic of, 123; medical definition, 123
Eco, Umberto, 244n38
Edison, Thomas, 171
Eisenzweig, Uri, 92, 241n1, 243n13, 245n22, 247n7
empiricism, 10, 33, 34, 58, 94, 97, 223; Cuvierian, 64, 240n5; "empirico-transcendental doublet," 87, 97–100, 103, 125, 231n7; inductive, 11; observation and, 102; positivism and, 98
Encyclopédie méthodique (Académie des Sciences), 231n8
L'Enfant maudit (Balzac), 237n9
entoptic phenomena, 1–2
epistemology: of detail, 248n20; modern, 98, 231n7; nineteenth-century models ("Galilean" and "evidential") proposed by Ginzburg, 149–52; subject-centered, 223; of visible and invisible, 91. *See also* Balzac, visual epistemology; detective novels, scientific epistemology of; French novels, visual epistemology and; visual epistemology
Escoubas, Eliane, 134, 246n27
Esrock, Ellen, 235n8
Essais critiques (Barthes), 48

Essay Concerning Human Understanding (Locke), 110
Essay Towards a new Theory of Vision (Berkeley), 110
Euclid, 6
Evans, Arthur, 249n7
Evans, Henri, 233n27, 237n14
L'Eve future (Villiers de l'Isle-Adam), 171, 214–21; Alicia Clary character in, 214–15, 217; "beauty-hag" scene in, 220–21; "Danse macabre" scene in, 216; Edison character in, 214, 216–17, 219–21, 257n23; Evelyn Habal character in, 215–16, 220; Hadaly character in, 214, 215; Lord Ewald character in, 214–16; Sowana character in, 214
extrasensory perception, 210–11, 213
eye(s), 119, 173, 177, 181–82; anatomy, 162–63; camera-eye analogy, 161–62, 164; hysteria and, 207–8, 256n12; non-transparency of, 134; physiology, 34, 133–34; subjective optical phenomena and, 133–34. *See also* eyesight; *mouches volantes*; retina
eyesight, 51–52

Facino Cane (Balzac), 51, 123, 237n10
fantasmagorie, 42, 71, 76, 116, 177, 185, 238nn18, 19; fantasmagoria/panorama, complementary meanings, 56; two aspects, 215
Fargeaud, Madeleine, 240nn5, 7
Fechner, Gustav Theodor, 237n16
Felman, Shoshana, 240n10
Fenichel, Otto, 249n14
feuilleton sensationalism, 93
La Fille aux yeux d'or (Balzac), 59–60, 77, 115, 116; Henri de Marsay character in, 65, 67–76; —, "second sight," 78–81; Paquita character in, 71–72, 74–76, 78, 81, 241nn20, 21; plot, 61; seeing (describing) Paris, 61–67, 239n4
fin-de-siècle fiction, 177, 194–95, 215, 253n17; concerns over science and the occult in, 177; French modernity and, 202. See also *Claire Lenoir*, *L'Accusateur*, *Les Frères Kip*
"Five Orange Pips" (Doyle), 87, 100, 101
Fizeau, Armand-Hippolyte-Louis, 2
Flaubert, Gustave, 1, 2, 227nn1, 3
focalisation, 5, 239n4
Fortassier, Rose, 241n20
Foster, Hal, 227n4
Foucault, Jean-Bernard-Léon, 2
Foucault, Michel, 5, 6, 88, 91, 97, 98, 100, 115, 228n12, 231n7, 235n11; on natural history, 242n4. *See also* "empirico-transcendental doublet"
French novels, 13, 14, 90; visual epistemology and, 2–3, 10. *See also* fin-de-siècle fiction
Les Frères Kip (Verne), 155, 156, 158, 159, 170, 174, 177, 193–95, 201; colonial tropes in, 196–97; Flig Balt character in, 178, 181, 195–97; geographical displacement in, 197–98; Harry Gibson character in, 196–97; plot, 155, 178–79; Vin Mod character in, 178, 181, 195; visual uncertainty theme, 178, 180–81
Freud, Sigmund, 12, 207, 208, 255n3
Frolich, Juliette, 233n27

Gaboriau, Emile, 87, 92, 94, 100, 102, 112–13, 123, 144; influence of Poe, 114
Gaillard, Françoise, 63, 64, 227n3, 240n6, 250n20, 255n20
Galison, Peter, 4, 228n9
Gall, Franz Joseph, 93
"The Garden of Scopic Perversion from Monet to Mirbeau" (Apter), 208
Gauchet, Marcel, 255n2
Genette, Gérard, 5, 239n4
geographical displacement, and national boundaries, 195–99
Ginzburg, Carlo, 149–52, 248n17
Giraud-Teulon, Félix, 140, 141, 163, 164, 168, 174–76, 189, 227n2, 250n17, 252n37; on *presbytie*, 146–47; on "ragle" of desert, 252n4
Goethe, Johann Wolfgang von, 13, 14, 34, 134, 240n5
Goux, Jean-Joseph, 235n13
Gregory, Richard L., 228n15
Grivel, Charles, 245n22
Greenfield, Anne, 214–15
Grojnowski, Daniel, 170, 248n5, 249n13
Gunning, Tom, 247n8

hallucinations. *See* visual hallucinations
Hamon, Philippe, 255n1
Handbuch des Physiologie des Menschen (Müller), 73

Harries, Karsten, 229n20
Hartman, Geoffrey, 150, 245n16, 248n18
Heidegger, Martin, 13
Hello, Ernest, 192
Helmholtz, Hermann Ludwig Ferdinand von, 2, 10, 19, 34, 86, 97, 103, 105, 110, 111, 120–21, 124, 133, 139, 174, 176, 189, 228n15, 234n1, 247n9; empiricist theories of visual perception, 105–9, 132, 229n28, 234n29, 245n18; invention of ophthalmoscope, 119, 143; on retinal afterimages, 258n4; on snow blindness, 252n6; on subjective visual phenomena, 127, 133–34
Holmes, Sherlock, 85–86; knowledge of, 102–3; on reason, 100–101; "reasoning backwards" and, 98–99
Le Horlà (Maupassant), 203, 255n20
Hoveyda, Fereydoun, 92–93, 241n1, 247n6
Huenon, Roland Le, 65, 240n9
Huet, Marie-Hélène, 180, 252n7
Hugo, Victor-Marie, 2, 19, 47, 230n1
Hustvedt, Asti, 251n31, 257n20, 258n32
hypnosis/hypnotism, 208–9, 257n24; "altered perception" and, 210; hallucinations and, 211–12, 256n16, 257n19
Hypnotisme et suggestion (Wundt), 210–11, 256n16
hysteria, 207–8, 255n2, 258n32; visual manifestations of, 207–8, 255n3

"iconotope," 207, 255n1
idealism, 58, 69–70, 217, 220
illusion, 219; illusion/hallucination distinction, 211, 252n4
Illusions perdues (Balzac), 20, 61
induction/inductive reasoning, 95–98, 103, 105, 111; pure, 108
Inquiry into the Human Mind on the Principles of Common Sense (Reid), 20–21
Irwin, John T., 243n20

James, Tony, 58, 239n24, 252n4, 256n16, 257n19
Jameson, Fredric, 236n14
Jay, Martin, 8, 227n4, 229n21, 230n32, 234n28, 240n14, 242n10
Jean-Jacques Rousseau: la transparence et l'obstacle (Starobinski), 70
Jones, Caroline, 4, 228n9
Jouffroy, Théodore, 232n10
Jouvences sur Jules Verne (Serres), 202
Judovitz, Dalia, 229n20
Julie; ou, La Nouvelle Héloïse (Rousseau), 69–70, 72–74, 77

Kadish, Doris Y., 241n21
Kalifa, Dominique, 246–n5
Kant, Immanuel, 97
Kepler, Johannes, 7, 9
Kipling, Rudyard, 254nn7, 8
knowledge, 229n17; light and, 117; physiology and, 98; surveillance and, 127
Krauss, Rosalind, 127, 246n24
kris knives, 193–95
Kühne, Willy, 158, 160, 168, 175, 252n37

Lacan, Jacques, 6, 11, 12, 144, 208, 221, 224, 229n22, 230n33, 243n20; concept of visual mastery, 12–13
Larmore, Charles, 229n23
Lathers, Marie, 258n26
Latour, Bruno, 202, 254n6; on "Pasteurization" of France, 254n16
Lavater, Johann Kasper, 93
Leibniz, Gottfried Wilhelm, 24, 80, 241n27
Leroux, Gaston, 91, 137; writing habits, 138
Lettre sur les aveugles (Diderot), 12–13, 79
Lévi-Strauss, Claude, 240n5
Levin, David Michael, 227n4
Levine, George, 228n11
light, 13, 77, 118, 120–21, 134, 225; objective nature of, 1–2; as physiological effect, 73; "primary," 212; speed of, 2; temporality and, 174. *See also* light rays
light rays, 121; "extramissive," 6, 7; "intramissive," 7; "intromissive," 6
Lindberg, David C., 228n15
literature, and visual theory, 14–15
Locke, John, 9, 20, 25, 33, 80, 105, 110, 232n10
Logic (Mill), 106–7
Lombroso, Cesare, 199, 203, 254n10, 256n12, 257n24
Louis Lambert (Balzac), 20, 24, 35, 59, 80; Louis Lambert character in, 27–32, 36, 47, 53, 60, 78, 104; "second sight" in, 29–30, 34
Louis XVIII, 41, 47

Machamer, Peter K., 229n15
La Maison du chat-qui-pelote (Balzac), 65
La Maison Nucingen (Balzac), 35–40; Bixiou character in, 37–39; Godefroid de Beaudenord character in, 35–38; plot, 35; story of storytelling, 37–38
Malebranche, Nicolas de, 2, 110
Manns, James W., 232n10
Mariotte, Edme, 33
Les Martyrs ignorés (Balzac), 231n6
Massey, Lyle, 8, 229n23
Matlock, Jann, 235n11, 255n2
Maupassant, Guy de, 203, 255n20
Le Médecin de campagne (Balzac), 50
Meininger, Anne-Marie, 42
Melville, Stephen, 13, 227n4, 230n34
Ménard, Maurice, 23
Merleau-Ponty, Maurice, 11–14, 221, 223, 229nn22, 29, 258n1
Mesmer, Franz, 209
Mesmerism, 209, 213
Messac, Régis, 93–94, 97, 137, 241n1, 243n14, 246n4
Micale, Mark, 255n2
Miller, D. A., 128–29, 246n26
Milner, Max, 173, 182, 235n10, 238n19, 248n5, 253n19
Mirzoeff, Nicholas, 228n8
Mitchell, W. J. T., 227n5
Mitterand, Henri, 6, 228n14, 238n20
modern novel, the, 3–4; realist, 19; romantic, 19
"Molyneux's problem" (Locke), 110
Monadology (Leibniz), 24
Monsieur Lecoq (Gaboriau), 87, –97, 104, 109, 123–24, 144; Absinthe character in, 118, 121–22; Gévrol character in, 115–18, 121, 126, 128, 132, 245n18; indirection of vision in, 134–35; Lecoq character in, 99–100, 115–16, 121–22; —, consulting an oracle, 131–33; —, focus and, 129–31; —, as observer, 119–20, 126–27, 245n18; —, panoptical plan of, 127–28; —, vision of, 117, 118; —, visual quest of, 124–29; M. d'Escorval character in, 122–23, 134–35; Mai character in, 124–25, 127–30, 133; murder/crime scenes as spectacle in, 114–15; plot of, 113; Tabaret character in, 99–100, 131–33; as visual bildungsroman, 112–16, 131
Moretti, Franco, 245n11
Morgan, Michael J., 244n1
Les Mots et les choses (Foucault), 88, 98
mouches volantes, 133, 138, 139, 247n9
Moutin, L., 256n13
Müller, Johannes, 73, 110
Muller, John P., 243n20, 247n14
"The Murders in the Rue Morgue" (Poe), 85, 87, 99, 114, 138, 253n2; Dupin character in, 85–87, 91, 93, 95, 98, 114, 135
"The Musgrave Ritual" (Doyle), 244n10
Le Mystère de la chambre jaune (film, dir. Podalydès, 2003), 137, 246n1
Le Mystère de la chambre jaune (novel, Leroux), 137–38, 144, 147, 149, 247n15; conservatism of, 150–51; empiricism in, 147–52; Joseph Rouletabille character in, 91–92, 139–48, 150, 151, 247nn12, 15, 248n20; Larsan character in, 145, 146, 149–52; Mathhilde Stangerson character in, 139, 140–42, 145, 151, 248n19; narrative form of, 152; plot of, 139; Sinclair character in, 145; yellow room/closed room/blind spot motif of, 138–44, 247n7

Narcejac, Thomas, 92
narrative, 38, 224, 250n23; "democracy," 40; design, 244n10; perspective, 239n4
Neefs, Jacques, 230n1
New Essays on Human Understanding (Leibniz), 80
Newton, Isaac, 9, 33, 77, 237–n16; optics of, 14
Nicephore, Niepce, 251n32
nineteenth century, 157, 205, 228n11, 235n11, 251n31, 253n1; atavism and, 202–5. *See also* Balzac, nineteenth-century naturalists and; detective novels, nineteenth-century; epistemology, nineteenth-century models; fin-de-siècle fiction; optics; nineteenth-century; science/the sciences, nineteenth-century
Noiray, Jacques, 187, 195
nouveau roman, 2, 222–25
Le Nouvel hypnotisme (Moutin), 209
Nye, Robert, 254n10
Nykrog, Per, 234n30

objectivity, 1, 4, 7–8, 228n9, 235–36n13. *See also* subject/object dualism
observation, 86, 89–90, 133; relation to theory, 90; scientific (objective), 126, 177. *See also* Cuvier, on relation between observation and theory
occult/occultism, 171, 184–85, 205, 213, 234n30, 252n37. See also *Claire Lenoir*, science versus occult theme; "scientific gaze"/"occult vision" alliance
"ocularcentrism," 230n32
"Of Seeing" (Reid), 21
ophthalmoscope, 119, 143, 156, 167, 169, 190, 195
optical illusions, 105, 243n36
optical perception, theories of, 19
optics, 4, 5, 51, 138, 224, 229n17, 231n8, 233n20; in antiquity, 6–7; classical, 7–9, 13; empiricist theories of, 9–10, 104–9; fixing images and, 174; geometrical, 12–13; nineteenth-century, 11; *nouveau roman* and, 222–25; philosophy and, 11–13; physiological, 12–15, 19, 40, 57, 105, 124, 143, 157, 161–62, 170, 176, 189; and seers, 21. *See also* Descartes, optic theories; visual epistemology
Optiks (Newton), 9
l'optique Romanesque, 6
optiques, 5
optogram(s)/optagram fiction, 15, 159, 160, 168, 172–74, 176, 180, 182, 183, 186, 191–92, 199, 200, 202, 205, 222, 249n12, 252n37; definition of, 158; "optogram fantastic," 194–95, 202; photography and, 158–60, 180–81, 248n5, 249n13; trope in novels, 156–57, 249n7. *See also* retina; retinal afterimages
Otis, Laura, 201, 254n14
"Ottysor." See *Claire Lenoir*, "Ottysor" figure in

panopticon, 125, 126; plan in *Monsieur Lecoq*, 127–28; social, 128
Pasteur, Louis, 194, 201, 202
Pastore, Nicholas, 229nn15, 26, 244nn2, 3
Paulson, William, 230n1, 241n26, 244n4
La Peau de chagrin (Balzac), 20, 24, 49–51, 239n21; *antiquaire* in, 51–54, 57, 237n14; antique shop passage, 58; post-Cartesian thought and, 55–56; Raphaël de Valentin character in, 53–54, 59, 60, 238n20; —,perceptions of, 54–55, 57–58
Peirce, Charles Sanders, 109
Peiresc, Nicolas-Claude Fabri de, 33
Le Père Goriot (Balzac), 20, 59, 62; Eugène de Rastignac character in, 59–61
Perron, Paul, 65
perspectivalism. *See* "Cartesian perspectivalism"
Phéline, Christian, 254nn11, 15, 18
"phénomènes d'optique," 57
phenomenology, twentieth-century, 11, 12, 14, 223–24
phonograph, 171
photography, 170, 171, 173, 181, 202, 248n5; anthropometric, 199; death and, 251n32; fetishizing function, 258n26; technology, 156–58, 248–49n6; vision and, 159. *See also* psychophotography
physics, 53, 138
Physiologie et pathologie fonctionnelle de la vision binoculaire (Giraud-Teulon), 140, 146
"pictorial turn," 227n5
Picturing Science, Producing Art (Galison and Jones), 4
Plato, 6
Podalydès, Bruno, 137
Poe, Edgar Allan, 85, 98, 112; influence on Gaboriau, 114
Ponnau, Gwenhaël, 253n17
Porta, J. B., 234n29
Porter, Dennis, 128
positivism, 100, 157, 187; materialist, 191; positivist scientism, 172, 251n31. *See also* empiricism, positivism and
Pour un nouveau roman (Robbe-Grillet), 48
Prendergast, Christopher, 61, 62, 239n4
presbyte, 144–47, 248n16
Priestman, Martin, 114, 246n25
private detectives ("private eyes"), 138, 246–n5
Proni, Giampaolo, 109
Proustian modernism, 3
psychopathology, 157, 207
psychophotography, 186
"The Purloined Letter" (Poe), 98, 144, 247n14; Dupin character in, 98, 99, 243n20

racial classification systems, 201–2
Raitt, A. W., 187, 188, 217–18
realism, "second sight" of, 77–81
La Recherche de l'absolu (Balzac), 52
Recherches sur les ossemens fossils de quadrupédes (Cuvier), 87; *Discours préliminaire* to, 88–89, 102
reductionism, 218–19, 228n11
Reid, Thomas, 20–21, 38, 110, 232nn10, 11, 233n23, 236n7; on visual deception, 232n12; on visual perception, 25–26
retina, 164, 174–75, 190, 234n29, 251n34, 252n37; as "frame" (*parergon*), 168; photochemical reactions in, 176–77; retention of retinal images by corpses, 155–56; rhodopsin (retinal violet) and, 158, 161, 163–64, 169–70, 173–75, 177, 181; yellow spots (*fovea centralis*) on retina, 140
retinal afterimages, 33–35, 39, 43, 163, 183, 191, 222–25, 249n12, 258n4; hysteria and ("hysterical afterimage"), 207–9; as "ocular specters," 57; privileging of, 234n4; as woman/spectacle, 214–21
Rifelj, Carol de Dobay, 258n30
Robbe-Grillet, Alain, 48, 49, 221, 225, 236n1
Robert-Houdin, Jean Eugène, 1
roman judiciaire, 182
roman policier, 85–86, 94, 99, 103, 104, 109, 111–12, 116, 119, 129, 136, 174, 182, 194, 222, 245n22, 249n14; definitions of, 92, 241n1, 243n14; "delayed decoding" of hermeneutic function and, 113, 244n10; as *genre scientifique*, 92; seeing/observing distinction in, 86–87; spectacle of crime scenes and, 114–15
roman-feuilleton (serial novel), 112
Rosa, Guy, 230n1
Rousseau, Jean-Jacques, 69, 71, 77, 240n14; idealism, 74; metaphysics, 73; "principle of immediacy," 78
Rumford, Benjamin Thompson, 237n16

Saint-Amand, Pierre, 241n21
St.-Beuve, Charles, 231n3
Saint-Hilaire, Geoffrey, 63, 88, 102, 240nn5, 7
Samuels, Maurice, 238n18
Sartre, Jean-Paul, 12, 230n30
Sayers, Dorothy, 92, 242n11
Schor, Naomi, 248n20
science/the sciences, 214, 228n11, 250n21; methodologies, 64; nineteenth-century, 20, 231n7, 237n12, 246n4; promise of in late nineteenth century, 171–72; science/literature relationship, 5–6, 104
"scientific gaze"/"occult vision" alliance, 165, 167
"scopic regimes," 14
scoptophilia, 161, 249–50n14. *See also* Balzac, scoptophilic impulses of
"The Scoptophilic Instinct and Identification" (Fenichel), 249n14
Scott, Walter, 93
second sight. See *voyance* (second sight)
Les Secrets de la Princesse de Cadignan (Balzac), 60, 239n2
Séraphîta (Balzac), 20, 24, 51, 59, 77–78, 80; as optical bildungsroman, 52–53; Séraphîta character in, 31, 47, 60, 78, 241n22
Serres, Michel, 144, 179, 202, 228n11, 252n5
shadow(s), 134, 172–73, 180
Showalter, Elaine, 255n2
sight. *See* vision
Silverman, Kaja, 230n31
Simon, Claude, 49, 221, 224–225
Simon, Gérard, 7, 229nn15, 17
Soemmering, Thomas, 140
Southall, Christine Ladd-Franklin, 237n12
Spallanzani, Lazzaro, 165
Le Sphinx des glaces (Verne), 179–80
spiritism, 206, 212–14
Splendeurs et misères des courtisanes (Balzac), 20, 61
Sprenger, Scott, 239n2
Starobinski, Jean, 5, 70, 240n13
Stendhal, Marie-Henri, 230n1
stereoscope, 97
Stewart, Garrett, 157, 248n1
A Study in Scarlet (Doyle), 91, 98–99, 101–3, 109, 244n8
Sturken, Marita, 228n8
subject/object dualism, 1–2, 6–7, 11, 13, 15, 119, 120, 163, 176–77, 186; in Balzac, 58
subjectivity, 2, 4, 11, 219, 224, 232n10, 235nn11, 13, 253n17; corporeal (physiological), 11, 177. *See also* subject/object dualism

Sully, James, 106
Summers, David, 8, 229n24
Surveiller et punir (Foucault), 125
Swain, Virginia, 235n13
Swedenborg, Emanuel, 51–52, 237n13
S/Z (Barthes), 68, 244n10

Taine, Hippolyte, 191
Taton, René, 229nn15, 25
Techniques of the Observer (Crary), 10, 234n4
Theory of Colors (Goethe), 9–10, 12, 14, 134
Thiher, Allan, 228n11
Tortel, Jean, 244n6
Tortonese, Paolo, 191
Totem and Taboo (Freud), 202
Tourette, Gilles de la, 210, 211
transcendentalism, 98
Treatise on Physiological Optics (Helmholtz), 10, 97, 105, 111, 129, 176, 229n28, 234n1
Triptyque (Simon), 224–25
Trousson, Raymond, 241n19

Une Ténébreuse affaire (Balzac), 60, 81, 111
"Ursule Mirouet" (Balzac), 209, 256n14

Van Dine, S. S., 114
Verne, Jules, 4, 15, 155, 196, 206, 221, 252n4; polar fiction, 179–80; as "pre-Pasteurian hygienist," 254n6; themes of communication in, 179
Vernois, Dr., 160, 183, 202, 249n13
Victor Hugo and the Visionary Novel (Brombert), 19
Villiers de l'Isle-Adam, Auguste de, 2, 4, 15, 155, 168, 170, 187, 196, 206, 214, 221, 249n12, 250n20; illusionism of, 188–89, 217–19; "metaphysical dualism" of, 219–20; philosophical antirealism of, 215–16; subjective idealism of, 217
Villiers de l'Isle-Adam et le mouvement symboliste (Raitt), 217
Vinge, Louise, 233n26
vision, 13, 30, 73, 91, 137, 149–50, 224, 229n17; binocularity, 212; communicability, 176–77; conception, 250n24; empiricist theories, 9–10, 77, 118, 177; idealist theories, 10, 77; "innate" theory, 105, 111, 233n24; privileging of, 230n32; psychology, 11, 12; restored, 244n3; "slow vision" (*vision lente*), 103–5; subjective phenomena of, 1–2, 176–77, 223. *See also* Cheselden; eyesight; photography, vision and; visual epistemology; visual perception; "visuality"
La Vision et ses anomalies (Giraud-Teulon), 163, 176
visual epistemology, 127, 192; 225, 230n1; in Balzac, 48–49, 58; French novels and, 2–3, 10; overview of debates, 6–10
visual hallucinations, 187, 188, 205, 211, 257n19; distinction from illusions, 252n4; under hypnotism, 211–12; images, 212–13; as optical phenomena, 257n17; reality and, 189, 190
visual perception, 25–26, 54, 97, 119, 156, 209, 219, 224, 230n1; empiricist theories, 104–11; gradualist theory, 110–11; nineteenth-century discoveries, 127. *See also* extrasensory perception
"visual studies," 3, 6. *See also* literature, and visual theory
"visuality," 3–4, 171, 223; Cartesian, 124
Vitoux, Pierre, 239–40n4
"Voir aveuglément" (Rosa), 230n1
voyance (second sight), 10, 25, 26, 28, 31, 39, 40, 47, 60, 70, 165, 209–10, 233n24; antimaterialist aspect, 233n27; definition, 30; distinguished from clairvoyance, 234n30; moral, 239n2. *See also* Balzac, theory of second sight; *Les Chouans* (Balzac), second sight (*la seconde* vue) in; realism, "second sight"

Wade, Nicholas J., 229n15, 244n37
Wheatstone, Sir Charles, 97
Whewell, William, 231n7, 243n15
Wittman, Blanche, 209–10
women/women's bodies, 258n32; epistemology of subjective projection and, 257n25; recreation of through light, 257n23; retinal afterimages and, 214–21
Wundt, Wilhelm, 211–13, 256n16, 257n19

Zola, Emile, 15, 19, 231n3, 238n20

Acknowledgments

In *The Practice of Everyday Life*, Michel de Certeau uses an optical metaphor to describe the many debts that underwrite any intellectual project: "Every particular study is a many-faceted mirror . . . reflecting the exchanges, readings, and confrontations that form the conditions of its possibility, but it is a broken and anamorphic mirror (others are fragmented and altered by it)." My general thanks go to all whose work has contributed to my own broken mirror.

But of course I also want to acknowledge the people who directly invested their energies in helping me write this book, beginning with Ora Avni. Her generosity, humor, trust, and skill as an advisor continue to sustain and inspire me. From the project's start, it received support from the Yale French Department. Thanks to Albert Feuillerat and the Ecole Normale Supérieure for sponsoring a fruitful year of research in Paris; to Yale University and Paul C. Gignilliat for a dissertation writing grant; and to the community of teachers and friends who gave feedback and support, including Peter Brooks, Ned Duval, Georges May, Charles Porter, Patricia Armstrong, Susie Brubaker, Leon Sachs, and Daryl Lee.

I want to thank Jann Matlock, Tom Conley, Maggie Flinn, and Maurie Samuels for welcoming me into the dynamic atmosphere of Harvard's department of Romance Languages and Literatures; I continue to take inspiration from their energy and high standards.

Larry Kritzman and Nelly Furman deserve my warmest thanks for organizing the French Cultural Studies Summer Institute at Dartmouth. They created an atmosphere that combines intellectual intensity with genuine concern for personal and professional development. In addition to their feedback on my work, I also received generous time and attention from visiting Institute professors, especially David Bell, Françoise Gaillard, and Timothy Reiss. Thanks, too, to my fellow participants, including Nanette Fornabai, Drew Jones, Andrew Sobanet, Thérèse De

Raedt, and Matthew Tiews—and especially to Jim Berkley, who patiently read and skillfully improved two long chapter drafts for my book.

John Anzalone also took the time to share with me his expertise on the fin de siècle and its literature. Given that he has never even met me, his generosity—in responding to queries, aiding my research, and giving invaluable feedback on long chapter drafts—is particularly appreciated. His is the kind of collegiality that makes this profession a pleasure. Others whose feedback has also contributed to my thinking on this project include Ralph Sarkonak, Scott Sprenger, Philippe Bonnefis, Carlos Alonso, Robert Harvey, Charles Stivale, and Gerald Prince. Thanks, too, to Dr. Aashish Gandhi for sharing his ophthalmological expertise.

I cannot imagine a group of colleagues more supportive than the ones I have at the University of Illinois at Urbana-Champaign. Both in and out of my field, I have encountered a community of respectful exchange, genuine interest, sage advice, and sane professionalism. Thanks to the participants in my faculty seminar on Descartes's optics, especially to Rachael Delue and Joseph Valente for their intelligent responses to my work. My research on this project was supported by a humanities release time grant from the University Research Board. The entire French Department has made my work life a positive experience and I extend my sincere thanks to Suzanna Fagyal, Karen Fresco, Alain Fresco, Doug Kibbee, Laurence Mall, Jean-Philippe Mathy, Adlai Murdoch, and Emile Talbot. Inparticular, I deeply appreciate the generous and inspiring mentorship of Armine Mortimer and Larry Schehr.

Many thanks go to Josué Harari, who was instrumental at the start of my graduate career and again in the support of this project; I continue to admire his intellectual energy and professional rigor. I also want to thank warmly Peg Flynn for translating this book's citations with such impressive grace and skill. And thanks to Eric Halpern and the staff at the University of Pennsylvania Press for their expert ushering of my manuscript into book form.

This book is dedicated to my parents, who taught me to love languages and literature. *Obrigada* and *merci* to them and to my entire extended family of Reynaldos, Goulets, Andersons, and Estys. Finally, my unbounded thanks go to Jed Esty, for all that he brings to my work and my life.

Earlier versions of portions of some chapters appeared in journal articles: portions of Chapters 1 and 2 in *French Forum* (2001); Chapter 7 in *SubStance* (2005); Chapters 7 and 11 in *Nineteenth-Century French Studies* (2005); Chapter 10 in *Yale French Studies* (2005). I want to thank the editors of these journals for permission to reprint them.